# Lady Randolph Churchill

## A Biography 1854–1895

RALPH G. MARTIN

CASSELL · LONDON

CASSELL & COMPANY LTD
35 Red Lion Square, London WC1
*Melbourne, Sydney, Toronto*
*Johannesburg, Auckland*

© 1969 by Ralph G. Martin
First published in Great Britain 1969

Also published in the United States, under the title
*Jennie: The Life of Lady Randolph Churchill.*
*The Romantic Years 1854–1895*

S.B.N. 304 93430 5

PRINTED IN GREAT BRITAIN
BY EBENEZER BAYLIS AND SON, LTD.
THE TRINITY PRESS, WORCESTER, AND LONDON
F.569

For my dear friends
Bob Nisenson and Larry Tajiri
who left their own heritage:
*give love and help,*
*and live life with the full zest it deserves*

# Acknowledgments

I am deeply and personally grateful to Martin Gilbert, Fellow of Merton College, Oxford, whose help was constant, advice invaluable and criticism important; to Robert Rhodes James, whose assistance was vital to making the whole project possible by opening the first doors to important research sources and material; to Sir Shane Leslie and his charming wife, who gave me so much of their time and memory and made available to me letters, documents, and photographs; to the Duke of Marlborough for so graciously giving me permission to examine and copy the enormous file of family letters and papers held in the Muniments Room of Blenheim Palace; and to the Duke's private secretary, Mrs Eva Sharpe, for her constant co-operation; and to Miss K. M. Gell and her staff at the Muniments Room, Charles G. Dennis and Helen Wannerton, for their kindness and their patience; to Peregrine Churchill for making freely available his large collection of family letters and photographs, and for permitting me to make quotations from *The Reminiscences of Lady Randolph Churchill* and other material in which he holds the copyright; to Mrs John Sloane and her husband, for allowing me access to the Jerome family bible and albums and for giving me copies of Jerome family pictures; to Mrs Oswald Frewen, for freely permitting me use of her husband's diaries, as well as of the family letters; to Prince Clary of Venice and the Countess Kinsky in London, for their excellent background information on Count Kinsky; to Allen Andrews, who was so kind as to make available to me the then-unpublished manuscript of Moreton Frewen's collection of letters, entitled *The Splendid Pauper*; to Mark Goulden, who helped me gain entrance to so many important research facilities in London; to Thomas Blackburn, managing director of the *Daily Express*, and Andrew Edwards of Beaverbrook Newspapers Ltd., who permitted my examination of their files and provided copies of material I requested; and to Michael Wybrow and his dear wife in Guildford, England, who provided me with lardycake and gave me unlimited use of their excellent Churchill library—one of the finest private libraries of its kind—and who helped me on some of the early research.

My gratitude also to Miss Marie Berry, Executive Secretary of the New York Genealogical and Biographical Society; Dr Blake McKelvey, city historian of Rochester, New York; Mrs Margaret H. Merhoff and Mrs Dorothy S. Facer of the Wayne County Division of Archives and History in Lyons, New York; Rex Schaeffer, Library Director of the Rochester *Times-Union*; James Kelly, historian of Brooklyn, New York; Mrs Kenn Stryker-Rodda, archivist of the Long Island Historical Society; Wayne C. Grover, archivist of the United States; Mason Tolman, Associate Librarian, and Ida M. Cohen, Senior Librarian, of the New York State Library; Alexander P. Clark, Curator of Manuscripts, Princeton University; Donald W. Marshall, town historian of Bedford, New York; Mrs Miner C. Hill, Oyster Bay Historical Society; Miss Lenore Wysong, Empire State Society, Sons of the American Revolution; Dr E. Taylor Parks, Historical Office of the State Department of the United States; Mrs Elaine Mann, National Museum of Racing, Saratoga Springs, New York; Gertrude Annan, New York Academy of Medicine; Timothy Beard, Genealogical Room of the New York Public Library; Rutherford Rogers, chief of the Reference Department of the New York Public Library; G. Gelman, editor of the Wallingford (Connecticut) *Post*; Gerald Harrington Miller, town clerk of Wallingford; Mrs Graham Wilcox, Curator of the Stockbridge Library Association, Stockbridge, Massachusetts; J. Guadagno of the Museum of the American Indian; Hope Emily Allen, historian of Pompey, New York; Virginia S. Hart, Chief of Information of the Bureau of Indian Affairs, United States Department of Interior.

My appreciation also to Robert Mackworth-Young, Librarian at Windsor Castle; R. J. Hill, Lord Chamberlain's Office at St. James's Palace; Cleanth Brooks of the U.S. Embassy in London; Miss A. J. Fraser, Public Record Office in London; Miss M. Winder, Wellcome Historical Medical Society in London; the Staff of the Main Reading Room and the Manuscripts Room in the British Museum, who were most kind and patient; the Registrar of Somerset House in London; R. Rickinger of the Austrian Institute in London; Dr Helmut Rumpler, Historiches Institut, Vienna; Mlle Nelly Coadou and Mme Claire Launois of the Institut Français du

Royaume-Uni; the staff of the London Library and the Department of Archives in Paris.

For varied help and information, my thanks to Clara Booth Newell, Mrs V. Colby, Mrs Margot Levy, Hugo Dyson, Michael O'Connell, Adrian Bergson, Elsie Herron, Mrs A. Verne Flint, Russell Bryant, Mrs S. B. Morgan, Doris M. Nesbitt, Mrs Sarah S. Dennen, Ray Rebhann, Emil Steinhauser, A. M. Keebler, Marion E. Snedeker, Kay Halle, Vera Curtis, Mrs Arthur A. Corcoran, Dr J. M. Spitzer, Dr Robert Edelman, H. A. Cahn, Mrs Alice L. Parker, D. W. Smythe, Jacqueline Bray, Erno Straus, Samuel Clarke, John Quinn, Charlotte Young, Len Slater, Mrs Meryl Riecken, Mrs Eleanor Claar, Philip Rosenberg, Carl Foreman and Alan Pizer.

My thanks, as always, to Director Ruth P. Greene and her staff at the Oyster Bay Public Library; particularly my deep gratitude to the very patient Mrs Christine Lane, whose help has been constant and invaluable, and to the other staff members, Mrs Annette S. Macedonio, Helen Baldwin, Ellen Coshignano, Gene McGrath, Patricia Stirrat, and Rosemary Burlew. As always, too, my thanks to Romana Javitz and her staff at the Picture Collection of the New York Public Library.

My personal thanks again for help beyond the call of friendship to Paul S. Green; Mrs Pearl Bernier and the staff of Colony Offset Printing Company in Boston; Ruth Tropin; Peggy Leder; Sidney Shore; Abba P. Schwartz, former Under-secretary of State, U.S. State Department; Ed Plaut; David Lewin of the *Daily Mail*, and his secretary Jean Cagienard; Irma Remsen; and to Mrs Mari Walker who again, as always, had the difficult job of translating my handwriting, my notes, my tape recordings, and my manuscript into finished copy.

I am very grateful for permission to reprint extracts from the following. *My Early Life* by Winston S. Churchill (Odhams Books Ltd., The Hamlyn Group); *My Life and Loves* by Frank Harris (W. H. Allen and Arthur Leonard Ross as executor of the Frank Harris Estate); *Winston S. Churchill: Youth 1874–1900* by Randolph S. Churchill (Heinemann).

My warm appreciation to my good friend Harry Sions, who gave the manuscript the benefit of his sharp editorial wisdom; Mrs Betty Copithorne, whose comments were similarly penetrating; and to my wife, Marjorie Jean, who was involved in some of the early research and criticism and who had the tedious job of deciphering the difficult handwriting in the letters of Lady Randolph Churchill.

A special note of thanks to my dear friend Howard Byrne, who believed in this book long before anybody else and who always placed the full facilities of his offices and the resources of his staff of Transatlantic News Features Ltd. at my disposal—my added thanks there to L. S. Symons and Mrs Zena Fry.

A final personal note of thanks to Elizabeth Ruth Martin, Maury Martin, and Tina Suzanne Martin for their special help.

R.G.M.

# Contents

# Illustrations

# Prologue

Even in her hospital bed, this woman of sixty-seven looked almost a generation younger, her face nearly free of wrinkles, her smile dazzling, and her eyes, 'great wild eyes', still luminous and eager.

In her time, she had been 'the most influential Anglo-Saxon woman in the world'.[1]

Out of her strength, she helped transform a social dilettante husband into one of the most important men in the British Empire; out of her love and ambition, she helped shape her son Winston into one of the great men of his century.

She sent her son the books that moulded his style of writing and speech; used her enormous influence to get him transferred from one war to another; got him his early assignments as a war correspondent; acted as agent to sell his first story and his first books; campaigned alongside him in his early elections; opened doors for him to all the important people of his time. But most of all, she gave him her courage and her stamina.[2]

It was a brassy kind of courage. In the last dramatic scene of her life, the doctor told her he would have to amputate her infected leg. This was a woman whose lovely legs and tiny feet were her special vanity—she had even displayed her collected evening shoes in a glass case. Yet, her answer came calmly and quickly: 'Make sure you cut high enough.'

Her stamina was also remarkable. In the course of a lifetime, Jennie was editor and publisher of an international literary magazine; organized a hospital ship for the Boer War and travelled with it for its first shipload of wounded; was a pianist of professional ability; took turns as playwright, author, reporter; directed national expositions and theatricals; single-handed conducted political campaigns at a time when most women were not even permitted to attend the theatre alone.

She married three times and characterized her second marriage as romantic but not successful, her third as successful but not romantic. At sixty-three, she had married a man younger than

Winston, but her beauty was still so extraordinary that the marriage caused only a minimum of surprise.[3]

Jennie had few saintly qualities. She was, of course, what her world was. It was a world of hypocritical morals, as faked as the bustle, thinly gilded with pretentious propriety. She was also what her parents were: a snob like her mother, a sensualist like her father.

But what made her unique in her time was the drive, the special force that was her own. A Prime Minister's wife once said of Jennie, 'she could have governed the world.'[4]

In a sense, she almost did.

# I

Leonard Jerome may well have served as the model for many of the men in his daughter's life. He was a man of considerable charm and extraordinary energy, a tall, handsome, bony-faced man with an impressive walrus moustache. He was also a fanatic lover of the horse and the race as well as of the woman and the chase. Nearly all the men Jennie loved, including the three she married, had most of those qualities, particularly the fierce zest for living.

At various times, Leonard Jerome was lawyer, newspaper editor, U.S. Consul at Trieste, art collector, part-owner of *The New York Times*.[1] Newspapers called him 'The King of Wall Street', because he was a fabulous speculator who could make and lose millions of dollars, and then make them again. They also called him 'The Father of the American Turf', because, almost single-handedly, he raised the social status of horse racing in the United States.

His private passion was music, and he financed the careers of many promising young singers—particularly if they were female and pretty. When the current love of his life was the famous singer, Jenny Lind, he had the audacity to persuade his unknowing wife to name their second daughter 'Jennie'.

Of his four daughters, Jennie was Leonard Jerome's favourite. When he was dying he said, 'I have given you all I have. Pass it on.' Much of what he gave her was a pattern of living, a conviction that life must be lived to the hilt, a sense that it was a waste to move through time without love.

That was part of his own heritage. The early Jeromes were among the thousands of Huguenot Protestants who fled France in search of religious freedom. But some failed to find it even in England and the Reverend William Jerome was burned at the stake in 1540. His descendants sailed to America. The first Jerome to become an American was an Englishman named Timothy, who came from the Isle of Wight in 1710.[2] In the strange completion of a circle, it was on the Isle of Wight, 164 years later, that Jennie Jerome took her first romantic step towards becoming an Englishwoman.

B

Timothy Jerome arrived at Meriden, Connecticut, with a royal grant for a monopoly on the salt-making in the area. He died rich and was buried on Buckwheat Hill overlooking the land he owned.[3] An inventory of his estate included a top hat, a punch bowl, a silk handkerchief, a large number of books, and four slaves named Pomp, Prince, Rose, and Jenny.[4]

During the American Revolution, Timothy's son Samuel fought alongside his own five sons. One of them, Aaron, married a cousin of George Washington. Since Washington had no lineal descendants, Leonard Jerome later claimed, 'We are the nearest of kin!'[5]

Aaron's son Isaac was also a soldier and a farmer, a quiet, conservative man, but his wife was a young Scotswoman, bright, witty, and ambitious. Her name was Aurora and she was the daughter of Reuben Murray, a soldier in the American Revolution,[6] a ready wit, a writer and balladeer, a tall, commanding figure full of drive and imagination who had made and lost several small fortunes. Isaac and Aurora Jerome had nine sons and three daughters.[7] Their fifth son, born in 1817, was Leonard Walter.

The Jeromes lived on a farm in the hill country of Pompey, New York. Isaac wanted to keep his sons on the farm, but the energetic Aurora insisted on packing the boys' bundles and sending them out to seek their fortunes. Like his brothers, Leonard first worked at his farm chores. Later he got a job in the village store for a dollar a week and learned to bargain with the shrewd farmers who came to exchange their produce for stores.

Two of Leonard's older brothers had gone to the College of New Jersey (which later became Princeton), and Leonard followed them there in 1836. A handsome boy who made friends easily, Leonard was involved in a number of college pranks. His most spectacular feat was to organize a group of a hundred students to return to the campus a huge cannon that had been captured during the War of 1812. The cannon is still there in the quadrangle, a prominent symbol of Princeton tradition.[8]

Princeton records also reveal that Leonard Jerome was suspended from school 'for going to Trenton without permission'.[9] He was caught tarring the seats in the prayer hall and sabotaging the chemistry teacher's test tubes so that they exploded in class. Perhaps in an attempt to compensate for all this ungentlemanly behaviour, Jerome later offered Princeton an annual sum of $5,000 to be

4

awarded to the best gentleman in the graduating class.[10] (*The New York Times* applauded the gesture and recommended that a similar award be offered in Congress, where, they felt, it was even more needed). Princeton, however, rejected the award because 'all Americans are equally born gentlemen'.

Family financial pressure forced Leonard to transfer to the less expensive Union College in Schenectady, New York, where he sang a loud clear tenor in the college chorus and graduated near the top of his class. One of his cousins, who attended Union College several years later, was James Roosevelt, father of Franklin Delano Roosevelt.[11]

Leonard Jerome soon went to work for his uncle, Hiram Jerome. A former law partner of Abraham Lincoln, Hiram had become the first judge of the Wayne County Court in Palmyra, New York. Palmyra was then a thriving town of broad streets, gay shops, and elegant hotels facing the Erie Canal, where the painted packet boats passed in a continual flow. Leonard not only became a partner in his uncle's practice but was appointed notary public for the county and bought 170 acres of land north of Mud Creek. He and his younger brother Lawrence double-dated the Hall sisters, Clarissa and Catherine.

Clarissa, who later shortened her name to Clara, was a quiet young woman with a full figure and a substantial inheritance. She had a lovely oval face, brooding black eyes, beautiful black hair carefully parted in the middle. Some called her secretive and shy; her aunts claimed they could not tell what the girl was thinking and that she was a judicious flirt 'who would fall into moods'.

The Hall sisters had been orphaned early, and now lived with their aunts. Their father, Ambrose Hall, a tall, strikingly handsome man, had been a wealthy landowner and a prominent member of the New York State Assembly. Their mother, Clarissa Willcox, came from a Massachusetts family of early settlers. All the Hall women had black hair, dark features, and high cheekbones, which they referred to as 'Hall-marks'. The whispered family legend was that these features were a result of Indian blood, that their grandmother had been raped by an Iroquois.[12]

These Hall-marks seemed to become accentuated with age. In her later years, Jennie's mother Clara looked so much like an Indian

5

that her kin referred to her as 'Sitting Bull', just as they called Aunt Catherine 'Hatchet Face'. Even when Jennie's blonde sister died, a member of the family noted that 'a strange change in her face gave her the look of an Indian. . . .' A nephew insists that Jennie herself took on the same look at her death.[13]

Uncle Hiram crimped the Jerome-Hall courtship by moving his law practice to Rochester and taking his nephews with him. A Rochester socialite[14] later remembered the Jerome brothers as 'screamingly funny boys . . . very popular with the ladies owing to the dashing manner in which they rode high-spirited horses'. Lawrence Jerome, however, soon married Catherine Hall, but Leonard Jerome took five years before proposing to Clara.

They were married on April 5, 1849. Leonard was thirty-two and Clara was twenty-four. The Jerome brothers bought houses alongside each other and built a connecting passage so they could visit without going outside. They lived in the fashionable Third Ward, the 'ruffled-shirt ward', separated from the business district by the Erie Canal. Houses there were large, post-colonial homes, some with pretentious façades of Greek revival architecture, and most fitted with the newest convenience, the Bates Patent Chamber Shower Bath.

Rochester was a major shipping point for wheat and had a thriving upper-crust society with its own snobberies. Clara Jerome fitted in easily, decorating her home with red plush, expensive ormolu mirrors, white marble fireplaces, and carpets from Brussels. Clara's money also helped her husband buy the Rochester *Daily American*, which resulted in his deeper involvement in Whig politics. Political activity led to political patronage, and Leonard was soon offered an appointment as Consul to Ravenna. He turned down the appointment, however, because he had become involved in a telegraph line company in New York. To be close to his new business, he sold his interest in the Rochester newspaper in 1850 and moved with his wife to Brooklyn.

Brooklyn, then a legally independent city, had a population of some 120,000, and thirty-five miles of paved and lighted streets. Streetcars wouldn't arrive until 1853. The Jeromes lived in the section later known as Brooklyn Heights, where Jerome had rented a fifteen-room red brick house on Henry Street just a block from the East River. His older brother Addison, a New York stockbroker, moved in with them, and the two men commuted by ferry across the river to Wall Street.

Near the Jerome home was Plymouth Church, made famous because its preacher was one of the country's loudest and most dramatic voices against slavery, Henry Ward Beecher. Beecher's sister, Harriet Beecher Stowe, later wrote 'the little book that started the Civil War'.[15] In one of his most powerful sermons, Beecher yelled, 'Sarah, come up here!' A small mulatto girl came to the pulpit and took his hand as Beecher said, 'This little girl is a slave, and I have promised her owner 1200 dollars, his price for her, or she will be returned to slavery. Pass the baskets!' People threw in money, watches, and jewelry, and Beecher was able to announce, to their thunderous applause, that Sarah was free. Despite a notorious and scandalous affair with the wife of one of his parishioners, Beecher stayed on as pastor for some forty years, and kept his 2,800 church seats almost always full.

After a short time, Leonard sold his telegraph company and joined Addison in a full-scale plunge into stockmarket speculation. Leonard called Wall Street 'a jungle where men tear and claw', but he thrived in it. When the New Haven Railroad was involved in a scandal over forged stock, Jerome helped lobby for and pass a railroad-reform bill to 'clear up the chaos'. He soon got a Wall Street reputation as a man who knew how to get things done.[16] A rival was even quoted as saying, 'That damn fellow has cashed in on honesty.'

Courage and a calculating coldness were the prime requisites of a Wall Street speculator. Jerome made much, because he was willing to risk much.

'How's business today, Leonard?' a friend remembered asking him.

'Oh, dull,' said Jerome, 'confoundedly dull. I have only made $25,000 today.'[17]

He specialized in 'selling short'—selling stock he did not yet own, to be delivered at a future date. The expectation was that in the interim the price would drop and he could then buy the stock more cheaply to fulfil his sale.

Leonard and Addison spent most of their evenings in Manhattan, either working hard or playing hard. Clara Jerome felt very much on the fringe. Her husband flourished financially and she had a houseful of servants and all the clothes she could buy, but she never really knew how to create excitement, as Leonard always did. Nor was she able to compete with her husband's diversions. Even her interest in music was so minimal that she seldom accompanied him to concerts. [18]

Clara was further restricted when her first child was born on April 15, 1851, a daughter they named Clarita. Less than a year later, Leonard blithely announced that they were all going to Trieste, where he had been appointed U.S. Consul, and that a Miss Lillie Greenough would accompany them.

Lillie was one of the several Rochester girls who had fallen in love with Leonard, and she was coming along, he said, to study Italian singing techniques. Clara was not overjoyed. Lillie even moved into their Trieste villa with them, but Clara branched out on her own, collecting her own covey of courtiers.[19] A visitor described her as 'an elegant brunette with American vitality and Paris gowns'. Soon Clara summoned enough courage to banish Miss Greenough and her piano to the attic.

Trieste was then the Austro-Hungarian Empire's only outlet to the Mediterranean, a city-state replete with Italian counts. Leonard was not impressed. 'They spoke more languages than I,' he wrote, 'but surely it is more important to think clearly in one idiom than to chatter in five.' He continued his special interest in the opera (a visitor wrote that Jerome had gone to see Verdi's new opera, *Rigoletto,* some thirty times), in opera singers, his small white yacht, a pair of prize Lipizzaner stallions, and Lillie.

The Trieste interlude lasted only sixteen months. Back home there had been a national election, and Democratic President Franklin Pierce replaced the Whig President Millard Fillmore. Jerome's resignation was promptly accepted. After a tour of Europe, the family was in Brooklyn by November 1853 in a rented house at 8 Amity Street, directly on the promenade facing the river view of New York.

Lillie was gone and Clara was pregnant again. But Leonard had renewed an earlier relationship with the Swedish Nightingale, Jenny Lind. Of her many admirers, Jenny Lind once remarked that Leonard Jerome was the best looking. Of Jenny, Leonard said, 'Her voice is indescribable, like the dawn. Who wants more?'[20]

According to the family Bible belonging to Leonard's parents, the second daughter of Leonard and Clara was born on January 9, 1854.[21]

'Why not name her Jenny?' Leonard asked his wife.

Clara refused at first, but then reluctantly agreed to Jeanette. Only months later did she realize why he had insisted on the name.

They lived at Amity Street four more years. Jennie (as she was always called) had no memories of Brooklyn, but she must have walked along the promenade, gazed at the sailing ships and paddle-boats, fed the pigeons, occasionally watched volunteer firemen racing along with their ruffled shirts, high top hats, and long-tailed coats. It was in Brooklyn that still another Jerome daughter, Camille, was born in November 1855.

Leonard Jerome became a millionaire during the Panic of 1857, again by selling short. According to Oliver Guthrie, New York society now knew Jerome as 'a great Don Juan, a great sportsman, and a beautiful whip'. But he also increased the fund he had settled on his wife, bought her a magnificent diamond necklace, rented a summer home in Newport, and bought a yacht so that he could sail there to visit his family.

Newport was the summer site of elegance, and the hub of its society was the Vanderbilt family, who later built a seventy-room stone Italian palazzo called 'The Breakers'. The Breakers had hot and cold running water (also hot and cold running saltwater) from silver taps. Bathtubs were carved out of solid marble, and the dining room was large enough for a dinner party of two hundred.[22]

Cornelius Vanderbilt was a big, bumptious man, a strong friend and a rough enemy, and he had taken a liking to Jerome. The two had been allies in the fight for control of the Harlem Railroad.[23] Many years later, Jennie was an honoured guest at The Breakers, staring at the huge chandeliers and marvelling at the sixteen foot-men wearing silk breeches. The friendship between the Jeromes and Vanderbilts lasted several generations.[24]

The Jeromes moved to Paris in 1858, settling in an apartment on the Champs-Elysées. Leonard Jerome noted briefly in a letter to his brother, 'We have been to the Grand Ball at the Tuileries and were presented to the Emperor and the Empress. It was universally conceded that Clara was the handsomest woman there. I never saw her look so well.'

Clara was blooming. 'I have found the court I want,' she wrote.

9

But Archduke Maximilian, whom she had known in Trieste, was more critical of the circle which gathered round Napoleon III.[25] 'The whole impression is of a makebelieve court occupied by amateurs who are not very sure of their parts.' One of these amateurs was Clara Jerome. She collected French aristocrats in small dinner parties and attended a series of salons that were 'delightful' and 'intimate'. Another pregnancy slowed her pace only slightly. Leonard, however, was bored. 'Paris is not as agreeable to me as New York,' he wrote his brother. 'I think I shall spend next summer at the Isle of Wight. It is a great place for yachting, horses. . . .'

Their fourth child was another daughter, and they named her Leonie. In 1859 Jerome brought them all back to New York.

New York was the nation's largest city, with a population of some 500,000, but Fifth Avenue was still unpaved north of Twenty-third Street, and most of Manhattan was rolling farmland spotted with summer estates. Jerome bought a piece of land on the southeast corner of Twenty-sixth Street in Madison Square, the new centre for the sedate and the social. The Square's six acres had once been a paupers' burying ground, the site of the city circus, a playing field for the first organized baseball club, and was still the address of the fanciest bordello in town, 'The Louvre', which advertised itself as 'the most refined of its sort in the world'.

Madison Square had begun its transformation when four-story private homes started to take over the fringes. Delmonico's Restaurant added splash to the area. Newly completed a few blocks away was the spectacular Fifth Avenue Hotel, with 'a perpendicular railway intersecting each story' (later known as an elevator), a central heating system, and the startling innovation of indoor toilets—which some critics considered 'not only unsanitary but immoral'.[26]

Jerome had promised his wife, 'I'll build you a palace yet.' And he practically did.[27] His plot of land was close to the splendid new house of Mrs Schermerhorn, who had snubbed the Jeromes earlier. To outshine their neighbour, Clara insisted they design their house in the style of Napoleon III's Paris. The handsome six-story, red brick house trimmed with marble, with a steep mansard roof, tall windows, and delicate ironwork contrasted sharply with the more simple brownstone homes on the Square. It had a white and gold ballroom that could accommodate some three hundred people, a breakfast room that could seat seventy, a huge drawing room that Clara decorated in flaming red.

Leonard lavished most of his attention on the adjacent stable. Built at a cost of some $80,000, it was three stories high, thickly carpeted and panelled with black walnut. 'Except for the Emperor's Mews in Paris, it is doubtful if any stable in the world . . . surpassed Jerome's,' reported the New York *Tribune*.

Attached to it was an equally unique private theatre that seated six hundred. 'As you entered, you were received by liveried servants, and by them, conducted to your seat where you found yourself surrounded by the most brilliant assemblage, and, on the stage, as amateur actresses supporting the fair singer, the fashionable beauties of that day.' That opening-day party for Jerome's theatre was in the tradition of the grand gesture—walls of roses and gardenias, fountains spouting champagne or eau de cologne.[28]

For Jerome, all this grandeur was a form of direct competition with his good friend August Belmont. Belmont was the renowned Rothschild representative in the United States. He was a short, heavy-set man with a limp (caused by a duel) and a foreign accent which many mistook for French, although his heritage was German and Jewish. Like Jerome, Belmont was a self-made millionaire with a razor mind and a biting wit, and both men were connoisseurs of women, horses, art, and good food. Belmont was married to the lovely daughter of Commodore Perry, and the costume balls at the Belmont home on Fifth Avenue were the social affairs of the season.[29]

One of the fashionable beauties for whom Belmont and Jerome competed was Mrs Fanny Ronalds, a Boston divorcee who had been a celebrated concert singer. Frank Griswold discreetly noted the contest in his privately printed memoirs:

There were two outstanding men at that time who were most prominent in all social and sporting events. They both drove coaches and four, and had large racing stables; both were married and in the prime of life. These two men fell desperately in love with Mrs. R—. L— and A— were rivals who kept the house of their lady filled with flowers and attempted to satisfy her every desire. She proved to be an accomplished general, for she managed these two great men with much skill.

Both men helped manage her money and multiply it. Both taught her how to handle plunging horses, and Leonard let her give a concert in his private theatre. Both also helped her produce the most

11

sensational ball of many seasons, at which Fanny wore a harp-shaped crown lit up by tiny gas jets from a holder hidden in her hair.

Twenty years later, Jerome and Belmont lunched together with their friend Frank Griswold, who recorded the conversation:

'August,' said Jerome, 'do you remember Fanny's celebrated ball?'

'Indeed, I ought to,' replied Belmont. 'I paid for it.'

'Why, how very strange,' said Jerome slowly. 'So did I.'

Jennie was not quite six years old when she first met Fanny, but the early memory lingered. 'Mrs Ronalds, who was as gifted as she was lovely, and shared the reputation of being the reigning beauty, gave me a species of small dog-cart and two donkeys which rejoiced in the names of "Willie" and "Wooshey".' The donkeys, of course, were kept at Newport.

The Jerome residence in New York was more of a display place than a home, and little girls were trained to sit gingerly on fine furniture, and never, never venture outside unless surrounded by servants. Little girls were supposed to move and act like little dolls, a studied part of the museum atmosphere. The upbringing of children was largely left to maids and nurses and teachers.[30]

Clara Jerome's major concern seemed to be clothes. Her diamonds and gowns now needed an inventory to keep them in order. William Allen Butler wrote a poem entitled 'Nothing To Wear' about women such as Clara:

> Miss Flora McFlimsey, of Madison Square,
> Has made three separate journeys to Paris,
> And her father assures me, each time she was there,
> That she and her friend, Mrs. Harris . . .
> Spent six consecutive weeks without stopping
> In one continuous round of shopping.
> And yet, though scarce three months have passed since the day,
> This merchandise went in 12 carts up Broadway,
> This same Miss McFlimsey, of Madison Square,
> The last time we met, was in utter despair,
> Because she had nothing whatever to wear!

Jennie cared more for horses than for clothes, and spent as much time as she could in her father's stable. Her father insisted that his daughters learn to play the piano, and Jennie's first teacher was Stephen Heller, a friend of Chopin. It was Heller who told her that if she practised seriously enough, she might someday be a concert pianist. Her father's theatre made its own impact on the imaginative Jennie. When there was a rehearsal in progress, young Jennie was often an avid audience, and the dramatic excitement of an opening night stirred the entire household.

In 1860 Jerome was an organizer of the Grand Ball for the Prince of Wales. The visiting Prince was nineteen, handsome, and bored. The Duke of Newcastle, his guide and guard, noted disapprovingly that the way American women pressed themselves upon the Prince was 'not in strict accordance with good breeding'. One of the would-be admirers was seven-year-old Jennie, who announced her determination to attend the ball and dance with the Prince. It was a tearful night for Jennie when she was not permitted to go. As for the Prince, it was reported in the gossip sheets that he escaped the watchful eye of the Duke of Newcastle one night 'and disported himself riotously in the most luxurious brothels.'

Clara Jerome kept her daughters within a strict social framework. 'Unlike most American children, we were seldom permitted to go to boy-and-girl dances,' Jennie later wrote.[31] But there was a costume ball given by August Belmont which Jennie did attend, and there exists a photograph to prove it. She was costumed as a *vivandière*. 'For days I did not sleep with the excitement of anticipation, but on the eventful night I was found in a flood of tears, the explanation being that I did not look "at all as I thought I was going to"— a situation which alas! has often repeated itself.'

The fun for Jennie was not on Madison Square, but at the Jerome summer house at Newport, a charming seaside villa. 'We were allowed to run wild and be as grubby and happy as children ought to be,' Jennie wrote. Harnessed to a cart filled with half-a-dozen children, Willie and Wooshey tore up and down Bellevue Avenue 'at the risks of our necks and everyone else's'. To urge the donkeys on, Jennie used a stick she called 'The Persuader', which featured 'the business end of a tack' at its tip. 'The cart and its occupants soon became a terror to the smart folk in their silks and feathers. These were delightful days.'

Clara Jerome unhappily told her husband that Jennie 'should have been a boy'. Yet to some extent, Clara encouraged Jennie's behaviour. The regimen for her daughters included 'plenty of milk, plenty of sleep and plenty of flannel'; to that, Clara added plenty of exercise, fresh air, and cold baths. 'Strong women make beautiful women,' she said.

One of their frequent summer visitors at Newport was Fanny Ronalds. Leonard Jerome often brought her along with him from New York on his new steam yacht named *Clara Clarita*, the interior of which was furnished in pale blue silk and hammered silver.[32] Clara seems to have become accustomed to her husband's extra-marital relationships: she was quoted as having said to Fanny when they first met, 'I don't blame you. I know how irresistible he is.[33]

Fanny not only filled in as occasional substitute wife in the Jerome family, but also as substitute mother. Her own three children were apparently living with her former husband or away at school, so she gave some of her maternal love to Jennie and her sisters, who soon 'allowed her to become a favourite'. Long afterward, Jennie fondly remembered how Fanny Ronalds used to sing to the children in the evening before bedtime. Her relationship with Fanny would last their lifetimes, for Fanny had all the qualities Jennie admired most: beauty and talent and force and sensitivity.

Jennie's mother Clara had mainly beauty. It is small wonder that the many-faceted Leonard Jerome sought elsewhere for fulfilment. It is even less surprising that Jennie sought, and found, in other women the model of the mother she wanted.

Lillie Greenough, who had since married, summed up the lack in Leonard's life when she wrote him, 'I love you more than ever because I feel you are never getting as strong love from anyone else.' If Leonard didn't, it was hardly because he wasn't trying. His newest protégée was seventeen-year-old Adelina Patti, whose voice reminded him of Jenny Lind. Jerome launched her musical career in his theatre and helped sponsor her first concert tour.

Jennie liked Adelina, too, but she liked young Minnie Hauk more. Minnie reportedly was Leonard Jerome's illegitimate daughter by an earlier romance. Jerome and Belmont both financed Minnie's musical education, promoted her sensational début when she was only fifteen, and later put her under Adelina Patti's private tutelage. Minnie and Jennie looked very much like sisters, and Clara Jerome wrote on the back of Minnie's picture, 'So like Jennie, but less good-looking.'

Minnie reminisced in her memoirs[34] that 'I was quite at home' in the Jerome house and remembered how warmly the Jerome girls accepted her. She also commented on the beautiful horses the girls had and their habit of riding many miles before breakfast. 'They rode like Amazons.'

Jerome had bought the old Bathgate estate at Fordham, in Westchester County. With 230 acres and a small racetrack of its own, the estate offered Jennie and her sisters even more freedom than Newport. Before Jennie was ten, the horse had replaced Willie and Wooshey, and at Bathgate Jennie had all the space needed to ride and race in the wild, free way she loved.

Jennie's younger sister Camille died of a sudden fever in 1863 at the age of six. The shock tightened Jennie's relationship with her older sister, Clarita, then twelve, and with Leonie, not quite five. Leonard's brother, Addison, also died about that time.

The country seemed full of death, for the Civil War had begun. 'I remember nothing about it,' Jennie reminisced, 'except that every little Southerner I met at dancing school was "a wicked rebel", to be pinched, if possible.' Her father, however, was deeply committed to the Union and must have brought his involvement home with him. Believing that one of the causes of the tragic war was the Negro's untenable position in American life, he helped with the government plan to start a colony of five thousand American Negroes on Haiti. When the government refused to support the Negroes financially while they organized themselves, and when he learned they were being maltreated on the island, Jerome withdrew.[35] (The scheme was finally a fiasco and most of the Negroes were returned.) Jerome also was Treasurer of the Union Defense Committee and paid for many of their activities. He personally contributed $35,000 towards the construction of the warship *Meteor*, served as an adviser to the government on its proposed Bank Bill, and was founder of the fund for families of the killed and wounded in New York's Draft Riots of 1863.[36]

The police had been unable to control the Draft Riots, and New York was overcome by looting mobs. Armed with torches, guns, and pikes, they roved in packs of several thousand, beating and hanging and burning Negroes, whom they blamed for the war. One gang broke into a Negro orphanage and threw children out of the windows. Jennie could not have been so sheltered that she did not hear of all this. And surely she must have known that her father, who owned a one-fifth interest in *The New York Times*, had manned one of the

15

two new breech-loading machine guns given by the Army to the *Times* when a mob threatened to destroy the building. (Jerome never had to fire—when word of the guns at the windows reached the rioters, they moved on to the *Tribune*, singing 'We'll hang old Horace Greeley to a sour apple tree'. Two hundred police arrived to help the newsmen beat them back.[37])

Jennie was eleven years old when President Lincoln was assassinated. 'I remember our house in Madison Square draped from top to bottom in white and black and the whole of New York looking like one gigantic mausoleum.'

When the war ended, Jerome turned his full attentions again to music, art, money-making, women-chasing, and horse racing. 'People like Belmont and Jerome do not enter Society,' wrote Mrs Frank Griswold, 'they create it as they go along.' As part of the creative process, the two formed The Coaching Club in an attempt to revive four-in-hand driving as a fashionable sport. '[Jerome's] horses were trained to caper and rear as they turned into the street,' a reporter noted. 'Gay and laughing ladies, in gorgeous costume, filled the carriage. Lackeys, carefully gotten up, occupied the coupe behind. Jerome sat on the box and handled the reins. With a huge bouquet of flowers attached to his buttonhole, with white gloves, cracking his whip, and with the shouts of the party, the four horses would rush up Fifth Avenue on towards the Park, while the populace said to one another, "That is Jerome".'[38]

With Belmont's help, Jerome also elevated horse racing from the rowdy to the social. On his Bathgate estate, he built the most elaborate racetrack in the country, sporting a grandstand seating 8,000 people, a luxurious clubhouse with a glittering ballroom, dining rooms, overnight guest rooms, and facilities for such diversions as trapshooting, polo, sleighing, and skating.

Opening day of the Jerome Racetrack on September 25, 1866, was described by the New York *Tribune* as 'the social event of all time . . . a new era in the horse-racing world'. Among the special guests was General Ulysses S. Grant. Adelina Patti and Fanny Ronalds were also there, and, it might be mentioned, so was Jerome's Madison Square neighbour, the madame of The Louvre. All three horses in the race were sired by the famous Lexington, and none had ever lost a race. One of them was Kentucky, for whom Jerome had paid forty thousand dollars. Clara Jerome left early, feeling faint, but Leonard insisted on keeping Jennie with him. Kentucky won, and Jerome lifted Jennie onto the horse's back while the crowd cheered. For twelve-year-old Jennie it was one of the unforgettable moments of her life.

Jerome built a small cottage near his racetrack, where his family could spend winter weekends. He even had an area flooded and frozen so that Clarita and Jennie could waltz on the ice while a band played in the cold air. Clarita, by then a young lady of fifteen, was a less venturesome skater than Jennie, who was called the 'madcap'. Fanny Ronalds, a superb skater, was often there, too, showing Jennie how to do figure eights in a shortened hoop skirt.

Jerome, Belmont, and Leonard's cousin and partner, William Travers, known as 'The Stammering Wit of Wall Street',[39] founded the American Jockey Club. *The New York Times* credited Jerome with 'weeding out the blackguards who then controlled the Turf'. It was then that reporters started referring to Jerome as 'The Father of the American Turf'.

When he wasn't racing horses, Jerome was racing yachts. He and his brother Lawrence proposed the first international yacht race across the Atlantic, with a ninety thousand dollar stake, winner take all. At the victory party with the Royal Yacht Squadron at Cowes on the Isle of Wight, observers noted that the Jerome brothers were the 'life and soul of the party'. During the dinner that night, Lawrence Jerome had a note delivered to him in a royal envelope, which he had picked up during a tour of the Queen's summer home earlier in the day. The Royal Yacht Squadron watched him open it, toss it carelessly aside, and then remark loudly to Leonard, 'I am so sorry I cannot dine with the Queen, as we have a previous engagement which it would be ungentlemanly to break.' The Royal Yacht Squadron's reaction was apoplectic. Lawrence finally pretended to let himself be persuaded to accept the Queen's invitation.[40]

After returning to New York, Leonard Jerome maintained his tradition of the grand gesture with a dinner at Delmonico's where each lady found a souvenir under her napkin—a gold bracelet.[41] 'One rode better, sailed better, banqueted better when Mr Jerome was of the company,' noted a commentator of the time.[42]

Newspapers and magazines and gossip sheets were full of Jerome happenings. Clarita read them and passed on the nuggets to twelve-year-old Jennie. For Jennie, at least, all this notoriety and adventure made Jerome seem even more a romantic figure. Besides, her father somehow always found the time to take Jennie to the opera or a concert or a matinee, 'to improve my mind.' Father and daughter enjoyed each other deeply. Clarita's mind took a different turn; she shared her mother's concern for clothes instead of shows and spent more time having her hair fashionably frizzled by her French maid.

Clara Jerome had found herself unable to compete with Mrs August Belmont, described in the press as the 'Queen of High Life', whose high style, French manner, exquisite jewels, and flamboyant parties were constantly discussed. More than that, Clara could no longer countenance the publicity of her husband's flagrant affairs. She therefore told Leonard that she was moving with her daughters to Paris, permanently. He could visit them whenever he wished.

# 2

The year was 1867, and Jennie was thirteen years old. The impending break in her parents' marriage must have been traumatic, but Clara Jerome probably assured her daughters that their father's absence was only temporary. Indeed, she counted on her husband soon tiring of his many women and finally returning to his family.

They moved into an elegant apartment in the Rue Malesherbes, the most fashionable section of Paris. At forty-two, Clara was still a handsome woman, although she now needed flounced gowns to hide her growing plumpness.

Paris had a population of some two million people, but it seemed like a city freshly finished. Napoleon III had transformed a medieval town into a city of grandeur. He had built the best of the boulevards, created the famous Les Halles markets in the city's heart, designed the Etoile, given the Bois de Boulogne its final shape, and completed the monumental design of the Louvre—doing more in five years than his predecessors had done in seven hundred. A historian described his regime as 'a government of cheap bread, great public works and holidays'.[1]

By the time the Jerome women settled into their new home, the extravagant new Paris Exhibition was in full swing, the city full of national costumes and visiting royalty.[2] 'Never had the Empire seemed more assured, the court more brilliant, the fêtes more gorgeous,' Jennie later wrote. 'The light-hearted Parisians revelled in the daily sights of royal processions and cavalcades. The Bois de Boulogne and the Champs Elysées were crowded with splendid equipages. . . .' Her mother's awed respect for any royalty had made its imprint on Jennie, and she used to watch and wait for the Empress driving in her daumont, 'the green and gold liveries of the postilions and outriders making a brave show.'[3]

The importance of all this was intensified for Jennie when in 1869 Clarita made her debut at the Imperial Court. For fifteen-year-old Jennie, it was as if Clarita were being given a key to freedom. No more governesses, no more rigid rules about bedtime and cold baths, no more 'little girl' clothes. Everywhere outside was the world of romance and adventure, and the door was open. Jennie could hardly wait for her own years to race by.

Jennie described in loving detail how Clarita looked in her low-cut dress of billowing white tulle, and the way her blonde hair hung in ringlets on her neck. Then she continued,

When the company was assembled, the doors were flung open and *Sa Majesté l'Empereur* was announced. Then, after a pause, *Sa Majesté l'Impératrice* appeared, a resplendent figure in green velvet, with a crown of emeralds and diamonds, spiked with pearls, on her small and beautifully shaped head. The Emperor and Empress walked around in the circle of curtsying and bowing guests, addressing a few words here and there, and proceeded to the ballroom.

Jennie not only actively identified herself with every step of her sister's debut, but thereafter served as a messenger, intermediary, and sister-confessor for the cluster of Clarita's beaus. One was the Duc de Lescera, a Spanish relative of the Empress, whom Clara Jerome had vetoed because he was a Catholic—she wanted only Protestant proposals for her daughters. Jennie one day acted as the Duke's guide through a side window into the drawing room. Mrs Jerome unexpectedly marched into the room while the Duke and Clarita were together. Clarita and Lescera froze. Mrs Jerome was so nearsighted, however, that she mistook Lescera for one of the servants and ordered him to deliver an immediate message to the cook about dinner that night. 'Oui, Madame,' said the Duke, and gratefully exited.

At the end of 1869, Jennie was almost sixteen, mature and ripe beyond her years. She was not simply budding, she was flowering. She had a figure that men's eyes lingered on, and her eyes had a dazzle and a magnetic impudence. Dreams of romance now held priority over horses, but her sister's complicated love life discouraged Jennie about marriage. 'I am never going to marry,' she told her father. 'I'm going to be a musician.'[4] She did practise at the piano four hours a day, but that was not a sufficient outlet for her energies. She was, after all, at the age of greatest susceptibility, open and warm, ready to accept any of the romance and wonder of life.

Her father was an ideal escort, particularly at this time. His need for her then was as great as her need for him. *Harper's Weekly*[5] had commented that if Leonard Jerome had been born in another age, 'he would have led charges of dragoons.' But Jerome had charged too deeply into the stockmarket, badly misjudging its ability to absorb his huge amount of surplus railroad stock.[6] The price dropped suddenly, and Jerome found himself badly battered, most of his huge fortune gone.[7] He told his family nothing of the disaster but leased his Madison Square house to the Union League Club and came to Paris.

Jennie gave him the lift and love he needed. He took her horseback riding, to picnics, parties, the theatre, opera, concerts. He was still an impressively handsome man, sophisticated in the ways of the world, and he gave her a grown-up look at the swirl of society that she had never had before.

Jennie soon found other men, older men, buzzing around her. Fanny Ronalds had come to Paris, so Leonard Jerome found it necessary to ask his good friend, the Prince de Sagan, a descendant of the Marquis de Talleyrand, to substitute as escort for Jennie. Sagan was charmed by the fresh, lovely Jennie on their frequent rides in the Bois de Boulogne. Mounted on a fiery chestnut horse, she remembered, 'I fancied myself vastly.' The Prince impressed Jennie enormously and she described him well:

He was a remarkable looking man, about forty-five, with snow-white curly hair which stood out like a lion's mane, and through which he had a habit of passing his fingers. With a well set-up figure, irreproachable clothes, a white carnation in his button hole and an eyeglass to which he attached a black moiré ribbon which became the fashion, he was undoubtedly the ideal Parisian beau. His name, his fetes, his extravagances were on all lips. . . .

Jennie looked like a woman, rode like a woman, acted like a woman. The Prince, who was not the fatherly type, obviously made her feel like a woman.

After all, what was Jennie's frame of reference? Her father, with whom she felt closest? Certainly by then she was fully aware of the way of his life. Her sister Clarita? Jennie was completely informed of every detail of her many romantic manoeuvrings. Her mother? Clara Jerome had instituted a steady series of soirees, always fringed with a variety of suitors. The social circle of the Imperial Court? Emperor Napoleon set the pace, and everybody knew that he was a man of many women, had fathered a number of illegitimate children, and always seemed to be in the process of disengaging himself from one mistress in order to move on to another.

It was hardly surprising to Jennie, then, that the Duc de Persigny, a close friend and political ally of the Emperor, was also married, the father of five children, and yet one of Clara Jerome's most attentive suitors. Nor did Persigny's courtship of Clara deter him from playing the gallant to both Clarita and Jennie. During one dance, the Duke's interest in Jennie was so obvious—and Jennie's responsive smile so flirtatious—that the Duchess de Persigny walked over to Jennie and publicly boxed her ears. Such was the morality of the day that even while her ears were being boxed by the indignant Duchess, Jennie knew—as all the Court knew—that the Duchess had so many extramarital affairs that even the Emperor had felt obliged to warn Persigny about it.

Leonard Jerome did complain to his wife about the wildness of his daughters. 'Well, dear,' she responded, 'they are *your* daughters.'[8] Her point was well taken, of course, but they were also daughters of their time. The values, rules, and goals of women of their class were, with varying emphasis, also theirs.

The standard was the Empress Eugénie, whom each of the Jerome women viewed from her own perspective. Clara saw the Empress Eugénie in terms of her incomparable social prestige; Clarita was overwhelmed by her elaborate wardrobe of some three hundred dresses and her magnificent jewels; ten-year-old Leonie saw her as the fairy queen come true; and Jennie marvelled at her being not only the handsomest woman in Europe but a woman of power, who could move men, influence decisions of state, change history.

Marie-Eugénie Ignace Augustine de Montijo was tall, beautifully formed, and elegantly graceful. The Austrian Ambassador, Prince Metternich, himself a connoisseur of women, called her 'all fire and flame'. On the other hand, Maxime de Camp described the Empress Eugénie as 'superficial . . . always preoccupied with the impression she made, parading her shoulders and bosom, her hair dyed, her face painted, her lips rouged . . . with no passion but vanity . . . enveloped in a sovereignty which she didn't know how to wear. . . . To be in her proper sphere, she only lacked the music of the circus, the cantering decorated horse, the hoop through which to jump and the kiss to the spectators. . . .'[9]

There was a romantic story that the reason Eugénie did not marry until she was twenty-six was that she had had a frustrated love affair with a young man who preferred her sister. The story added that Eugénie even tried to poison herself and that the whole affair soured her on men. When she married Charles Louis Napoleon, he was some twenty years her senior, a short, squat man, with a disproportionately large head, a sharply-cut goatee, and a needle-point moustache. Napoleon had originally offered Eugénie his bed but not his throne. Only when she indignantly refused, did he propose marriage.[10] Their marriage, however, did not impede Napoleon's parade of mistresses. After two miscarriages, Eugénie gave birth to her only child, the Prince Imperial. After that, her relationship with Napoleon was purely platonic.[11]

'Destiny always has a sad side to it,' the Empress wrote her sister. 'For instance, I, who was always longing to be free, have chained my life; I shall never be alone, never free. I shall be surrounded with the etiquette of court, whose principal victim I shall be.' Then she added, 'Papa said to me one day, when we were talking politics: "*Las mujeres a hacer calceta!*" [Women are for knitting stockings]. I know very well I am not destined for that!'[12]

Eugénie showed an increasing favouritism for foreigners, particularly the Americans living in Paris. Her grandfather was an American, William Kirkpatrick, who had served as U.S. Consul at Malaga. Napoleon similarly enjoyed Americans. When he was still the young Pretender to the French throne, he had spent a happy, romantic exile in the United States and had even outlined a novel he hoped to write about a French grocer who emigrated to America.

Clara Jerome and her daughters were swept into the inner circle of the Empress. Eugénie found in Jennie the warmth and laughter that she herself had seldom had, and she and Jennie became close friends. For Jennie, this was another substitute mother–daughter relationship of considerable importance. She learned from the Empress not only the extravagances of power, but the loneliness of it. She learned, too, that majesty without love is hollow.

It was the Princess Mathilde who had introduced Eugénie to Napoleon. Mathilde was the daughter of the old roué King Jerome of Westphalia and a niece of Napoleon Bonaparte. She was a cousin of Louis Napoleon and had been engaged to marry him, but her father broke it off when Napoleon failed in his early coup to regain power. Instead, her father arranged a marriage for her with an immensely wealthy Russian, from whom she was soon separated. After Louis Napoleon became Emperor, he again proposed marriage, but Mathilde refused him. 'I refused . . . without any hesitation and without the slightest regret,' she said. 'I should have been unable to give up my independence, and I should have felt that my heart was not in it.' To a close friend, Mathilde later added, 'If I had married him, I should have broken his head open to see what was inside.'[13]

Jennie was fascinated with Princess Mathilde and called her 'undoubtedly the most brilliant and intelligent woman of the Second Empire'. When Jennie knew her, Mathilde was in her late forties, a handsome, animated woman with a lively, piercing glance, a woman in the full flush of life, always surrounded by men.

'The Princess loved to surround herself with all those possessing wit and talent,' Jennie later wrote, 'and her salon had a world-wide reputation, comparing easily with the famous salons of the eighteenth century, with the added attraction and glamour of royalty and great wealth. . . . It was there that some of the young and pretty Americans in Paris . . . had the privilege of meeting such men as Dumas, Sardou, Théophile Gautier, Baudry and other habitués of the house.' Some of the others included Proust, Guy de Maupassant, Anatole France, and Gustave Flaubert.

Sixteen-year-old Jennie was deeply impressed with the ease with which Mathilde could talk with men of intellect. Her soirees sparkled, unlike the dreary, formal 'Little Mondays' of Empress Eugénie's set.[14] It was the difference, Jennie decided, between a bitter, lonely woman and a woman who loved life and loved love. Mathilde's men were always much younger than she was, but she once advised a friend who was tempted to marry a much younger man: 'You are in love with him; he is good-looking and he pleases you; keep him at your side but do not marry him.'[15] Those words meant little to Jennie then, but later they would mean more.

Jennie was also impressed with Mathilde's imagination and taste in decorating her two homes, a flair that Jennie soon found within herself. In fact, she saw in Prince Mathilde many facets of the woman she herself wanted to become.

If Empress Eugénie represented the majestic mother to Jennie, and Princess Mathilde the exciting aunt, Princess Pauline Metternich seemed like the older sister with whom Jennie most easily identified and whom she probably most admired. The Princess was about a dozen years older than Jennie, but the two had much in common: extraordinary beauty, strong will, warm heart, capricious moods, passionate speech, wit, and vivacity. 'Her repartee and *bons mots* were on everybody's lips,' said Jennie, 'her dresses were the models all tried to copy and her company was eagerly sought by the greatest in the land.'

The Princess and Jennie also shared a love of music and the theatre. It was Pauline who was mainly responsible for presenting the first performance of *Tannhäuser* in Paris. And she organized theatricals and ballets and revues where she herself played some of the parts and sang some of the songs. One listener noted how surprised she was to hear Princess Pauline sing 'broad—very broad—Parisian songs . . . with more dash and spirit than one has ever heard in any theatre.'[16]

Pauline was married to the handsome Austrian Ambassador, who was a chronic woman chaser. She herself became the discreet favourite of Napoleon III.

Jennie's friend, the Duc de Persigny, was a caustic critic of the role that upper-class society played in French government— particularly the circle close to the Empress. He called them 'brilliant and frivolous, chivalrous and war-loving, but lacking the virtues needed in a free state.'[17]

The war-loving quality was quite in evidence by 1870. Prussian Chancellor Otto von Bismarck, the most calculating mind in Europe, had made Prussia the new centre of the North German Confederation. 'We could not have set up the German *Reich* in the middle of Europe without having defeated France . . .' he said.[18] Napoleon, already a sick man with a stone in his bladder, did not want war, but the Empress did, and so did most of the Court. Napoleon's misadventure in Mexico had cost the French dearly in men, money and material, and he knew that there were now horses without harnesses, cannon without ammunition, and machine guns without men who knew how to fire them. Besides, the French Army could only muster 300,000 men in the field with no reserves, while the Prussians had almost 500,000 ready men and large reserves. But when told that the Prussians represented the race of the future, Empress Eugénie answered icily, 'We are not there yet.'[19]

Meanwhile the Imperial social life never stopped. Jennie described the scale and style of one Royal weekend at Compiègne.

It was much smaller than usual (less than a hundred people), on account of the Emperor's bad health and political worries.

There was a *grande chasse* or stag hunt on the first day, at which all the guests appeared, riding or driving. Those who hunted wore the royal colors, the men in the green coats and the gold hunt buttons, the ladies in flowing green habits and three-cornered hats. The stag on this occasion was brought to bay in a lake, the Prince Imperial giving him the *coup de grâce*. At night there was a *curée aux flambeaux* in the courtyard of the chateau, the whole party assembling on the balconies in the glare of the innumerable torches. The carcass of the deer lay in the center, covered with its skin; the *hallai* was sounded; at the signal, the hounds were unleashed, and in a moment, every vestige of the stag had disappeared.

The men then escorted their ladies into the dining room where the table was set with Napoleon's magnificent initialled gold dinnerware. Since Napoleon disliked lingering over his meals, everyone ate quickly. Afterward, the Emperor staged one of his grand lotteries of prizes, which were usually rigged so that the most prominent guests won something. The American Ambassador, for example, seldom went home empty-handed. At this party, Clarita won an inkstand filled with gold Napoleon coins, while Clara won some valuable pieces of Sèvres china.

That spring of 1870, Leonard Jerome wrote from New York, 'Everyone is getting tiresome here.' His solution was to take Jennie and Clarita for a vacation to Nice. Clarita reported to their mother, still in Paris:

Papa was very tired last night when he got here, but this morning he looked so fresh and handsome that we told him the ladies would all be after him. . . . We have arranged a little surprise for Pa. He has gone out and said he wouldn't be home till four. So Jennie and I have arranged a little salon so prettily, and brought home flowers to make it look 'homey'. . . . I suppose Jennie told you what a charming day we passed at Cannes . . . . there was Lord-Someone-or-Another and his father, the Earl-of-Something-Else. . . . Madame Rothschild, from Vienna, asked me if I knew Mrs. Belmont. . . .

But even in the comparative calm of Cannes there was increased talk of the coming war with Prussia. Collision finally came on a point of pride—because Bismarck wanted it to come. He manœuvred a touchy political situation in Spain into a war crisis and then heightened the crisis by carefully editing a telegram from the French government to make it seem like a stinging insult to the German government. Unaware that the telegram had been altered, King William of Prussia sent a stiff reply to France. Bismarck called it 'a red rag to the Gallic bull'.[20]

Paris in the summer of 1870 was in high fever. 'The war, the war, there is no other topic,' noted a young American woman. 'Utter strangers would stop to discuss the situation. The confidence in the generals and the army was immense. It was to be one long but straight march to Berlin; not a soul doubted it. . . . I shall never forget the excitement.' Thousands packed the Place de la Concorde night after night with scenes of frenzied dancing. Boulevard windows were so thick with waving flags that one could hardly see the faces behind them. Anyone who dared openly question the wisdom of the war was called a 'Prussian spy' and jeered and hooted at and chased. One mob overturned a beer cart and everybody filled glasses and toasted, '*Vive l'Empereur . . . Vive la France . . . Vive l'Armée!!!!*' Another stopped a bus and asked an opera singer inside to stand on top of it to sing the 'Marseillaise'. 'There was a profound silence when she sang the first note,' an American onlooker observed, 'but all Paris seemed to take up the chorus after each stanza. . . . There were real tears in the singer's eyes, and her voice trembled with genuine emotion. . . .'[21]

Jennie had persuaded her mother to let her wander the streets and share in the excitement. Clara sent along Jennie's childhood nurse, Dobbie, a large American Negro woman who was visible in any crowd because of her green turban and red shawl. Jennie knew little of the real meaning of the war. The Duc de Persigny had filled in some of the background for the Jerome women, and the Empress had given them her highly emotional point of view. But Jennie was caught up in the drama of the moment, the deeply charged patriotism of the people. She was not a watcher; she was a participant, a sixteen-year-old girl who cried and clapped and cheered and waved.

Walking home from the Opera one evening, Jennie and her mother and sister saw crowds of men marching to the cry of, '*des chassepots . . . des chassepots . . .*' (*Chassepots* were the new French rifles supposedly superior to the Prussian guns.) 'Poor devils,' Jennie wrote many years later, 'they soon had them, and all the fighting they wanted.'

27

The Germans crossed the border into Alsace on August 4. Napoleon III went to see his cousin and former fiancée Princess Mathilde and fell weeping into her arms. Then he took his son, the Prince Imperial, and went to the front to take command. Jennie thrilled to the news that the Prince had received his baptism of fire by pulling the lanyard of the first French artillery shot of the war.[22]

The Prussian advance was so methodical that French towns were notified in advance that they would soon be occupied and that the Prussians expected them to furnish particular supplies. The list included everything from one-and-a-half pounds of bread per soldier for a specified number of soldiers, plus one pound of meat and a quarter pound of coffee, to five cigars and either a pint of wine or a pint of beer per soldier. Towns unable to provide the supplies were burned to the ground.

After three successive major defeats, Napoleon wired home from the battlefront, 'Hasten preparations for the defence of Paris.' Paris became a city in panic. If there was one pervasive sound, it was the steady pounding of drums. Men and boys of all ages drilled in the streets, even at night under the gas jets. Some 40,000 oxen and 250,000 sheep were brought in from all directions to pasture in the Bois de Boulogne. Food was packed into warehouses to prepare the city for siege. People clustered in crowds everywhere, noisily trading rumours. Everyone kept an eye out for Prussian spies, and all foreigners became suspect.

Most foreigners had left Paris by August. Among the few to remain were the Jerome women. Leonard Jerome wired his family from New York to flee to London. 'Unfortunately my mother was laid up with a very severe sprain, and could not put her foot to the ground,' Jennie wrote, 'so we tarried. Besides we were incredulous of the Prussians ever reaching Paris, and every day we put off our departure. Our house became the rendezvous of the few of our French friends who had not gone to the front.' Their most frequent visitor was still the Duc de Persigny, and the news he brought grew increasingly ominous. Prussia was advancing with three main armies, all reinforced with superior artillery. Then one day he rushed in, crying, '*Tout est perdu; les Prussiens sont à nos portes!*'

That was not exactly true. The Prussians were not yet at the Paris gates, but it was time to leave. Trains were moving irregularly, but he had managed to secure space for them to Deauville. They would have to pack within an hour, he said; they might tie some valuables in a sheet or a tablecloth. Since there were no cabs, Persigny rushed out to find a cart to carry the injured Clara.

Up to then, war for Jennie had meant flag-waving and songs, a game represented by a war map stuck with brightly coloured pins. Now, suddenly the game had come alive, the drama had turned into fear edged with panic. Jennie tried to pull her mother away from her frenzied watering of the flowers and helped organize the packing. Clarita was more concerned with scribbling a short note to the Marquis de Tamisier, with whom she was currently in love. Jennie, more than anybody, kept the group in gear. Their maid Marie helped carry things to the train and then was sent back with instructions to pack the trunks and take them on the next day's train to Deauville. She never came. Their own train was the last out of Paris.

The end came for Napoleon III in the sleepy town of Sedan, where he surrendered his army of 80,000 troops.[23] Only seven months before, seven million Frenchmen had given their Emperor an overwhelming vote of confidence in a special plebiscite. Now they denounced him,[24] voted his Empire at an end, and proclaimed a new French Republic.

Friends of the Court finally persuaded the Empress to escape to England and join her son, who had been sent there earlier. Wearing a black veil and a dress of black cashmere, she went unannounced to the office of her dentist, a 46-year-old American, Dr Thomas Evans. Together with another American friend, Dr Crane, Evans managed to get a carriage and take the Empress to Deauville.

The Jerome women were still there waiting for passage on a ship across the Channel.

While at Deauville, a friend of ours, M. de Gardonne, called on us unexpectedly and asked if he might spend the day in our rooms—in fact, hide there [Jennie wrote]. He begged that on no account were we to mention his name or let anyone know we had seen him. Naturally we thought this very strange, and my mother grew suspicious; but he impressed upon us that it was for 'state reasons', of which we would hear later. After dinner, when it was quite dark, he departed as mysteriously as he had come.

Later they learned that Gardonne had helped arrange for the Empress's escape from Deauville aboard a British yacht.[25] 'I took her on board,' Gardonne wrote, 'and the only remark she made was,

"I know I am safe now, under the protection of an Englishman."
She also said, "Poor France," and became very hysterical for a
time.' After a rough crossing, the Empress landed on the Isle of
Wight.

The Jerome women were able to leave soon afterward.

# 3

The Jerome women felt like refugees when they arrived in Brighton. It was a resort out of season, the sky bleak, the winds brisk. They stayed at the Norfolk Hotel, still without clothes or servants, waiting further word or direction from Leonard Jerome. Jennie remembered always the sorrow she felt as she walked along the stony beach. 'Our friends scattered, fighting or killed at the front; debarred as we were from our bright little house and our household goods, it was indeed a sad time.'

They all felt as the Prince Imperial did when he wrote to the Princess Mathilde: 'I find England very dismal. The grey skies make me long for France more than ever. I hope 1871 will be happier; it cannot be worse.'[1]

Leonard Jerome sailed immediately to England, swept his family into London, and settled them all into Brown's Hotel near Piccadilly.[2] As quickly as possible, they got clothes and governesses and established a routine of living that included the usual intensive piano practice. 'A winter spent in the gloom and fogs of London did not tend to dispel the melancholy which we felt,' Jennie wrote. They made few English friends that first year, and Clarita developed a fever which the doctors diagnosed as typhoid but which she described as frustration. Her Marquis sent messages by balloon[3] from the besieged Paris, but their romantic future seemed more dim than ever.

The Duc de Persigny came to call, and the Jeromes were saddened by the once-dashing diplomat now 'broken-hearted, ill and penniless'. When Leonard Jerome found the Duke selling his few possessions, he insisted on setting Persigny up in a room at Brown's and paying all the bills. 'If it were not for you,' Jerome told him, 'my wife and daughters might yet be caught in a starving city.'

The Jerome rooms became a haven for a vast variety of French refugees, each of whom brought his own rumours to trade. They all knew that the Empress had sold her jewelry, plus some royal real estate in Italy, and had settled in the country village of Chislehurst in Kent. She had leased a simple three-story house called Camden Place from a man who had been the trustee for the Emperor's former mistress, Harriet Howard. Unknown to the Empress, Camden Place held tender memories for the Emperor—he had paid heavy court to another young lady who had lived there, and was said to have been engaged to her for a short time.[4]

But now the Emperor had warmer feelings for his wife. From his prison in Prussia, on January 30, 1871, he wrote:

Dearest friend, Today is the anniversary of our wedding. . . . I want to tell you that I am very fond of you. In good times, the links between us may have grown loose. I thought them broken, but stormy days have shown me how solid they are, and now, more than ever, I am reminded of the words of the Evangelist: 'For richer, for poorer, in sickness and in health, to love, cherish, and obey. . . .'[5]

After seeing his family safely settled, Leonard Jerome had a United States government mission to perform. Paris was under siege. After Napoleon's surrender, the Government of National Defence had taken control with the public promise, 'Not an inch of our soil will we cede, not a stone of our fortresses.' The United States wanted Jerome to forward special proposals to Bismarck concerning an easing of the siege. They gave him a diplomatic passport and assigned the famous Civil War Generals Sheridan and Burnside to accompany him.

The three Americans found the city starving. The food hoarded in warehouses was long since gone, and so were the cattle and horses in the Bois de Boulogne. Some two months before, the Christmas menu at a Paris restaurant had listed: soup from horsemeat, mince of cat, shoulder of dog with tomato sauce, roast donkey and potatoes, mice on toast.[6] Sewer rats were considered 'far more delicate than young chickens', according to young Charles Joseph Bonaparte, who stayed in the city throughout the siege.[7]

*The Paris Journal* described the purchase of the rats at the Rat Market in the Place de l'Hôtel de Ville:

. . . as the rats are shut up in a big cage, one has to choose the animal one wants out of the crowd. With a little stick the dealer makes it go into a smaller cage where it is alone, and then a bulldog is brought along. The little cage is shaken and the rat escapes; but it is promptly seized by the formidable teeth of the dog, which breaks its back and drops it delicately at the purchaser's feet.

One gourmet said that rat tasted like a 'mixture of pork and partridge. . . .' Writing about his daily diet, a man named Labouchère noted in his diary:

... I have a guilty feeling when I eat dog, the friend of man. I had a slice of spaniel the other day; it was by no means bad, something like lamb, but I felt like a cannibal. Epicures in the dog-flesh tell me that poodle is by far the best, and recommend me to avoid bulldog, which is coarse and tasteless. . . .

Dog sold for four francs a pound, when it was available, compared to horse at forty centimes a kilo. Cats were considered more of a delicacy, and the price was twenty francs a pound. A statistic supplied to the Chronique du Siège notes that the Parisians had eaten 25,523 cats during the siege, not counting strays. Mule was also considered superior to beef, but antelope wasn't thought as good as stewed rabbit. When the zoo was closed, some elephant's trunk circulated at eight dollars a pound. Camel kidneys were much cheaper. Bread 'seemed to have been made from old panama hats picked up in the gutter'.[8] Jerome did not tell his daughters that a piece of bread was the price for a prostitute.

The prolonged siege so angered Bismarck that he ordered his troops to fire on the starving women and children of Paris, who often approached Prussian soldiers for food. When somebody suggested that his Prussian soldiers might refuse to do that, Bismarck answered, 'Then you'll have to shoot the soldiers for disobedience,' and added, 'I attach no great importance to human life, because I believe in another world.'[9]

The only plentiful food in Paris was mustard and champagne.[10] More Parisians—approximately 65,000—died of starvation and disease than of battle wounds. Of these, 3,000 were babies. After a four months' siege and a bombardment from heavy guns in the last few weeks, an armistice was arranged so that the dead could be buried.

Jerome visited the American Ambassador, Mr E. B. Washburne, the only foreign representative who stayed in Paris throughout the siege. Washburne told him that the theatres had been turned into hospitals, then back again into theatres when human souls seemed sicker than bodies.[11] He described how Victor Hugo held recitals of readings from his books, and how hard the entertainers worked to stir the faint blood of the people.[12]

Jerome reported to his family that he had found their house intact, except for a cellar wall which had been blown open by a shell. The maid Marie was still there, guarding her mistresses' clothing.

He also described his visit with the two Civil War generals to Bismarck's headquarters in a large villa in Versailles. Bismarck worked and slept and smoked his endless cigars in a single over-heated room, changing only from his doeskin-lined uniform to his dressing-gown, frequently working through the night and then sleeping to noon. He provided his guests with a simple dinner on tin plates, with candles stuck into wine bottles and one of his officers playing the piano.

The American group accomplished nothing, but it mattered little because soon it was all over. Paris surrendered. Bismarck dictated his terms to a French lawyer, and peace was signed at Versailles on February 26, 1871.

Upon his return to London, Jerome told his family of all he had seen in Paris, describing in dramatic detail the starvation, the despair, the courage. What affected seventeen-year-old Jennie most deeply and lastingly was the story of Paris's surrender. As the Prussians prepared to march down the Champs Elysées, the people emptied the streets, shuttered their windows, and waited in the dark silence of their defeat. Even the Bois de Boulogne was bare—the trees had long ago been cut down for fuel. Masses of Prussian troops wearing their spiked helmets marched past the Arc de Triomphe and down the deserted boulevards singing 'Die Wacht am Rhein', the drum and fife corps playing in perfect unison. That day the Prussian soldiers were seen waltzing with one another in the Place de la Concorde.[13]

Had the Jerome women stayed in the United States, Jennie's life would have consisted almost entirely of the youthful gaieties of the rich. Those would still be the frame of her emerging womanhood, but the Paris interval had imposed a new understanding of the world.

Leonard Jerome decided to go again to Paris to safeguard his valuable collection of Italian paintings. Clara insisted on going along, even though Paris was in turmoil. When they arrived, they selected their favourite paintings and managed to pack and ship them just before the real riots of 'Bloody Week' started. The mob had moved on to the Palais de Justice and the Hôtel de Ville, set them afire, and after throwing furniture out the windows, held auctions on the lawn.

Auctions were still taking place the next morning when Clara ventured out to view the scene for herself. Outside the smouldering Tuileries, Napoleon's initialled gold dining plates were being offered for sale; Clara bid for them and bought them, then hired a wheelbarrow to carry the plates to her surprised husband. (Clara's grandson Winston later used those plates.[14])

It is easy to classify Clara Jerome as a social snob, a woman of limited imagination, firm prejudice, and pronounced ambition. She was. But she also had courage and high style—valuable attributes for the wife of Leonard Jerome and a resident of 1870 London.

England in 1870 was still in the Victorian Age, with the Prince of Wales running gaily around the rim and Queen Victoria sombre in the centre. For the Queen, the guiding words were duty and self-denial. Her 'dear Albert' had died nine years before, but she still wore the black silk dress of mourning, still had his clothes laid out every night on his bed at Windsor Castle, still ordered a fresh basin of water placed in his room every morning. And over her bed hung a framed photograph of Albert's head and shoulders, taken after he died.

Victoria had once complained to her daughter that, even in the happiest marriages, 'the poor woman is bodily and morally the husband's slave. That always sticks in my throat' Still, Albert was much the stronger personality, and she a most willing follower. Soon after her first pregnancy, she gave him the keys to all her secret boxes and papers, allowed him the final word on all formal decisions—in effect made him her permanent prime minister.

After Albert's death, she suffered a nervous breakdown that lasted two years, then became a virtual recluse. For a long time, her pre-occupation seemed to be setting up memorials to her dead husband.[15] She seldom made public appearances, held few receptions—at which no refreshments were served. All that her guests had to look forward to was their chance to kiss her 'soft, small, red hand'.[16] Court life was strict, stuffy, and dull. The public was royally bored.

The British people had loved her once, loved the young Queen who was fascinated by the glitter of court ceremonies. And when she married Albert, mothered nine children, and reigned with pomp and ceremony, the people respected her. But when she became a

D

widow, sad and sour and solitary, they ignored her, mocked her, even demanded her abdication.

Disraeli, of the purple waistcoat and the flowery speech, had said that England was 'a country of two nations', the classes and the masses; and that was true. It was also partly true, as *The Spectator* had printed, that 'The country is once more getting rich. The money is filtering downwards to the actual workers.'

Not enough, however. Charles Dickens died in 1870 but Oliver Twist did not. Too many children still went hungry. Almost half the country's children were not in school. They worked in the factories at the age of ten, in the mines at twelve, six days a week. The legal age of consent for girls was thirteen, and many were soon part-time prostitutes, as were their mothers. The white-slave traffic travelled from England to Paris, and not vice versa.

Workers in the ugly, sprawling industrial towns of the Midlands and the north-west saw little of the growing prosperity at this time; many were even charged for the use of water and the cost of cleaning the lavatories. As for women factory workers, when somebody tried to campaign for shorter working hours for mothers on Saturday, one newspaper editorialized: 'To pretend that women wish to have their hours of work restricted by legislation is not honest.' Yet a favourite tune was, 'Home, Sweet Home.'[17]

Jennie, of course, knew nothing of all this. England to her was Brown's Hotel, governesses, piano lessons, French aristocratic refugees, Hyde Park, the opera, and some carefully selected young people in British high society. It would be years before she really learned about the other England, where a quarter of the people couldn't write their names and more than half couldn't read. She lived in the world of the 'upper 10,000', highly social, quite stuffy, with a rigid schedule of 'seasons'. Besides the London Season, there was the Hunting Season, the Shooting Season, and the Season at Cowes.

Fortunately for the Jerome women, their entry into London society was considerably eased by the sponsorship of the Duc de Persigny, who had once been French Ambassador to England. The Emperor had been released from his comfortable Prussian prison and had joined his wife at Chislehurst in Kent. The collected gaggle of French aristocratic refugees quickly integrated into the London Season.

36

Although the London Season officially started in the spring, the prime period was summer. A Paris visitor was dazzled by how this 'race of gods and goddesses descended from Olympus upon England in June and July . . . appeared to live on a golden cloud, spending their riches as indolently and naturally as the leaves grow green.'

It was a steady round of opera, ballet, theatre, and parties, with little variation in the schedule. Most of the entertaining, however, took place at home. For the many social Charitable Committees, there were breakfast invitations, usually from 8:30 to 10. Guests left promptly after the meal because most of them had to get ready for luncheon elsewhere. These luncheons ran into several courses with matched wines, often much more formal than today's dinners. More informal were the afternoon teas, always at five, usually featuring one of the accomplished guests at the piano. Jennie was often on call.[18]

A *Punch* joke on the subject of amateur pianists told of two matrons, one asking the other:

'Do your daughters play, Mrs. Jones?'
Mrs. Jones: 'No.'
'Sing?'
'No.'
'Paint in water-colours?'
'No,' said Mrs. Jones, smiling. 'We go in for beauty.'[19]

Beauty was essential, conversation desirable, piano-playing optional. The best female guests managed all three.

Dinner was usually the high point of the day, and the preparations were elaborate. Seating arrangements represented an art, equal to the selection of the various wines to suit the several courses of the lavish menu. The meal usually consisted of a thick soup or a sherry-fortified clear soup, one or two fish dishes, a choice of four entrées, followed by some poultry or game, then puddings, sweets, cheese, and dessert. Thanks to the influence of the Prince of Wales, champagne gradually took the place of claret as the main dinner wine.

Hostesses invariably checked each other to avoid conflicts of dinner dates, and particularly of parties, since most of their guests came from the same two hundred governing families of England, whom Winston Churchill called 'that brilliant and powerful body'. Invitations were usually sent three weeks in advance, and the only excuses for non-attendance were death or contagious disease.

The rules were precise: all guests were to arrive no sooner or later than fifteen minutes after the time specified on the invitation, and all guests divided into male and female groups immediately after dinner. The women gathered in the drawing room, while men lingered behind at the table for their cigars and drink and manly conversation. Social 'tail' of the evening was the arrival of other guests after ten, followed by some scheduled entertainment, such as a brief recital by an opera singer or a dance.[20]

'To make a ball successful,' Lady Cowper once told Lady Nevill, 'three men should always be asked to every lady—one to dance, one to eat and one to stare—that makes everything go off well.' Competition for guests and entertainers was incessant, with three or four balls—or 'drums' as they were called—almost every night. The challenge to a guest was to transform night into day, crowd in as many parties as one could.

Even the afternoon social parade in Hyde Park had the fixed pattern of a pirouette. The time and place were between five and seven in the afternoon on a broad southern avenue that led past the Albert Gate and paralleled Rotten Row—a contraction of the French, *Route du Roi*, the Avenue of the King.

Rotten Row is actually nothing more than an unsurfaced road of loose sand and gravel, but nonetheless, the Row was regal. In a House of Commons debate, it was jokingly suggested that houses be built on both sides of the Row, so that ladies in the balconies could look at the riding gentlemen. The need to be seen was a matter of first importance.

All proper coaches had meticulously uniformed coachmen, usually dressed in blue coats with brass buttons. 'It was not etiquette to handle the reins oneself in the afternoons,' noted the Countess of Warwick in her memoirs,

so we sat . . . chatting and behaving as if the world we knew, bounded by the Smart Set, was a fixed orbit, as if London—our London—was a place of select social enjoyment for the Circle, as if nothing could change in this best of delightful worlds. Then there would be a clatter of faster horses, and down this mile of drive came the well-known royal carriage, the beautiful Alexandra, Princess of Wales, bowing right and left as only she could bow, and hats were raised and knees curtseyed before seats were resumed and interrupted chatter continued.[21]

Jennie was among those who curtseyed to the Princess of Wales. Accompanied by a governess, she made the Hyde Park walk part of her ritual. There is little likelihood that it ever crossed her mind that one day she might compete with this Princess to whom she curtseyed for the affection and attention of the Prince of Wales.

In 1871, the Prince was thirty years old and had been married to the Princess Alexandra of Denmark for eight years. His taste in women was as varied as his taste in clothes, and he often set the style in both categories. The fashionable constantly copied the cut of his clothes, the shape of his goatee, his habit of cigarette-smoking after dinner. After an attack of rheumatism, Prince Edward was forced to shake hands stiffly, his elbow pressed against his side. Within a short time, the watchful fashionable men of London even copied that. Everyone knew that the Prince always travelled with two valets while two others stayed behind to clean and care for his huge wardrobe. As for his women, the British penny-press gave special space to his Paris sprees with a beautiful French actress, Mademoiselle Hortense Schneider, and a prominent prostitute called 'Skittles'. Popular gossip often named him as one of the 'persons unknown' in several celebrated divorce cases and certainly there were many affairs that were hushed up. In fact, it was on a trip to settle one of his son's affairs that Albert, Queen Victoria's Consort, caught the fever from which he died. It was said the Queen never forgave Prince Edward.

The Queen once confided to a friend that sometimes she could hardly bear to be in the same room with her son. She also refused him access to any important papers or to make any important decisions. Disraeli agreed with her. The Prime Minister called the Prince 'Chitter Chatter' and advised the Queen not to let him see any private papers because 'he lets them out and talks to his friends about them'.[22] During the Franco-Prussian War, Prince Edward had pleaded with his mother to let him act as her emissary to try to negotiate a peace. 'I cannot bear sitting here doing nothing whilst all this bloodshed is going on,' he wrote her. But she refused. One of the classic cartoons of the day showed him at Windsor, standing in a corner like a bad little boy in a schoolroom, with his mother glaring at him.[23]

Denied any prerogatives of power, the Prince became more completely a 'heavy swell' and an habitué of the racetracks. When his mother pointedly asked him not to attend the Ascot Races, he wrote her:

I am always most anxious to meet your wishes, dear Mama, in every respect, and I always regret if we are not quite *d'accord*—but I am past 28, and have some considerable knowledge of the world and society; you will, I am sure, at least I trust, allow me to use my own discretion in matters of this kind. . . .[24]

But the most serious mother-son arguments concerned his parties—wild affairs that lasted until dawn, with guests tobogganing down the stairs on trays or engaging in slapstick battles with soda-siphons. Unwanted as guests were the literary people or intellectuals, because the swells 'did not want to be made to think'.

'We acknowledged that pictures should be painted, books written, the law administered,' wrote the Countess of Warwick:

We even acknowledged that there was a certain class whose job might be to do these things. But we did not see why their achievement entitled them to recognition from us, whom they might disturb, overstimulate, or even bore. On rare occasions, if a book made a sufficient stir, we might read it, or better still, get somebody to tell us about it, and so save us the trouble.[25]

Most of the parties were at Marlborough House, the Prince's London home. His social group was called the Marlborough House Set, and it was quite fitting, therefore, that one of the Prince's newest recruits, a young man who became a particular favourite of his, was the second son of the Duke of Marlborough, Lord Randolph Churchill. Lord Randolph was a pop-eyed young man with an intense face and a handsome moustache. He was fresh out of Oxford by way of a Grand Tour of the Continent.

Marlborough House became the important meeting place for the fashionable beauties, particularly the Americans, in whom the Prince was especially interested. Of the many women who wandered into the Prince's orbit, few denied him their favours. In return, many of them came away with such expensive princely gifts as a gold sharkskin cigarette case with a diamond-and-sapphire clasp.[26] *Town Topics* said of the Prince, 'He wastes nothing, and gives no favours without the assurance of favours in return.' It added, 'The attentions of H.R.H. to any woman means indignity and scandal.' Such gossip was grist for the public mill, and the public loved it. To them, Prince Albert Edward of Wales was 'good old Bertie'. 'The Prince of Wales is loved,' said Lord Granville, 'because he has all the faults of which the Englishman is accused.'

The Cowes Season began with the end of the London Season in

the first week of August. With its wooded shores, cliffs of coloured sands, chalk downs, and well-kept flower gardens whose fragrant scents tempered the sea air, the Isle of Wight's physical setting resembled an impressionist painting. Here Queen Victoria had spent her young womanhood, and here she would come to die. Here also were the 300 members of the Royal Yacht Squadron, the most exclusive yacht club in the world, housed in a castle built by Henry VIII.

'In those days,' Jennie wrote,

it was delightfully small and peaceful. No glorified villas, no esplanade or pier, no bands, no motors or crowded tourist-steamers. . . . The Royal Yacht Squadron lawn did not resemble a perpetual garden party, or the roadstead a perpetual regatta. People all seemed to know one another. The Prince and Princess of Wales and many foreign royalties could walk about and amuse themselves without being photographed or mobbed.

But in that first week of August, the Solent yacht clubs held regattas of such sweep and magnificence that they transformed the sleepy island into the social centre of all Europe. It was *the* place in England to see and be seen.

*Graphic Magazine* described for Jennie the newly expanded social world in which she would soon move:

For the fashionable beauty, life is an endless carnival, and dress a round of disguises. She does everything and the wings of Mercury might be attached to her tiny bottines, so rapid are her changes of scene and character. She is a sportswoman, an athlete, a ballroom divinity. She is alternately a horsewoman, a huntress, a bold and skilful swimmer; she drives a pair of horses like a charioteer, mounts the roof of a four-in-hand, plays lawn tennis, is at home on a race course or the deck of a fast yacht. She is aware of the refinements of dining and has a pretty taste in vintages. She is a power at the theatre or the Opera; and none is more brilliant at a supper party. Of the modern young lady à *la mode*, who wields alike the fiddle-bow, the billiard-cue and the etching-needle, who climbs mountains and knows the gymnasium, none but herself can be the prototype.

*Graphic*, of course, was focusing on a highly favoured few. More generally, the Victorian woman was not only considered the weaker sex in body and mind, but was presumed to have a purity and spirituality that needed to be protected from male coarseness. Women of polite society were expected not to travel either by cab or railway without a chaperon or to attend any public entertainment unescorted.[27] Except for the flouting, fashionable beauties, most of whom filtered into the Marlborough House Set, the Queen kept her women in a strict social straitjacket.

Sex was a dirty word, but an increasing number of society women smuggled Swinburne's poems into their bedrooms. One magazine referred to the poet as 'Swineborn' and classified his sensual writings as the 'Fleshly School of Poetry'.

Jennie's occasional contact with young men was still carefully chaperoned and restricted entirely to parties and dances. Typical of her limited social correspondence was a note from the young French Prince Imperial, who was two years younger than she and lived with his parents in Chislehurst: 'Will you please forgive my negligence in the last few days? . . . I got measles from a young lady with whom I danced a mazurka, and I really should not dance with any other girl.'

Leonard Jerome rented Rosetta Cottage at Cowes, a small house with pretty gardens facing the sea. It was often a rough sea, as the Jeromes discovered one day when they were invited for a cruise around the island in the Emperor's yacht. Most of the small group became sick and remained in their cabins. The young, gangly Prince Imperial unsuccessfully tried to lift everyone's spirits with jokes. Only the Empress seemed to flourish in the fierce sea, but it was the Emperor whom Jennie best remembered: 'I can see now the Emperor leaning against the mast looking old, ill and sad. His thought could not have been other than sorrowful and, even in my young eyes, he seemed to have nothing to live for.'

The Emperor's long moustache had begun to droop badly now, his hair was ragged around his ears, his speech softer and more hesitant than ever. He spent his time developing long-range schemes for old-age pensions for the French people and outlining drawings for an economical stove for poor families. He also conceived a plan to abolish war by which a council of nations would meet regularly to decide critical issues on the basis of international law. While he kept his social life carefully cloistered, limited to a few old friends and an occasional visit to Queen Victoria, his great pleasure was in the time spent with his son. He had already enrolled the Prince Imperial in the Royal Military College at Woolwich.

Napoleon's staff organized a stratagem for a Royalist return to France through Switzerland to spark a Bonapartist uprising. But Napoleon was too sick to mount a horse. He told his old associates he would not return to France even if the Army revolted in his favour; he would return only if recalled by a plebiscite. Organizing a *coup d'état* was something 'one does in one's youth', he said.[28]

Later in the autumn of 1871, Jerome took his family back to France. 'But what changes in Paris itself!' Jennie wrote.

Ruins everywhere: the sight of the Tuileries and the Hôtel de Ville made me cry. St.-Cloud, the scene of many pleasant expeditions, was a thing of the past, the lovely chateau razed to the ground. And if material Paris was damaged, the social fabric was even more so. In vain we tried to pick up the threads. Some of our friends were killed, others ruined or in mourning, and all broken-hearted and miserable, hiding in their houses and refusing to be comforted.

The statues at the Place de la Concorde, representing the most important towns of France—Strasbourg, Lille, Nancy, Orleans—swathed in crepe, . . . reminded one daily, if one needed it, of the trials and tribulations France had just gone through. Only the embassies and a few foreigners, principally Americans, received or entertained. . . . A few opened their houses, but the French on the whole were shy of going out at all, and if Paris had any gaiety left in those days, it was owing to her cosmopolitan character.[29]

What does an energetic seventeen-year-old girl do in a sad city? Her younger sister Leonie had been sent off to school in Weisbaden, and Clarita was still mooning over the Duc de Lescara, toward whom her mother would not relent. Persigny returned to Paris, but Jennie no longer saw him as anyone to flirt with—he was just an old man of fifty, bitter and boring. He would die that year. Dismayed by Clarita's stolen romance with the Marquis, Mrs Jerome was more watchful than ever of Jennie and established stricter limits on her social life. So Jennie went riding in the Bois with her father or his friends, and with little else to do, studied music and languages more intensively.

Paris seemed so quiet for Clara Jerome, too, that she welcomed her husband's suggestion that they all return to Cowes in the summer of 1872. Jerome continued on to New York alone.

The time had come for Jennie's debut. During Regatta Week at the start of the August season she would be presented to the Prince and Princess of Wales at the Royal Yacht Squadron Ball.

Her dress, of course, had to be white. Dressing was an ordeal. A maid pulled the corset laces as tightly as pain would permit. A seventeen-inch waist was a thing of pride, but anything over twenty-one inches was considered an enormity. The tight lacing also

43

caused an artificial enlargement of the bust—augmented when necessary by padding of horsehair or inflated rubber. For Jennie that was not needed. To offset the artificially enlarged curve of the bust (well-exposed by an extreme decolletage), there was an even more artificially enlarged posterior, produced by the bustle hidden under a full flounce, and further complicated by the yard-long trailing skirt. All this extra fabric and artificial enlargement was in sharp contrast to the dress material stretched over the woman's flanks and loins with an almost violent tightness. Whatever the attractions of the bigger bust and the exaggerated posterior, it is true that statistics indicated a considerable increase of marriages in the 1870's.[30] The only make-up permitted Jennie, however, was a little powder on her nose—she could keep the puff wrapped in her handkerchief.

Throughout the presentation, her manner was easy, her enjoyment obvious. It was a gay evening and Jennie danced through the hours, never lacking for partners. A British guest described her vitality as 'American'.

Throughout the Cowes Season, Clarita and Jennie applied the same vigour to piano duets at dinner parties. 'Such a lovely sight it made, those two young heads, one blonde and one dark, bent raptly over the keys,' an admirer recorded years later.[31]

The two sisters were kept so busy socially that they seemed to have little time for writing letters—either to Leonie at school in Weisbaden or to their father in New York. Jerome complained:

Mrs. Clit, Miss Clarita, and Miss Jennie,
  Dearly beloved, it is nearly two weeks since I had a letter. You must be sure to write me particulars of all that is going on. I have no doubt you will see many nice people and will have Cowes all to yourselves as far as Americans are concerned. Did you get the tent from London? And do you make it lively and have you secured the Villa Rosetta for another year? etc. I rather like the idea of Cowes next summer and a yacht. Don't forget while sitting under your own vine and eating up your own fig tree that I am awfully disappointed if I don't get my weekly letters.[32]

# 4

By the time of the 1873 Cowes Week, the Jerome women were firmly entrenched on the scene. Clara Jerome felt her position strong enough on the Cowes social list to pick and choose most selectively among the many invitations. But one of them was obviously a must: a deckle-edged invitation from the officers of the guardship *Ariadne* to a ball on board in honour of the Czarevich and the Czarevna of Russia.

The invitation read:

To Meet
Their Royal Highnesses, the Prince and Princess of Wales
and
Their Imperial Russian Highnesses
the
Grand Duke Cesarewitch and Grand Duchess Cesarevna,
Captain Carpenter and the officers of H.M.S. 'Ariadne'
request the honour of the Company of
MRS. and MISSES JEROME
On board, on Thursday, August 12th, from 3:30 to 7:30 P.M.
DANCING
Boats will be in attendance at the RYS Landing Place.
R.S.V.P.

Jennie long afterward wrote between the lines of the invitation:

To meet—Randolph.

Until then, the social life at Cowes had been a steady hum, but this was high spectacle and Clara was all aflutter about it. Barges took the guests from shore to ship, the women having to negotiate the ship's ladder with their full skirts. Canopied with bobbing lanterns, the ship's deck was draped with the national colours of Britain and Imperial Russia, and a Royal Marine Band played in the background.

The two sisters were quickly crowded around by admirers. Both bare-shouldered and beautiful, they effectively complemented each other: Clarita, blonde and dreamy; Jennie, dark and sparkling. Jennie was swiftly swept away into her first dance, a waltz with a

45

lieutenant, then again surrounded by a host of admirers wanting a place on her dance-card.

Her friend Frank Bertie pushed through the crowd, bringing with him a pale young man. Jennie had noticed him before, standing aside and staring at her. She had smiled slightly at him, and when he simply kept staring, she had blushed. 'Miss Jerome,' said Frank Bertie very formally, 'may I present an old friend of mine who has just arrived in Cowes, Lord Randolph Churchill.'[1]

He was slim, not tall, with a large head and a walrus moustache, attractive but not handsome. He had held his courtesy title since he was eight years old (when his father became the Duke of Marlborough), and he looked the part. Impeccably dressed, almost dandified, he had the elegant polish of his class but also much of its pomposity. His manner with strangers was brusque and his sense of humour occasionally cutting. At twenty-three his was the life of the pleasure-seeker of turf and town. He had neither deep convictions nor high ambitions. In fact, he had hardly any deep passions except for the horse and the hunt.

His mere membership of the Marlborough House Set served as intriguing credentials as far as Jennie was concerned. It provided him with an aura of attractive danger. If he belonged to the Set, he could hardly be *too* proper! The floor was full of pompous dandies, but beneath the surface of this one there might be something special.

After proper small talk, Randolph rather reluctantly asked Jennie to dance. Like most Churchills, he was not a man of music, and he detested dancing. But it seemed the only way he could keep with him this strikingly lovely young woman in the white dress with the fresh flowers and the dark hair.

Lord Randolph had such noticeable problems in matching his feet to the intricate figures of the quadrille, that he finally admitted to Jennie that dancing made him dizzy, and wouldn't she prefer sitting somewhere? In this case, she definitely would. So he found some seats on the open deck in the soft breeze and they sat and sipped champagne and talked.

Lord Randolph had a way of speaking with great rapidity and vehemence and a compelling intensity. It was as if his words were trying to catch up with his thoughts. It intrigued Jennie. A beautiful woman who knows she's beautiful, who always has been openly admired for her beauty, is often more captivated by the man who regards her as someone with a mind as well as a body. They had much to talk about, much to interest each other. They had travelled to the same countries; they both loved horses; they had both mingled with the great of the world. Jennie had a lively mind and was easily bored. He obviously did not bore her. When he wished, Lord Randolph could be charming, witty and jaunty. This was one of those nights.

The two talked so long, so oblivious to the dance and the dancers, that Jennie's mother searched them out. Without many words, she clearly indicated that there was such a thing as spending too much time with one man at such a ball. But before the evening was over, Jennie had persuaded her mother to invite Lord Randolph, along with their mutual friend, Colonel Edgecumbe, to dinner the next night.

Jennie seemed particularly nervous the following day. She insisted that she and Clarita spend extra time rehearsing their piano duet and even asked Clarita to decide what dress she should wear.

The evening air was gentle, with an occasional breeze and bright stars, and the lights of the many boats flickered in the harbour. The small dinner was very pleasant, and afterward Jennie and her sister 'played duets at the piano and chattered merrily'. When Colonel Edgecumbe commented to Lord Randolph on both the performance and the players, Randolph answered quietly and seriously, 'I admire them both tremendously. And, if I can, I mean to make the dark one my wife.'[2]

After their guess had gone, Jennie asked her sister in private what she had thought of Lord Randolph. Clarita had not been very impressed. She thought he had been trying too hard to be clever, and she didn't particularly like his fancy moustache. 'I'm sure you'd like him if you knew him better,' Jennie answered while she brushed her hair. Then she suddenly stopped brushing, looked at her sister very seriously and added, 'Please try to, Clarita, because I have the strangest feeling that he's going to ask me to marry him. . . . I'm going to say yes.' Clarita was incredulous and laughed out loud.

The next day, Jennie was so unusually quiet that her mother commented on it to Clarita. It was then that Clarita mentioned Jennie's confession of interest in the young nobleman. Clara was not happy about it. She was aiming higher for Jennie than a mere second son who stood so slight a chance of succession to the dukedom.

But Jennie already had arranged her next rendezvous with Randolph. It was ostensibly a meeting 'by accident'. During their conversation the night before, she had told him of her daily habit of walking along a certain path at a certain time. Naturally, he was there. For the first time, they were quite alone.

He was supposed to leave the next day for Blenheim. Could he see her again that night? She would ask her mother. Perhaps he might come to dinner again.

Forewarned of Jennie's interest in the young Churchill, Clara regarded this new request most critically. 'Are we not inviting that young gentleman rather often?' she asked. But Jennie persisted, and her mother scribbled on a small, printed card:

Mrs. Leonard Jerome
The Misses Jerome
I shall be most happy to see you
at dinner this evening truly yours
C.H. Jerome.

(Lord Randolph later preserved that card in a black metal box in Blenheim Palace among his most intimate possessions.)

After dinner that night, Mrs Jerome unwillingly excused herself with a headache, and Clarita more willingly excused herself with a smile. In a short memorandum to herself, Jennie remembered the night as being beautiful and described how she and Randolph strolled into the garden, 'when, finding ourselves alone for a moment, he asked me if I would marry him and I said yes. We agreed not to say anything to my mother, as she would not understand the suddenness of it.'

It was probably not so matter-of-fact—not with these two passionate people. There must have been many promises made and sealed, love freely given, dreams shared.

Randolph postponed his departure another four days. Just before he left, they broke the news to Mrs Jerome. 'She thought we were both quite mad,' Jennie later commented, 'and naturally would not hear of anything so precipitous.'

At Blenheim, when Randolph told the news to his mother, the consternation was even more intense. Those were the days when the great houses of England had closed their doors to 'dollars and

48

impudence'.[3] As Jennie herself later put it, 'In England then, the American woman was looked upon as a strange and abnormal creature with habits and manners something between a Red Indian and a Gaiety Girl.'

The Duchess of Marlborough was a commanding woman. She was, after all, formerly Lady Frances Anne Emily Vane, eldest daughter of the Third Marquess of Londonderry. *The Complete Peerage* described her as 'a woman of remarkable character and capacity, judicious and tactful'. Few denied the quality of her character, but many questioned her judiciousness and tact. Her face had more strength than beauty and her eyes were hard or warm, depending on whom she looked at, but they were never lacklustre. 'She ruled Blenheim and nearly all those in it with a firm hand,' Jennie wrote later. 'At the rustle of her silk dress, the household trembled.'[4]

Joined with a frequent temper and an occasional rage, the spirited Duchess had breathed new life into the moribund Blenheim. Her entertainments were lavish and exciting. She also produced two sons and six daughters (three other sons died in infancy). As a mother, she was both domineering and devoted. Her grandson Winston later wrote of her: 'She was a woman of exceptional capacity, energy and decision.'

But her eldest son, the Marquess of Blandford, was a sharp disappointment both to her and to the Duke. He had married a beautiful, pious, stupid woman who now bored him, and he openly showed his boredom by hedge-hopping with any other beautiful woman he could find. He was a restless, unhappy man, a rebel against the propriety of his parents. The Duke and Duchess, therefore, had turned their hopes and love to Randolph. At the very least, Randolph always had been a warm, affectionate son.

Most of Randolph's early life had followed the fixed upper-class pattern. When he was only ten, he rode his first pony on a fox hunt and came back 'blooded' with the fox's brush. As soon as he was old enough, he bought and bred his own hounds, raced his own horses. Everything else was subsidiary, including school.

For the English aristocracy, the horse was a symbol of social, political, and economic dominance. Those who rode and those who owned horses viewed society as composed of 'a small, select aristocracy, booted and spurred to ride, and a large, dim mass, born, saddled and bridled to be ridden.'[5]

49

At Eton, Randolph had been called 'a scug'. A scug was an untidy, ill-mannered, and morally undeveloped boy, a shirker at games, bumptious and arrogant. If not naturally vicious, a scug was considered degenerate. One teacher called Randolph 'idle to the extreme'; another called him a 'little blackguard'. He liked to recline langorously with his feet on the desk, where he had carved his name, and he seemed to dress for effect, getting particular pleasure from the startled looks when he wore a gaudy violet waistcoat. One of his few close friends, later Lord Redesdale, insisted that he had no real evil in him, that he was 'the most delightful of boys, bubbling over with fun and the sweetest devilry'. However, Randolph did manage to organize one of the largest of the groups of personal 'fags' to do his bidding. He had fifteen lower-form boys to fulfil his every wish.

Even his father wrote of his 'pain and displeasure . . . to find you ignore every promise you have made to me as to your conduct.' And, in another letter: '. . . To tell you the truth, I fear that you yourself are very impatient and resentful of any control . . . and allow both your language and manner a most improper scope. . . .'

As to Randolph's manners, a family friend noted that Randolph called attention to his needs at the Eton dinner table by banging his spoon. The battered spoon later became a family memento. Randolph himself wrote about his manners in a letter home, describing the local parade by the Prince of Wales and his new bride, Princess Alexandra. When determined to crash through the parade line and reach the royal coach, 'Several old genteel ladies tried to stop me but I snapped my fingers in their face . . . crying "Hurrah" and "What larks!" I frightened some of them horribly.'

He then added that he charged through the barricade and broke it ('. . . it was a second Balaclava'), knocked down the police in front of him, lost his hat, and pushed on to the door of the carriage. He was perfectly certain, he said, that the Prince of Wales bowed to him, all of which made him shriek louder.

In a biography of his father, Winston Churchill was most generous when he wrote, 'He dreamed no dreams at Eton.'[6] It took Randolph a long time to dream any dreams at Oxford, either. In fact, it took him a long time to be admitted. Despite the help of a crammer, he failed on the first try. 'The truth is, he does not care for scholarship and is horribly inaccurate,' the tutor reported to the Duke.

Oxford is so close to Blenheim, that after Randolph went up to Merton[7] he practically lived at home, making full use of his hunting hounds. At Merton he organized a select social group of students called 'The Blenheim Harriers'.[8] They hunted regularly and kept a careful account of their kill. Of his own accomplishments one season, Randolph recorded, 'Killed altogether last season twenty-nine brace of hares and one fox.'

His sister Cornelia later wrote of the fun he had at Oxford: 'luncheons in his rooms . . . gatherings full of fun and amusement . . . and many a party, which I, as a girl, accompanied. . . .'

Classmates called him 'Gooseberry' Churchill because of his protruding eyes. Among other things, 'Gooseberry' was fined for smoking while in academic dress, and again for breaking the windows of the Randolph Hotel.[9] He was also once arrested for drunkenness.

Years later, Frank Harris, wrote in his notorious autobiography that Louis Jennings, one of Churchill's closest friends, had told him of a far more serious incident: A small group had had a lively discussion of the master-servant relationship, and Randolph had expressed his views so well that the group had cheered him. As the party broke up, one of the members filled a huge stirrup-cup of champagne for Randolph and he drained the drink. Randolph insisted to Jennings later that he remembered nothing more of what happened that night.

'Next morning,' Jennings reported Randolph having told him,

I woke up with a dreadful taste in my mouth, and between waking and sleeping was thunder-struck. The paper on the walls was hideous—dirty—and, as I turned in bed, I started up gasping: there was an old woman lying beside me; one thin strand of dirty grey hair was on the pillow. How had I got there? What had happened to bring me to such a den? I slid out of bed and put on shirt and trousers as quietly as I could, but suddenly the old woman in the bed awoke and said, smiling at me, 'Oh, Lovie, you're not going to leave me like that?'

She had one long yellow tooth in her top jaw that waggled as she spoke. Speechless with horror, I put my hand in my pocket and threw all the money I had loose on the bed. I could not say a word. She was still smiling at me; I put on my waistcoat and coat and fled from the room. 'Lovie, you're not kind!' I heard her say as I closed the door after me. Downstairs I fled in livid terror.[10]

Randolph described to Jennings how he rushed frantically to the doctor, who examined him and then treated him with a strong disinfectant. But, after a 21-day incubation period, a syphilitic sore became apparent. The doctor treated him with mercury, pronounced him cured, and warned him to abstain completely from alcoholic drink. But the cure proved only temporary.

Syphilitic treatment was still highly primitive, not far removed from the so-called 'Greek water', an arsenic treatment which had been granted a patent by King George II more than one hundred years before. Those unable to afford the half-guinea for a bottle used the cheaper substitute called 'Hot Hell Water' and often died of arsenic poisoning.

About that time, when he was twenty years old, Churchill's whole tone of life seemed to change. He suddenly gave up the Blenheim Harriers, turned seriously to a study of history and law, wrote Latin verse, and helped organize a chess club. He also discovered Gibbon's *Decline and Fall of the Roman Empire*, and was so fascinated by it that he read it again and again, memorizing whole pages.[11]

A frequent visitor at Blenheim in the 1860's was the family friend, Benjamin Disraeli, leader of the Conservative Party and soon to be Prime Minister. It was Disraeli who told the Duchess that 'it rested with Randolph to become a distinguished man'.

But that seemed increasingly unlikely. After his graduation, Randolph returned to Europe, this time on a Grand Tour through France, Italy, and Austria that lasted eighteen months. If he had indeed received any doctor's order to avoid alcohol completely, he no longer followed it, and he smoked cigarettes 'until his tongue hurt'. On his return to England, he seemed oppressed by dark moods. Even the hilarity of the Marlborough House Set failed to pull him out of his depression. The future seemed vague and un-shaped. The army, maybe, or the diplomatic service, perhaps, but not for a while. He was a young man with neither purpose nor direction.

Then he met Jennie.

Randolph's mother soon conceded that she would be unable to sway her son's decision to marry this American girl but hoped her husband might have more influence in the matter. Not only did Randolph have extraordinary affection and respect for his father, but his father represented Randolph's sole source of income. The Duke was on a fishing and shooting trip in Scotland when Randolph wrote him from Blenheim. Part of his long and carefully worded letter said:

I must not keep you in ignorance of a very important step I have taken—one which will undoubtedly influence very strongly all my future life. I met, soon after my arrival at Cowes, a Miss Jeanette Jerome, the daughter of an American lady who has lived for some years in Paris and whose husband lives in New York. I passed most of my time at Cowes in her (Jeanette's) society, and before leaving asked her if she loved me well enough to marry me; and she told me she did. I do not think that if I were to write pages I could give you any idea of the strength of my feelings and affection and love for her; all I can say is that I love her better than life itself, and that my one hope and dream now is that matters may be arranged that soon I may be united to her by ties that nothing but death itself could have the power to sever.

I know, of course, that you will be very much surprised, and find it difficult to understand how an attachment so strong could have arisen in so short a space of time, and really, I feel it quite impossible for me to give any explanation of it that could appear reasonable to anyone practical and dispassionate. I must, however, ask you to believe it as you could the truest and most real statement that could possibly be made to you, and to believe also that upon a subject so important, and I must say so solemn, I could not write one word that was in the smallest degree exaggerated, or that might not be taken at its fullest meaning.

He then apologized for not having written to his father before proposing to Jennie, but explained that he could not restrain his emotion. He added that they had broken the news to her mother before he left Cowes. '. . . And she [Jennie] said in her letter that her mother could not hear of it. That I am at a loss to understand.'

Randolph then got down to the hard fact:

I now write to tell you of it all, and to ask whether you will be able to increase my allowance to some extent to put me in the position to ask Mrs. Jerome to let me become her daughter's future husband. I enclose you her photograph, and will only say about her that she is as nice, as lovable, and amiable and charming in every way as she is beautiful, and that by her education and bringing-up she is in every way qualified to fill any position.

To reinforce his argument,

Mr. Jerome is a gentleman who is obliged to live in New York and look after his business. I do not know what it is. He is reputed to be very well off, and his daughters, I believe, have very good fortunes, but I do not know anything for certain. He generally comes over for three or four months every year. Mrs. Jerome has lived in Paris for several years and has educated her daughters there. They go out in Society there and are very well-known.

I have told you all I know about them at present. You have always been very good to me, and done as much and more for me than I had any right to expect; and with any arrangement that you may at any time make for me, I shall be perfectly contented and happy. I see before me now a very happy future, almost in one's grasp. In the last year or so I feel I have lost a great deal of what energy and ambition I possessed, and an idle and comparatively useless life has at times appeared to me to be the pleasantest; but if I were married to her whom I have told you about, if I had a companion, such as she would be, I feel sure, to take an interest in one's prospects and career, and to encourage me to exertions and to doing something towards making a name for myself, I think that I might become, with the help of Providence, all and perhaps more than you had ever wished and hoped for me. On the other hand, if anything should occur to prevent my fondest hopes and wishes being realized (a possibility which I dare not and cannot bring myself to think of), how dreary and uninteresting would life become to me! No one goes through what I have lately gone through without its leaving a strong impress on their character and future. Time might, of course, partially efface the impression and recollection of feelings so strong as those I have tried to describe to you, but in the interval, the best years of one's life would be going, and one's energies and hopes would become blunted and deadened.

Finally, he concluded with:

I will not allude to her. I believe and am convinced that she loves me as fully, and as strongly as possible, as I do her; and when two people feel towards each other what we do, it becomes, I know, a great responsibility to assist in either bringing about or thwarting a union so closely desired by each.

Randolph's letter demonstrated insight into his own potential, but more than that, it stated clearly why he had chosen Jennie—not simply for her beauty but for the strength he knew she had and he needed. He counted on her to 'encourage me to exertions and to doing something towards making a name for myself'.

The Duke replied quickly. 'My dearest R.,' he wrote, 'You have indeed taken me by surprise, and to use a Cowes speech, you have brought up all standing.' After some short, noncommittal generalities, he continued, 'Your letter is in a very affectionate tone and I appreciate all your feelings but I cannot say more. I only hope you will be willing to be guided by your mother and me.'[12]

This was not the answer Randolph had hoped to get. But his father could not then be more encouraging, for he was after all the seventh Duke of Marlborough, and his was a heritage among the richest in England. The first Duke of Marlborough had been John Churchill, who commanded the English armies for Queen Anne and fought France in ten campaigns. He won every battle he engaged in, took every fortress he besieged. His greatest victory was the Battle of Blenheim in 1704, when he broke the French line on the left bank of the Danube with a cavalry attack. The grateful Queen Anne presented him with the royal manor of Woodstock, rich in history for more than a thousand years. Here the Saxon and Norman and Plantagenet kings had held Court. From the time of Henry I, there was scarcely an English king or queen who did not stay in the manor house. Here the Black Prince was born and here Princess Elizabeth was imprisoned for nearly a year by her sister Mary Tudor. And it was here that the Roundheads besieged the Royalist forces during the Civil War, and then ravaged the place.

When Queen Anne gave the manor to Marlborough, the manor house was an old ruin and Parliament voted £250,000 towards the cost of a new home, not only as a personal reward to the victor of Blenheim, but as a massive national memorial. 'It was his achievements, not himself, that were to be recognized by a grateful country,' Winston Churchill wrote in a biography of his ancestor.[13]

Set in 2,700 acres, the building finally had 320 rooms, soon filled with treasures of the world. King George II said of it, 'We have nothing to equal this.'

One approaches Blenheim through the arched stone gateway at the edge of the town and down the winding drive until one reaches a scene out of time, a setting as of a King Arthur legend. The peaceful lake, the enormous old trees, and the palace itself, spread over a huge area, severe and symmetrical with an almost ominous power. Winston Churchill called Blenheim 'an Italian palace in an English park'. He was referring to the balanced wings, the geometrical flower beds, the matched monuments. But the heritage of Blenheim is constructed of the bones and hot blood of England.

If there was ever a woman to match a man, it was the wife of the first Duke of Marlborough. Some say the Duchess not only ruled her roost but occasionally helped run the British Empire. As Queen Anne's closest confidante (until she angered the Queen), Sarah was even credited by some with master-minding the final decision to make war with France. The poet Alexander Pope wrote scathingly of her:

> Offend her, and she knows not to forgive;
> Oblige her and she'll hate you while you live.

She was also highminded. When she read a biography of her

famous husband, she remarked in a letter: 'This History takes a great deal of pains to make the Duke of Marlborough's extraction very ancient. This may be true for aught I know. But it is no matter whether it be true or not in my opinion. For I value nobody for another's merit.'

Despite her sometimes disagreeable character and her commanding presence, Sarah's numberless possessions attracted many suitors after the Duke's death. To one of them, the eminent Duke of Somerset, she wrote: 'If I were young and handsome as I was, instead of old and faded as I am, and you could lay the empire of the world at my feet, you should never share the heart and head that belonged to John, Duke of Marlborough.'[14]

Since Sarah gave the Duke no sons, the dukedom passed to a nephew, Charles Spencer—Spencer thereby becoming part of the family name. The Spencer family crest was a griffin, the fabulous half-eagle, half-lion; the Churchill crest was a lion.

After Spencer and then the third Duke, the fourth Duke succeeded to the dukedom at the age of twenty and held it for fifty-eight years. He hired 'Capability' Brown to create at Blenheim an artificial lake of a hundred acres, the largest such lake on any British private property. He also collected antique gems, staged elaborate amateur theatricals, and had Sir Joshua Reynolds paint the family portraits. The fourth Duke, however, became a confirmed hypochondriac. For three full years he maintained complete silence, not saying a single word. He broke his silence when he was informed of the scheduled arrival of a noted woman author. 'Take me away,' he roared, 'Take me away. . . .'[15]

The most noteworthy comments on the fifth and sixth Dukes concern their fantastic extravagance, which necessitated their selling the most important Blenheim art treasures. The sixth Duke ended up so broke that he was forced to live in a remote corner of the palace.

The seventh Duke, John Winston, the father of Randolph, was described as 'a man of formidable façade who was gentle and understanding but with an obstinacy and singlemindedness that characterized the Churchills.'[16] Unlike his immediate predecessors, the seventh Duke led a useful life of public service. He was Conservative Member of Parliament for Woodstock and later served as Lord President of the Council.

With his eldest son and successor seemingly so irresponsible, Marlborough had pinned high hopes on Randolph. And now, here was a letter from Randolph asking his permission to marry an American. Who were these Jeromes, anyway? Marlborough sent off a stream of inquiries to key contacts in various countries.

While Randolph was trying to obtain his parents' approval for the marriage, Jennie was using all her powers of persuasion on her mother. At first, her mother was firmly opposed to the idea. She already had written her husband a hurried resumé of what had happened, using such phrases as, 'hasty . . . rash . . . headstrong . . . unconsidered . . . impulsive', and adding, 'You must return to England by the next boat.' Clara Jerome felt that Lord Randolph simply wasn't good enough for Jennie, Lord or no Lord, Marlborough or no. Still filled with romantic memories of the Imperial Court of Napoleon III, she envisioned a long parade of Princes and other royalty just waiting to pay court to her daughter.

Jennie enlisted the strong support of Clarita. With incessant arguments and tears, the girls pursued their mother relentlessly. The combined force of two daughters was too much for Clara Jerome. Finally, but reluctantly, she consented to the marriage. She wrote her husband of her view and also answered Randolph, who had written her a pleading letter: 'I must acknowledge that you have quite won my heart by your frank and honourable manner.' But toward the end of her letter, she also added, 'I hope you will listen to your father's advice, whatever it is. He can only have your happiness at heart. As a good son, your first duty is to him.'

Marlborough, in the meanwhile, had begun to receive reports about Leonard Jerome. A London lawyer wrote:

I am advised . . . that the gentleman named is at the present time doing one of the most extensive stockbroker's businesses in New York but that he lives very extravagantly and it is not unlikely that his income, large as it is, may be absorbed in his expenditure.

Another contact reported:

I know Leonard Jerome of New York slightly. He has been a successful speculator and is what would be called by boon companions a 'jolly good fellow'; but I have never heard that he holds a prominent position in either public or social life. Still, I believe he is a thoroughly respectable person.

An American friend contributed:

Jerome is a well-known man with a fast reputation, has been a large stock speculator and was a few years ago supposed to be well cleaned out and managed to hold onto some purchases of real estate heavily mortgaged. As to his social position, I don't know what to say "*comme ça*" not good except among a fastish set. The daughters, who have been abroad several years with their mother ... are, I hear, much admired.

One correspondent noted that Jerome's credit on the stock exchange was good, that nobody would 'hesitate to execute any order of his.' But another discussed his lavish expenditures, 'the worst inference being that he spends as much as he makes.'

Such reports were enough for the Duke. On August 31, he finally wrote Randolph:

It is not likely that at present, you can look at anything but from your own point of view but persons from the outside cannot but be struck with the unwisdom of your proceedings, and the uncontrolled state of your feelings, which completely paralyzes your judgment. Never was there such an illustration of the adage, "*love is blind*" for you seem blind to all consequences in order that you may pursue your passion; blind to the relative consequences as regards your family and blind to trouble you are heaping on Mamma and me by the anxieties this act of yours has produced. . . .

Now as regards your letter I can't say that what you have told me is reassuring. I shall know more before long but from what you tell me and what I have heard, this Mr. J. seems to be a sporting, and I should think vulgar kind of man. I hear he drives about six and eight horses in New York (one may take this as a kind of indication of what the man is).

Everything that you say about the mother and daughters is perfectly compatible with all that I am apprehensive of about the father and his belongings. And however great the attractions of the former, they can be not set off against a connection, should it so appear, which no man in his senses could think respectable. . . . I am deeply sorry that your feelings are so much engaged; and only for your own sake wish most heartily that you had checked the current before it became so overpowering.

May God bless and keep you straight is my earnest prayer. Ever your affectionate father,

Marlborough.

That was crushing for Randolph. A double-barrelled blow came from his sister Cornelia and his brother Blandford. Cornelia wrote a long letter, part of which said:

. . . when one feels how serious a step marriage is, one can't help feeling anxious that you should have chosen hastily . . . and whether affection so quickly found would be likely to last and get stronger, as one sees how miserable marriage is when the reverse is the case. All I can say is one can't be too careful in taking a step which is so irrevocable. . . . I am

58

afraid that there are many difficulties in the way, and that money will be a great obstacle. . . . Do, dearest Randolph, think calmly and sensibly over the whole matter, and do not let yourself be carried away by what might only be a passing fancy. . . . I think that when one hears people say that marriage is a mistake, and indeed madness, it is a hasty, ill-considered marriage that has made them say so.

Since Cornelia was staying with the Duke in Scotland, her words were particularly meaningful.

Blandford was much more blunt. He sent his younger brother a poem he had written, entitled, 'An Elegy on Marriage.'

> Twas yours and not another's hand that built
> The funeral pyre near which you tarry.
> The dagger's plunged into its bleeding hilt
> Thy fate is sealed if thou dost marry . . .
>
> Remorse shall seize upon thy stricken soul
> When tinselled charms begin to pall,
> Thy part is strife, a fractious grief thy whole
> If thou dost thus in weakness fall . . .
>
> Perambulators and the babies' rusks
> Shall be among thy chiefest cares.
> See thou to the bottle that it sucks,
> Revolt? Thy spirit will not dare.
>
> And when thy better half shall whine or fret
> Because thou dinest not at home,
> Perchance the scene will turn into a pet,
> Then! Wilt thou at thy fortunes moan! . . .

It went on like that for fifteen stanzas, all of which pointed up the perils of a marriage in haste repented at leisure.

Randolph was infuriated. He sent copies of Blandford's poem to Cornelia and to the Prince of Wales. Cornelia answered soothingly:

You must not think he means to be unkind. It is only his love of writing pieces that makes him give expression to such ridiculous sentiments, and I think he fancies himself enormously. You know him as well as I do and can make allowances for him. . . .

The Prince of Wales, with even more extensive experience of marriage and mistresses, replied that Blandford's poem 'is certainly one of the most extraordinary productions I have ever read'. But he advised Randolph not to take it too seriously, that he himself would write to Blandford.

Another letter came from his parents. His father had gone from

Scotland to Cowes, where his mother had joined him. The Duchess wrote the letter, which the Duke, who was a little tired, dictated.

Your mother and I are only anxious for your happiness. I am quite willing, my dear boy, to give you credit for all you say . . . to make allowances for the state of mind in which you say you are. I only hope it will not lead you . . . to treat your mother and me ungratefully. . . .

You must imagine to yourself what must be our feelings at the prospect of this marriage of yours. You cannot regard yourself alone in the matter and disassociate yourself from the rest of your family. . . . Under any circumstances, an American connection is not one that we would like. . . . you must allow it is a slightly coming down in pride for us to contemplate the connection. . . .

In New York Leonard Jerome similarly had qualms. After receiving his wife's letter about the rushed romance, he was highly sceptical. He had a strongly biased opinion against the inbreeding and overbreeding within the British aristocracy, and he felt this was not a fit match for his fiery and beautiful daughter.

'You quite startle me,' he wrote Jennie.

I shall feel very anxious about you till I hear more. If it has come to that—that *he* only 'waits to consult his family' you are pretty far gone. You must like him well enough to accept for yourself which for you is a great deal. I fear if anything goes wrong you will make a dreadful shipwreck of your affections. I always thought if you ever did fall in love it would be a very dangerous affair. You were never born to love lightly. It must be *way* down or nothing. . . . Such natures if they happen to secure the right one are very happy but if disappointed they suffer untold misery. . . .

Jennie was at her best in a situation such as this. It was a romantic drama and she was the heroine. The accumulating obstacles only sweetened the prize. The opposition only fortified her determination. Life had generally been smooth for her. Now for the first time she was forced to fight for what she wanted, fight for the man she loved. And she discovered that she was most effective when she was doing battle for a cause.

Leonard Jerome read his favourite daughter's protestations of her love, and ultimately he wrote her:

You know my views. Great confidence in you, and still greater in your mother; and anyone you accept and your mother approves, I could not object to, provided he is not a Frenchman or any other of those Continental Cusses.

He would have preferred to take the next boat to England and survey the situation himself, but the Duke's financial reports on Jerome were quite accurate. A financial scandal early in 1873 had rocked the stockmarket and panicked the country. Stephen Fiske described an evening at a restaurant with Leonard Jerome host to a large group of friends. A waiter delivered a telegram to Jerome, who excused himself to read it silently. Only after dinner was over did Jerome apologize for his rudeness in reading the telegram, and added, 'But, gentlemen, it is a message in which you are all interested. The bottom has fallen out of stocks and I am a ruined man. But your dinner is paid for and I did not want to disturb you while you were eating it.'[17]

Jerome was not quite ruined. He long ago had settled a sufficient sum of money on his wife to assure her financial independence. He also had salvaged some real estate. And out of the wreck of his major speculations, he recovered enough to keep him going on Wall Street, but on a much slower and smaller scale. His greatest ruin was in his loss of status. He was no longer one of those who ruled Wall Street, no longer in the top group of Vanderbilt, Gould, and Fisk.

Jerome, however, wrote little of the financial problems that were preventing an immediate trip to Europe. He had seldom discussed his financial affairs with his wife, 'who hates money, or thinks she does.' But the likelihood of Jennie's formal engagement, too, hinged on the money question. 'I telegraphed your mother immediately that I was "delighted" and that I would arrange £2,000 per year for you which she says in her letter will do,' Jerome wrote.

I cannot imagine any engagement that would please me more. I am as confident that all you say of him is true as though I knew him. Young, ambitious, uncorrupted. And best of all you think and I believe he loves you. He must. You are no heiress and it must have taken heaps of love to overcome an Englishman's prejudice against 'those horrid Americans'. I like it in every way. . . . I must say I have been very happy all day. I have thought of nothing else.

To his wife, Leonard outlined suggested terms of the dowry. By this time, Clara and her daughters were again at their house in Paris.

Learning of the Duke's disapproval of the match, Clara Jerome promptly wrote Randolph:

Of course, dear Randolph, he [Leonard] knows nothing of you except what I have written, which I need not say was most favorable. Taking for granted that what I said must be true, and listening to his daughter's earnest appeal, who thinks all her happiness in life depends on her marrying you, he gives his formal consent. I must say that my husband has not the slightest idea of any opposition from your father. And I wrote him very particularly what you told me at Cowes, that there would be none. I can only repeat that both Mr. Jerome and myself have too high an opinion of our daughter and too much love ever to permit her to marry any man without the cordial consent of his family. . . .

If your father gives his consent, I shall wish you to see more of each other before taking such an important step, and if there is any engagement at all, it must be a long one.

She appended a financial comment from her husband: 'If the settlement of £2,000 a year and the allowance of one-third of all my fortune later is satisfactory, this can all be easily arranged.'

However, nothing was to be easily arranged, and money was one of the critical keys. Randolph's financial dependence on his father made any marriage without Marlborough's consent impossible, for he had neither the inclination nor the training to hunt for a job. And Jennie, though possessed of some 'original, if arrogant, opinions', would not dream of disobeying her parents.

Blandford at this time followed up his poetic advice with some perishable prose. In a greater attempt at brotherliness, he addressed it, 'My dear old chap. . . .'

I feel that what I am about to say is like words scattered at a raging gale. . . . You are my only brother and what you do affects me far more than anything that can befall anyone else. . . .

I don't care if your demoiselle was the incarnation of all physical beauties on God's earth, my opinion is the same. . . .

Do you marry for a fortune? No!

Do you marry to get children? No!

Do you marry because you have loved a woman for years? No!

You really only want to marry because you are in love with an *idea*.

. . . Damnation! . . . here you are a sensible man, no longer a child . . . you are a d——d fool. Excuse my plain speaking, old chap. . . .

The Prince of Wales in the meanwhile had written Blandford and sent a copy to Randolph. The letter so impressed Randolph that he asked the Prince's permission to forward it to the Duke and Duchess. The Prince hesitated, then agreed only to let Randolph apprise his parents of the contents, without showing them the letter itself. He must have worried that the Duchess might pass the letter back to his own mother the Queen. But the Prince did write Randolph, 'I quite understand how low you must feel under all this suspense.'

Leonard Jerome had now heard of the Duke's disapproval of the proposed marriage and cabled his wife, 'CONSENT WITHDRAWN.'

At this low point in their ebbing fortunes, it was Jennie who served as their common source of strength while Randolph vacillated between exhilaration and despair. Jennie gently chided him for it, and Randolph answered, 'You certainly have great powers of perception. I cannot but own that there is a great deal of truth in what you say about my being one moment very despairing and another moment very sanguine. I cannot help it; I was made so.'

In another letter, he explained some of the antidotes for his moods:

When I feel very cross or angry, I read Gibbon, whose profound philosophy and easy though majestic writing quiet me down, and in an hour, I feel at peace with all the world. When I feel very low and desponding, I read Horace, whose thorough epicureanism, quiet maxims and beautiful verse are most tranquillizing. Of late, I have had to have frequent recourse of my two friends, and they have never failed me. I strongly recommend you to read some great works of histories. . . . Novels, or even travels, are rather unsatisfactory, and do no good, because they create an unhealthy excitement, which is bad for anyone. I wonder whether you will understand all this, or only think me rather odd.

But she did not think him odd; she prided in his mind and boasted of his intellect.

Fortunately for Randolph, reports were still flowing to the Duke about the quality and character and cash of Leonard Jerome, and the details now seemed more favourable. These reports added strength to the unceasing pressure of his favourite son—who was desperate enough to propose that he might even seek a job, 'in England or out of it'.

The Duke demurred but eventually felt compelled to acquiesce—provisionally—'for the sake of his son's peace of mind and his own authority.'

The great question is still unsolved, whether you and the young lady who has gained your affections are, or can be, after a few days' acquaintance, sufficiently aware of your own minds to venture on the step which is to bind you together for life. What I have now to say is that if I am to believe that your future is really bound up in your marriage with Miss Jerome, you must show me proof of it by bringing it to the test of time. I will say no more to you on the subject for the present, but if this time next year you come and tell me that you are both of the same mind, we will receive Miss Jerome as a daughter, and, I need not say, with the affection you could desire for your wife.

Reporting to Jennie, Randolph referred to his father's 'unnecessary rigamarole and verbosity', and added:

. . . I do not mind telling you that it is all humbug about waiting a year. I could and would wait a good deal more than a year, but I do not mean to, as it is not the least necessary; for though we have only known each other a short time, I know we both know our minds well enough, and I wrote a very long and diplomatic letter to my father yesterday, doing what I have done before, contradicting him and arguing with him, and I hope, persuading him that he has got very wrong and foolish ideas in his head. You see, both he and my mother have set their hearts upon my being a Member for Woodstock. It is a family borough, and for years and years a member of the family has sat for it. The present Member is a stranger, though a Conservative, and is so unpopular that he is almost sure to be beaten if he were to stand; and the fact of a Radical sitting for Woodstock is perfectly insupportable to my family. It is for this they have kept me idle ever since I left Oxford, waiting for a dissolution [of Parliament]. Well . . . a dissolution is almost sure to come almost before the end of the year. I have two courses open to me: either to refuse to stand altogether unless they consent to my being married immediately afterwards; or else, and this is still more Machiavellian and deep, to stand, but at the last moment to threaten to withdraw and leave the Radical to walk over. All tricks are fair in love and war. . . .

Finally, came good news:

The clouds have all cleared away, and the sky is bluer than I have ever seen it since I first met you at Cowes. It is exactly six weeks tomorrow since we met on board the *Ariadne,* and I am sure I seem to have lived six years. How I do bless that day, in spite of all the worry and bother that has come since, and I am sure you will not regret it. I have not had a further conversation with my father since I wrote you, for I think it is best to leave things for the present as they are. Our early golden dreams of being married in December won't quite become realized, but still it won't be very long to wait; and I shall be able to see you from time to time, and write as often as I like; in fact, we can be regularly engaged, and all the world may know it. . . .

Jennie dutifully wrote to her prospective mother-in-law, and Randolph was quick to compliment her on it.

My dearest, what a nice letter you wrote to my mother, she was so pleased with it. You have the happiest and nicest way of expressing yourself of anyone I know. You will be happy to hear that my father is very much struck with your handwriting, which he assures me has a deal of character.

Now he was also able to reassure her that his father had

promised to give his consent to our marriage when he is sure we are fond of each other. As to the year, I have every right to say that I do not think he will insist on it. . . .

There are three new elections to come off, owing to death vacancies; and if they go against the government, as they very probably will, we are sure to have a dissolution, and then I shall become a Member for Woodstock.

But, after all, public life has no great charms for me, as I am naturally very quiet, and hate bother and publicity, which, after all, is full of vanity and vexation of spirit. Still, it will all have greater attractions for me if I think it will please you and that you take an interest in it and will encourage me to keep up to the mark.

To stir her interest in politics, he wrote in another letter, 'I advise you to get a copy of today's *Times* if you can, and read Disraeli's great speech. He has made a magnificent one to the Conservatives of Glasgow . . . it is a fine specimen of perfect English oratory.'

Jennie not only read Disraeli's speech but everything about British politics she could. On Randolph's recommendation, she also read Gibbon and Horace. She was determined to make her mind a match for his.

For Jennie, life was more exciting and fruitful than it was for Randolph. Paris was seething with rumour and whisperings by Royalists and Bonapartists wanting to be back in power. To dampen any smouldering fire, the new French Assembly accused Marshal Bazaine of treason for having surrendered his army to the Prussians. Jennie attended the Bazaine trial at Versailles, and wrote her partisan impressions:

A long, low room filled to suffocation with a curious crowd, many of whom were women, a raised platform, a table covered with green baize and holding a bottle of water, a few chairs arranged in semi-circles, completed the *mise-en-scène*, which seemed a rather poor one for the trial for life or death of a Marshal of France.

She related that some women had jumped onto their chairs and peered through their opera-glass to get a better look at Bazaine, so that the gendarmes 'pulled the offenders down unceremoniously by their skirts', reproving them by saying, '*C'est pas gentil*.' And Jennie added, 'Nor was it.'

What had impressed her was how impassively Bazaine sat while his defence lawyer dramatically gestured toward him, exclaiming that Bazaine was no traitor but merely an imbecile. 'How the mighty have fallen!' Jennie wrote.

65

I thought of him and his wife in the glittering throng of Compiègne only three years before, and of him again as the Commander-in-Chief of a huge army, which now he was supposed to have betrayed and sold. I say supposed, for although he was found guilty and condemned to death [later commuted to twenty years' imprisonment], there were many who believed in him and thought him a hero. . . . I doubt if posterity will place a halo around his head.

Somewhere in her long letter about the trial, Jennie incorrectly used the word *prorogue*. Randolph chided her for it. Instead of accepting his correction, Jennie consulted a young French nobleman, Count de Fénelon, whose name she had seemed to mention often in her letters. Fénelon agreed with her definition of the word. Randolph's reply was sharp:

. . . Hang *le petit* Fénelon, little idiot! What do I care for him. He may be a very good authority about his own beastly language, but I cannot for a moment submit to him about English. . . . To prorogue means to suspend something for a definite time, to be resumed again in exactly the same state, condition and circumstances. Therefore to talk about proroguing the Marshal's powers would mean that they were to be suspended for a certain time and then resumed again exactly as before. Parliament is prorogued; L'Assemblée is prorogued; that does not in the least mean that the powers of either are lengthened or increased in any way, but that they are temporarily suspended.

Jennie, however, refused to let the matter drop. She showed Randolph's letter to her mother, who merely commented, 'What a very English letter.' Then she again consulted Fénelon, and continued her semantic cause. Randolph finally answered,

I am looking forward particularly to utterly suppressing and crushing *le petit* Fénelon. We must really, tho', drop this argument when I am with you, as it is likely to become a heated one, I fear. We will therefore 'prorogue' it.

Jennie complained about the tone of his letters, and he responded,

My darling Jennie,
You heap coals of fire upon my head by YOUR DEAR LOVING LETTER received this morning. I remember now I did write a rather cross letter last Tuesday, but you must make allowances for me as I have been awfully hustled and worried. . . . I hope your sister is quite well, comforts you and sticks up for me when you abuse me to her or doubt me. . . .

Jennie then informed Randolph that her father had arrived in Paris and planned to visit his future son-in-law in England.

Randolph promptly wired 'Miss Jeanette Jerome' on January 1, 1874:

HAS YOUR FATHER STARTED? WHERE DOES HE STOP WHEN IN LONDON? HAVE LEFT SANDRINGHAM. MY AUNT DANGEROUSLY ILL IN IRELAND.

His aunt's illness came at the worst time for the young lovers, because Randolph had finally received permission from his parents to visit Jennie in Paris. But Lady Portarlington was a favourite aunt, and his parents depended on him to be in Ireland with them. First, however, he had to meet his future father-in-law. In his daily letter to Jennie, Randolph wrote:

I am just going to dinner with your father, and then I am off to Ireland. There is no change in Lady Portarlington's state, and I doubt whether she will be alive when I arrive. It is very, very sad; and I do so dread a house of mourning. . . . I have been going about with your father all day. . . . I had a very pleasant afternoon . . . and helped him to make his different purchases. . . . I really like him so much, the more I see of him. I am sure we will always be the best of friends. I had it all out with him about the abuse of me that had been sent from America. I am glad to find that such nonsense does not seem to have made any impression on him. Fancy people saying that I drank!!!! What next?

P.S. You will not get a letter from me till Sunday night or Monday morning, as the post takes longer going from Ireland. But, really, *you* might write a little more. It makes me think your head is full of everything and everybody else but me. . . .

Before he left for Ireland, Randolph sent another telegram to Jennie, saying that he had dined that night with her father, and, 'AFRAID THERE IS NO CHANCE OF MY BEING IN PARIS MONDAY.'

Throughout that month, Randolph's depression deepened considerably—his Aunt Alice would seem to get better, he would prepare to leave, then she would slip into another crisis, and he would unpack again. He set specific dates for his arrival in Paris several times and each time had to postpone the trip.

His letters to Jennie poured forth in a daily stream:

. . . These ups and downs are more trying and depressing than anything you can imagine. I am so unhappy and low. . . . There are only my father and mother and Lady Londonderry here. . . . I don't think I ever witnessed anything so trying. Everyone is in a state of continual apprehension, never knowing what to expect from one moment to another. I would give anything to be with you, darling, quiet and happy. I was thinking last night, what would I do, if, supposing we were married, and you were to fall ill like this? I am sure I should go quite mad. . . .

. . . I should be more distressed than I am at your loneliness if I did not

F

know that you have Kevenhuller to pass your time with. He must be very charming, as you write so much about him. . . .

. . . My darling Jennie, I am sure you don't care for me as much as you did. I don't wonder; I am not wonderfully brilliant when I am with you that you should remember me very much when I have been away. I don't think, if we had been prevented from seeing each other for a year, we should have had a chance of being married . . . you seem to let anything come between you and your letter to me. It is never the least trouble to me to write to you, because I love you and am always thinking of you. I wish it was the same to you. . . . I am certainly a fool. I began this letter intending to say nothing reproachful, and I find I have written ten pages. I can't help it. . . .

. . . Try to write one letter in which that . . . Austrian should not appear. It would be curious to see if you could do it. I don't think you could. . . .

. . . My dearest, I hope and trust you are really not looking ill or worried, as you say. I wish you could get out of that horrid habit of sitting up so late. You can't imagine how bad it is for you. If you could go to bed early, you will soon get into the habit of going to sleep after a few nights; but you never do anything I ask you—at least, not often. *Good-bye, darling, dearest, loving, good, affectionate Jennie.* . . .

Here I am detained again, at the very last moment. I'd actually started; but I'd left my aunt in the most critical state. A sudden relapse had come on and everyone was much alarmed. I could not bear the idea of disappointing you, but, still, I did not like to leave the house at such a moment. If she had died . . . it would have looked so unfeeling, my having to go off. . . . My mother was quite sorry at my being obliged to stay, on your account, and insisted on telegraphing herself to you, that you might know it. . . .

(The telegram read: GRIEVED TO SAY RANDOLPH CANNOT LEAVE HIS AUNT TILL THIS CRISIS IS OVER. DUCHESS OF MARLBOROUGH.)

Really, my dearest, you must not get afraid of my getting tired of you. . . . So far, dearest, from my learning to do without you, this prolonged separation of ours is showing more forcibly than ever before that I *cannot* get on or do without you. . . .

Do try to amuse yourself, and do something to make the time pass. Go to Fontainebleau and play, and anything to occupy your thoughts; even try Kevenhuller, if he can amuse you. . . .

. . . I cannot bear you to think that my letters have been 'cold'. I am sure it is only your fancy. They may, and most probably have been, stupid, as I have nothing to write about except this sad illness, which could not interest you much; but I am sure they were never cold. I could not write you so if I wished to. . . . I don't know what I would not give to get away, but here I am tied by the leg. She is still alive and conscious, but that is all one can say. There is no hope of the slightest recovery; but how long this state may last, it is impossible to say. . . . Yet, every evening and morning follow each other and she is still alive. . . .

A month after Randolph had arrived in Ireland, his aunt died. The funeral at Emo Castle was one of much pomp and ceremony. The night after the funeral, Randolph hurried across the Irish Channel and on to Dover, intending to take the first boat the following morning to France.

Just then the news came that Parliament was dissolved. Gladstone's Liberal Party had been enervated by factionalism among its leaders. A Conservative Party leader referred to the Prime Minister's administration as 'a range of exhausted volcanoes . . . not a flame flickers on a single pallid crest. . . .' The tide that had swept the Liberals into power in 1868 now turned against them, and the Government lost a series of important by-elections. Finally, Gladstone, old, exhausted, and ill, used poor political judgment in attempting to override a Parliamentary action and then found that on the pinprick of a legal technicality, he had consented to the dissolution of Parliament.

So Lord Randolph was suddenly called back to Blenheim to begin his campaign for Member from Woodstock. The situation allowed no postponement—that very afternoon there was to be an open-air meeting of all the farmers in his area, and his attendance was mandatory.

'It was perfectly impossible to get any letter off by last night's post, as I have not had a moment to spare,' he wrote Jennie from Blenheim.

Since ten this morning, I went and saw several people at Woodstock, and had, on the whole, satisfactory answers and assurances of support. It was a most fortunate circumstance that the Annual Coursing Meeting, which my father allows every year in the Park, had been fixed for today; all the farmers were there, and as they had a good day's sport, were all in great spirits. I took the chair at their dinner at the Bear Hotel, and you cannot imagine how enthusiastic they were for me. They all go as one man. I hear nothing certain as to any opposition; there are no end of rumours, but no one as yet has appeared publicly; I suppose we shall know for certain tomorrow.

I am off now to a part of the borough four miles distant, to see more people, and I have a large meeting of my committee at four in Woodstock. I think that I may say that for the present everything is satisfactory. There are 1,071 voters, and I do not think that more than 800 will poll; out of these I calculate at least on 460, which will be enough. But this is, of course, mere guesswork; it is all still very uncertain, and I am glad I lost no time in arriving.

His Liberal opponent was George Brodrick, who had been a don at Merton when Randolph was an undergraduate there. In 1868, when running for Parliament from Woodstock, Brodrick had charged the Duke of Marlborough with bribery, intimidation, and dishonest interference with the vote. After that, Randolph had refused to attend any more of Brodrick's lectures. Called to explain his absence from Brodrick's lectures, Randolph had said, 'How, sir, could I attend the lectures of one who has called my father a scoundrel?'[18] Whatever his memories, Randolph again met Brodrick, and wrote Jennie, 'We shook hands and were very friendly. The contest will be a hard one and the result doubtful; it is impossible to say how the labourers will go. However, I have made a very good start and have nothing to complain of as yet.'

The politically inexperienced Randolph needed help, and Edward Clarke, a well-known Tory barrister from London, came to his aid. Meeting Clarke at the station was the retiring Member of Parliament, Henry Barnett, who fully outlined all of Randolph's handicaps. Clarke soon catalogued them himself:

He had little knowledge of literature, none of science, no familiarity with political history and very slight acquaintance with foreign affairs. . . . Lord Randolph Churchill was a rather nervous, awkward young man who certainly seemed to have the most elementary ideas about current politics. We had some talk about the subjects he was going to deal with in his speech. I wrote out four or five questions which were to be put in friendly hands and asked from the back of the room, and gave Lord Randolph the answers. . . . When we came to the meeting, Lord Randolph was very nervous. He had written out his speech on small sheets of paper, and thought if he put his hat on the table and the papers in the bottom of the hat, he would be able to read them. This of course he could not do. There was a rather noisy audience who gibed at him and shouted to him to take the things out of his hat, etc., and the speech was far from a success. But the questions and answers went very well; then I made a speech, and, taken together, the meeting went off very well.[19]

Clarke also edited Churchill's campaign speech for the press, and Randolph later wrote him, 'I really am confident that many of the votes, if not the majority, may be attributed to your excellent speech.'

Randolph's letter to Jennie failed to mention the disturbance at the meeting but said:

We had a great meeting last night which was very successful; we had a speaker down from London and I made a speech. How I have been longing for you to be with me! If we had only been married before this!

I think the reception you would have got would have astonished you. The number of houses I have been into—many of them dirty cottages—the number of unwashed hands I have cordially shaken, you would not believe. My head is in a whirl of voters, committee meetings and goodness knows what. I am glad it is drawing to an end, as I could not stand it very long; I cannot eat or sleep. . . .

Brodrick must have been sleeping even more poorly. Randolph had all the Marlborough money and influence on his side. The Duke had rented the town's three leading hotels for his son's cause, and that left Brodrick with what Randolph described to Jennie as 'a wretched, low, miserable pothouse'. Coming to help Brodrick was a bright young man named Asquith.[20] But Woodstock was a family borough, and in one way or another many of the local people were dependent on the Marlboroughs. Not all were, however, and Randolph was realistic, if not pessimistic.

'How this election is going,' he wrote Jennie,

I really can form no opinion and the uncertainty of it makes me quite ill. Yesterday I was canvassing all day in Woodstock itself. People that I think know better than anybody tell me it will be very close. You see, with the [secret] ballot, one can tell nothing—one can only trust to promises, and I have no doubt a good many will be broken. Our organization and preparations for Tuesday are very perfect, and the old borough has never been worked in such a way before. . . . I have a presentiment that it will go wrong. I am such a fool to care so much about it. I hate all this excitement. . . . I saw my opponent today in church. He looks awfully harassed. I feel quite sorry for him, as all his friends here are such a disreputable lot. . . .

Interspersed among his letters to Jennie, Randolph kept up a barrage of telegrams, several of them in French, one of which worried aloud, 'I BELIEVED ALL GOES WELL, BUT IT IS GRAVE ENOUGH.' But on February 4, he sent her a telegram which read: 'I HAVE WON A GREAT VICTORY BY 569 VOTES AGAINST 404. GREAT ENTHUSIASM. EXPECT ME SATURDAY.'

Jennie's excitement was almost explosive. She exultantly showed everyone the victory telegram and constantly quoted Randolph's remarks about everything.

He now wrote her:

. . . Ever since I met you, everything goes well with me—too well. I am afraid of a Nemesis. I always hoped I should win the election, but that under the ballot and against a man like Brodrick I should have that crushing, overwhelming victory never entered into my wildest dreams. It was a great victory—we shall never have a contest again. The last two contests—in '65 and '68—were won only by 17 and 21 majorities; so just conceive the blow it is to the other side. You never heard such cheering in all your life. The poll was not declared till eleven, and hours of suspense were most trying; but when it was known, there was such a burst of cheers that must have made the old Dukes in the vault jump. I addressed a few words to the Committee—and so did Blandford—and was immensely cheered; and then they accompanied us, the whole crowd of them, through the town and up to Blenheim, shouting and cheering all the way. Oh, it was a great triumph—and that you were not there to witness it will always be a source of great regret to me. . . .

. . . There is nothing more to be done except to pay the bill, and that I have left to my father. . . .

Leonard Jerome wrote his future son-in-law a letter on Jockey Club stationery from New York:

You are very good indeed to write to me the particulars of your canvass. They are interesting indeed. You do not tell me how much you were pelted with eggs and stones etc. That I suppose you leave to my imagination. But the great fact of your election, I assure you I appreciate, and I congratulate you most heartily. It is really a great thing, great to anyone; and just at this period of your life, it is immense. It opens to you a magnificent field—a field wherein, with only half an effort, you are bound to play no ignoble part.

. . . I think of the many talks we shall have in the course of time. You will find me quite ready to impart to you, if not words of wisdom, at least my notions of the problems of life gathered from experience. . . . Could we have 'a few words in private' you might get a liberal dose tonight, but situated as we are, that may not be. What a fortunate fellow you are.

Jerome hoped Jennie and Randolph would visit him in America after their wedding that summer. 'I will take you on the rounds of this "great republic" and do my best to implant in your bigoted Conservative brains some liberal Yankee notions (including a buffalo hunt).'

The victory had created for everyone, including the Marlboroughs, a warmer, more amenable mood. The situation seemed even more agreeable when the Duke went with Lord Randolph to Paris to meet Jennie. Jennie charmed him. She played the piano for him—Beethoven's 'Sonata Appassionata'—and even talked about British politics, backed up by a surprisingly large fund of information. The Duke was openly impressed and pleased. Jennie was similarly pleased with her future father-in-law. As for Mrs Jerome, she found the Duke 'a perfect dear'.[21]

The Duke of Marlborough's income from his Oxfordshire estates then totalled about £40,000 a year. Considering the size and upkeep of his estate and allowances to his daughters and two sons, this was not a great fortune. In fact, he had felt forced to sell the ancestral Marlborough gems for some £36,000, as well as a major part of Blenheim's famous Sunderland Library.[22]

Nonetheless, he offered a preliminary wedding present to his son: '. . . I observe your bills,' he wrote.

Therefore, if you wish me to clear you, it must be done at the expense of the fund I have proposed to put into settlement, and I will go so far as to raise now £2,000 to clear your present and previous debts, without charging you the interest so that I shall be giving you actually £1100 . . . and in addition to this, I will pay your annual expenses for the representation of Woodstock. . . . I shall have done as much as my means and income will admit of. . . . As you must be well enough aware, my income is not large enough to bear the continual and heavy charges which are continually accruing. . . .

Randolph himself could offer Jennie only his title, a town house in London, and two fine horses (but not his own carriage).

The Duke advised him that he was forwarding to his lawyer Jerome's proposed marriage settlement and then commented, 'I do not wish to say anything harsh or unkind, but the inference is not hopeful unless Miss Jerome takes the finance department under her own control. . . .'

Randolph sent his gratitude for 'your offers *most* kind and *most* liberal and more than I at any time expected . . . in clearing off my debts before starting on what one may call a new life. . . . I did not like Mr J. should think I had married Jennie to get my debts paid. . . ' Then he added:

I am quite decided that Jennie will have to manage the money, and I am quite sure she will keep everything straight, for she is clever, and like all Americans, has a sacred, and I should almost say, insane horror of buying anything she cannot pay for immediately.

Actually, though Jennie had learned about many things, money management was not among them.

There was only one item left to settle—the details of the dowry. Lord Randolph never concerned himself with money matters, but the Duke did. His ancestors had left him financially strapped. Unfortunately, Leonard Jerome was in similar financial straits, and

while he was far from flattened, he now had to consider more carefully which money went where. Consequently, the dowry negotiations were long and legal and messy. Jerome wrote to the Duke and
the Duke wrote to Randolph and all of them wrote their lawyers,
who all then wrote to each other.

Marriage, then, was arranged not simply by informal family
agreement but by contract, often incredibly detailed, full of all
kinds of clauses and whereases intended to anticipate every eventu-
ality. Particularly in the great families of England, such a contract
was an accepted formality, making marriage an economic union as
well as a physical one. No one really questioned its need, even those
who resented it.

Randolph stayed in Paris, and wrote long, daily letters to his
'dearest Papa' and constantly asked his father's advice on all the
qualifying clauses in the contract. Things became not only increasingly complicated but increasingly bitter. '. . . Affairs are come
to a most unpleasant pass,' he wrote his father. 'Mr and Mrs
Jerome and myself are barely on speaking terms and I don't quite
see what is to be the end of it. . . . I think that his conduct and Mrs
J's is perfectly disgraceful . . . and I am bound to say that Jennie
agrees with me entirely. . . .'

Leonard Jerome returned to Paris for the final negotiations. With
his two daughters pressuring him in one direction, his wife in
another, and Randolph set in the centre glaring, it was not a friendly
family picture. Finally it was agreed that if Jennie died before
Randolph and there were children, the money would be appor-
tioned among them. If Jennie died before Randolph and there were
no children, half the money would go to Randolph and the other
half to the Jerome family. Jubilantly, Randolph wrote his father the
good news:

. . . I must thank you for your letter to him, which was so nice in every
part. I really don't think there is anyone who can write such nice letters as
you can. Mr. Jerome was immensely pleased with it, and I have no doubt
it had the effect of making him behave properly. . . . Please don't be very
angry with Mr. Jerome, though I cannot be surprised if you think he
behaved rather curiously. . . . The fact of the matter is that Mrs. Jerome
twists him round her finger. She was furious at the whole of the after-
dinner agreement, and declared that Mr. Jerome did not know what he
was doing, and tried to make him back out of it. When, however, for two
days, I would not speak to her or him, except to tell them both my mind,

74

when Mr. Jerome became so worried, he actually never came down for dinner or breakfast, and when he finally declared he was going to London the next morning, and America the next day, she became frightened and alleged all the difficulties could easily be overcome. You will not tell anybody except Mama about this, will you? It is not very pleasant. Poor Jennie has been most awfully worried about it all, and I believe she had several hours up with her mother. . . .

That, however, was not the end of it. The lawyers took over, and negotiations reached an incredible nadir of haggling over who should pay for the telegrams and postage ($61), the title search on the Madison Square property (then under lease to the Union League Club of New York), and even the charges for preparing the abstract (£102 15s. 6d.). There was also a major wrangle over an allowance for Jennie. To Marlborough's lawyer, Jerome wrote: 'I have conceded considerably more than Lord Randolph declared to me by letter . . . was entirely satisfactory (and nearly all required by his father . .).'[10]

The pile of legal letters grew. One dated February 23, 1874 and written to Lord Randolph by one of Marlborough's lawyers in Savile Row noted,

The Duke says that such a settlement cannot as far as you are personally concerned be considered as any settlement at all, for as I explained in my former letter, Miss Jerome would be made quite independent of you in a pecuniary point of view, which in my experience is most unusual. . . . Although in America, a married woman's property may be absolutely and entirely her own, I would remark that upon marrying an Englishman, she loses her American nationality and becomes an Englishwoman so that I think that the settlement should be according to the law and custom here. . . .

That, too, was resolved, and the fathers-in-law-to-be exchanged more friendly letters. Jerome wrote:

In regard to the settlement, . . . I beg to assure you that I have been governed purely by what I conceived to be the best interests of both parties. It is quite wrong to suppose I entertain any distrust of Randolph. On the contrary, I hope there is no young man in the world safer. Still, I can but think your English custom of making the wife so entirely dependent upon the husband, is most unwise. In the settlement, as it is finally arranged, I have ignored American customs and waived all my American prejudices, and have conceded to your views and English customs on every point, save one. That is a somewhat unusual allowance of money to the wife. Probably the principle may be wrong, but you may be very certain my action upon it in this instance by no means arises from any distrust of Randolph. . . .

Randolph was then able to report to his mother, 'Things are all going now as merrily as a marriage bell.'

The wedding would take place in Paris on April 15, 1874. That was also the Duchess's birthday, but the Duke and Duchess excused themselves from attending. The Duchess was presumably not well. The absence of both Randolph's parents was not only unusual—it was incredible. Randolph was their favourite son. Despite their early disapproval of the marriage, they had given their final consent and their blessing. Even if one of them were ill, the other would have been expected to participate in the wedding.

Leonard Jerome tried to put the best possible face on the awkward situation. In a letter addressed 'Dear Duke', he noted,

I am very sorry you are not able to come over for the wedding. We had all hoped to have the pleasure of seeing both yourself and the Duchess. . . . I have every confidence in Randolph, and while I would entrust my daughter to his sole care alone in the world, still I can but feel reassured of her happiness when I am told that in entering your family, she will be met at once with 'new affectionate friends and relatives. . . .'

Blandford, however, did come, as did three of Randolph's sisters and his aunt, Lady Camden. Leonard Jerome arranged a resplendent family dinner for all of them the night before the wedding.

The trousseau had long ago been ready: twenty-three French-made dresses, seven Paris bonnets, piles of delicately embroidered white underlinen. 'These will have to last me a long time,' Jennie told Clarita and Leonie, thinking of her limited budget.

The night before her wedding, Jennie wrote: '. . . This is the last time I shall wind this clock . . . this is the last time I shall look in this old mirror. Soon nothing will be the same for me anymore: Miss Jennie Jerome will be gone forever.'

On the wedding morning, Randolph received a letter from his father:

I must send you a few lines to reach you tomorrow, one of the most important days of your life, and which I sincerely pray will be blessed to you, and be the commencement of a united existence of happiness for you and your wife. She is one whom you have chosen with rather less than usual deliberation, but you have adhered to your love with unwavering constancy, and I cannot doubt the truth of your affection, and how I hope that, as time goes on, your two natures will prove to have been brought not accidentally together. May you both be 'lovely and pleasant in your lives' is my earnest prayer. I am very glad that harmony is again restored, and that no cloud obscures the day of sunshine; but what has happened will show that the severest faith is not without its throes, and I must say ought not to be without its lesson to you. . . .

. . . We shall look forward shortly to seeing you and Jeanette here, whom I need not say, we shall welcome into her *new family*. . . .

It was a morning wedding, and the maid hurried in early with a breakfast tray for Jennie. The corset had to be pulled more tightly than usual, but not so tight as to cause the bride to faint at the ceremony. A hairdresser arrived to arrange her thick black curls.

Jennie's dress was of white satin with a long train, all lavishly trimmed with Alençon lace. She wore white silk stockings, white satin slippers, and long white kid gloves. There was a knot of white flowers at her breast and a fine tulle veil covering her from head to foot. Her only jewelry was a string of pearls, a wedding gift from her father.

As his best man, Randolph had chosen Francis Knollys, secretary to the Prince of Wales. Jennie's bridesmaid was her sister Clarita. The ceremony was swift and simple. The marriage certificate read:

I hereby certify that Lord Randolph Henry Spencer Churchill, bachelor of the parish of Woodstock and the county of Oxford, now residing at Paris, Hotel d'Albe, and Jennie Jerome, spinster, of the city of Brooklyn, in the state of New York, U.S.A., were duly married according to the rites of the Church of England in the House of Her Most Historic Majesty's Ambassador at Paris this 15th day of April in the year of our Lord one thousand eight hundred and seventy four. . . .[24]

The brief wedding was startlingly unadorned. This, after all, was one of the first great international marriages of the time. Considering the prestige of the families, the historic nobility of the Marlboroughs and the national eminence of Jerome, one would have expected the social splash of the season. Despite his diminished fortune, Leonard Jerome certainly had the friends and funds to stage an elaborate wedding. Instead, there was just a simple ceremony in the British Embassy before a handful of people, with the Duke and Duchess of Marlborough conspicuously absent.

Certainly it was not the way Mrs Jerome would have wanted it. In addition to her hopes of steadily rising social splendour, this was the first marriage among her daughters, and no wedding preparations could have been too lavish for her. In contrast, the later weddings of Jennie's sisters were to be most lavish affairs. Nor could it have been the ordinary wish of Jennie, whose recent memories were still captivated by Napoleon III's Imperial Court.

Furthermore, why had Clara Jerome, hardly blissful about Jennie's less-than-royal choice, suddenly become instrumental in eliminating all settlement obstacles?

Was there a connection with the birth of Winston Churchill seven months later? It is a fact, of course, that Jennie's second son was also a seven-months baby. But is it not also possible to imagine that the two lovers, with passions intensified by their long separation and the fear their chances of marriage were dribbling down the legal drain, might determine to force the marriage, or simply let their emotions overwhelm them.

Anyway, there they were, after a hearty wedding breakfast, climbing into a beautiful coach with handsome grey horses. Jennie wore a dark blue-and-white striped travelling dress with a stylish bonnet. She held a lovely, fragile parasol of white lace frills mounted on a tortoise-shell stick rimmed with gold, a gift from her father. 'Thought it looked like the sort of bit of nonsense you liked,' he told her.

The last comment Jennie made to her mother before leaving was 'Why, Mama, don't cry, life is going to be perfect . . . always . . .'[25] It would not be, for her future held heartbreak as well as splendour, terror as well as triumph.

# 5

'This was a love match if ever there was one, with very little money on either side,' wrote Winston Churchill of his parents' marriage. 'In fact, they could only live in the smallest way possible to people in London society.'[1]

That was only partly true. Randolph and Jennie did feel a financial pinch, but such was their ignorance of money and budgets that it scarcely interfered with the extent of their social life. Everything to them seemed gay and glittering.

The Duke of Marlborough had given them a 37-year-lease on a four-story house at 48 Charles Street in London, a graceful building complete with balconies and window boxes.[2] It would not be available, however, until the late summer of 1874, so for the intervening months, the young Churchills had rented a house at 1 Curzon Street. Randolph suddenly cut short their French honeymoon in order to attend the opening of Parliament. Since the Curzon Street house was not quite ready, the young couple decided to visit Blenheim Palace.

They were met at the station by the assembled townspeople, who unhitched the horses from the Churchill carriage so that they themselves might pull the young couple to the palace. Woodstock was a quiet place of small, old houses and a single main street. The people waved and cheered as the Churchills went by. Through the town, under the tremendous stone archway, past a porter holding a long wand topped by a red-tasselled, silver knob—and then the park and palace of Blenheim. Jennie gazed at it with awe and expectancy; the view of the monumental bridge across the valley, miles and miles of magnificent park, green glades edging an ornamental lake, the palace partly hidden by the trees in the distance, and the trees themselves, thousand-year-old oaks once part of a royal forest where many kings had come for their private pleasures.

For Jennie it was overwhelming, the hugeness of it, the splendour and formality, the dramatic suddenness of it.

They moved up the broad and shallow steps, past the oversize

79

doors, and into the immense hall, with its domed ceiling so high that Jennie had to crane her neck to see the painting of the first Duke of Marlborough, dressed in a Roman toga and driving a chariot.

The initial impression of grandeur, however, was quickly over-ridden by the less pleasant reality. Alexander Pope had written of Blenheim:

> See, sir, here's the grand approach;
> This way for his Grace's coach:
> There lies the bridge and here's the clock;
> Observe the lion and the cock,
> The spacious court, the colonnade,
> And mark how wide the hall is made!
> The chimneys are so well designed
> They never smoke in any wind.
> This gallery's contrived for walking,
> The windows to retire and talk in;
> The council chamber for debate,
> And all the rest are rooms of state.
> 'Thanks, sir,' cried I, ''tis very fine,
> But where d'ye sleep and where d'ye dine?
> I find by all you have been telling,
> That 'tis a house, but not a dwelling.'

The first Duchess, Sarah, had referred to Blenheim as 'a wild and unmerciful house'.[3]

'We slept in small rooms with high ceilings,' complained the American guest who later became mistress of the palace. 'We dined in dark rooms with high ceilings; we dressed in closets without ventilation; we sat in long galleries or painted saloons.'[4] Horace Walpole had likened it to 'the palace of an auctioneer who has been chosen King of Portugal', and Voltaire had called it simply 'a great mass of stone'.[5]

Jennie's nephew, Hugh Frewen, who played there as a child, called Blenheim 'a bastard of a building'.[6] One of his strongest memories was the clatter of eating from gold plates. 'I always worried for fear some of the gold would chip off and get mixed with the vegetables.' He also remembered that there was about it a 'palace smell . . . rather like the weighty smell of locked-in history . . . with hints of decaying velvet.' All visiting children were kept outdoors as much as possible, an understandable system in a palace filled with irreplaceable Brussels tapestries, Meissen china and countless mementoes each worth a fortune.

Formality and order ruled at Blenheim, guided by tradition. The Duchess dictated everything to her guests, including the train they must take for their arrival and the time of their departure. 'When the family were alone at Blenheim,' Jennie remarked later,

everything went on with the regularity of clockwork. So assiduously did I practise my piano, read or paint, that I began to imagine myself back in the schoolroom. In the morning an hour or more was devoted to the reading of newspapers, which was a necessity, if one wanted to show an intelligent interest in the questions of the day, for at dinner, conversation invariably turned on politics. In the afternoon a drive to pay a visit to some neighbor, or a walk in the gardens, would help to wile away some part of the day. After dinner, which was a rather solemn full-dress affair, we all repaired to what was called the Vandyke room. There one might read one's book, or play for love a mild game of whist. . . . Many a glance would be cast at the clock, which sometimes would be surreptitiously advanced a quarter of an hour by some sleepy member of the family. No one dared suggest bed until the sacred hour of eleven had struck. Then we would all troop out into a small anteroom, and lighting our candles, each in turn would kiss the Duke and Duchess and depart to our rooms.[7]

Even breakfast was a ceremony, women dressing in velvet or silk and no one beginning to eat until everyone was assembled. Luncheon was dignified, formal, with rows of entrée dishes filling the table and the Duke and Duchess carving joints of meat for the whole company, including governesses, tutors, and children. The children filled food baskets for poor or sick cottagers in the surrounding area, a traditional family gesture of *noblesse oblige*.

Afternoon tea was solemn. The gold tea service was used mainly in honour of visiting royalty. Yet no matter who the guests were, the exchange of tea-time small talk always concluded when the hostess said, 'I am sure you must need a little rest.' It took a visiting Princess to answer icily one day, 'Thank you, it is now half-past five. I will go to my room at seven.'

'Furs and hot-water bottles kept us warm,' wrote one guest.[8]

The Duchess sat, evidently racking her brains for some subject of conversation, but was unsuccessful in finding any sufficiently interesting. . . . The Duchess seems a kindhearted, motherly sort of person—neither clever nor at all handsome. The Duke also is a 'plain' man in all its meanings, but it is in itself an immense merit to be a religious Duke of Marlborough, and this, His Grace has[9].

For Jennie, however, the Duke was not 'plain' and the Duchess was not 'motherly'. Jennie got along far more easily with her father-in-law, seeing in him a man of grace, courtesy, and kindness, the

81

*grand seigneur*, with an acute sensitivity toward his heritage. Marlborough told her the story of the French Ambassador touring Blenheim during the time of the fifth Duke. The Ambassador expressed curiosity in the sources of the various art treasures, impressed by the fact that so many had been gifts. 'The house, the tapestries, the pictures—were they all given? Was there anything that had not been given?'

Highly irritated, the Duke quickly led the French Ambassador out to the south side of the palace, showed him the stone trophies and the effigy of Louis XIV, and said simply, 'These were *taken*, not given, by John, Duke of Marlborough, from the gates of Tournai.'

Despite the Duke's pride in the past, Jennie observed that the family rarely looked at the magnificent art surrounding them. 'If familiarity breeds contempt,' she remarked, 'it also engenders indifference.'

Blenheim was occasionally opened to tourists who came to stare more appreciatively at the art treasures. On those days, the Marlboroughs remained in their private rooms. But not Jennie. 'Occasionally, for fun, some of us would put on old cloaks and hats, and, armed with reticules and Baedekers, walk around with the tourists to hear their remarks, which were not always flattering to the family,' she wrote. 'One day, we nearly betrayed ourselves with laughter at one of my compatriots exclaiming before a family picture: "My, what poppy eyes these Churchills have got"!'

Jennie recorded only one other excitement during her initial stay at Blenheim. It occurred one day while the family was out shooting with the Lord Chief Justice, Sir Alexander Cockburn. His gun went off by accident, the bullet just missing her head. 'I must be careful,' he calmly apologized.

It was still May when the young Churchills moved into their home in Curzon Street. The early swing of the London social season had just begun and would continue ceaselessly until the end of July. Curzon Street was in the middle of Mayfair, the heart of London's most fashionable district, not far from Piccadilly and quite close to Marlborough House on Pall Mall where the Prince of Wales lived. The Churchills were a young couple gifted with all the graces: beauty, charm, social position, wit, intelligence, spirit, and energy; and the Prince himself had provided them social entrée everywhere.

Soon after Jennie and Randolph had settled in Curzon Street, the

Duchess of Marlborough arrived to help her daughter-in-law pay her preliminary visits to the city's social leaders. 'The Duchess came for me at two, and we went off in grand style in the family coach,' Jennie wrote her mother. 'The Duchess was very kind, and lent me some rubies and diamonds, which I wore in my hair, and my pearls on my neck. I also had a bouquet of gardenias which she sent me.'

The Set had a prim rule about newlyweds. Before presenting themselves socially, young married couples were required to hibernate for a few months. The young Churchills violated that rule—as they would so many others—by appearing at a ball in honour of Czar Alexander II. Notified that they had been married barely a month, the Czar looked at Jennie, and indicated rather shocked surprise at the social breach.

Jennie soon discovered other rules: 'Having been brought up in France, I was accustomed to the restrictions and chaperonage to which young girls had to submit; but I confess to thinking that as a married woman I should be able to emancipate myself entirely.' She learned, however, that a lady never travelled alone without taking her maid with her in a railway carriage. 'To go by oneself in a hansom was thought very "fast",' she noted. 'Not to speak of walking, which could be permitted only in quiet squares or streets. As for young girls driving anywhere by themselves, such a thing was unheard of.'

But Jennie had a way of disintegrating strictures. Freed first from her mother's watchful eye, and now from the formality of her mother-in-law's palace, Jennie went the blithe way of her own sweeping wings. With a high spirit let loose and a loving, indulgent husband who also relished the swiftness of free flight, the horizon was unlimited.

Jennie envisaged her life as a never-ending schedule of fun: garden parties, the fashionable races at Ascot and Goodwood, the regatta at Henley, the pigeon-shoots at Hurlingham,[10] the Princess Cricket and Skating Club. ('. . . There's a slight loss of lady-like complacency among female beginners, but none are so ill-bred as to remark their tumbles.') And of course the balls, the opera, the concerts, theatre, the ballet, the new Four-in-Hand Coaching Club, and the sequence of parties that lasted until five in the morning.

Jennie's sister Clarita (who now called herself Clara) came to visit for part of the summer in 1874 and reported to their mother, 'I don't know why, but people always seem to ask us [to parties] whenever H.R.H. [His Royal Highness] goes to them. I suppose it is because Jennie is so pretty. . . .' At one of the Prince's exclusive affairs, to which women came decorated as cards, he asked Jennie to come as the Queen of Clubs. Almost as much as Jennie's beauty, the Prince enjoyed her fresh wit and frankness. Discussing the bridegroom of an Anglo–American marriage, the Prince told Jennie, 'The family is very poor, but it is in its favour that it came over with the Conquerer.'

'That's all very well,' said Jennie, 'but if I were the girl, I'd prefer to marry into a family that had done a little conquering on its own account.'[11]

The Prince had a particular fondness for American women. 'I like them because they are original and bring a little fresh air into Society,' he said. 'They are livelier, better educated and less hampered by etiquette . . . they are not as squeamish as their English sisters and they are better able to take care of themselves.'[12]

With the Prince around, they had to. He had a notorious reputation with women and was accused of being 'a prominent actor in almost every scene of aristocratic dissipation and debauchery which has been encountered in the British metropolis.'[13] He seemed to make a speciality of the wives of friends, and he was seldom to be denied. His early attention to Jennie was noticeable, and he made it more obvious by inviting the Churchills to most of his frequent parties. Most British society, however, regarded the Anglo–American marriage 'as experimental as mating with Martians'.[14] Jennie aptly described the reactions of British women toward the American female invader:

Anything of an outlandish nature might be expected of her. If she talked, dressed and conducted herself as any well-bred woman would, much astonishment was invariably evinced, and she was usually saluted with the tactful remark: 'I should never have thought you were an American.' Which was regarded as a compliment.

As a rule, people looked upon her as a disagreeable and even dangerous person, to be viewed with suspicion, if not avoided altogether. Her dollars were her only recommendation, and each was credited with the possession of them—otherwise what was her *raison d'être*? No distinction was ever made among Americans. They were all supposed to be of one uniform type. The wife and daughters of the newly-enriched California miner, swathed in silks and satins, and blazing with diamonds on the smallest provocation; the cultured, refined and retiring Bostonian; the aristocratic Virginian, . . . all were grouped in the same category, all tarred with the same brush. . . .

Shortly after the Churchills' marriage, there was a sudden increase in Anglo–American unions. The American press was generally scornful of this marital quest for English titles. 'They should have sought noble hearts instead of noble names,' was a typical comment. *Town Topics* once noted in its columns that there was a Polish Prince looking for an American beauty with ten million dollars. 'He is Prince Poniatowske, and a Polish Prince is about as marketable as last year's hat. I strongly advise Ward to bring on additional Dukes.' However, observing the significance of the American woman in England, Lord Palmerston prophetically remarked, 'Before the century is out, these clever and pretty women from New York will pull the strings in half the chancelleries in Europe.' Minnie Stevens became Lady Paget, Consuelo Iznaga (of Cuban and American parentage) became Lady Carrington,[15] Mrs Arthur Post became Lady Barrymore, all of them with pretty faces to match their attractive fortunes.

These were only a small influential sprinkling of the flood that followed, and Jennie knew them all. There was, in fact, an obvious kinship among them. Outstanding among the American beauties circulating the same parties with Jennie were a Mrs Standish and a Mrs Sandys. So often were the three together that the press dubbed them 'The Pink, the White and the Black Pearls'. Raven-haired Jennie, of course, was the Black Pearl and generally acknowledged as the most gifted and the prettiest.[16]

She was also the most individual. For the Gold Cup meeting of 1875, she daringly wore her wedding dress, newly embellished with crêpe de chine trimmings. The low decolletage of some of her other dresses caused even more comment. And to the theatre, where traditionally women wore only black, Jennie insisted on wearing a pale blue dress, even though Randolph begged her to change because it was 'so conspicuous'.[17]

At one fancy-dress ball, Clara introduced a young nobleman to Jennie. 'Introducing him to me, she [Clara] pretended I was her mother,' wrote Jennie.

Later in the evening I attacked him, saying that my daughter had just confided to me that he had proposed to her, and that she had accepted him. To this day I can see his face of horror and bewilderment. Vehemently he assured me that it was not so. But I kept up the farce, declaring that my husband would call on him next day and reveal our identity, and that meanwhile I should consider him engaged to my charming daughter. Deficient in humour and not over-burdened with brains, he could not take the joke, and left the house a miserable man.

'Generally speaking,' Jennie added, 'there is no doubt that English people are dull-witted at a masked ball, and do not understand or enter into the spirit of intrigue which is all-important on such occasions. . . .'

A woman's social success greatly depended on her gift for badinage, and it was a gift Jennie had in abundance. To counter the constant flow of aggressive flattery from most men, she displayed a special talent for arch banter, a lilt and a quip and a laugh that made her everywhere popular, with women as well as men.

Jennie's mother was in Paris, with her own social circle, and Clara continued to write: 'Jennie and R. have quite decided to come to Deauville . . . and R. after depositing Jennie and I with you, will go off for a cruise with the Duke on his new yacht.' As an afterthought she added, 'You must not think that we are at all fast. . . .' But 'fast' is what they were, and 'fast' is what they wanted. 'We seemed to live in a whirl of gaieties and excitement,' Jennie commented.

Typical of their style was a small dinner party featuring a parlour game called 'thought reading'. Blindfolded in the middle of the room, Randolph heard Lady de Clifford tell him, 'Don't resist any thought that comes into your head; do exactly as you feel.' Without hesitating, Randolph grabbed and embraced her. Lady Jeune described him then as 'a great schoolboy, full of fun and mischief. . . . I have seen him lie back in his chair and roar with laughter at things he had done and said.'[18]

Lady Jeune was originally Mary MacKenzie who married a Colonel Stanley in 1871 and lived for a year in Utah and Nevada where her husband helped operate a mining company. After her husband's death, she married Sir Francis Jeune, a Privy Councillor, and quickly became one of the prominent hostesses of London. George Smalley quoted a noted socialite who told him, 'I go to Lady Jeune's because I never know whom I shall meet, but I always know there will always be somebody I shall like to meet.' Lady Jeune's thesis was that the interesting people are the exceptional people, and among her good friends was Theodore Roosevelt.

To Jennie and Randolph Churchill, the social life counted for almost everything. Even Randolph's seat in Parliament seemed mainly a social gesture. His maiden speech about a railway works at Oxford was very 'maiden' indeed. Benjamin Jowett, the Master of Balliol, said at the time, 'It is only the speech of a foolish young man who will never come to any good.'[19]

*Punch*'s Parliamentary correspondent Henry Lucy was more perceptive than Jowett in his analysis: '. . . The young Member was so nervous, his voice so badly pitched, his delivery so faulty, that there was difficulty in following his argument. But here and there, flashed forth a scathing sentence that made it worthwhile to attempt to catch the rest.'[20]

Disraeli described Randolph's speech more kindly to both the Duchess and Queen Victoria:

Lord Randolph said many imprudent things, which is not very important in the maiden speech of a young member and a young man; but the House was surprised, and then captivated by his energy, and the natural flow, and his impressive manner. With self-control and study, he might mount. It was a speech of great promise.[21]

Perhaps Disraeli was kind because he well remembered the reaction to his own first effort. He had stood wearing his black velvet coat, purple trousers with gold braid running down the outside seam, a scarlet waistcoat, and white gloves outside of which he wore diamond rings. Disraeli's friends insisted this dandified dress was part of a deliberate pattern to attract attention. 'At heart, I think he always despised that sort of thing,' said his friend Lady Nevill. He did attract attention, but he was so laughed at by the Members of the House, that he finally sat down, his speech unfinished. 'I will sit down now,' he said then, 'but the time will come when you will hear me.'[22]

A similar 'dandy' and wit, Randolph Churchill wore a smartly cut dark blue frock coat with coloured shirts, and sometimes startled his friends by wearing tan shoes and an excess of jewelry. His favourite was a large diamond ring in the shape of a Maltese Cross that Jennie had given him.

Like Disraeli, too, Lord Randolph could be impertinent and blunt. While women often found this fascinating, men found it a little frightening. Randolph often seemed to be dancing on the edge of hysteria, his nerves taut, his speech brittle. And since he had learned so well from Gibbon 'to finger the phrase and marshal the paragraph',[23] guests could never be completely sure what devastating remark might come from him, almost at whim. Buttonholed at his club once by some boring friend who seemed unable to finish his story, Randolph rang the bell for a footman whom he told to 'listen until his Lordship finishes', while he himself left.

Lady Jeune told of another example of his annihilating arrogance. Churchill had quarrelled with an old friend who had been his classmate at Eton. 'Every time they met,' she wrote, 'I had to go through the same little farce of introducing them to each other, Lord Randolph saying to him in a very innocent, irritating manner: "Ah! Yes, I believe I do recollect you at Eton".'[24]

Jennie's warmth complemented her husband's cutting coldness. It was Jennie who gave Randolph whatever resilience and calm sureness he thereafter occasionally showed. He, in turn, gave her the polish of his class and access to the most brilliant and important people of their time, while broadening her political education so she could ask pertinent and intelligent questions.

Disraeli had become Prime Minister the year the young Churchills were married. He was seventy years old and his wife had died the previous year, but he enjoyed Lord and Lady Randolph and visited them often. Jennie appreciated Disraeli's wit, which could be cutting to rude people he disliked. When one young woman tapped him with her fan, Disraeli turned to Jennie and asked, 'Who is that little ape?' But he was always charming and kind to Jennie. Comparing the effect of sitting next to Disraeli or Gladstone, one woman wrote: 'When I left the dining room after sitting next to Gladstone, I thought he was the cleverest man in England. But when I sat next to Disraeli, I left feeling that *I* was the cleverest woman!'

Jennie always enjoyed Gladstone as a dinner companion. However,

having once started him on his subject, an intelligent 'yes' or 'no' was all that was required. But if you ventured a remark (to which he listened in grave silence) he had a disconcerting way of turning sharply round, his piercing eye fixed inquiringly upon you, and his hand to his ear, with the gesture so well known in the House of Commons. His old-world manner was very attractive, and his urbanity outside the House remarkable.[25]

At one of the Churchills' parties, the Prince of Wales noted that Jennie and the Prime Minister had been in deep conversation for an extended period of time, and afterward asked her, 'Tell me, my dear, what office did you get for Randolph?'[26]

But the truth was that at that time Lord Randolph wanted no office. He just did not find politics fun. He considered himself as merely one of the Members of the House who supplied Disraeli's majority, with slight need for either his vote or his voice. Compared to his frenetic social life, parliamentary politics seemed too calm, too formal, and too sluggish.

The social world was also most important for Jennie. With other prominent society newcomers, she was presented to Queen Victoria at Court. The Queen was reported to have taken a poor view of Anglo–American marriages.

'I was dreadfully frightened,' Jennie wrote. 'Making my curtsies for the Queen quite put me out. As I went to kiss her hand, she pulled me towards her and kissed me, which proceeding so bewildered me that I kissed her in return, and made comical little bows to the other Royalties instead of curtsies.'

Of course Jennie was awed by the experience, but years later she fondly remembered a comment made by a maid of Mrs J. Comyn-Carr upon first seeing the Queen: 'So that's the Queen? Who'd have thought she'd look so much like an old apple woman?'

Years after the Prince Consort had died, one of the Queen's daughters wrote her husband Crown Prince Frederick of Prussia:

Mama is dreadfully sad . . . and she cries a lot; then there is always the empty room, the empty bed, and she always sleeps with Papa's coat over her and his dear, red dressing gown beside her and some of his clothes in the bed! . . . Poor Mama has to go to bed, has to get up alone—for ever. She was as much in love with Papa as though she had married him yesterday . . . and is always consumed with longing for her husband. . . .

It was her daughter Alice who brought John Brown from Scotland to be the Queen's manservant. He was a rugged, mountain of a man, a rough-talking Highlander who liked his pipe and his whisky. In Jennie's social circle, rumours soon whirred like arrows: Did you know that John Brown slept at Windsor in a bedroom right next to the Queen's? Did you know that John Brown was quoted everywhere saying, 'The Queen and I'?

Their intimacy increased after John Brown saved the Queen from a would-be assassin. One cartoonist depicted Brown putting his boots on the mantelpiece in the Queen's room. Another showed him leaning against the vacant throne, pipe in hand, while below him the British lion roared. *Punch* parodied the court circular by reporting the daily routine of John Brown instead of the Queen's. One of the many critics commented on the coarseness of the former stableboy, observing that the Queen 'clings to him with more warmth and tenacity than becomes a lady who carried her sorrow for a deceased husband previously to such an extravagant pitch.' And every woman in Jennie's set knew about the scraps of a letter from the Queen found in John Brown's room which were pieced together to read, '. . . you are so indescribably dear to me, so precious and so adored that I can't bear you misunderstand things. . . .' And she signed it, 'Your own ever-loving and devoted one.' Much of all this was hashed together into a best-selling pamphlet called *Mrs John Brown*.

Years later, when Prince Edward became King, one of the first things he did was smash the china figurines of Brown that the Queen had kept in a cabinet. Brown not only had boxed the Prince's ears when he was a boy but once kept him waiting two hours before letting him see his mother.

With the beginning of August, the London Season was over and Jennie Churchill's life changed completely. She was pregnant, and her world was suddenly quiet. 'We are very humdrum and stay a great deal at home,' Clara wrote their mother. Home was now their own house in Charles Street, in a 'très chic' location, as Jennie said, just three houses from Berkeley Square, and complete with butler, footman, and housemaid. It was a famous street. Lady Nevill had lived there for thirty-eight years, and that was enough to make it a social centre. In 1792, 'Beau' Brummel had lived just a few doors away from the Churchill's new home. Bulwer-Lytton had a house in Charles Street, with a room fitted as an exact replica of a Pompeian apartment.[27]

'You see, dear Mama,' Jennie wrote,

now that we have this house, we must look after it, and tho I should be delighted to pass September in Paris with you, I think I had better be in London till after my confinement. . . . We only mean to furnish at the present, two bedrooms and the sitting room downstairs, which we shall use also as a dining room. . . . There is one good thing, we have our *batterie de cuisine* and china, glass and plate and linen, all things which are very expensive. . . . I am so delighted to have a fixed abode at last, and it is such a nice house. . . . Randolph had no settlement made on him when he married, and this of course, makes a settlement. If anything was to happen to him, this house comes to me. . . .

She had another mercenary note: 'I do so hope Papa will be able to give me the £2,000 he promised. . . . And, of course, he need not send it all at once, but gradually, as it is convenient.'

Jennie must have chafed at having to live quietly. After all, she was only twenty-one and the past few months had been filled with high excitement and her rising importance as a welcomed young woman of beauty and wit. September and October of 1874 were among the most inactive, contemplative months of her life.

There were a few parties and dances, but Jennie became tired of sitting with the chaperons, so the young Churchills went to Blenheim for a change of scene. There is a Visitor's Book at Blenheim Palace, an enormous volume bound in heavy red leather, worn at the edges. It has the signature of the first Duke of Marlborough, dated 1708, and then the signatures of most of Europe's royalty, the kings, the queens, the emperors, and their collective royal kin, as well as those of the prime ministers of Britain and the leading social, literary, and political luminaries of European history. The name of Jennie Spencer-Churchill makes its first official entry on October 22, 1874.

November was a peaceful month at Blenheim but it was climaxed by the annual St. Andrew's Ball. Her grandniece, Anita Leslie, claims that Lady Randolph was dancing when suddenly she had to hurry away while the party was still at its height, '. . . past the endless suite of drawing-rooms, through the library, "the longest room in England," down the longest corridor in the world, the quarter-mile of dark-red carpet that led to her bedroom. . . .' In his book on Blenheim, historian David Green states that Jennie was out on a shooting party when she suddenly felt ill and hurried back to the palace. The facts are that while out on a shooting party with her husband on a Tuesday, she fell. 'A rather imprudent and rough drive in a pony carriage brought on the pains on Saturday night,' Randolph wrote to his mother-in-law. 'We tried to stop them, but it was no use. They went on all Sunday.'

They had put her up quickly in a room on the ground floor, just outside the Great Hall. It had once been the room of Dean Jones, a fat cleric with a florid face who had served as chaplain to the first

91

Duke. Since that time, several guests swore they had been wakened in the night by a blaze of light to see the ghost of the cleric bending over them. That Saturday night, the small room had been converted into a ladies' cloakroom, the bed covered with the feather boas and velvet capes of guests who had come for the ball.

Since there were few trains on Sunday, the London obstetrician failed to arrive when needed, and a local Woodstock doctor, Frederic Taylor, performed the historic delivery on November 30. 'The baby was safely born at 1:30 this morning after about eight hours labour,' Randolph continued. 'She [Jennie] suffered a good deal poor darling, but was very plucky and had no chloroform. The boy is wonderfully pretty so everybody says dark eyes and hair and very healthy considering its prematureness.'

He had an upturned nose and protruding Churchill eyes, and they named him Winston Leonard Spencer-Churchill, after his American and English grandfathers.

Attending Jennie were her mother-in-law, Randolph's Aunt Albertha, Lady Clementine Camden, and Randolph's sister-in-law, Lady Blandford. Lady Camden was named godmother, and Randolph asked Leonard Jerome to be godfather. As the birth was unexpected at that time, there was no layette ready at Blenheim. So young Winston Churchill started out life in clothes borrowed from a local solicitor's wife, whose own expected baby had not yet arrived. However, much of Winston's layette had been ordered in London.[28]

Early the next morning, the bells of Woodstock Church rang to announce the arrival of a new Churchill. 'A merry peal was rung,' according to the signed document handed to Jennie as the first written record of her son's birth.

To make it even more official, the *Times* of London reported at the head of its birth notices:

On the 30th Nov., at Blenheim Palace, the Lady Randolph Churchill, prematurely, of a son.

The young family spent Christmas at Blenheim with the Marlboroughs, and the baby was baptized in Blenheim Chapel by the Duke's chaplain. Shortly afterward they moved back into their home in Charles Street.

One of the clichés compounded by biographers of Winston Churchill presses the point that his mother ignored him as a child until he grew old enough to be interesting. Like many such clichés, this is a half-truth. The real intimacy between mother and son did develop during Winston's early manhood, when indeed he was interesting, but it is also true that Jennie's concern for her child was constant, as her many letters and memoranda fully testify. But as Lady Randolph Churchill, she had become basically adapted to the British way of life and one of the most permanent fixtures in this way of life, particularly among the upper classes, was the institution of 'Nannies'. One recent sociologist has termed the system a 'prostitution of maternity', but that is unfair. It is true, nonetheless, that nannies were paid more in love than in money.

In his novel *Savrola*, Winston Churchill described a nanny:

She had nursed him from the birth up with a devotion and care which knew no break. It is a strange thing, the love of these women. Perhaps it is the only disinterested affection in the world. The mother loves her child; that is maternal nature. The youth loves his sweetheart—that, too, may be explained. The dog loves his master, he feeds him; a man loves his friend, he has stood by him perhaps at doubtful moments. In all there are reasons; but the love of a foster-mother for her charge appears absolutely irrational. It is one of the few proofs, not to be explained even by the association of ideas, that the nature of mankind is superior to mere utilitarianism, and that his destinies are high.[29]

Winston's 'Nanny' was Mrs Elizabeth Ann Everest, a plump, friendly 41-year-old widow who liked to wear dark silks and a bonnet. 'My nurse was my confidante,' Winston later wrote. 'Mrs Everest it was who looked after me and tended all my wants. It was to her I poured out my many troubles.' As for his mother, 'She shone for me like the evening star. I loved her dearly—but at a distance.' She would come up to kiss Winston goodnight, usually dressed for dinner, shimmering like 'a fairy princess from afar'.

Victorian children were seldom seen and almost never heard. Nannies provided a physical barrier between children and parents. Jennie bridged that barrier more than most mothers in her social set, although she did exempt herself from the chores of early motherhood. She also happily maintained a total ignorance of the art of housekeeping, 'the ignorance I often had cause to bemoan'.

Jennie was desperately trying to become as British as she could. She was aware of the focus on her every action. She was, after all, one of the very first American women to make such a prominent international match.[30]

But something happened to Jennie at this time that was not revealed in her letters. She was more than just a social butterfly. From the letters of her sister Clara, who stayed with her then, it appeared almost as if there was an element of frenzy in her social life. In most of her accounts of their intense socializing, Clara makes no mention of Randolph's presence. Indeed, at most of the reported parties, Clara and Jennie were on their own, always the instant focus of a variety of men. Clara's letters to her mother in Paris revealed much:

... Lord Hartington took me to lunch in a private room with the royalties, the Prince himself giving his arm to Jennie. . . . Jennie took her Sir William Cumming all to herself, he being the swell of the party and does not let anyone else talk to him. . . . Sir Cumming . . . began *très sérieusement à faire la coeur* to Jennie last night. . . . There was a party for the Prince [afterward Emperor Frederick] and Princess of Prussia . . . we came away about three o'clock . . . escorted by a whole troop of men!

At a dance after the races, '. . . Jennie wore her dark blue and the men were all *very* nice to us. . . .'

Where was Randolph Churchill all this time? He was certainly not being kept busy in Parliament, where he had only made two speeches the first year. Had there been a rift because of the Prince's obvious amorous advances to Jennie? Or had Jennie discovered the dark secret of Randolph's syphilis?

The second stage of syphilis manifests itself in headaches, fevers, recurrent illness coming suddenly and diminishing slowly, annoying rashes, and pimples on the genitals, the palms of the hands, and the soles of the feet. Sores appear and disappear repeatedly on the mouth, and the lymph glands of the groin become swollen and tender. Even if Randolph did not confess the nature of his illness to her, she had the right to expect the truth from Dr Robson Roose, who was not only Randolph's doctor but hers.[31]

There might have been an added factor in the rift. Medical opinion agrees that sexual guilt can cause frigidity, which may evolve into a strong aversion to the opposite sex. That may well have been the case with Randolph Churchill, and may explain the frenetic behaviour of his beautiful twenty-one-year-old bride.

The Jeromes made separate trips to Charles Street to inspect their new grandson, Leonard travelling from New York and his wife coming from Paris. 'The Baby is *too* lovely,' Clarita had written her mother. 'He is so knowing. I wish you could see him on the piano stool, playing the piano!' Still a handsome woman, Mrs Jerome had her own salon on the Rue de Roi de Rome, catering mostly to minor royalty, faded diplomats, unappreciated artists, and unpublished poets. She soon returned to them, but Leonard Jerome lingered awhile in London. Fanny Ronalds had deserted the court of the Bey of Algiers to set up her salon in Cadogan Place. It was occasionally highlighted by the Duke of Edinburgh playing the violin and His Royal Highness, the Prince of Wales, playing the piano while Fanny sang the songs of 'dear, dear Arthur Sullivan'.

Jennie and Fanny Ronalds became close friends in the course of time. Fanny was a sophisticated adviser and offered needed warmth. Her long relationship with Jennie's father was an added fillip. For a troubled Jennie trying to handle some extramarital affairs, Fanny served as a familiar model of the easy morality of the time.

Despite the obvious tension in their marriage, Jennie and Randolph maintained a proper social face. They took Leonard to the races, which they all equally loved. 'R. is in very good humor as he made £200 at the Derby and Jennie £20 on her own book,' Clara gleefully wrote her mother. Leonard probably supplied his daughters with some extra money while he was there: 'Boxes of hats and gowns seemed to arrive every hour,' he wrote. Leonard also met for the first time the Duke and Duchess of Marlborough. His reactions are unreported.

There is, however, no lack of report on the growing strain between the Duchess and Jennie. Clara wrote to her mother about some of the signs. '. . . I can't tell you how jealous Randolph says the Duchess is of Jennie and I. She is always very kind and amicable but *une certaine aigreur* in the way she talks. . . .'

The Duchess exacerbated the tension to a critical point the first year after the marriage. Blandford, who had campaigned in both prose and poetry against Randolph's marriage, now became increasingly captivated with his American sister-in-law. His own marriage had long ago grown sour. His wife, Lady Albertha Hamilton, related by blood to many of the great peerages of the realm, was a confirmed practical joker. At various times she served slivers of soap among the cheese for her guests, and put inkstands

95

over her bedroom door to drop onto her husband's head as he entered. But if her sense of fun was acute, her wit was not.

Blandford, a middle-sized man with a smooth face, a strong jaw, and a formal manner, was also a French scholar, a connoisseur of art, a student of science, a constant correspondent with the great minds of his time, and a devoted lover of beautiful women. So taken was Blandford with Jennie that he gave her a ring, and Jennie made the mistake of showing it to her mother-in-law. The Duchess exploded. Blandford had no right to give Jennie that ring, said the Duchess, because it belonged to his wife. Jennie promptly repeated that to Randolph, who promptly told Blandford, who promptly wrote his mother an unprecedented letter, blisteringly angry, which said in part:

Well acquainted as I am with the intense jealousy that you often display in your actions and the mischief which you so often make . . . I should not have thought you would have allowed yourself to be so carried away as to descend to mistruth to substantiate an accusation [so] as to give colour to a fact.

To try to calm the situation, Jennie offered to return the ring, but the issue had become a matter of family principle. The Duke stepped in, writing to Randolph:

Your mother has received today the enclosed correspondence.
I have only three words to say upon it.
1st. You have grossly misrepresented facts to Blandford.
2nd. You have while being received with kindness, yourself, wife and child dishonourably and treacherously abused the confidence which you yourself pretended you shared with [your] mother about Blandford.
While you were much aware that she never entertained any motives but those of the truest affection for you both.
3rd. You have thus induced your brother to pen to his mother an unparalleled letter, which I do not trust myself to characterize in words.

Randolph's answer was hardly meek:

My dearest Papa,
I most respectfully remark with regard to your letter of this afternoon that I think you have formed a hasty judgment of the enclosed correspondence. I venture to think that expressions such as '*dishonourable*', '*treacherous*' and '*liar*' are hardly applicable to me. As long as these expressions remain in force further communications between us are not only in your remark useless but impossible.

In contrast with the warm and loving relationship that had

existed between Randolph and his parents, this exchange came as a terrible blow, particularly to the Duchess. She might have understood Blandford's explosion, as she and the Duke had always made obvious their displeasure at Blandford's actions, and this could be seen as Blandford's resentment finally reaching bursting point. But Randolph's response was an injury for the Duchess that would never heal. It was smoothed over in the course of time, but it was always there and always sensitive. In perhaps typical motherly fashion, the Duchess transferred all the blame and hostility to her daughter-in-law. This hostility, like the injury, was often carefully camouflaged and sometimes even seemed to disappear, but it was a live coal, buried deep, always ready to flare again.

# 6

Lord and Lady Randolph had been swept into the social vortex of the Prince of Wales. Where he went, they went. In the course of nine months, a newspaper critic commented that the Prince attended thirty plays, twenty-eight race meetings, and more than forty social functions.[1] Just as Gladstone had continually urged the Queen to let the Prince help her in the 'visible duties of the monarchy',[2] Gladstone's successor, Disraeli, continued to encourage the Queen in her refusal, commenting that the Prince was 'a thoroughly spoilt child who can't bear being bored'.[3]

Disraeli had suggested that the Prince might be sent to live in Ireland where he could hunt, socialize (out of sight and sound), and perhaps even learn something about government administration. But the Prince decided he would prefer a long trip to India. He assembled a group, more social than political, to accompany him. The Queen and Disraeli both objected to the make-up of the group, as well as to the itinerary, and Disraeli proposed a parliamentary allotment for expenses which the Prince felt was too meagre. In support of the Prince, Randolph wrote a letter to *The Times* defending the trip. Disraeli called this letter 'a mass of absurdities'. The issue became rather heated, and Disraeli commented in a letter, 'I dined this evening at the Somers'. . . . There were the Randolph Churchills; he glaring like one possessed of the Devil, and quite uncivil when I addressed him rather cordially. Why?'[4] The situation straightened enough, however, for the Prince and his party to make their trip. Jennie and Randolph did not join them. The reasons may have been partly financial, but Randolph might well have had more personal grounds for not going. The Prince's attention to Jennie had become increasingly obvious.

Randolph would not have wanted to become another 'Sporting Joe'. 'Sporting Joe', who was going with the Prince to India, was the Earl of Aylesford, a champion polo player, whose lovely Welsh wife had been having a prolonged but intermittent affair with the Prince. 'Sporting Joe', however, did not let the affair interfere with his friendship for the Prince. Randolph was not then as compliant. This attitude could well have explained Randolph Churchill's strange behaviour in the sensational scandal that followed.

While the Prince of Wales and 'Sporting Joe' and their group were in India, Randolph's brother Blandford moved his horses and himself to the inn closest to Lady Aylesford's house. Word of this soon travelled to India, and it was even intimated that Lady Aylesford was pregnant with Blandford's child. (Blandford's wife at this time played one of her more pointed practical jokes by serving him his usual breakfast tray—but instead of his poached egg underneath the silver cover there was a small pink baby doll.)[5] The Prince and 'Sporting Joe' were equally outraged at Blandford's intrusion on their mutual preserve. The Prince insisted that Blandford had openly compromised the good Lady and should therefore divorce his wife and marry her.

Randolph entered into the argument, but in a surprising way. Ordinarily one might have expected him to intervene as a soft-spoken mediator, a friend of both parties. Instead, he openly threatened to publish some love letters that the Prince had written to Lady Aylesford unless the Prince withdrew his adamant support of 'Sporting Joe' on the matter. Randolph even went so far as to visit Princess Alexandra to warn her of the undesirable publicity of any proposed divorce suit, suggesting she persuade the Prince to pull out of the affair. 'I have the Crown of England in my pocket,' Churchill later told Sir Charles Dilke.[6]

But the Marlboroughs counselled Randolph to be cautious in any row with the Prince of Wales. At the Queen's request, the Prince had forwarded Randolph's threatening letter to her, and now Randolph faced the royal wrath. Randolph was in Holland when he received a demand from the Prince for either an apology or a duel to be held in Rotterdam. Ironically, it was Lord Knollys, en route home from India, who two years before had served as best man at Randolph's wedding, who delivered the message from the Prince. Randolph refused to fight against his future Sovereign and offered to duel with anyone of the Prince's choice. In the interim, Jennie wrote him: 'Do you think the Queen will have an interview with Disraeli? If so perhaps you will have one with him ... and you may get him on your side (in a way) before HRH returns. Am I talking nonsense? ...'[7]

'Even Jennie's iron nerves began to fray,' reported a member of the family.[8] Then Queen Victoria intervened. 'What a dreadful, disgraceful business,' she wrote the Prince of Wales. '. . . Poor Lord Aylesford should not have left her. I *knew* last summer that this was going on.'[9]

Randolph received a royal emissary, the distinguished Lord Hartington, later to become the Duke of Devonshire. George W. Smalley, who was present when Hartington arrived, afterward described the events that followed and said of Hartington, 'There are Dukes and Dukes. This was the greatest of all. None was more sagacious, none had a sounder judgment of affairs and of men.' A tall man with a long face and a high nose, who was seldom angry but often bored, Hartington belonged to one of the great governing families of England and was immensely wealthy. His life was given to public service and he held more Cabinet offices under more governments than any other man in his time. Three times Hartington would be offered the position of Prime Minister, always to refuse it. He was above ambition, above corruption, and was therefore perfect for this delicate assignment. What made him even more suitable was his experience in these matters: he himself had for thirty years been maintaining a quiet extra-marital affair with a beautiful Duchess.

Smalley reported that Hartington said he would do nothing for either side until he first saw the Prince's letters to Lady Aylesford. Randolph gave them to him.

'Are there any more?' Hartington asked.
'No.'
'I have your authority to make such use of these letters as I think best?'
'Yes.'

Lord Hartington then walked to the fire, put the letters through the grate, saw them become ashes, and said, 'I do not think it will be necessary to carry this much farther.' Then he notified Randolph, 'You are at liberty to say what you like and do what you like. I have acted in what I consider to be the interests of both sides.'

'Hartington', Smalley commented, 'is the only man I know who could have done it without question. But that is because he is Hartington.'[10]

Whispers and rumours about the episode spread everywhere. The major mystery was Lord Randolph's role. Why had he reacted so intensely when his friendly mediation might have solved it all quietly? The most plausible explanation seems to reside in Randolph's resentment of the Prince's feeling for Jennie, and the fact that everyone knew of it. Jennie's other escorts could easily be dismissed as 'flirtations', but the Prince's attention toward any woman attracted an enormous social spotlight, and Randolph became angered by the glare.

The Prince was similarly angered. He let it be known that he would not visit any home in which the Churchills were guests. It was a strict boycott, seldom broken. In one instance, Randolph and Jennie were guests at a ball given by Lord Fitzwilliam when the band stopped playing at the height of the festivities and there followed the hush that always preceded the royal entry. The harassed host begged Jennie and Randolph to leave quickly, and the two were rushed through the servants' quarters, down through the basement to the back stairs. When the Prince arrived, he couldn't understand why the gaiety had gone out of the party.

British society, which had so warmly welcomed the Churchills, now just as coldly ostracized them. There were a few exceptions. When the Prince reprimanded John Delacour, saying, 'I hear you are continuing to see the Randolph Churchills,' Delacour answered, 'I allow no man to choose my friends.'[11] And the American-born Duchess of Manchester coolly informed the Prince, 'I hold friendship higher than snobbery.' Then she added smilingly, 'I couldn't possibly, Sire, even for you, neglect poor Jennie. We were at school together.'

Without describing the details, Winston Churchill's biography of his father said, '. . . Lord Randolph incurred the deep displeasure of a great personage. The fashionable world no longer smiled. Powerful enemies were anxious to humiliate him. His own sensitiveness and pride magnified every coldness into an affront. London became odious to him.' It became odious to Jennie, too. She had been so near the summit of Society, and suddenly she was a social pariah. 'Most people in the course of a lifetime get to know the real value of the Mammon of Unrighteousness,' she wrote, 'but few learn their lesson so early. We both profited by it.'[12]

Winston regarded the incident in retrospect as 'a spur' to his father. 'Without it, he might have wasted a dozen years in the frivolous and expensive pursuits of the silly world of fashion;

without it he would probably never have developed popular sympathies or the courage to champion democratic causes.'[13] There is little question that the incident 'altered, darkened, and strengthened his whole life and character', and that it converted 'a nature originally congenial and gay' into a man of 'stern and bitter quality' with 'a harsh contempt for what is called "Society" and an abiding antagonism to rank and authority.'

As for Jennie, she realized that her own future impact on Society could no longer depend on her beauty or personality or her husband's heritage or friends, but strictly on the weight of accomplishment. That realization, more than anything else, tightened their marriage. No more parties, no more balls, no more suitors, and only a few friends. All they truly had left was each other, and their need was great. Toward the end of the crisis with the Prince, she had written Randolph, '. . . if we are to have all these worries—do for Heaven's sake let's go through them together. As long as I have you I don't care what happens. . . .'[14]

'Randolph felt in need of solace and distraction,' Jennie wrote. So did she, and nobody knew this better than her father. He sent them a sympathetic invitation to come to the United States 'to sail and drive and see what I have left in the way of horses'.

Leonard Jerome was then fifty-eight years old and still an attractive man. That was the year he had imported polo from England, introducing it at Jerome Park in New York. He himself was unable to play after having strained his back by impulsively challenging (and beating) a weightlifter at a circus.

Jennie and Randolph arrived first in Canada, and went from there to Niagara Falls and Newport before going to New York. With them was an intimate friend of Randolph's named Harry Tyrwhitt.[15] 'Although the life there was a great contrast to that of Cowes, savoring more of the town than of the country,' Jennie said of Newport, 'we found it one of the most fascinating of places, and the hospitality and kindness shown us by the friends of my family were most gratifying.'

In the United States 1876 was a presidential election year and Rutherford Hayes barely won. Jennie understood the Hayes character when she heard his nickname: 'Queen Victoria in Breeches.' Much wilder news that year came from the West, news of everything from Custer's Last Stand at Little Big Horn to frequent and daring stagecoach robberies. Mark Twain had written: 'This country is fabulously rich in gold, silver, copper, lead, coal, iron, quicksilver . . . thieves, murderers, desperadoes, ladies, children, lawyers, Christians, Indians, Chinamen, Spaniards, gamblers, sharpers, coyotes. . . .'

Newspapers in New York were lively and unrestrained. They played up horrifying crimes, such as those which left bodies dismembered by 'THE HUMAN FIEND . . . A THIRST FOR BLOOD'. Some criminals were even caught trying to steal the bones of Abraham Lincoln to hold for ransom. Central Park was described as 'a ruffian's refuge where ladies, children and the unprotected generally are at the mercy of villains.' On the same page with advertisements promising 'ugly girls made pretty' with French corsets, or 'beautiful artificial teeth for only eight dollars', there was the item, '150 FINE PLATES AND ENGRAVINGS OF THE ANATOMY OF THE SEXUAL ORGANS.' And, in the Page One personal column:

7th Avenue Car. Saturday evening, seven o'clock . . . Was the fall in my lap when getting out accidental. If not, address, in honor, BACHELOR Box 139, appointing interview.

Broadway between Madison Square and Forty-second Street was called The Rialto. It was a street lined with theatres, a roof-garden Casino for light opera, and the vast yellow brick of the Metropolitan Opera House. Streetcars were still horse-drawn, but the elevated was being built on Third Avenue where Jennie's father used to race horses, and the Brooklyn Bridge spanned the river which once had only ferries to connect Brooklyn with Manhattan.[16]

'We went also to Saratoga,' wrote Jennie, 'where the beauty of the ladies, and the gorgeousness astonished the men.' An article in *Harper's Magazine* that year noted that 'The fountains of Saratoga will ever be the resort of wealth, intelligence and fashion.' Jennie, however, thought the obvious wealth too rich for their pocket. 'Having found the hotel at that place absurdly expensive, I asked my father to remonstrate with the proprietor, who replied: "The Lord and his wife *would* have two rooms, hence the expense." '

Philadelphia was more fun. The hundredth anniversary of American Independence was being celebrated with a Centennial Exposition featuring everything from the greatest steam engine ever built to the first public demonstration of Alexander Graham Bell's telephone, from the hand of the unfinished Statue of Liberty to

George Washington's false teeth. Other demonstrations included an automatic baby feeder, an eagle eating live chickens, and the new typewriting machine.

One of the places that particularly interested Jennie was the Women's Pavilion featuring a woman operating a six-horse-power steam engine, which powered a press producing a weekly eight-page magazine that boasted, 'No masculine hand had any part in its production.'

'For heaven's sake, keep them diverted,' Leonard Jerome asked his brother Lawrence, who served as their guide. And so he did. Acting as a volunteer salesman for products at various outdoor booths, Lawrence not only kept the young couple laughing but collected huge crowds, sold many items, and even accepted the commission from appreciative booth owners.[17] Had Lawrence done anything like that in England, he would have been thought drunk, insane or at best eccentric. Public fun in England was strictly for the 'lower classes'.

Jennie might have sighed at the contrast. America was her childhood, Europe her adolescence; and she had flowered as a mixture of both. Years later, she remembered of this visit that she had been 'invigorated and refreshed by contact with the alert intellects of my compatriots'. But that has the settled sound of time. How different it must have been when she was actually there, free from the vice of British formality. How exhilarating to come from an old city to a growing one, from austere in-laws to a warm, laughing, vibrant father who could never say no to her.

There had been, of course, the fairyland quality of the past few years, emperors and princes and the high minds of Europe knowing her, dancing with her, calling on her. That now seemed lost, the social future bleak. She felt free and alive in America; going back to England held a chilly uncertainty. Yet there was no choice—she could not ask Randolph to stay in her country. Some Englishmen had become Americans, but Randolph was a Member of Parliament. He had no other trade or talent.

Upon their return to England, the young Churchills' bleak future seemed brightened. The Duke of Marlborough had accepted an appointment as Viceroy to Ireland, a position he had previously refused. Disraeli had pressed it on him again, urging that the social air of Dublin Castle might prove more friendly to his family than that of England. The particular point was that Randolph would accompany his father as an unpaid private secretary. It was a happy solution to all the problems brought on by the Aylesford affair.

'Not being in favor with the Court, from which London society took the lead,' wrote Jennie, 'we were nothing loath to go.' Jennie looked forward to Ireland. She had heard the Irish were a people of warmth and passion, that theirs was a country of rich speech, green fields, mist, and mystery.

They arrived in December 1876. It was a dramatic entry, full of the panoply and pomp that royal Britain attached to a Viceroy—full dress parade, carriages with outriders and postilions, the booming of cannons. Jennie didn't know where this new twist in her road would wind, but she was eager for the adventure.

# 7

Jennie, Randolph, and Winston moved into 'The Little White Lodge', a low, white building with green shutters and veranda. Set in Phoenix Park, it was only a few minutes' walk from Viceregal Lodge, the home of the Viceroy. This enormous park of 1,700 acres, an ancient place of dramatic duels and tame deer, was originally set up as a hawking ground for the viceroys, then became the great public pleasure grounds of Dublin.

Preceding the Duke of Marlborough as Viceroy had been the Duke of Abercorn, better known as 'Old Magnificent', a delightful and handsome man who scented his beard and had the debutantes pass by in a kissing review, asking the pretty ones to return for an encore. What made Marlborough's replacement of Abercorn embarrassing was that Abercorn's daughter was Blandford's wife, deserted in the Aylesford scandal. Nevertheless, the Marlboroughs and the Churchills moved in for a three-year stay.

Jennie liked Ireland. She viewed the green island with the romantic eyes of a 23-year-old woman of privilege. Instead of a poor, rocky land, it was for her a lovely, lonely place with stone fences lining the green meadows 'like veins on a time-worn hand'. Instead of the wretched hovels, she saw the slender, circular stone towers that had given shelter from foreign raiders during the Middle Ages, the profusion of flowers and sea-swept rocks, the bright oats stacked next to black peat. Instead of the hopelessness of hungry people, she saw barelegged colleens in red petticoats riding sideways on the backs of donkeys. For Jennie, it was a singing land of poetically lilting names—Inishmore, Tipperary, Limerick, Blarney, MacGillicuddy's Reeks.

She would soon learn the harsher truth of Ireland, but now she knew only the pleasure. Hers was primarily the outdoor life: sailing on the lakes of Killarney and the wide stretches of the loughs, trout fishing in Galway and Connemara, snipe shooting at Lord Sligo's place in Westport and shooting near Muckross Abbey, catching lobsters in the natural harbours of the irregular coastline, week-ending at Lord Portarlington's home near Emo (where Randolph had spent so many weeks waiting for his aunt to die), hard riding in the wild woods and open fields. Riding, in fact, became such a passion for Jennie that she 'begged, borrowed or stole any horse she could find', to go whenever she could. With a brown mare she had bought in Oxford, she could manage most of the 'trappy' fences of the Kildare country, as well as the banks and narrow doubles of Meath 'as though to the manner born'.[1]

Riding often and everywhere gave her the outlet she needed for her enormous physical energy, as well as a sense of freedom—freedom from the watchful eye of her mother-in-law, freedom from the polite but dull duties at the Viceregal Lodge, and the freedom of feeling that she belonged to herself.

Randolph occasionally rode with her. Once she was going through an opening in a fence when the heavy gate swung and caught the horse broadside.

Luckily I fell clear, but it looked as if I might be crushed underneath him, and Randolph, coming up at that moment, thought I was killed. A few seconds later, however, seeing me all right, in the excitement of the moment he seized my flask and emptied it. For many days it was a standing joke against him that *I* had the fall, and *he* had the whiskey.

One photograph of Jennie shows her wearing a closely fitting black riding habit and a rakishly set, black silk hat. Winston, two years old when the family went to Ireland and six when they left, retained that image through his adulthood. 'My picture of her in Ireland is in a riding habit, fitting like skin and often beautifully spotted with mud.'[2]

Lord D'Abernon remembered her differently. The former Sir Edgar Vincent, D'Abernon was a statesman and philosopher, former Ambassador to Berlin, an international banker in Turkey, and regarded by many as one of the most handsome men in England. He wrote:

I have the clearest recollection of seeing her for the first time. It was at the Viceregal Lodge at Dublin. She stood on one side, to the left of the entrance. The Viceroy was on a dais at the farther end of the room surrounded by a brilliant staff, but eyes were not turned on him or his consort, but on a dark, lithe figure, standing somewhat apart and appearing to be of another texture to those around her, radiant, translucent, intense. A diamond star in her hair, her favourite ornament—its lustre dimmed by the flashing glory of her eyes. More of the panther than of the woman in her look, but with a cultivated intelligence unknown to the jungle. Her courage not less great than her husband's—fit mother for descendants of the great Duke. With all these attributes of brilliancy such kindliness and high spirits . . . she was universally popular. Her desire to please, her delight in life and the genuine wish that all should share her joyous faith in it, made her the centre of a devoted circle.[3]

He and Jennie were to be intimates for a long time.

Jennie was impressed with all the men of Ireland: their warmth and wit, their conviction that life and living were more important than form. 'During those three years we lived there,' she wrote, 'I cannot remember meeting one really dull man. From the Lord Chief Justice to the familiar car-man, all were entertaining.'

Randolph Churchill was away at Westminster much of the time. Jennie wrote him dutiful letters: '. . . Winston is flourishing, though rather cross the last two days—more teeth, I think. Everest has been bothering me about some clothes for him, saying that it was quite a disgrace how few things he has, and how shabby, at that. . . .'[4]

In his first three years as a Member of Parliament, Randolph spoke a total of one-and-a-half hours on the House floor, his speeches unimportant and unimpressive. On January 28, 1878, he wrote Jennie from London:

. . . I am sure the debate will be very stormy. I am in great doubt what to do. I think I could make a telling speech against the Government, but old Bentinck got hold of me today and gave me a tremendous lecture. Of course I have my future to think of. . . . It is very difficult. . . .

It did not seem much of a future then, but that made it easier to surrender on various points of principle. The Duke of Marlborough was finally able to persuade Randolph to sign a full and formal apology to the Prince of Wales. The Queen and Lord Chancellor, however, had prepared for Randolph an even more contrite letter of apology, and he signed that, too.

That still did not heal the rift. Jennie, therefore, seldom went with Randolph to London. She had no wish to suffer any snubs, or defend herself against sneers. During that summer of 1878, however, she did accept an invitation to the 'Peace with Honour' banquet given for Disraeli (who had been created Earl of Beaconsfield three years before), and for Lord Salisbury, who had returned from a Berlin Conference where peace had been made with Russia over the Dardanelles. Jennie accompanied the Duchess of Wellington. 'It was a wonderful sight,' she said of the banquet, 'and the enthusiasm was boundless when Lord Beaconsfield, looking like a black sphinx, rose to speak. It was on that occasion that, pointing with a scornful finger at Mr Gladstone, he declared that he [Gladstone] was "inebriated with the exuberance of his own verbosity".'

Another newcomer to Parliament, elected the year after Randolph, was Ireland's fiery Charles Stewart Parnell. Like Randolph, his initial speeches were characterized by bad delivery and obvious nervousness. But unlike Randolph, his convictions were strong and his passions intense, particularly when he insisted on Ireland's right of self-government: 'Ireland is not a geographical fragment,' he said, 'She is a nation.'[5] Parnell gradually organized a small band of Fenian followers in Parliament to obstruct all proposed legislation until their own demands were met. Randolph once remarked, 'How very troublesome the Fenians are', and called them 'a great, secret, army'. He overestimated their strength, however.

Born in the United States as a movement to export revolution to Ireland, Fenianism had become more of a symbol than a breed. Its uprisings were few and frustrated. The most formidable of them, in 1867, just seven miles out of Dublin, resulted in 960 arrests and practically destroyed the movement. Another Irishman, the brilliant Isaac Butt, accepted leader of Parliament's sixty representatives favouring Home Rule for Ireland, was a more moderate man. He believed in the power of words and reason; Parnell believed in force. Parnell saw the House of Commons as an English institution and hated it; Butt loved the House.

Randolph and Jennie knew both men. Butt, however, was their good friend and had begun to influence their opinions on the Irish issue. Other Irish friends, Lord Justice Fitzgibbon and Father James Healy, also worked to convert the Churchills to the cause of Home Rule.

Jennie must have been impressed by the fact that these Irish leaders thought of her not only as a woman, but as a thinking person, as someone worthy of conversion. Men of experience, older and wiser than she, they easily might have considered her simply a charming lady to be hand-kissed and ignored. That they did not, and that she felt capable of debate with them, gave her a growing sense of individuality, even apart from her husband.

While the Churchills remained unconverted on Irish Home Rule, Lord Randolph's familiarity with that crucial issue not only made him strongly sympathetic to Irish problems but served as a springboard for his future. In one of his early speeches, which had been in answer to an Irish Member of the House who had sneered at the first Duke of Marlborough, Randolph had retaliated by calling Dublin 'a seditious capital'. He now publicly apologized, saying, 'I have since learned to know Ireland better.' Then in an inflammatory speech at his home borough of Woodstock, Randolph blamed a generation of British misgovernment and neglect of Ireland as the real cause of the crisis between the two peoples. 'There are great and crying questions which the government has not attended to,' he warned, 'and as long as these matters are neglected, so will the government have to deal with obstruction from Ireland.'[6]

This unprecedented criticism from a Tory aristocrat caused considerable furore in the press. Newspaper editorials blistered Randolph as a traitor to his country and his class. In obvious disapproval of Randolph's Woodstock speech, Disraeli wrote to the Duke of Marlborough that the seeds of the Irish Home Rule movement seemed to him a menace 'scarcely less disastrous than pestilence and famine'. A family friend asked Marlborough for an explanation of Randolph's remarkable speech. 'The only excuse I can find for Randolph,' the Duke replied, 'is that he must either be mad or have been singularly affected with local champagne or claret. I can only say that the sentiments he has indulged in are purely his own.'[7]

Jennie, however, believed as her husband did. It was true that she and Randolph had lost most of the fire of their early love and that their marriage had been pulled together by the social disaster of their encounter with the Prince. But more important in maintaining a sense of unity was their abiding mutual respect. Churchill knew the strength of his wife's will, the extent of her energy, and the value of her astuteness; Jennie was keenly aware of the potential of Randolph's intelligence and passions, however fitful. Certainly Randolph himself, at this unsure time in his political career, could not have stood against the austere force of his father and the pleading of his mother had he not had Jennie's full support.

Famine had come to Ireland with the failure of the potato crop in 1877, resulting in two years of hunger, terror, and ruin. Official aid being insufficient, the Duchess started a Famine Fund. It was largely aimed at supplying the basic essentials to the aged and the ill, with a sum of money to help keep at least a few families out of the workhouse and provide food and clothing for children in school. Jennie and Randolph both joined in the effort and travelled throughout the country, from the moors to the mountains. They were profoundly moved by the despair, especially in southern Ireland. 'In our walks, we had many opportunities of seeing the heart-rending poverty of the peasantry who lived . . . more like animals than human beings,' Jennie wrote.

They found people living in one-room huts furnished only with some straw and blankets, eating nothing but potatoes and salt, and having meat but twice a year, at Easter and Christmas. Pigs could not be raised because there was no garbage to feed them—garbage was a luxury. 'There are many houses in this parish at present,' wrote one priest at the time,

in which the last pound of meal has been consumed, the last bed-covering worth a shilling has been deposited in the pawn office, and the last fire of turf collected from the saturated heap upon the bog has died upon the hearth, the dying embers being a vivid emblem of that death from starvation which is already creeping upon the threshold.

Together the Churchills toured almost every county in Ireland. What they saw and learned had a permanent effect upon them both.

The experience was particularly significant for Jennie. This was the first time she had been drawn outside of herself. While it was true that she and Randolph lived on limited funds compared to others of their social level, it was still a financial pinch of the gentlest kind, a pinch with a wink in it. She had never seen the horror of hunger, of children without shoes, of homes warmed by huddled bodies for lack of coal. It was a new view of an old world that shocked and hurt her. She never forgot. Nor would she ever let Randolph forget.

Her son, however, also demanded attention. '. . . Winston has just been with me,' she wrote Randolph, 'such a darling he is. "I can't have my Mama go—and if she does, I will run after the train and jump in," he said to me. I have told Everest to take him out for a drive tomorrow, if it is fine.'[8]

Mrs Everest, whom Winston called 'Woom' or 'Woomany', was the one who took him to the pantomime, helped teach him to read, and introduced him to the 'tangle of arithmetic'. In *My Early Life*, Winston wrote of the latter:

These complications cast a steadily gathering shadow over my daily life. They took one away from the interesting things one wanted to do in the nursery or the garden. They made increasing inroads upon one's leisure. . . . My mother took no part in these impositions, but she gave me to understand that she approved of them and she sided with the Governess almost always.[9]

British tradition relegated Jennie's job with Winston to that of overseer, at a prescribed distance. Children appeared briefly at breakfast, at lunch, and shortly before bedtime. Nannies, at that time especially, cultivated in children a sense of strain because they repeatedly emphasized that all children must be on their best behaviour during any appearance before parents. Parents were to be regarded as special personages of unpredictable moods. Any undesirable behaviour on the part of a child, whether a sob or a sudden laugh, could cause immediate banishment to the nursery and even the deprivation of dessert. Thus children of this time and this class found they could really relax only with their nannies.

Commenting on a British children's book at the time, a London critic wrote: 'Little boys and girls ought not to regard themselves, as these stories teach them to do, as possible personages. . . . They should be left to the happy humility of unspoiled children who do not discover that they are worth thinking about. . . .'

While Jennie deviated somewhat from the pattern of the upper-class British parent, Randolph followed it in the extreme. She demonstrated love and concern, but Randolph seemed to determinedly maintain a distance from his son. Part of that, too, was the standard of British upper-class fathers. But Randolph Churchill's attitude toward Winston, from his earliest years to the time of his death, was more — or rather, less — than austere reserve — it was calculated coldness. Children of a disappointing marriage, of course, are often the objects of resentment, and if Winston had been conceived before the marriage, guilt may have further embittered Randolph.[10] Moreover, had there been no marriage and no son, the nature of Randolph's illness might have remained secret and his shame unexposed. In the family, however, it was also said that Randolph generally disliked children. Whatever the origin, the fact is clear: Randolph Churchill did not like his son.

Although the marriage was still intact, it was severely rent. Jennie was happy to go riding with nearly any attractive and interesting man. One of her most frequent escorts was Colonel Forster, then Master of the Horse to the Viceroy. Jennie wrote of him only that he was 'a beautiful rider, and many were the pleasant hunting days we had together'.

Hunting trips seemed to consume an increasing amount of time. Jennie went on many, but primarily for the ride. She had a particularly strong aversion to the killing of any living creature. Years later, she described the way a young, charming-looking woman killed a stag:

With the aid of a powerful pair of field-glasses, I watched her stalk. . . . First she crawled on all fours up a long burn; emerging hot and panting, not to say wet and dirty, she then continued her scramble up a steep hill, taking advantage of any cover afforded by the ground, or remaining in a petrified attitude if by chance a hind happened to look up. The stag, meanwhile, quite oblivious of the danger lurking at hand, was apparently enjoying himself. Surrounded by his hinds, he trusted in their vigilance, and lay in the bracken in the brilliant sunshine. I could just see his fine antlered head, when suddenly, realizing that all was not well, he bounded up, making a magnificent picture as he stood gazing round, his head thrown back in defiance. Crash! Bang! and this glorious animal became a maimed and tortured thing. Shot through both forelegs, he attempted to gallop down the hill, his poor broken limbs tumbling about him, while the affrighted hinds stood riveted to the spot, looking at their lord and master with horror, not unmixed with curiosity. I shall never forget the sight, or that of the dogs set on him. . . . If these things must be done, how can a woman bring herself to do them?

During this hectic time in Ireland Jennie still managed to maintain a smooth relationship with her in-laws. From the first time they met, she and Marlborough shared a mutual admiration. As for the Duchess, Jennie was an obvious asset during the considerable entertaining that was required of the Duke's position. Jennie also had worked hard for the Duchess's Famine Fund, for which the Duchess had received flattering appreciation from Queen Victoria. But most of all, the cooling relationship between Jennie and Randolph had strengthened Randolph's ties to his mother. The Duchess was most happy to have it that way.

On April 15, 1879, Randolph wrote to his mother from London: 'I write to wish you very many happy returns of your birthday tomorrow, which is also, as perhaps you may remember, our wedding day; and having been married five years, I begin to feel highly respectable.'

The importance of respectability was certainly one of the pressures that kept his marriage intact and one reason he blinded himself to the constant rumours about Jennie and her men.

While Randolph was away at Westminster, Jennie had met the visiting Empress Elizabeth of Austria. Now forty-two, Elizabeth had once been considered the most beautiful princess in Europe. She was an eccentric, who always carried a large fan to hide her face from the crowd, and who for a time had lived on a diet of blood and milk. On one occasion during her youth, she had received her Greek teacher wearing black, flowing clothes and hanging upside down from a trapeze. Her father had once told her, 'If you and I had not been born princes, we would have been performers in a circus.' On her arrival in Ireland, Elizabeth converted her boudoir into a gymnasium. She wore a riding habit so tightly fitted that whenever she fell from a horse, she had to be unbuttoned before she could stand up.

Elizabeth had married the Emperor Franz Joseph when she was only sixteen. Not only had she been infected by him with syphilis, but she had passed on the disease to their only son, the Crown Prince Rudolph. Once this was discovered, the Emperor refused her nothing. He catered to her every whim, even let her choose his mistress.[11] Perhaps Randolph catered to Jennie's whims out of his guilt, for her influence over him continued, despite her affairs.

Randolph's trips to London increased considerably, both in quantity and duration. During his stays in London, Randolph wrote often to his mother but less often to his wife. The tone of affection was marked in the letters to his mother; those to Jennie were mainly of politics.

Even when Randolph was back in Ireland, he and Jennie rode separately as often as they rode together. In his memoirs, Winston Churchill noted, 'She and my father hunted continually on their large horses; and sometimes there were great scares because one or the other did not come back for many hours after they were expected.'[12]

One of the favourite friends of the young Randolph Churchills for many years was Lieutenant-Colonel John Strange Jocelyn. She had met him at Blenheim Palace on that first day she signed the Guest

Book. Strange Jocelyn was the third son of the third Earl of Roden, born in Dublin, educated at Harrow. He and his wife had a 8,900-acre estate close to the shores of the Irish Sea.[13]

Jennie was again pregnant in the summer of 1879, and her second son was born in Dublin on February 4, 1880. John Strange Jocelyn was asked by the Randolph Churchills to be a godfather,[14] and they named the boy John Strange Spencer-Churchill.

# 8

Women had few legal rights in England in 1880. So long as a wife remained under her husband's roof, she was legally subject to him. As late as 1899, a man suffering from syphilis could legally insist upon sexual intercourse with his wife and could not be accused of rape if he forced her. For any upper-class woman of the time, the stigma of divorce was overwhelming. To the outside world the strange thing was that here was a country ruled by a woman, and yet the Victorian Age represented the last stand of British male supremacy.[1] For example, the first British Marriage and Divorce Act was passed in 1857, but society women generally steered clear of it, because the stigma was too strong. While the Queen had no qualms about inviting men to Court ceremonies who were known to be unfaithful to their wives, she would never—until 1887—invite any woman who had the temerity to petition for divorce, no matter how justified the woman's reasons.[2] The Married Women's Property Act would not pass Parliament for another two years. Until then, a husband could demand and collect the whole of his wife's income and spend it any way he wanted—even if she had left his bed and board, and even if their children were starving.

Private lives were considered private, with only a single social rule—no scandal. Divorce meant scandal, and scandal damaged society's image with the mass of people. 'We saw to it,' said Lady Warwick, 'that five out of every six scandals never reached the outside world.'[3] As soon as it seemed there might be an appeal to the Divorce Court, social pressure converged on the couple to avoid the final step. If the name were famous enough, such pressure often came from the highest quarters.

But there were other factors. Jennie, of course, was not unfamiliar with compromised marriage. Her own mother, after all, had nearly always been cognizant of her husband's flagrant infidelity and had made no attempt at divorce. The London society of which the Churchills were a part abounded in such situations, where marriage merely served as a social convenience long after love had gone.

Moreover, if Jennie did not respect Randolph as a husband, she did respect his other qualities—his courage, his charm, his wit, and his potential. Jennie was then only twenty-six years old, and she felt a lingering tenderness for Randolph. Leaving her husband then would have meant abandoning him at a time of his greatest need.

Divorce for Randolph was similarly out of the question. He still loved Jennie in his own way, and there were never any other women connected with him in whispered scandal. He needed Jennie as an anchor, a source of strength, a sympathetic adviser. He always had been physically frail, but now the recurrent spectre of syphilis also kept him mentally insecure.[4] In addition, divorce would have seriously crippled any political future Randolph hoped to have.

In March, 1880, Jennie and Randolph and their ménage of two children, nanny, cook, and servants set up house at 29 St. James's Place, a very desirable address.[5] It was a small, prestigious street, set in an area of quiet dignity. The cream of the social élite were gathered there. St. James's Palace and Marlborough House were just on the other side of Pall Mall; at the bottom of St. James's Place, in the cul-de-sac bounded on one side by Green Park, was the lovely home that had belonged to Lord Spencer, the noted Home Secretary in the time of Pitt and Burke. Next door to the Churchills lived Sir Stafford Northcote, who replaced Disraeli as leader in the House of Commons, after Disraeli's elevation to the House of Lords in 1876. A man of dignity and patience, with a puckish sense of humour, Northcote was too tolerant of the turbulent spirit of his times to maintain a position of party leadership. Lord Randolph later made Northcote his personal target for political destruction, and succeeded. They must have been interesting neighbours for one another.

Britain had a General Election in April 1880. The country had changed significantly during the previous generation. The population had jumped from 27 to 35 million and liberalized election laws had extended the franchise. After its success with Russia over the Dardanelles, Disraeli's government had suffered some severe setbacks, particularly over the Afghan and Zulu wars (in the latter of which the Prince Imperial, son of Napoleon III, was killed). There had also been unemployment and discontent in rural areas following the arrival of cheap wheat from America. The Tories seemed to be in serious trouble everywhere. Even the family borough of Woodstock

117

no longer seemed safe, and Randolph hurried there to work for votes.

'The outlook here at the outset was very alarming,' he wrote his mother. 'I think I must attend more regularly this session. Hall hit me rather hard on account of my slack attendance.'

In *My Early Life*, Winston Churchill reported his boyhood estimate of the election:

In 1880 we were all thrown out of office by Mr. Gladstone. Mr. Gladstone was a very dangerous man who went about rousing people up, lashing them into fury so that they voted against the Conservatives and turned my grandfather out of his place as Lord-Lieutenant of Ireland. . . . Lord Beaconsfield [Disraeli] was the great enemy of Mr. Gladstone, and everybody called him 'Dizzy'. However, this time Dizzy had been thoroughly beaten by Mr. Gladstone, so we were all flung out into Opposition and the country began to be ruined very rapidly. Everyone said it was 'going to the dogs'.[6]

Randolph, however, had won, but by a mere sixty votes. 'Starting with many advantages,' his son later wrote, 'he was still, at thirty-one, obscure. . . . His party was now humbled in the dust. . . . Grave and violent dangers beset the State, and no one troubled to think about an undistinguished sprig of the nobility. Nevertheless his hour had come. . . .'[7]

That summer of 1880 Winston was six years old and a troublesome boy. Jennie wrote her mother that he was a 'most difficult child to manage'. It was probably partly a little boy's frustration with the seeming lack of parental affection. Randolph Churchill was involving himself more deeply in politics and Jennie faced the delicate job of again ingratiating herself with London society after a three-year absence. Winston and his baby brother Jack were still primarily looked after by Mrs Everest. Many years after, Winston Churchill would write, 'If there be any, as I trust there are some, who rejoice that I live, to that dear and excellent woman, their gratitude is due.'

Jennie occasionally took over, particularly when Mrs Everest was ill or on holiday. On one such night, Winston was unable to fall asleep and Jennie exhausted herself playing 'Pirates and Indians' with him.[8]

Vacation plans soon had to be made, but since Parliament was not expected to recess till September, Jennie sent Winston and Jack to Ventnor, on the Isle of Wight, for the month of August. Mrs Everest had a sister who lived there. Her sister's husband was a prison warder who filled Winston with all sorts of exciting stories of prison mutinies, and took him for long walks out on the cliffs overlooking the sea. One day, Winston wrote, 'We saw a great splendid ship with all her sails set, passing the shore only a mile or two away.' 'That is a troopship,' the prison warder told him, 'bringing the men back from the war.' Then there was a sudden storm and Winston afterward learned the ship had capsized and three hundred soldiers had drowned. He was told divers had gone down searching for the bodies, 'and it made a scar on my mind—that some of the divers had fainted with terror at seeing the fish, eating the bodies of the poor soldiers. . . .'

Winston then wrote what was probably his first letter: 'My dear Mama I am so glad you are coming to see us. I had such a nice bathe in the sea today. love to papa your loving Winston.'[9]

Shortly after his return from Ventnor, he was sent away to school for the first time.

It appeared that I was to go away from home for many weeks at a stretch in order to do lessons under masters. The term had already begun, but still I should have to stay seven weeks before I could come home for Christmas. . . . I was no more consulted about leaving home than I had been about coming into the world. . . .

The fateful day arrived. My mother took me to the station in a hansom cab. She gave me three half-crowns, which I dropped onto the floor of the cab, and we had to scramble around in the straw to find them again. We only just caught the train. If we had missed it, it would have been the end of the world. However, we didn't, and the world went on.

St. George's was a fashionable, exclusive school that prepared boys for fashionable, exclusive Eton.

It was a dark November afternoon when we arrived at this establishment. We had tea with the Headmaster, with whom my mother conversed in the most easy manner. I was preoccupied with the fear of spilling my cup and so making 'a bad start'. I was also miserable at the idea of being left alone among all these strangers in this great, fierce, formidable place. After all, I was only seven, and I had been so happy in my nursery with all my toys. I had such wonderful toys: a real steam engine, a magic lantern, and a collection of soldiers already nearly a thousand strong. Now it had to be all lessons.[10]

Winston soon learned that St. George's was a school where flogging was a regular practice. 'Two or three times a month the whole school was marshalled in the Library,' he remembered,

and one or more delinquents were haled off to an adjoining apartment by the two head boys, and there flogged until they bled freely, while the rest sat quaking listening to their screams. How I hated this school, and what a life of anxiety I lived there for more than two years.

Winston was once flogged for taking sugar from the pantry. Afterward he was reported to have found the Master's straw hat and kicked it to pieces. In her *Life of Roger Fry*, which purportedly describes St. George's, Virginia Woolf described floggings by a sadistic headmaster with a hatred of red-haired boys.[11] Red-haired Winston, however, kept the fact of the headmaster's sadism to himself and wrote his parents, 'I am very happy at school.'

In those next years, Jennie lived with a different anxiety. London was always a part of it. Their house was expensive, Winston's school was expensive, everything was expensive, and their income never seemed to cover everything. 'London is very gay now,' she wrote her mother.

I haven't been to many balls; as I simply cannot afford to get dresses and one can't wear always the same thing. Besides I was not bidden to the one I wanted to go to [because of the Prince] and I did not care about the others. . . . Money is such a hateful subject to me just now . . . don't let us talk about it. . . .

Fortunately, Jennie was able to furnish her house 'on the cheap'. She had a collector's instinct as well as a decorator's flair, and she had made the rounds of the Dublin antique shops during her Ireland years, buying mostly choice pieces from ancestral homes. Blandford referred to her collection as 'Jennie's stage props'. Her most expensive acquisitions were silk panels for her drawing room—but they were soon ruined by the damp.[12]

Mrs Jerome had left Paris to live again with her husband in New York, and Jennie wrote them there:

. . . Our money affairs are pretty much like everyone else's, it seems to me, hard up, notwithstanding Papa's most generous 'tips'.
Randolph is obliged to spend so much in a political way, going to these meetings etc., and this big public dinner in Woodstock will cost a lot . . . the building alone costs £120. . . . But this demonstration is of great importance to R. and the thing must be well done with Lord Salisbury and a lot of big swells coming. You don't know how economical we try to be. I've not bought but one winter dress, and that we bought in Woodstock for twenty-five shillings and made over by my maid—dark red thin flannel. . . .
P.S. R. sends his best love—Bye and bye couldn't you send me a barrel of American eating apples to St. James's Place? I'm so fond of them.

Up to then, Jennie Churchill was many things: beautiful, fascinating, witty, but her positive impact upon others had been primarily social and mainly among men. She had broken out of the small, rigid frame that limited the mind and activity of the average Victorian society woman. Her conversations were not confined to the female trivia of her time, and few topics were beyond her ken. Yet the hard fact was that at twenty-seven she was neither a successful wife nor a successful mother. But the year of 1881 was a turning point in her metamorphosis, just as it was for Randolph. It was as if both had suddenly realized that success in politics could influence so much else—their self-respect, their position in society, and particularly their marriage. Their common enthusiasm for the nature of politics and the rewards it offered could generate a way of life to be discussed and planned together. Jennie had a gift for the written word, and could help her husband with his speeches—read them, listen to them, suggest changes, and perhaps even write some of them. Randolph also relied on Jennie for her manipulative mind and her intuitive judgment of people.

Lord Randolph Churchill, the quiet back-bencher, meekly accepting most party orders, suddenly became aggressive, sarcastic, gay, heedless of consequences. The social dilettante who seemed to care little about anything suddenly became a political figure with the principles and courage of a Scarlet Pimpernel.

He was still ill-equipped, however, to cope with a new-found future, having had only the slightest background in foreign affairs and almost none in political history, except for the Irish question. As a speaker, too, he appeared to be ill-suited to success. His voice was guttural, with 'a curious rolling effect, as if his tongue was too big for his mouth.'[13] (Winston Churchill later copied his father's voice and style.) It was also rather disconcerting that Randolph used head movements instead of arm movements to emphasize a point. And his physical figure, too, was hardly impressive: slim, slightly smaller than medium height, his main distinction a fashionable walrus moustache, but one that seemed disproportionate to his face.

Yet what gave his speech particular force and made one forget the face and the figure and the guttural sounds was a smouldering fury that often exploded. It was the same fury of the small boy who, as Shane Leslie described it, once 'took a silver spoon, twisted it, stamped on it, bit it and crushed it out of all recognition'. The direction of this fury was unpredictable. Neither his enemies nor his friends knew what he might say or do next, nor whether his reason might be lofty or confused, based on conviction or self-sacrifice.

Attacking a government pamphlet on one occasion, Randolph threw the pamphlet down on the floor of the House and stamped on it, to the long, loud cheers of his fellow Tories. After that speech, Jennie wrote in a letter to her sister, 'Everyone . . . rushed up and congratulated me to such an extent that I felt as tho' I had made it.'

His humour was barbed, his phrasing incisive, his mode of thought cynical and sparkling, his charm persuasive. At a political meeting in Paddington, a woman in the audience asked a question that caused an uproar. Churchill asked for quiet, then said, 'Gentlemen, there is only one reply to a lady when she argues with you— Silence.' The audience laughed in approval. It was little wonder that he soon gathered around him a small circle of kindred spirits. He and three others became a pressure group in the House and were soon nicknamed the 'Fourth Party'.[14] A long-time family friend, fifteen years older than Randolph, Sir Henry Drummond Wolff, was the most flippant and unflappable of the four. Jennie, who had met Wolff at Cowes before her marriage, later described him as 'the best of the company . . . with a pink-and-white complexion that a girl might have envied, and a merry twinkle which hid behind a pair of spectacles . . . a godsend if anything went wrong, and a joke from him saved many a situation.' It was Wolff whose warmth always gave the group's meetings the tone of a family gathering.

Then there was John Eldon Gorst, a serious, calculating man in his late forties, a Member of the House for fourteen years, and a close friend of Disraeli. In her *Reminiscences*, Jennie said of Gorst that he always seemed stern but that 'he could make himself very pleasant'.

I remember [Gorst] defending me in some trivial case in the County Court, and winning it; the appearance of a Queen's Counsel in silk gown and wig creating a sensation. Randolph accompanied us, and we drove away in a four-wheeler, feeling very triumphant until the wheel came off and we were ignominiously precipitated into the street.[15]

A see-saw member of the Fourth Party, Arthur James Balfour, moved in and out, depending upon the political climate. Thirty-two years old, Balfour served as secretary to his uncle, Lord Salisbury, whom he kept fully posted on Lord Randolph's plans. Balfour seemed to need nobody. Among contemporary public figures, his blood was the bluest—he was a Cecil and the son of a prominent Member of Parliament, his wealth was extensive, and behind his bland face and indolent, charming demeanour worked 'the finest brain that has been applied to politics in our time'.[16] He had entered Parliament through a family-controlled borough, as Randolph had, at the age of twenty-six.

Balfour was later quoted as saying that one of the reasons he joined the Fourth Party in the House was that the front benches gave him more room for his legs. Six feet tall with a willowy figure, Balfour always seemed to be sitting on his spine. *Punch*'s Henry Lucy described the position by saying that Balfour appeared to be trying to discover 'how nearly he could sit on his shoulder blades'. Winston Churchill in later years called Balfour 'the most courageous man alive. I believe if you held a pistol to his face, it would not frighten him.' Still, some Irish members of the House called him 'Miss Balfour' and even 'Clara', because of his unmistakable effeminacy.

Jennie particularly admired Balfour's knowledge of music, and the two of them frequently played Beethoven and Schumann piano duets. She saved this note from him, written at the House of Commons:

I'm groaning and swearing on this beastly bench: while you are listening to Wagnerian discords, I am listening to Irish grumblings—there is a great deal of brass in both of them; otherwise there is not much resemblance! I *am* sitting next———, I *might* be sitting next you! I am an unhappy victim. . . .

She and Balfour shared their mutual interest in music with Gorst, and the three of them often went together to concerts, particularly the 'Monday Pops'. 'My fashionable and frivolous friends, spying the three of us walking together, often teased me about my "weird" companions,' Jennie wrote, 'one solemn with beard and eye-glass, the other aesthetic with long hair and huge spats.'

Jennie was practically a fifth member of the Fourth Party. 'Many were the plots and plans which were hatched in my presence by the Fourth Party,' she said. 'How we used to chaff about the "goats" as we called the ultra-Tories and followers of Sir Stafford Northcote! Great was to be their fall and destruction.'

Lady Jeune described one of the group's meetings at her house when 'Randolph looked like a great schoolboy, full of fun and mischief, his busy brain devising means by which he could upset his political opponents, and then bubbling over with fiendish glee at the traps he was setting for the unaware politicians of his own side. . . .'

Five months after the General Election, in August 1880, the Liberals solemnly rebuked the Fourth Party for 'obstruction', noting that since the election the Fourth Party, collectively, had made 247 speeches and asked seventy-three questions.

A junior member of the Liberal Government found himself being chaffed at one of Jennie's soirees because he was absenting himself from the House that night. The guest finally admitted that he had asked permission to come to the party and was told that he could stay as long as he liked—provided he managed to keep the four members of the Fourth Party away from the House.

The first cartoon about the Fourth Party featured a faithful likeness of Randolph which emphasized his popeyes and showed him gazing upward while his three bewildered companions murmured, 'We wonder where he is taking us to?' Parliamentary critic Lucy described the group's mood as 'one of youth, as of boys playing at politics, and in their undisciplined revels plucking the beards of grave and reverend seigneurs. . . .'

House members always expected the unexpected from Lord Randolph. Who else but he would ride a bicycle on the terrace of the awesome House of Commons, just to get some exercise? Or accept a bet that he could run back and forth across Westminster Bridge while Big Ben was striking midnight, and do it? Who but Randolph would tell another Conservative Party member in the lobby, 'You had much better join us. Sitting up there behind the old Goat [Northcote] you will never have any fun at all.'

Always the dandy, his frock coat open, looking correct yet frivolous, Randolph could pose his questions in the most charming but insinuating way and invariably evoke an emotional reaction from Gladstone. The Prime Minister's was the classic manner of speech and debate, and it was his eloquence that was largely responsible for his great victory in overthrowing the Disraeli Government. But he was easily provoked, although he quickly regained his calm to answer the question at length. Then, as soon as Gladstone had concluded, another Fourth Party member would pop up with still another question. And so it went.

Gladstone had serious problems with Turkey and Greece and Cyprus and South Africa, problems that would still plague Winston Churchill's Government in the next century, but the Fourth Party's point of most concentrated attack was the Irish question. Unrest in Ireland had intensified, and the Gladstone Government seemed unable to cope with it.[17] The Fourth Party was convinced that coercion was unnecessary to quell the Irish troubles, that proper education and social welfare were more effective. It was a concept central to the Fourth Party's doctrine of 'Tory Democracy'.

Charles Stewart Parnell was soon attracted into Randolph's orbit. Parnell felt strongly that Lord Randolph was more likely to be genuinely touched by the Irish cause than any of his Conservative Party compatriots. By aligning himself with Churchill now, Parnell shrewdly calculated that he could stir the Liberals into moving in his direction.[18] Parnell's support would give the Fourth Party a strength out of proportion to its size, particularly since Gladstone's Liberal parliamentary majority was unruly and unpredictable. And the Fourth Party would provide a critical weight to the House's Irish group, as a motion for adjournment 'on a matter of urgent public importance', required forty supporters. Parnell had a personal following in the House of thirty-seven; with the addition of the Fourth Party, the Irish group would have its necessary forty.

Churchill soon moved into the corner of the coveted front bench of the House, the focal point of House attention. In one of his more celebrated speeches, he said:

People sometimes talk too lightly of coercion. It means that hundreds of Irishmen, who if the law had been maintained unaltered and had been firmly enforced, would now have been leading peaceful, industrious and honest lives, will soon be borne off to prison without trial; the others will have to fly the country into hopeless exile; that others, driven to desperation through such cruel alternatives, will perhaps shed their blood and sacrifice their lives in vain resistance to the forces of the Crown. . . .

Of this performance, Henry Lucy wrote: 'Few spectacles have been more sublime than that of this young man of fashion devoting himself assiduously to the affairs of the state, sitting up long hours in the House of Commons, and doing violence to a naturally retiring disposition by bearding the Premier. . . .'[19]

Randolph began to put more sting into his speeches against the elderly Gladstone. He called Gladstone's Government, 'these

125

children of revolution, these robbers of churches, these friends of the lawless, these foes of the loyal. . . .'

'On one occasion,' Jennie noted,

I had been at the House hearing Randolph make a fiery attack on him [Gladstone], this he answered with equal heat and indignation. The hour was late, and Randolph and I had just time to rush home and dress to dine at Spencer House with Lord and Lady Spencer. The first person I met as I went in was Mr. Gladstone, who at once came up and said: 'I hope Lord Randolph is not *too* tired after his magnificent effort.'

Dinner at the Gladstones often featured readings from Shakespeare and Macaulay. The typical gentleman of the day was still the Gladstone type: devoted to duty, an excellent landlord, anonymous contributor to charities, regular attendant at church.

Jennie sometimes sat next to 'picturesque and dignified' Mrs Gladstone in the Ladies Gallery at the House of Commons. For special debates, the small gallery might be filled with fifty women crowded 'into the small dark cage to which the ungallant British legislators have relegated them'. The Ladies Gallery in the House— or 'parliamentary cage', as it was called—had three rows. Jennie described how the ladies in the front row had to sit

in a cramped attitude, their knees against the grills, their necks craned forward, and their ears painfully on the alert if they wish to hear anything. . . . Those in the second row, by the courtesy of the first, may get a peep of the gods below. The rest have to fall back on their imagination or retire to a small room in the rear, where they can whisper and have tea. . . .
Next to speaking in public oneself, there is nothing which produces such feelings of nervousness and apprehensions as to hear one's husband or son make a speech. There is no doubt, however, that the frequent recurrence of it minimizes the ordeal, particularly if the speakers are sure of themselves. In this respect I can claim to be specially favored, though Randolph, even after years of practice and experience, was always nervous before a speech until he actually stood up.
. . . [That] reminds me of a painful sight, . . . a young member of Parliament with more acres than brains, who sat for a family pocket borough. Shutting his eyes tight and clenching his hands, he began in a high falsetto voice . . . and for thirty minutes he recited, or rather gabbled, the speech he had learned by heart, while his wife, with her eyes riveted on him, and with tears pouring down her cheeks from nervousness, unconsciously, with trembling lips, repeated the words he was uttering.[20]

Jennie did not suffer from such fears. She had a tough, hard mind, which she used to full advantage. By the spring of 1881, she had helped Randolph acquire a supreme self-confidence he had never known before. He relied on her more for that than for anything else. It was this self-confidence that imparted to Randolph Churchill an aura of excitement and a political magnetism that propelled him suddenly into national prominence.

In a letter to her mother, Jennie wrote,

You will be glad to hear that R. has been covering himself with glory and I'm told he has made himself a wonderfully good position in the House. ... When this Government goes out (which they say will be soon) I fancy R. and his boon companion Sir Henry Drummond Wolff must be given something. ...

Disraeli was less reserved in his predictions. He told Sir Henry James, a Liberal Party friend of Randolph's, that the Conservatives would soon be swept into power again. 'When they come in,' Disraeli said, 'they will have to give him [Randolph] anything he chooses to ask for, and in a very short time they will have to take anything he chooses to give them.'[21]

Disraeli served as the early adviser for Randolph's group, and remarked to them, 'I wholly sympathize with you, because I never was respectable myself.' The former Prime Minister, though now a member of the House of Lords, was still titular head of his Party and the man to whom the Fourth Party went for final advice on key questions, the man who served as intermediary to forge a compromise with their own Conservative Party leadership in the House of Commons. He still sat in Parliament as he always had, impassive, his crossed legs covered by his long frock-coat, his body slumped, his arms folded across his chest, his chin drooping as if he were about to fall asleep. But he was acutely aware of everything.

Disraeli died at the end of April, 1881. Young Winston later recalled:

I followed his illness from day to day with great anxiety, because everyone said what a loss he would be to his country and how no one else could stop Mr. Gladstone from working his wicked will upon us all. I was sure Lord Beaconsfield was going to die, and at last the day came when all the people I saw went about with very sad faces because, as they said, a great and splendid Statesman, who loved our country and defied the Russians, had died of a broken heart because of the ingratitude with which he had been treated by the Radicals. ...[22]

With Disraeli's death, Lord Randolph became even less temperate. His attacks on Gladstone became more bitter, more personal, often vitriolic. One friend said to him: 'You will kill Gladstone one of these days.'

'Oh no!' answered Randolph, 'he will long survive me. I often tell my wife what a beautiful letter he will write to her, proposing my burial in Westminster Abbey.'[23]

In the meantime, there was happy news from Jennie's sister Clara, who had become engaged to be married. Moreton Frewen came from an old Sussex family and was known as one of the best gentleman riders in England. A tall, assured sportsman, he had also spent a year driving cattle in Colorado, had explored the buffalo trails of Texas, and had known every one there from Buffalo Bill to Sitting Bull. 'A bad man with brown eyes need not be feared,' Frewen once wrote, 'but the fellow with grey eyes or grey-blue whose eyes grew darker as they looked down a gun—that was the sort of man to reckon with.' Moreton described himself as 'lean and hard and tough as pinwire'. He had a natural gift of the gab, all of it highly opinionated, and moved easily into the Leonard Jerome circle in New York. 'My predestined father-in-law, Leonard Jerome, one of the kindliest of men, was the centre for a brilliant côterie to which I had entrée.' Of his future mother-in-law, Moreton had less kindly comment. He called her 'Sitting Bull', because 'she looked like a hatchet-faced squaw, and she never got up during my courting visits.'[24]

To his future sister-in-law Jennie, whom he carefully called 'Lady Randolph', Moreton wrote,

For fear you may think me ungracious enough to bear malice, let me write you a few lines to say how right and reasonable you were to oppose Clara's selection. I should have thought you a careless sister indeed had you done otherwise. Still, I am not inclined to admit that she is doing a foolish thing. . . .[25]

Jennie did not consider Frewen good enough for her sister, and she made her opinion known. Clara was four years older than she, but Jennie never had any compunction about expressing her views on anything to anyone. She felt that Frewen offered neither the security nor the stability that her sister needed. Earlier that year, Moreton had been one of the more active suitors of Lily Langtry, who had caught the public imagination throughout England after her 1881 début in *She Stoops To Conquer*. Langtry had a classic profile, golden hair, and a startling figure, and crowds followed her wherever she went. (Lord Houghton had introduced Jennie to Lily Langtry, saying, 'I am proud to introduce the two most beautiful women in Europe to one another.') Women at all levels of society were soon wearing their hair in Langtry knots, buying Langtry shoes and Langtry hats. 'The Jersey Lily' was seen riding in the park long after dark with the Prince of Wales. King Leopold II of Belgium came to call for her at the unusual hour of nine in the morning, and Crown Prince Rudolph of Austria deluged her with flowers. Frewen gave Lily a beautiful horse named Redskin, but bowed out of the competition with royalty. He later wrote, 'But I had the joy of seeing her ride my horse when out exercising with H.R.H. Anyway, lilies can be dreadfully boring when not planted in bed!'[26]

His association with Langtry was only one factor in Jennie's opposition to Frewen; but Jennie was in London and Clara and he were together in New York. The marriage plans were set.

Frewen and Clara were married in New York's Grace Church in 1881. The young couple spent their honeymoon in Moreton's pine-log house on a beautiful knoll overlooking the Powder River in Wyoming. They lived entirely on fresh meat and fish, a far cry from the elegant sustenance on which Clara had been bred. But she still kept her French maid. Moreton invited Jennie to come and visit their Big Horn home:

I can promise your husband A-1 shooting and a glimpse of the nicest life in the world. What an incongruous century this is: we've got a telephone connecting this house with our store and post office twenty-five miles below on the river, and last week there were a lot of Redskins—more naked than ashamed—talking to one another through it. I never saw such ludicrous astonishment. . . .

Visiting the Churchills later in London, Moreton wrote to his wife that he admired the 'quiet force' of Randolph, '. . . but Jennie is an angel as she has whooping cough and the children too and R. is ill and rather snappish but she takes it all so well.' In another note, contrasting Jennie and Leonie, Frewen commented, 'Jennie has not got Leo's depth of character.'

Jennie's character was soon to be strengthened with the tests of time and tragedy. Randolph's syphilis had been in remission, but now suddenly worsened. It had reached the stage of recurrent headaches and fevers, lowering his threshold of irritability. His friends saw it as a kind of subterranean hysteria, and Jennie had the added job of soothing her husband and calming the ruffled feelings of puzzled friends.

'It was a most bewildering enterprise to follow the course of his friendships,' wrote Lady Jeune.

Sometimes he was inseparable from his friends; at other times he would hardly speak to them, and although this added greatly to the excitement of a visit he might happen to pay, it had its drawbacks in the fact that you were never certain for twenty-four hours when the change from one extreme to the other might take place.[27]

One by one, Randolph cut himself off from some of his closest associates, even breaking bitterly with Gorst on the Irish issue. It reached a point where Lord Hartington felt impelled to denounce Randolph publicly as 'vile, contumacious and lying'. Instead of responding with his customary scorn, Randolph dispatched an emissary to Hartington to demand a retraction or satisfaction in a duel. His emissary was even stranger than his demand—Captain O'Shea, an Irish Member of the House of Commons, and the husband of Parnell's mistress. Hartington apologized for his language, and the incident was closed. Friends, however, regarded Randolph's behaviour as still another sign that he was poised at the edge of a breakdown.

As his illness worsened, Randolph insisted on spending more time at Blenheim—back with his horses and his dogs, back with the scenes of his boyhood. Now that the Duchess felt renewed control over her son, she made life increasingly bitter for Jennie. In a letter from the Palace that winter, Jennie confided to her mother:

I quite forget what it is like to be with people who love me. I do so long sometimes to have someone to whom I could go and talk. Of course, Randolph is awfully good to me and always takes my part in everything, but how can I always be abusing his mother to him, when she is devoted to him and would do anything for him—The fact is I *loathe* living here. It's not on account of its dullness, *that* I don't mind, but it is gall and wormwood to me to accept anything or to be living on anyone I hate. It is no use disguising it, the Duchess hates me simply for what I am— perhaps a little prettier and more attractive than her daughters. Everything I do or say or wear is found fault with. We are always studiously polite to each other, but it is rather like a volcano, ready to burst out at any moment...[28]

Jennie rented a small cottage near Wimbledon in the spring of 1882, and she and Randolph stayed there for several months, out of

Leonard Jerome

Clara Jerome

The Jerome house in Henry Street, Brooklyn

The Jerome house in Madison Square

Jennie (*left*) and her sisters Clara and Leonie.
A fourth sister, Camille, died at the age of six

Jennie with her mother

Lord Randolph Churchill at about the
time of his marriage to Jennie in 1874

Jennie at about the time of her
marriage

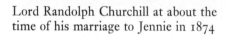

The Seventh Duke of Marlborough     The Duchess of Marlborough

Blenheim Palace

The room at Blenheim Palace in which Winston Churchill
was born, 30 November 1874

The announcement of Winston Churchill's birth in *The Times*

# Nº. 28,176.

## BIRTHS.

On the 30th Nov., at Blenheim Palace, the Lady RANDOLPH
CHURCHILL, prematurely, of a son.

On the 7th Oct., at Rangoon, the wife of HALKETT F. JACKSON, Esq.,
Lieut. and Adjutant 67th Regt., of a daughter.

On the 20th Oct., at Bombay, the wife of Capt. G. W. OLDHAM,
R.E., of a son.

On the 27th Oct., at Ranchi, Chota Nagpore, the wife of Capt.
NINIAN LOWIS, B.S.C., Assistant Commissioner, of a daughter.

On the 6th Nov., 1874, at Belgaum, India, the wife of J. CHARLES
M. PIGOTT, Esq., Lieut. 66th Regt., of a daughter.

On the 20th Nov., at Marlborough-terrace, Roath, Cardiff, the wife
of THOMAS J. ALLEN, of a daughter.

On the 21st Nov., the wife of POYNTZ WRIGHT, M.R.C.S.E., of a
daughter.

On the 22d Nov., at South-hill-park, Hampstead, the wife of ALBERT
STRAUBE, of a son.

On the 26th Nov., at Wolfang, Queensland, Australia, the wife of
HENRY DE SATGÉ, Esq., of a son.

Jennie with Winston, possibly the earliest photograph of the future statesman

Winston Churchill at the age of six

Possibly Winston Churchill's first letter to his mother

My dear mama
I am so glad
you are coming
to see us I had
such a nice
bathe in the
sea to day.
love to papa
your loving
winston

'The Fourth Party'. Lord Randolph Churchill, Arthur Balfour,
Sir Henry Wolff, John Gorst

Jennie with her two sons, Jack and Winston

Jennie (*standing*) with Winston (*at her side*) and Jack (*standing in front of her*). Clara Frewen (*seated left*) holding Oswald Frewen, Mrs Leonard Jerome holding Claire Frewen, Hugh Frewen, and Leonie Leslie (*seated right*) holding Norman Leslie. Shane Leslie is seated in front

The Marquis de Breteuil                    King Milan of Serbia

Lady Randolph Churchill

Lord Randolph Churchill

Lord Randolph Churchill in 1893, some two years before his death

Count Charles Andreas Kinsky

Jennie

public sight. It was a lovely house with a long, green lawn and a rose garden. This peaceful period drew them closer together again, and Randolph's disease again went into remission.

Early that summer, when he had recovered enough, Jennie took Randolph to New York to stay with her family. Her letters had revealed her need to be close to them, a need to return to her roots. In a letter to a friend, Leonard Jerome wrote of his son-in-law: 'frail but fiery . . . I think Jennie is wonderful for him, he draws on her strength. I love having them here. I believe in R.'[29]

These were the Elegant Eighties in the United States, a time of national tranquillity between wars. One era had ended five years before with the death of Sioux Chief Crazy Horse, the last of the warring Indians, and another with the withdrawal of the final contingent of Federal occupation troops from the South. James A. Garfield had been shot and killed in 1881, and the new President was Chester A. Arthur. If the Presidents then were nondescript, perhaps it was because the times demanded no great leaders.

The Churchills stayed in the United States for two months, long enough to see Edison's electric lights transform the streets of Manhattan. New York was then a city of small brownstone or red brick houses, of pot-bellied stoves and horse-cars, of organ-grinders and strolling bands and the ubiquitous wooden Indian. Men wore scratchy paper collars and preachers denounced baseball as a game for oafs and 'ill-mannered persons'. Harlem was a quiet suburb and the Bronx was considered countryside; a skyscraper was a building twelve stories high. But most people worked a twelve-hour day, six days a week, for an average of ten dollars, and many worked longer for less. Even a short illness spelled family disaster, and a father's death often meant orphanages for the children. Immigrants jammed the slums, each national group in its own ghetto, with some 500,000 of New York's two million population unable to speak English. Some sections of the city had so much violence and crime, so many gang wars that police seldom ventured into them unless they went in strength. A few teen-age street gangs had a thousand members, armed with guns, knives, and blackjacks. Murder on the Bowery was common and expected, but any thug found in the so-called respectable part of town could expect a thorough beating in the backroom of the nearby police station.[30]

None of these things penetrated the social conversation within the charmed circles of Astor or Vanderbilt. Novelist Edith Wharton said that talk among their members 'was never intellectual and seldom brilliant, but it was always easy and sometimes witty'. Conversation concentrated on 'food, wines, horses, yachts, cotillions, marriages, villas at Newport. . . .'[31]

The search for sensation became outlandish: a dinner eaten on horseback, with the favoured horse fed flowers and champagne; a banquet given in honour of a small black and tan dog who wore a diamond collar worth $15,000; fine black pearls placed inside oysters and served at a dinner party; monkeys alternating with seated guests at a dining-room table; a complete orchestra hired to serenade a newborn child.

But the most widely-discussed town topic was a social war between Mrs William Backhouse Astor and Mrs William Kissam Vanderbilt. Mrs Astor, 'a tall, formidable woman of commanding dignity', had long been the sole arbiter of New York society. It was she who had given the famous ball to which only four hundred guests were invited because there was room for no more in her ballroom. This limitation had prompted Ward McAllister's remark that there were only about four hundred people in fashionable New York Society. 'If you go outside that number,' McAllister had informed reporters, 'you strike people who are either not at ease in a ballroom or else make other people not at ease.' As far as Mrs Astor was concerned, the number did not include Mrs William Kissam Vanderbilt.

As pugnacious as she was plump, Mrs Vanderbilt made her supreme challenge. She had built, at a cost of three million dollars, a replica of a French chateau, and then announced she would inaugurate her new palace with a ball. In reporting on guests' preparations for the ball, *The New York Times* wrote that they had 'disturbed the sleep and occupied the waking hours of social butterflies, both male and female, for over six weeks'. Dress designer Lanouette estimated that the 150 gowns he had designed had cost more than $30,000 and had kept 140 dressmakers working day and night for five weeks. Naturally expecting to be invited, Mrs Astor's daughter Caroline organized a special dance for the ball. However, Mrs Vanderbilt gently let it be known that she could hardly invite the young Miss Astor since Mrs Astor had never called on her. Faced with her daughter's disappointment, Mrs Astor made the humiliating drive in her carriage up Fifth Avenue to call on Mrs William Kissam Vanderbilt, and the war was won.

The Churchills did not attend the Vanderbilt ball because Randolph was ready to return to England, as was Jennie. The social round would always be a part of her life, but its allure now seemed to pall before the exhilaration of politics. The Astor–Vanderbilt feud did not compare with the fury of the Fourth Party. It was good rediscovering the openness and love of her family, and she enjoyed the free vitality of the United States; perhaps her heart was still in America, but her spirit and ambitions were in England.

Just before Jennie and Randolph departed, the Irish troubles were again in the headlines. 'I remember a reporter calling at my father's house in Madison Square and telling me the news. We were greatly shocked and could hardly believe it until it was confirmed the next day. . . . Mr Burke . . . and his sister . . . we knew quite well.' Thomas Burke, the Permanent Under Secretary and an old friend of the Churchills, and Lord Frederick Cavendish, a close friend of Gladstone, had both been assassinated in Phoenix Park by a group called the Irish Invincibles.

When Jennie was in Dublin the following season for the Horse Show, she was invited by an official of the Kilmainham Gaol to meet the convicted assassins.

I confess that I did not feel any great desire for this entertainment, but being told that it was nearly impossible to get permission to see them, and that without exception no one was allowed in the prison, I began to feel more interested.

She was taken to a small room in the jail and stood behind the man who interviewed each murderer. As he was being led back, the youngest of them turned suddenly to Jennie and asked her to help his wife if he 'had to go'. 'This depressed me dreadfully,' Jennie noted afterward,

nor were my spirits raised by being taken round the prison by the Governor. . . . The tier upon tier of tiny cells, each containing a miserable-looking man, the food brought in baskets which I saw prodded through and through with swords for fear that something might be smuggled in them, were a more than unpleasant sight.[32]

The Inspector-General, however, arrived unexpectedly at the jail and Jennie was hidden in a bleak cell to avoid explanations. It was a cell without windows, and in the utter blackness Jennie was certain she saw 'the little beady eyes' of rats. 'The door opened just in time to save me from screaming.' But later she could not help laughing when she thought of the expression that would have appeared on the face of the Inspector-General if he had happened to visit her dungeon, especially as he had previously met her on a more social occasion. It would have made a fine dinner party anecdote, but Jennie revealed the story to no one for more than three years after the assassins were executed, for fear of compromising the Governor of the jail.

# 9

When Jennie came back to England, she and Randolph moved to a less fashionable though larger house at 2 Connaught Place early in 1883. Friends soon called the Connaught home 'House Tyburnia', because it sat in the square terrace of the new Tyburn area, the residential quarter of the new society. The more fashionable, more proper society was beyond them, over the invisible line that enclosed some 350 homes in Mayfair and Belgravia. The novelist Thackeray described Mayfair–Belgravia as 'that pale and polite district where all the inhabitants look prim and correct, and the mansions are painted a faint white-brown.'

The Connaught house faced onto Hyde Park and the site of Tyburn Tree. It was at Tyburn in 1724 that an estimated 200,000 people had watched the hanging of Jack Sheppard, one of the most celebrated of all English criminals. At the same place, Catherine Hayes, convicted of murdering her husband, was burned at the stake by a mob who refused to wait for a hangman. Here, too, the corpse of Oliver Cromwell, having been torn from its tomb at Westminster Abbey, was hung by a mob on the anniversary of the death of King Charles I. Shortly after the Churchills moved into their new house, a mass grave was uncovered in the cellar. Because of all this notoriety, the house was generally thought to be haunted.

The Connaught Place house was even more of a curiosity in being one of the first homes in England to be lit by electric lights. Since Randolph was a traditionalist in the home, the idea of having the electricity undoubtedly came from Jennie. 'The light was such an innovation that much curiosity and interest were evinced to see it, and people used to ask for permission to come to the house,' Jennie said. 'I remember the fiasco of a dinner party we gave to show it off, when the light went out in the middle of the feast, just as we were expatiating on its beauties, our guests having to remain in utter darkness until the lamps and candles, which had been relegated to the lower regions, were unearthed.'[1]

That was characteristic of Jennie, always restlessly seeking out the different and the new. Her home was striking evidence of her spirit. The traditional Victorian home, like the Victorian female body, was, as one critic observed, well covered. Window curtains three deep and elaborately fringed; and dark, dull, expensive wallpaper matching the dark, dull brown paint on most woodwork. Furniture was usually mahogany, massive and solid. Living rooms were cluttered with enormous clocks, huge vases, stuffed birds and wax flowers under glass domes.[2] Jennie, however, startled her friends—and set a style—by using white paint and simple panelling, delicate pieces of French and Italian furniture, art from China and Japan, as well as electric light.[3]

Randolph was politically on the rise again, but the rise and fall of his emotions were more and more marked. At times he seemed drained and dispirited. 'One evening I came home from the House of Commons very anxious and rather discouraged,' he wrote,

because ... among people whom I ought to look upon as my political friends, I had met nothing but gloomy looks; and I felt very much inclined to retire from the game, thinking I was doing more harm than good, and rather—to use a slang expression—disposed to cut the whole concern.

Upon recovering his self-confidence, he frequently acted recklessly, as when he referred to a parliamentary opponent as 'a damned fool'—unheard-of language in the House of Commons. The press called him 'Cheeky Randy' and 'Little Lord Random',[4] and mocked the way he perpetually twisted his walrus moustache. His popularity, however, was enormous. At outdoor rallies, he tailored his style of speech to his audience, often combining wit and abuse, epigram and harangue, while flailing his arms for emphasis.

His effectiveness in Parliament, too, was vastly broadened.

Lord Randolph dominated the House of Commons in all its moods. When it was gay, he stirred it into laughter; when it was flippant, no one could exceed him in droll irreverence; when it was united and determined, he spoke with seriousness and moderation; when it was angry, he fanned the flames until they spread into an ugly glow; when it craved a leader who would 'show them game', Lord Randolph Churchill stood in the van.[5]

When his popularity led to over-confidence, Jennie acted as a balance wheel. She wrote her mother, 'I am only so afraid of R.

getting spoilt . . . he would lose half his talent if he did. I keep reminding him of it.'

Jennie went with him on speaking tours around the country in the early 1880's, but was always exasperated when required to sit for hours with other politicians' wives who wanted to talk trivia when she wanted to talk politics. It was a bit more lively at Aston Park outside Birmingham, where a rioting group of Liberals threw potatoes, chairs, and stones at them.

Jennie was saved from the crush of another crowd by a Colonel Frederick Gustavus Burnaby, six-foot-four with a 47-inch chest. She described him as also having laughing eyes and a heavy dark moustache. 'He was a gentle-voiced amiable man, notwithstanding an enormous frame and gigantic strength.' Then she added cryptically, 'I had occasion to see a good deal of Colonel Burnaby.'[6]

Randolph's renewed success in politics animated their social life. 'We were bombarded with invitations of every kind,' Jennie wrote. 'The fashionable world, which had held aloof, now began to smile upon us once more.'

This fashionable world that the young Churchills re-entered had long been an inbred circle of several hundred people. One could neither push in nor buy in nor break in—one could only be born into it. By the 1880's certain specially favoured individuals—favoured by royalty or marriage or celebrity or wealth—were gradually admitted, on a conditional basis. If the drastic change could be attributed to one motive, it was the desire for novelty. 'In the old days we rather dreaded the social influence of a people we did not know,' Lady Dorothy Nevill, London's most celebrated hostess, commented, 'but many old families, both in mind and pocket, have been completely revivified by prudent marriages with American brides.' She described most of the American female influx as bright and vivacious, and added, 'it is by the American girl that we have been conquered.' Lady Nevill was an elderly but vital Victorian lady, well known for her quaint caps and quick wit. She loudly proclaimed her disapproval of 'the lip salve and muck' that some women then put on their faces, and she believed all women should wear veils and gloves so that their skin would not look 'like a bit of mahogany veneer. . . . I should think,' she added, 'that the young men would as soon think of kissing a kipper.'[7]

Lady Nevill was very fond of the young Churchills, who had been her neighbours in Charles Street. At her frequent parties she gathered together some of the most vibrant people in London, and Jennie and Randolph were often among them. She was also among the guests at a dinner party given by the Churchills on March 18, 1883 in honour of the Prince and Princess of Wales. The occasion marked the final reconciliation between the Prince and Randolph. Others attending included Mr Gladstone and his wife and a small group of similar distinction. 'The conversation proved so animated that there was no possibility for awkward thoughts, or looks, or even silences to occur.'

There was small question in Lady Nevill's salon that the gentle persuasion of Jennie had much to do with the Prince's decision to be reconciled with Lord Randolph. Shortly before his death, Disraeli had predicted that reconciliation would come about when Randolph was a rising star. 'The Prince is always taken by success,' he said. It was also the wish of Queen Victoria, who was concerned about any hostility between the royal family and a man who might soon be a Minister of the Crown. Four days before the dinner party for the Prince and Princess, Jennie was invited to the Queen's drawing room.

The Prince of Wales was pleased with his renewed friendship and let it be known: 'R. Churchill's manner was *just* what it ought to have been.' But he was even more pleased that his relationship with Jennie could be revitalized, and more openly. Prince Edward was soon giving Jennie presents of expensive jewelry.

Jennie was the Prince's frequent guest at the great, rambling, country home at Sandringham in Norfolk, even though Randolph did not always accompany her. 'One felt at home at once,' she wrote.

Indeed, the life was the same as at any pleasant country house. Breakfast, which began at nine o'clock, was served at small, round tables in a dining-room decorated with Spanish tapestries given by the late King of Spain. The men were in shooting get-up, and the ladies in any dress they chose to affect—short skirts and thick boots or elaborate day-gowns. No one cared or noticed. None of the Royalties appeared before midday, although the Prince of Wales joined the shooters, who made an early start after breakfast.

While the men were shooting, the women moved into the large hall to the writing tables, books, magazines, piano. Most often, too, they separated into cliques, usually formed on the first day and kept firm until the final day.

Country-house parties customarily lasted four nights, the guests arriving Tuesday and leaving Saturday. The discreet hostess usually took into account unacknowledged liaisons in assigning bedrooms, each of which had a name in a brass frame outside the door so that after-hours visitors would make no embarrassing mistakes.

The extravagances involved in country-house entertaining were so considerable that some friends of royalty could not afford it. In certain houses of unlimited wealth, it had become customary to have a royal suite refurnished for each visit and to replace the regular chef with a specialist. 'I could tell stories of men and women who had to economize for a whole year, or alternatively get in debt so that they might entertain royalty for one weekend,' wrote Lady Warwick in her memoirs. 'Added to the cost of entertaining guests was the cost of caring for accompanying servants, which might mean as many as four hundred more mouths to feed.'

A typical lunch for six might include cold pheasant, a couple of partridges, two hot roast fowls, and hot beefsteaks. Dinner always featured a choice of at least two soups, whole salmons and turbots, vast saddles of mutton and sirloins of beef, roast turkeys, several kinds of game such as woodcocks, plovers, and snipe, a large array of vegetables, perhaps some devilled herring and cream cheese, an assortment of pastries, the ever-present, enormous Stilton and Cheshire cheeses, a profusion of wines followed by nuts and preserved fruits, and then some port or madeira. Luncheon at Sandringham was usually served in a big marquee and was always animated.

Five o'clock was a feature at Sandringham. The simplicity of the day attire was discarded in favor of elaborate tea gowns. . . . Sometimes I played duets with the Princess, who was particularly fond of Brahms' Hungarian Dances, which were just then in vogue. Or it might be that we would go to Princess Victoria's sitting-room, where there were two pianos, and struggle with a Concerto of Schumann. The pace set was terrific, and I was rather glad there was no audience. . . .

Although no uniforms were worn at dinner, this was a ceremonious affair, with everyone in full dress and decorations.

*Queen's Magazine*, on the rules of etiquette at such dinners, noted, 'The guests are sent into dinner on their first evening according to their rank (except for their Royal Highnesses).' On the second night, however, it became the fashion for gentlemen to draw lots to determine which of the ladies they would escort in to dinner. 'Rather unpunctual in those days, I was always on the verge of being late,' Jennie remarked.

... When everyone was assembled, Their Royal Highnesses would be announced. . . . The dinner, which never lasted more than an hour, was excellent and admirably ordered, which is not always the case in royal households where indiscriminate profusion is often paramount. Conversation was fairly animated; there was none of that stuffiness which pervaded Windsor and made one fear the sound of one's own voice.
... The evenings were not prolonged. . . . The Prince would have his rubber of whist, while the rest of the company sat about and talked until the Princess made a move to go to bed, when the ladies would troop off together, stopping to laugh and chatter in the passages. . . .

The men, meanwhile, moved into the smoking room for a couple of hours before retirement. Prince Edward preferred company who played a good game of bridge or baccarat, knew how to tell good jokes, liked light music rather than classical. Lady Warwick, who knew the Prince intimately, summed up his taste when she said, 'As a class, we did not like brains.' Of the exceptions, Lady Warwick herself was one and Lady Randolph Churchill another.

Despite her deafness, Princess Alexandra was an astute woman who knew how to hide her intelligence, just as she knew how to hide the scar of a burn on her throat with a broad dog-collar of diamonds that soon created a fashion called 'La Belle Alexandrine'. Jennie also was said to have a distinguishing mark, a tattooed snake on her wrist, usually hidden by her bracelets. Tattooes were a fad at the time — the Prince of Wales had one, as did Czar Nicholas II.[8]

Princess Alexandra's resentment against the many women involved with her husband somehow never extended to Jennie, who always remained her good friend. Sometimes Jennie would be invited into the Princess's room.

On the perch in the center of the room was an old and somewhat ferocious white parrot, which I remember made disconcerting pecks if you happened to be within his radius.
At other times the Princess might surprise you by coming to your room, ostensibly 'to see if you had everything you wanted', but in reality to give a few words of advice, or to offer her sympathy if she thought you needed any.

In the midst of this calm sea came a rough shock for Randolph.

His father died suddenly in early July 1883. Randolph had dined with him just the night before. Marlborough had been the steadying influence that Randolph had relied upon, a source of solid, conservative opinion that leavened his own. This contrasted with Jennie's influence, which served as both a spur and a brake, depending upon his need and his temper.

Randolph and Jennie went to Blenheim for a time, where Randolph brooded over his father's death, and spent hours rereading the early letters his father had written him. The *Dictionary of National Biography* termed the Duke of Marlborough 'a sensible, honourable and industrious public man'. Jennie included this description of him in her own memoirs:

He had always been most kind and charming to me. If he seemed rather cold and reserved, he really had an affectionate nature. Although his children were somewhat in awe of him, having been brought up in that old fashioned way which precludes any real intimacy, they were devoted to him.

The formality of Randolph's relationship with his father was exceeded only by Randolph's relationship with his own sons. Years later, Winston wrote,

I would far rather have been apprenticed as a bricklayer's mate, or run errands as a messenger boy, or helped my father to dress the front windows of a grocer's shop. It would have been real; it would have been natural; it would have taught me more; and I should have got to know my father, which would have been a joy to me.[9]

Aside from generalized animosity toward his son, Randolph had little faith in Winston's potential. He felt that his son was a boy of small matter and less mind. Winston's school reports were mixed. He was good in English and history but little else. His teachers complained that he did not work hard enough, was often late to class, had little ambition. As for his conduct, it ranged from 'troublesome' to '*very* naughty'. In a letter to her husband, Jennie had written, 'As to Winston's improvement, I am sorry to say I see none.' She had made a similarly critical comment about Winston to Leonard Jerome, who promptly answered, 'Let him be. Boys get good at what they find they shine at.'

'My teachers saw me at once backward and precocious, reading books beyond my years and yet at the bottom of the Form,' Winston Churchill reflected. 'They were offended. They had large resources of compulsion at their disposal, but I was stubborn. Where my reason, imagination or interest were not engaged, I would not or I could not learn.'

School was loathsome. It seethed with brutality, yet somehow he could not or would not transmit to his parents the details of this brutality. How his father would have snorted at him had he complained! The practices of fagging and flogging were typical of the entire British public school system. 'I counted the days and the hours to the end of every term when I should return from this hateful servitude, and range my soldiers in line of battle on the nursery floor.'

He was nine years old then, and his private army of 1,500 toy soldiers represented a kind of final retreat, a make-believe world where he could convert his loneliness into dramatic action which he alone controlled. His soldiers were all of the same size, and he had arranged them as a British infantry division with a cavalry brigade.

He organized wars, manœuvred the soldiers into battle, committed heavy casualties with peas and pebbles, stormed forts, charged his cavalry, destroyed bridges, surrounded the enemy with real water obstacles.

His visiting cousins would watch with wonder, but Winston never allowed them to touch anything. However, when a plaything broke, he would let one of the younger children keep it. Among the things the other children thus collected was a mastless ship, a model theatre whose figures could be manipulated from the wings, and some tattered copies of boys' adventure magazines.

Toddling along with the children was three-year-old brother Jack Churchill. The two brothers would always be separated more by their difference of personality than by their difference in age. Nonetheless, Jack's admiration for his older, more adventurous, more successful brother remained so unbounded and uncritical that their family feeling was strong and affectionate.

Winston vented some of his frustration in make-believe battles, but more was manifested in his public behaviour. Some of his cousins remembered him as 'full of fun and quite unself-conscious'. Others, though, saw him as 'a little upstart' who had even taught Jack how to use a pea-shooter. His dancing teacher, Miss Vera Moore, called him 'the naughtiest small boy in the world'. The future Lady Barlow, then a little girl, remembered a party that year during which the footman came in to tell Winston, 'Your nurse has called for you, sir.' Winston told the footman, 'Tell her to wait.' The little girl asked with awe, 'Can you make your nurse wait?' And Winston answered, 'Everything and everybody waits for me.'

That year was one of rebellion, of antagonism toward a world that had given him little. At another children's party, Winston arrived dressed in a sailor-suit, protesting aloud. One of the young women wanted to know, soothingly, what was wrong. 'My clothes,' he said. 'I told them they were wrong, and of course they are!'

If Winston was in danger of being a prig, he was in greater danger of being a suppressed, embittered little boy, full of frustrations, and hungry for affection. He idolized his mother. She was still his own fairy princess, even more perfect in his imagination because he saw her so seldom. He considered every visit a privilege, every excursion a special pleasure. Jennie gave him little of herself then. In 1883, she was twenty-nine years old, but she wrote, 'I shall not acknowledge it to the world, twenty-six is quite enough!' Women considered thirty the deadly age, especially those who concerned themselves more with men than with children, more with love than with schools, more with the enticements of life than with its chores.

Jennie crowded her life that year with politics, the Prince of Wales, her husband's illness, her house, the pulsing whirl of an intense social life, and a new lover. During the summer of 1883, Count Charles Kinsky rode his own chestnut mare, Zoedone, in the Grand National and became the first amateur ever to win that race— despite 14–1 odds. They toasted him in all the racing clubs, named drinks after him, made him the social hero of the hour.[10]

The handsome, dashing Charles Rudolf Ferdinand Andreas Kinsky was twenty-five—four years younger than Jennie—had served as honorary attaché at the Austro–Hungarian Embassy in London since 1881, and had been made Imperial Chamberlain early in 1883. His father was Ferdinand, seventh Prince Kinsky, whom Jennie probably met when he toured Ireland with the Empress of Austria in 1879. Count Kinsky's mother was a Liechtenstein Princess, and the whole family was rooted deep in the heritage of European history.[11]

The most fashionable party place in London then was the New Club at Covent Garden, and Count Kinsky was host at a small dance attended by the Prince of Wales, the Duke of Braganza (who later became King of Portugal), the King of Greece, and Archduke Rudolph of Austria. Kinsky invited Jennie; there is no record of her husband being there. Jennie described the evening as 'most animated . . . we danced till the early hours of the morning, to the music of Tziganes, then a new importation'.

She wrote nothing more about that evening, but Count Kinsky had come into her life to stay. He was a fiery young man, highly romantic and impulsive. Emotionally, he and Jennie were a matched pair.

Nonetheless, Jennie was deeply conscious of her position and her children. She often had guilt feelings about Winston. His health was still 'very delicate', and his complaints about St. George's School were now frequent, so she found him a smaller, more informal school in Brighton, close to where the family doctor, Robson Roose, lived. The Brighton school was run by two kind ladies who promoted an atmosphere of permissiveness. Jennie also insisted to Randolph that they take Winston with them on their vacation that summer to the Austrian Alps.

They all went to Gastein, a well-known 'watering place' where the accent was on the simple life. There was little to do besides climbing mountains and taking mineral baths, but there were some interesting people. 'In our walks we frequently met Bismarck with his big boar-hound, two detectives following him closely,' wrote Jennie. 'One day as he was walking rather slowly, we tried to pass him, whereupon, much to my annoyance, the detectives rushed forward in a most threatening manner. I had no idea we looked like anarchists.'

One afternoon the Churchills were invited to tea with Emperor William I.

The Emperor was a fine-looking man, notwithstanding his age, and he had that old-world manner which is as attractive as it is rare. He was full of gaiety, and chaffed some of the young people present. It was a mystery to me how he survived what he ate and drank, although he was doing a cure. He began with poached eggs, and went on to potted meats and various strange German dishes, added many cups of strong tea, and ended with strawberries, ices, and sweet, tepid champagne. We talked *banalities*; it was not very exciting.

In a letter to his friend Wolff, Randolph also described the meeting:

The Emperor I must admit was very guarded in his conversation, which was confined to asking me how long I had been here, and whether I had come for my health. I imitated his reserve. My wife, however, sat by him at tea, and had much conversation which, I have ascertained, was confined to the most frivolous topics. I have reason to believe, though it is humiliating to confess it, that the fame of the Fourth Party has not yet reached the ears of this despot. I must say he is a very fine old fellow and the Germans seem to love him. There are several other Prussians and Austrians present; but I was rather bored on the whole and so was my wife. They wanted us to go the next night, when they had arranged some tableaux for the old boy, but I sent an excuse on the ground that I was in deep mourning. We did not come here to kowtow to monarchs.

Toward the end of their stay, Blandford, now the eighth Duke of Marlborough, joined them for some mountain climbing. Their father's death had brought the brothers close together again.

The new Duke had finally been divorced by his wife. Even though Lady Aylesford had given birth to his child in Paris, he had decided not to marry her.[12] Now he insisted that Randolph and Jennie join him at Blenheim for the rest of the year with Jennie acting as Blenheim's hostess. Jennie hesitated. 'My American efficiency will out,' she said, 'and they will call me bossy.' But they decided to go. Because of Randolph's recurring depressions, the attraction of Blenheim was strong. And Jennie was probably intrigued with the idea of being mistress of a palace.

As Blenheim's hostess, Jennie recalled she had had trouble remembering the names of the great governing families of Britain, their lineages and titles. It was equally difficult to keep straight the detailed protocol of servant duties. For example, if a fire needed to be lit, she *never* rang for the butler. If she did, he would inform her, coolly but politely, 'I shall send for the footman.'

One of their frequent guests was George Nathaniel Curzon, a Fellow at Oxford who later became Viceroy of India. Over six feet tall and proportionately broad, Curzon had a head too small for his large body, and a face incongruous to it—chubby and exceptionally young-looking. He could be cordial; but more often he affected the grand manner, his demeanour cold, hard, completely lacking the 'common touch'. His conversation, often bordering on the brilliant, flashed with wit and laughter and fine phrases. Margot Asquith considered him 'a remarkably intelligent person in an exceptional generation', but others regarded him as an intellectual fop, often obnoxious in his icy arrogance and limitless vanity. He was the subject of a widely circulated doggerel of which one version ran:

> I am a most superior person,
> My name is George Nathaniel Curzon.
> My face is pink, my hair is sleek,
> I dine at Blenheim once a week.

Curzon added his name to the long list of men who fell in love with Jennie. She appreciated his intelligence and natural eloquence, but she had too many prior claims on her affections to consider Curzon.[13]

The Fourth Party was in a kind of limbo in 1883, and Sir Henry Drummond Wolff proposed an idea. The primrose had been Disraeli's favourite flower, and Wolff was given one to wear on the anniversary of Disraeli's death. In Parliament that day, he was struck by the number of Members also wearing the primrose.

Why not start a Primrose League? 'Let's go off and do it at once,' Randolph answered.

The League became fully operational that winter and was a complicated affair with distinctive titles and badges and decorations. Men were Knights, women officers were Dames, and clubs were called Habitations. Randolph had his mother made president of the Ladies Grand Council and Jennie made a Dame.[1] 'As a Dame I was determined to do all I could to further its aims,' Jennie said. 'The wearing of the badge exposed me to much chaff, not to say ridicule, but we persisted.'

The Primrose League was a brash innovation, a kind of political-social organization through which Conservatives could gather, no matter what their class, to discuss issues, listen to their leaders, and participate in election work. Churchill's critics at first regarded the League as 'another of Randy's pranks', but it soon had almost two million members.

The most startling result of the Primrose League was that it put women into politics. British women in the 1880's were already reading 'Modern Love', going to the new colleges, some even practising as doctors.[2] They were not, however, emancipated enough for the House of Commons to pass an amendment to the Reform Bill of 1884 to the effect that 'words importing to the masculine gender' should be interpreted as embracing the fair sex. Englishwomen were still generally considered the 'fags and fans' of their pretentious men, waiting only for their husbands' command. Englishmen were supposed to show a similar reaction to their women as to their horses, using the same word to describe both. The word was 'fine'.[3]

It is not difficult to imagine that the force that created the Ladies

Grand Council of the Primrose League was the highly persuasive force of Lady Randolph herself. She knew from her own experience the stimulation and fascination of politics for women eager to escape the routine of running a household and to move away from personal problems into the realm of the unexpected, of association with people of all classes and kinds, of commitment to a cause. As a fifth member of the Fourth Party hierarchy, she would not have found it hard to convince them.

I became Dame President of many Habitations and used to go all over the country inaugurating them. The opening speeches were often quaint in their conceptions, a mixture of grave and gay, serious and frivolous—speeches from members of Parliament, interspersed with songs and even recitations, sometimes of a comical nature. The meeting would end with the enrollment of converts.

A strange medley, the laborer and the local magnate, the county lady and the grocer's wife, would troop up to sign the roll. Politics, like charity, are great levelers.

She told how Lady Salisbury rebuked a member who complained that some proposed entertainment might be attractive to the masses but was really slightly vulgar. 'Vulgar? Of course it is vulgar,' said Lady Salisbury, then president of the Ladies Executive Council, 'but that is why we have got on so well.'[4]

Jennie not only travelled the Primrose League trail for her own purposes, making her own speeches, but she also continued to accompany her husband on his major political trips. By the beginning of 1884, Randolph again had energized his passion for politics. Speaking in Blackpool, he made a blistering speech, one of his best:

Gentlemen, we live in an age of advertisement, the age of Holloway's pills, of Coleman's mustard, and of Horniman's pure tea; and the policy of lavish advertisement has been so successful in commerce that the Liberal Party, with its usual enterprise, has adopted it to politics. The Prime Minister is the greatest living master of the art of personal political advertisement. . . . Every act of his, whether it be for the purposes of health, or of recreation, or of religious devotion, is spread before the eyes of every man, woman and child in the United Kingdom on large and glaring placards. . . . For the purposes of recreation, he has selected the felling of trees; and we may usefully remark that his amusements, like his politics, are essentially destructive. Every afternoon the whole world is invited to assist at the crashing fall of some beech or elm or oak. The forest laments, in order that Mr. Gladstone may perspire. . . .[5]

So similar in style and tone were the speeches Jennie and Randolph made that some of their closer friends openly wondered about it. One friend of particular courage, Cecil Spring-Rice, made mention to the Dowager Duchess of Marlborough of this apparent wifely influence. The Duchess bristled and answered icily that the only real influence on Lord Randolph's career was his mother.

It was true that the Duchess was a growing influence. With the death of the Duke, she concentrated completely on furthering the fame and fortune of her second son. 'She idolized him,' observed George Smalley. 'She talked of him often to those whom she knew to be his friends, and she thought of him continually. She made sacrifices for him; to her they were none because they were for him. In him, her life centred....'[6]

Randolph, in turn, visited his mother more often, especially after she moved to her London house in Grosvenor Square. And when he travelled, his letters to his mother still were longer and more affectionate than those to his wife. Yet he continued to respect deeply Jennie's judgment and advice. The fight between Jennie and the Duchess for control over Randolph ended only with his death.

Whatever Jennie did, she did with high style. One of her widely copied social inventions was the 'dinner of deadly enemies'. A guest at her first such dinner, Smalley later described it:

It was thought a hazardous experiment. It proved a complete success. They were all well-bred people. They all recognized their obligations to their hostess as paramount for the time being. They were Lady Randolph's guests; that was enough. As guests, they were neither friends nor enemies. There were no hostilities. The talk flowed on smoothly. When a man found himself sent in to dinner with a woman he did not speak to, his tongue was somehow unloosed; it was a truce. In some cases, ancient animosities were softened. In all, they were suspended. The guests all knew each other; and as they looked about the table, they all saw that Lady Randolph had attempted the impossible, and had conquered. A social miracle had been performed.[7]

Part of the challenge was to eliminate all consciousness that these dinners had a political purpose. Yet there could hardly be any such dinner without political discussion, even argument. At one affair, attended by Joseph Chamberlain, Liberal Party leader and President of the Board of Trade under Gladstone, Randolph was expounding on the connection between class and character in the ruling of India: 'He [a typical member of the upper class] knew how to govern because he came of a governing class,' Randolph said. 'And he was a gentleman. Whereas now,' he added, looking directly at

Chamberlain, 'instead of gentlemen, you get men from—Birmingham and God knows where.'

Chamberlain was a man of elegant features who wore a monocle and faultless attire. A self-made millionaire, he had retired from business at thirty-eight, and gone into politics. After achieving a brilliant record as a reforming Mayor of Birmingham, he had moved into Parliament at the age of forty. The public called him 'Pushful Joe', and Randolph's verbal knife had plunged deep. But cool and smiling, Chamberlain simply noted that it was time to join the ladies. 'Instantly the clouds cleared,' said Smalley. 'India was forgotten. The two combatants walked up the stairs arm in arm, and the storm was as if it had never been.'

Jennie's own remarks often had a more caustic edge now. During one hectic political crisis, Lord Hartington told her he had not yet made up his mind whether to vote for or against Randolph the next day. 'I shall be a man or a mouse,' he told her.

'Or a rat,' she responded, with only the smallest smile.[8]

One reported comment that reached her was that a Mrs Stephens had told a Mrs Farquhar that she 'hoped little Lady Randolph had better manners than she had last year'. But that acerbic quality had become one of Jennie's weapons and she kept it sharp for ready use. She had started to paint seriously that year and was once cornered at one of her house parties by Joseph Chamberlain, Sir William Harcourt, and Sir Charles Dilke—all political rivals of Randolph. The three men begged her to paint their portraits. 'Where can you find more attractive models?' they asked.

'Impossible,' said Jennie smiling. 'I should fail.'

They wanted to know why.

'I could never paint you black enough,' said Jennie, still smiling.[9]

Sir Charles Dilke was an impressive-looking man with a brilliant political future and an obvious charm for women. When Mrs J. Comyns-Carr mentioned to Lady Lindsay that she would like to meet Dilke, she was told, 'There's always a waiting list, you know.' But Dilke was so smitten with Jennie that he got down on his knees and begged her to be his mistress. Jennie afterward related the incident to Lord Rosebery, pointing out how ridiculous Dilke looked on his knees, and Rosebery wrote the story in his private papers. Randolph heard of the incident and physically attacked Dilke. Reference to all this was obliquely made by Dilke, who, without supplying details, told of his friendship with Randolph which was ended when Randolph attacked him.

Dilke later was caught in a scandal involving prostitutes, bizarre sex practices, and adultery, and it killed his career.[10] Years after, Jennie wrote in a published essay that there were many British society leaders who could 'live down scandals, whereas the less-favored go under emphasizing the old saying, "One may steal a horse while another may not look over the wall".'[11]

She may have been referring to herself or the Prince of Wales or a dozen other people. As for Randolph, however, there were almost never any women remotely connected with his name. One of the few was Lady de Grey, a good friend of Jennie, 'a luxurious woman with perfect manners, a kind disposition and a moderate sense of duty.' She was also beautiful, perceptive, and charming. Emotionally, however, she was so high-strung and easily agitated that even the cry of the cuckoo made her feel ill. She hardly seemed a candidate for the affections of the even more volatile Randolph.[12]

It further seemed that the growing danger and doom of his syphilis had alienated him from all women, except his mother. Much whispered comment was made of the fact that Randolph took a great many short trips on the Continent without Jennie—always with individual men friends, always the same ones reappearing. They were not political friends, nor were they generally invited to the Churchills' dinners or parties—they were Randolph's personal friends.

'Randolph is a woman and I never seem to manage women,'[13] Lord Salisbury told a friend of Lady Leslie. Her friend added, 'Indeed, it is quite true that Lord Randolph has a feminine side, and a large side, to his nature.'

If there is any truth in this it could be held to explain many things—failure of his marriage with Jennie, her search for other men, his utter lack of relationship with his sons and his very strong ties to his mother. But if this were the case, it was certainly not so when he married Jennie, for theirs was initially a physical love.

At this time, Jennie was taking lessons in painting from Mrs E. M. Ward,[14] the wife of a noted artist. Among Mrs Ward's pupils were the Princess of Wales, the Duchess of Albany, and assorted other royalty. Jennie was occupied 'very violently' with her painting and was soon 'martyrizing many models, paid and unpaid, covering miles of canvas with impossible daubs, and spending a small fortune in paints and pigments.' Whenever he was home on holiday, Winston liked to watch his mother paint, and he soon tried it himself. It became one of the few subjects at school that he really liked and excelled in. From school he soon wrote how he had begun 'shading. I have been drawing little landscapes and bridges, and those sorts of things.'

Jennie was soon herself made a model of sorts, one of the so-called PBs, the Professional Beauties, an élite group of England's most beautiful women, whose photographs were sold in shops all over the country. 'The first time mine found its way into a shop,' she said, 'I was severely censured by my friends, and told I ought to prosecute the photographer.' Of course, she didn't—the flattery apparently counterbalanced the notoriety. In addition to the photographs, there were persistent publicity, interviews, and magazine articles about the PBs.[15] A poem about these women named a dozen of them. About Jennie, it said,

> Then Lady Randolph Churchill, whose sweet tones
> Make her the Saint Cecilia of the day . . .

The PBs became a highly prized asset at all social affairs. Hostesses would tack onto invitations, 'Do come; the PBs will be here.' Lily Langtry was one of the most celebrated PBs, and was once so crushed by her admiring crowd that she needed an ambulance to rescue her. 'Whatever happens, I do not intend to grow old,' Langtry told Lady Warwick.[16] The man who most approved of that sentiment was Leonard Jerome. He courted Langtry heavily when she came to New York, introduced her and Oscar Wilde to the city society at a round of his famous dinners. Langtry called him 'Uncle Leonard'.

Leonard's daughter Clara would have qualified as another PB, but she and her French maid and Moreton Frewen were far distant in their log house at Big Horn, Wyoming, with few visitors except bears, buffalo and such friends as Lord Queensberry and Buffalo Bill.

A number of Englishmen had invested heavily in American cattle and land. The Duke of Sutherland alone owned some 500,000 acres, and two English syndicates had bought seven million acres in Texas. But the big attraction for the British visitors was the hunting of American bear. Moreton's interest, however, was in his 45,000 head of cattle. But the story is that, wise as he supposedly was to the ways of the West, Frewen once stood on a hilltop and bought the same herd of 7,000 cattle three times while the herd was driven in a circle around the hill.

Something more serious at the time was Clara's pregnancy. The nearest doctor was in Cheyenne, two hundred miles away, a four-day trip by the Deadwood Coach. The child was still-born, and was sent back to the family burial plot in Greenwood Cemetery in Brooklyn. Clara went to recuperate in New York. Moreton stayed behind, until his father-in-law ordered him to return to Clara.

Leonie now announced her own marriage plans. Her fiancé was Lieutenant John Leslie of the Grenadier Guards, whom she had met four years earlier while visiting Jennie in Ireland. The romance had been discouraged because Mrs Jerome wanted at least one French son-in-law and Lady Leslie preferred an English bride for her only son. It hardly helped matters that the former Elizabeth Livingston of Staatsburgh, New York, who had married British socialite George Bentinck, had told the Leslies that Leonard Jerome was a dustman whose coach was used to remove offal. Lady Leslie's friends also informed her that Mrs Jerome was three-quarters Indian. Sir John Leslie promptly warned Leonard Jerome that his estates were his own, and not necessarily willed to his children. Jerome's answer was curt: 'Letter received.'

But the wedding gown was by Worth; the famous Bishop Potter of New York performed the service in Grace Church; guests included the Astors, the Belmonts, the Livingstons, the Van Burens. A society reporter noted, somewhat inaccurately, 'Mr Leslie [is] an intimate friend of Lord Churchill's, and his income amounts to 30,000 pounds a year. Miss Jerome is worth a quarter of a million in her own right.'[17] The press did not note the Leslie family's disapproval—the bridegroom's sisters were not even allowed to cable their congratulations.

Ritzman's in London meanwhile added the photographs of Leonie and Clara to their window display of Professional Beauties, but *Town Topics* commented, 'Pretty as these two heads are, neither can compare in beauty with the second sister, Jennie.'

The reunion of the Jerome sisters at Leonie's wedding was a short one, but that must have been the time when Jennie persuaded her sisters to move to England so that they could all live close together. Mrs Jerome would follow her daughters shortly.

Only Leonard Jerome stayed behind. He rented his house on Madison Square as a gaming club for $25,000 a year. The club specialized in baccarat and poker, and featured a big blackboard posted with racing results from Paris and London. Jerome moved to the Brunswick Hotel on Fifth Avenue, considered the headquarters of the aristocratic 'horsey set'. It was also the meeting place for Jerome's Coaching Club, which he still conducted wearing a whole bouquet in the buttonhole of his bright green coat.

Upon her return to England, Jennie found Randolph's health and disposition worsening. About that time, Randolph's friend Frank Harris came to visit. Born in Ireland, educated in Kansas, where he had become an American citizen, Harris was editor of the *Evening News*. 'While we were talking the door opened and Lady Randolph appeared,' Harris remembered.

Naturally, I got up as she called out, 'Randolph,' but he sat still. In spite of his ominous silence, she came across to him, 'Randolph, I want to talk to you!'
'Don't you see,' he retorted, 'that I've come here to be undisturbed?'
'But I want you,' she repeated.
He sprang to his feet. 'Can't I have a moment's peace from you anywhere?' he barked. 'Get out and leave me alone!' At once she turned and walked out of the room.[18]

It was a single, small incident. By itself, it might have little meaning, but it was part of a pattern.

Randolph's mind was now tormented and his health tortured. His syphilis apparently was entering the third stage.

During this stage, the disease can take many forms. Decay may penetrate to the bone or erode the membranes of the mouth and rectum or form dead areas in the liver, kidney, brain, or heart. No organ is immune to the danger. Erosion of the brain's fragile blood vessels or a gradual disintegration of the cerebrum can stretch out interminably. As the infection increases, the syphilitic brain gradually becomes detached from reality, disconnected from the evidence of its senses. It functions with intervals of fantasy that can be either pleasant or violent. These fantasies are often patterned on a distorted imitation of reality, but gradually they become progressively abstract and meaningless.

It was then Randolph decided to travel to India and Egypt—without Jennie. He was trying to escape something from which there was no escape.

# I I

Randolph's stay in the east lasted four months. With him was Thomas Trafford, his favourite travelling companion. Trafford had been in the Churchill party on Randolph's visit to the United States in 1876 and had accompanied him on a number of shorter trips. Friends had thought it strange that Randolph did not delay his departure a few weeks so that he could spend the Christmas holidays with his family at home. Jennie had wanted to go to India and was bitter about being left behind. Soon afterward, she met G. E. Buckle, editor of *The Times*, who had written a critical editorial about Randolph that morning. Buckle smilingly approached Jennie and asked if she would still speak to him, or whether she was too angry.

'Angry? Not a bit,' she said. 'I have ten volumes of press cuttings about Randolph, all abusive. This will only be added to them.'[1]

'I cannot remember one friend of mine who was really happy,' said Frances, Countess of Warwick, a close friend of Jennie who shared with her the unofficial title of the prettiest young matron in London. Both were women of sharp minds. They were both unhappy in their marriages and had competed for the intimacy of the Prince of Wales. 'Each of us knew that disillusion must follow . . . ,' she wrote. 'In the feverish search for pleasure, any woman might lose her lover.'[2]

Jennie was not lonely during those winter months. Lucille, the heroine of Winston Churchill's novel *Savrola*, was modelled after his mother.

. . . her life had been a busy one. Receptions, balls and parties had filled the winter season with unremitting labour of entertaining. Foreign princes had paid her homage, not only as the loveliest woman in Europe, but also as a great political figure. Her salon was crowded with the most famous men from every country. Statesmen, soldiers, poets and men of science had worshipped at the shrine. She had mixed in matters of State. Suave and courtly ambassadors had thrown out delicate hints, and she had replied with unofficial answers. Plenipotentiaries had explained the details of treaties and protocols, with remarkable elaboration, for her benefit. Philanthropists had argued, urged and expounded their views and whims. Everyone talked to her of public business. Even her maid had approached her with an application for the advancement of her brother, a clerk in the Post Office; and everyone had admired her until admiration itself, the most delicious drink that a woman tastes, became insipid.

Lucille's husband 'saw her less and less frequently', and she then took a lover.

Jennie saw much of the Prince of Wales during that time, and she saw even more of Count Kinsky. Kinsky was still the hero of the hour in England because of his victory in the Grand National. Every man wanted him at his table and a waiting list of women wanted him in their boudoirs. He had not only brawn but brain. He was handsome, charming, a rising diplomat with a talent for words, a sparkling pianist, a man with an easy laugh and a firm grip. Jennie's brother-in-law Moreton Frewen called Kinsky 'the best Austrian that ever was', and printed his photograph in his memoirs;[3] Leonie named Kinsky godfather to her second son. Randolph Churchill himself was proud to call Kinsky his friend through the years, despite the fact that Jennie's romance with the Count was an open secret all over London.

But it was still a furtive romance. Kinsky could only visit her when Randolph was away. Not only was she a married woman, but her husband had become one of the most important politicians in England.

Though Kinsky concentrated on Jennie, therefore, his attentions were not exclusive. He was a womanizer, and the women were always available. Jennie frankly exploited some of her own anxious admirers to stir up Kinsky's jealousy. One of them was an extremely handsome horseman and boxer named Peter Flower. Leonie hinted to Kinsky that Jennie liked Flower 'dangling about' and noted that Kinsky promptly went to Jennie and demanded an explanation.[4]

To help fill the big house at Connaught Place, Jennie invited her sister Leonie to stay while John Leslie was serving with the Guards in London. Clara had settled in Sussex, in a bleak and beautiful stone house, Brede Place, at the edge of the Frewen estates. Built in 1350, it had been occupied only by gamekeepers for more than two hundred years and still had wells from which the water was hauled and old-style privies. Moreton Frewen's anticipated fortune in cattle had disappeared in a severe drought. In the course of coming years, Moreton would spend most of his time away from home in every part of the world, searching for a fortune he would never find.

Leonie, also, was having her troubles, mainly with her mother-in-law, Lady Leslie. For many months, her mother-in-law refused even to recognize Leonie's social existence. A formidable woman of firm opinions, Lady Leslie also had a terrible temper. Relatives still remembered her as the headstrong Constance who jumped onto the windowsill of her Berkeley Square home and threatened to 'dash herself down if not yielded to in a dispute'. Her language could be similarly strong. Leonie noted in her diary that she had received 'a vile letter' from Lady Leslie and 'it makes me . . . feel so wretched. . . .'[5]

So there they were, the three Jerome sisters, an exceptional trio of beauty, talent, energy, and character—each woman undergoing a variety of misery in her marriage, each skimming along on a financial shoestring, each unable or unwilling to alter her way of life. They went everywhere together. A critic called them 'The Beautiful, the Witty, and the Good'[6] (Jennie, Leonie, and Clara in that order). Others called Clara 'beautiful, blonde, and brainless'; Jennie, 'flashing, brainy, and social'; and Leonie, 'the one with the most character.'

The three sisters shared a love of music and the theatre. Fanny Ronalds still held her Sunday afternoon salons for music lovers, and the Jerome sisters were often in attendance. They were also constantly at the opera. As they couldn't afford boxes of their own, their good friend, Covent Garden manager Harry Higgins, often let them sit in various boxes to 'paper' the house, where they 'could see without being seen'.[7]

Leonard Jerome's fortune had almost disintegrated. He had settled $10,000 a year on Jennie, part of the income from rental of the Madison Square house. In addition, he sent $2,000 a year now to the improvident Leonie and John. Moreton still pretended to provide for Clara, and occasionally did, but Leonard told his wife that he himself hoped to send $2,000 a year to Clara. He did rent a house for her in Aldford Street, close to Jennie. And Leonie soon moved to nearby Seymour Street.

But the three Jerome sisters lived as if money would always be available. It was true that Jennie spent little on jewelry. One of her few pieces, and her favourite, was a large diamond star which she wore low on the brow. It was remarkably similar to the diamond star worn by the heroine of one of Disraeli's novels, *The Divine*

*Theodora.* What Jennie and the others did not spend on jewelry, they spent on clothes. Leonie, however, was happy to accept Jennie's cast-off Worth gowns.[8]

Following in his famous father's tradition, Jean Worth in Paris was Europe's most distinguished dress designer. With his pointed beard and his steady smile, Worth was an impressive figure. He seldom met his clients, except a few favoured ones from the French Empire days, such as the Jerome women. He would study them as a painter might, until inspiration came. Quickly, then, he would outline the dress in the air, order special fabrics in particular colours from his anxious assistants, and make his expectant customers pose for him while his dress creation evolved. The cost was proportionate to the creation—up to five hundred dollars for a dress. He frankly confided to one of his clients that the reason he was so interested in every gown he made was that 'every Worth creation must be the advertisement for other Worth creations. Every costume has its advertising value'.[9] So strong was the female urge to insure the absolute uniqueness of each Worth dress, that Jennie's future sister-in-law Daisy, Princess of Pless, even had a fringe of real violets sewn into the train of a gown. (It was a gown of transparent lace, lined with blue chiffon and a sprinkling of gold sequins—which would seem to have been unique enough.)

The style in women's clothing had changed considerably in the ten years since Jennie's marriage. The huge bustle moderated gradually, then temporarily disappeared by 1878. Replacing it was a narrowed but highly elaborate skirt fitted tightly over the hips and thighs. Gone was the gown so full that a wind could almost carry a woman away, as Gladstone's daughter Mary once described in her diary. Gone too was the dress so heavily petticoated that it made tennis playing almost impossible—especially when the woman had to use one hand to hold down her hat. The bustle, however, reappeared in 1883, looking more like a camel's hump. The earlier bustle had shot out from the spine like a shelf, on which one could actually place a glass of water or a plate of soup. Back, too, was the wasp waist, which demanded that women corset their ribs so tightly into their liver that it often caused an anaemia called 'green sickness'. Dr Wardrop's heavily advertised corset featured a light, strong plate, for which he claimed medical approval, 'which gives the stomach flatness and grace. . . . The figure is entirely remodelled without undue pressure.' The crinoline, or hoop-petticoat, also had been improved to eliminate its 'creaking or rattling' and its tendency to sway from side to side as a lady walked. Jennie was one of the first to wear looser dresses of richly coloured material, falling in straight lines from a more natural girdle.

At an exhibition in 1882 of 'hygienic wearing apparel', the bloomers, introduced unsucessfully by Mrs Amelia Jenks Bloomer in the 1840's, were reintroduced, but it took another ten years before they came fully into vogue. Women outdid themselves with their cotton stockings, decorating them with horizontal stripes of green, yellow, or red.[10]

Single women were still not allowed to go anywhere without chaperones. Even married women were never expected to lunch alone in London, and no proper ladies, single or married, were ever expected to walk past the big-windowed private clubs from which men could watch them. In 1882, women were the subject of a national symposium entitled 'Our Freedom and its Results'. Mary Agnes Hamilton said that there were 'very large numbers of otherwise intelligent persons who did sincerely endorse the view that members of the female sex were not human, as members of the male sex were.'[11]

Little of this, of course, impeded Jennie. She was thirty years old and long before had broken barriers, stretched rules, ignored conventions. Just as she set her own style in clothing and house decoration, so she set her own pace. She was no fluttering female, and she seldom minced words or suppressed her feelings. 'Whenever I want to think of an outstandingly brilliant woman, my mind leaps immediately to Lady Randolph Churchill,' wrote Lady Warwick later. '. . . One never thought of giving a party without her. She was as delightful to women as to men. . . . Lady Randolph was like a marvellous diamond—a host of facets seemed to sparkle at once.'[12] Thomas Escott, editor of the *Fortnightly Review*, had commented, 'London possesses no more accomplished or charming hostess. . . .'

Wherever Jennie went now, she was questioned about Randolph. His letters to her from India and Egypt were educational rather than emotional. Though he dismissed the Suez Canal as a 'dirty ditch', he praised the elephant highly:

I think the elephant is the best mode of conveyance I know. He cannot come to grief; he never tumbles down nor runs away (at least not on the march); nothing stops him; and when you get accustomed to his pace, he is not tiring. You would not believe what steep places they get up and down or what thick, almost impenetrable jungle, they go through. If a tree is in the way, and not too large a one, they pull it down; if a branch hangs too low for the howdah to go under, they break it off. They are certainly most wonderful animals, and life in many parts of India would be impossible without them.

Letters to his mother were more exciting: 'I have had the great good fortune to kill a tiger. . . .' He told her of riding his elephant and coming across

the recently killed carcass of a pig, half devoured. Hersey, when he saw it, declared it was quite fresh, and that the tiger must be close by. You may imagine the excitement. . . . All of a sudden out bundled this huge creature, right under the nose of Hersey's elephant, and made off across some ground which was slightly open. Hersey fired and missed. I fired and hit him just above the tail. (A very good shot, for he only showed me his stern, and he was at least forty yards off). Hersey then fired his second barrel, and broke his shoulder, which brought him up (literally with a round turn). He took refuge in a patch of grass about fifty yards from us where we could just see bits of him. Heavens, how he growled, and what a rage he was in! He would have charged us but that he was disabled by Hersey's last shot. We remained still, and gave him four or five more shots which on subsequent examination, we found all told; and then, after about five minutes more awful growling, he expired. Great joy to all! The good luck of getting him was unheard of this time of the year; the odds were a hundred to one against such a thing. He was a magnificent specimen, nine feet seven inches in length, and a splendid skin—which will, I think, look very well in Grosvenor Square. . . .[13]

Randolph did not mention the possibility that the skin would look equally well at his own home in Connaught Place.

To Randolph, Jennie noted petulantly, 'You never mentioned me in your letter to your mother . . . ,' but throughout his four-month trip, Jennie kept Randolph posted on the family: 'The children are flourishing. I hear a much better account of Winston. . . . He is working so much harder this term.' Winston's handwriting also had improved slightly, she noted, and 'the spelling is not too bad. . . .'

Randolph also got reports from ten-year-old Winston, about the Christmas party, his stamp book getting filled up (but would his father please send him more stamps), how he was learning to dance 'and I like it very much', and that the dog Chloe 'is very fat indeed. I give her a run every day to take her fat down.' He also remarked how nice it was for his father to be 'sailing all over the sea', and had a variety of other questions: 'Are the Indians very funny?' 'Are there many ants in India if so, you will have a nice time, what with ants and mosquitoes. . . .'

Winston's father answered few of his letters.

Jennie kept her husband advised, too, on the course of British politics. Gladstone's Liberal government was in serious trouble on a number of issues: a fiasco in Sudan, a series of dynamitings in Ireland, trouble with Russia over the Afghanistan border, and the failure to reinforce General Gordon at Khartoum. Even the Queen sent her Prime Minister a bitter telegram about Gordon's death and Randolph wrote: 'Any Hindu who dies at Benares and whose ashes are thrown into the Ganges, goes right bang up to Heaven without stopping, no matter how great a rascal he may have been. I think the G.O.M. [Gladstone] ought to come here; it is his best chance.'[14]

In the strange way of politics, Randolph's four months' absence only increased his public popularity. In a *Punch* cartoon, Fourth Party members Wolff and Gorst stare sadly out to sea, crying, 'When *will* he come?' Commenting on this to Jennie, her father wrote:

I have watched with wonder Randolph's rise in the political world. Over and over he was smashed, pulverized, so ruthlessly squelched that he was considered done forever. And yet, little after, up he comes smiling, as though he had never been hit at all. I confess, I am amazed. So young! So reckless in experience, so impulsive! That he should have fought his way up through the fiery elements without, as the trotters say, a 'skip or a break', is indeed wonderful. I hope he will come home soon, and that he will find himself in accord with Lord Salisbury. . . .

It seemed likely that the Gladstone Government would soon fall. In that event, Salisbury would become Prime Minister and Randolph would inevitably be offered an important position.

One of England's men of distinction, Robert Arthur Talbot Gascoyne-Cecil, Lord Salisbury, had twice held the India Office and the Foreign Office and would serve three times as Prime Minister. He had firm opinions, a penetrating mind, a tactless manner. Leadership, he felt, belonged to the men of birth, wealth, and intellectual power. What he said, he usually said with virulence, and sometimes with imprudence and even insolence. He was not a man who measured his phrases.

A massive man—six feet four—with stooped shoulders, almost

bald but with a curly grey beard, Salisbury preferred solitude to society, liked to ride a tricycle in St. James's Park for exercise, hated hunting or shooting, and was always reluctant to visit the Queen because he thought she kept her residences too cold. An intellectual with a sharp interest in science, Salisbury had fitted up his own chemical laboratory; a melancholy and deeply religious man, he attended his private chapel every morning before breakfast.[15]

Curzon called Salisbury 'that strange, powerful, inscrutable, brilliant, obstructive deadweight at the top'. In the best of times, it would have been difficult to be 'in accord' with Salisbury. But these were the worst of times. Salisbury recognized Randolph for what he then was: brilliant but sick, irresponsible and unpredictable.

At his first appearance in the House after returning from his trip, Randolph was cheerfully greeted by the Tory Party, and even Gladstone walked over to shake his hand. So did Sir Stafford Northcote, whose resignation as the Tory Party leader Randolph had been demanding. Questioned as to what place he would give Lord Randolph if he were asked to form a government, Northcote replied, 'Say, rather, what place he will give me.'[16] Northcote's point was well made. Not only had Randolph demanded Northcote's dismissal, but he had insisted that if Salisbury became Prime Minister, he should give prominent posts to Fourth Party members. 'He had won no battle, negotiated no peace,' wrote Winston Churchill of that time. 'He had passed no great measure of reform; he had never held public office; he was not even a Privy Councillor; yet he was welcomed on all sides with interest or acclamation.'[17]

Winston wrote from school that he had been out riding with a gentleman who 'thinks that Gladstone is a brute and thinks that "the one with the curly moustache" [Randolph Churchill] ought to be Premier'. Jerome also wrote a complimentary letter:

... I want to congratulate you on your safe return from the East, and especially on the great good the trip seems to have done you. They all say you are in splendid condition. I should be glad to believe you would keep so, but I fear, from what I read of your doings lately, you will soon put yourself down again. A little less work and not quite so many cigarettes, I fancy, would be better for you. ...

I might indulge in some complimentary remarks on the 'wonderful rise of the young statesman' and how very gratifying ... but I know it would only bore you.

But Randolph was far less optimistic about his 'wonderful rise'.

When a friend told him that Salisbury could not form a govern-ment without him, Randolph answered, 'He can form a Ministry, if necessary, with waiters from the Carlton Club.'

After a defeat for Gladstone on a critical vote, Randolph jumped onto the bench in the House of Commons and like a small boy waved a blue handkerchief over his head, yelling taunts at the Liberals. But with Gladstone's overthrow imminent, Churchill's depression grew quickly deeper. 'I am very near the end of my tether,' he told a friend.

In the last five years I have lived twenty. I have fought Society. I have fought Mr. Gladstone at the head of a great majority. I have fought the Front Opposition Bench. Now I am fighting Lord Salisbury. I have said I will not join the Government unless Northcote leaves the House of Commons. Lord Salisbury will never give way. I'm done.[18]

Much of this sudden shift from boyish joy to deep depression was a typical symptom of his degenerative disease. The smell of Tory success was in the air, and Jennie was enthusiastic about her husband's new possibilities. She tried to buoy him up as best she could. The rumour was that Randolph would be offered the post of Secretary of State for India when the Conservatives came in.

Randolph had discussed India's problems at a banquet of the Primrose League, shortly after his return.

Our rule in India is, as it were, a sheet of oil spread out over the surface of, and keeping calm and quiet and unruffled by storms, an immense and profound ocean of humanity. Underneath that rule lie hidden all the memories of fallen dynasties, all the traditions of vanquished races, all the pride of insulted creeds. . . .

Home barely a month, however, Randolph decided he needed still another holiday abroad, this time to France. Going with him was his friend Sir Henry James.

Caught up in the political turmoil which might heighten their need of each other, Jennie and Randolph now wrote more affection-ate letters. 'Darling dearest petit R. . . .' 'Petit R.' was her most endearing nickname for him. And he answered, 'My dearest Jennie.'

Shortly upon Randolph's return from France in June, Gladstone resigned after a parliamentary defeat on an unimportant budget amendment. The Queen asked Lord Salisbury to form a govern-ment. Many felt that Randolph might now compromise his demands

M

for Northcote's removal and Fourth Party rewards. But he remained adamant. Salisbury seemed stymied. This angered the Queen, who wired Salisbury that she did not think Lord Randolph Churchill should be allowed to dictate his own terms, especially since he had never before held Cabinet office. Even the Dowager Duchess intervened, appealing to Randolph by letter to reconsider his demands and to reconcile himself with the new Salisbury government. Randolph refused, and his reinforced resolution won out. Northcote was eased upstairs into the House of Lords, and Fourth Party members Wolff, Gorst, and Balfour were all brought into the Government. As for Randolph, Salisbury appointed him Secretary of State for India after Queen Victoria said she had 'no insuperable objection'.

On being appointed to the India office, 'The Wasp from Woodstock' had to stand for re-election as an M.P. He had neither the time nor the energy to work for votes there, so Jennie took charge and single-handedly supervised his election campaign, to insure his seat in the House. It was a key election. Randolph Churchill's defeat at that particular time would have meant an enormous victory for the Liberals, who mounted an energetic campaign to overthrow him. True, it was a family borough, and Marlborough support had considerable meaning. But at first Jennie did not even have that vital help. When her brother-in-law had succeeded to the Dukedom, he had sold many of the family treasures at Blenheim. He and Randolph had quarrelled bitterly about it, and the new Duke was not anxious now to help Randolph's re-election. Though he permitted Jennie to stay at Blenheim, she had to maintain her committee rooms at the nearby Bear Hotel. Pressed by Jennie's pleas, he finally relented enough to loan her his carriages to help bring voters to the polls.

'We held daily confabulations with the friends and Members of Parliament who had come to help,' she wrote.

We were most important, and felt that the eyes of the world were upon us. Revelling in the hustle and bustle of the Committee rooms, marshaling our forces, and hearing the hourly reports of how the campaign was progressing, I felt like a general holding a council-of-war with his staff in the heat of battle. A. was doubtful, B. obdurate, while C's wife, a wicked abominable Radical, was trying to influence her husband whom we thought secure, to vote the wrong way. At once they must be visited and our arsenal of arguments brought to bear on them.

Jennie travelled in her sister-in-law's tandem, the horses decorated gaily with the ribbons of Randolph's racing colours, pink and brown. There were a thousand voters to be reached.

The distances to cover were great. . . . Sometimes we would drive into the fields, and getting down, climb into the hayricks, falling upon our unwary prey at his work. There was no escaping us. . . . Sometimes with these simple country folk a pleading look, and an imploring 'Oh please vote for my husband; I shall be so unhappy if he does not get in,' or, 'If you want to be on the winning side, vote for us; as of course we are going to win.[19]

The Primrose League was still in the embryonic stage in Woodstock, with no Habitation to supply Jennie with Primrose Dames. She therefore had to find her own workers. This was the first time that Primrose badges were worn in an actual political campaign. 'Party feeling ran high,' said Jennie, 'and in outlying districts we would frequently be pursued by our opponents, jeering and shouting at us; but this we rather enjoyed.'

Reception committees greeted her with jingling rhymes about her campaigning. One of them went this way:

But just as I was talking
With Neighbour Brown and walking
To take a mug of beer at the Unicorn and Lion,
(Because there's somehow a connection
Between free beer and election)
Who should come but Lady Churchill, with a turnout that was fine.

And before me stopped her horses,
As she marshalled all her forces,
And before I knew what happened I had promised her my vote;
And before I quite recovered
From the vision that had hovered,
'Twas much too late to rally, and I had changed my coat.

And over Woodstock darted
On their mission brave, wholehearted,
The tandem and their driver and the ribbons pink and brown.
And a smile that twinkled over,
And that made a man most love her
Took the hearts and votes of all Liberals in the town.

Bless my soul! That Yankee lady,
Whether day was bright or shady,
Dashed about the district like an oriflamme of war.
When the voters saw her bonnet,
With the bright pink roses on it,
They followed as the soldiers did the Helmet of Navarre.[20]

Randolph could not have been more pleased. 'I should be very glad if you could arrange to stay in Woodstock till Friday,' he wrote Jennie. 'If I win, you will have all the glory.'

Widely covered by the press, the election was considered important enough for newspapermen to send some six hundred 'result' messages on the final victory. Randolph had received a majority of 127 votes, more than twice the majority he had received five years before.

The lady from Brooklyn had travelled a long, strange road to where she now stood in front of the Bear Hotel in an English town, thanking the large, enthusiastic crowd for her husband's victory. One day her son Winston would stand at that same place thanking the people for his own victory.

'I surpassed the fondest hopes of the suffragettes,' Jennie reflected, and thought I was duly elected, and I certainly experienced all the pleasure and gratification of being a successful candidate. I returned to London feeling that I had done a very big thing, and was surprised and astonished that the crowds in the streets looked at me with indifference. ... I often think that these must be the sensations of a newly made Member of Parliament when he first goes to the House of Commons, fresh from the hustings of his own meetings, where his dullest and silliest inanity is listened to and applauded. In the House he finds his level, alas! only too soon, and in a cold and inattentive audience realizes that perhaps he may not be the born orator he was led to believe.

There was a note awaiting her from Sir Henry James:

You must let me very sincerely and heartily congratulate you on the result of the election, especially as that result proceeded so very much from your personal exertions. Everybody is praising you very much.

But my gratification is slightly impaired by feeling I must introduce a new Corrupt Practices Act. Tandems must be put down,[21] and certainly some alteration—a correspondent informs me—must be made in the means of ascent and descent therefrom; then arch looks have to be scheduled, and nothing must be said 'from my heart'. The graceful wave of a pocket handkerchief will have to be dealt with in committee.

Still, I am very glad.

The Prince of Wales also sent his congratulations, adding that reading some of Lady Randolph's speeches had converted him, in some respects, to her views. In answer, Jennie wrote, 'It is a further source of infinite satisfaction to Lady Randolph to know that possibly by action on her part she may have been fortunate enough to influence in any degree your Royal Highness's view on a subject of large political importance.'

In those days, when women were generally thought of in terms of kitchens and bedrooms, Lady Randolph Churchill's political campaigning received international attention. As Leonard Jerome proudly wrote to his wife, 'You have no idea how universally Jennie is talked about and how proud the Americans are of her.'

Paradoxically, Randolph's weakness had become Jennie's strength. If her husband had possessed the strength of a Salisbury or a Gladstone, Jennie would have been forced into the role of the assured social hostess, the tea-pourer, the smiling, decorative ornament in the background. She would have been a wallpaper wife, as were the wives of most leading politicians. But Randolph's lack was the irritating sand that created the pearl. It forced Jennie into areas where she otherwise would not have trodden. Even the Marlborough House Set, for all their irreverence of rules, could not have imagined that path for a woman.

Jennie was now not only the mistress of her house but often the master. Randolph's trips were so frequent and often so extended that she found herself in a role of increasing independence. Unlike other wives who went into a solitary confinement when their husbands were absent, Jennie kept her house alive with friends and parties. More and more, too, she was faced with daily decisions normally resolved by the man in the house. Decisions about money, decisions about the children's education, decisions and evaluations concerning her own purpose in life.

Jennie's successful electioneering prompted her good friend, the Baroness Angela Georgina Burdett-Coutts, to ask her to help conduct her new husband's first campaign for office. Jennie agreed.[22] The Baroness had lived through the entire Victorian era and the Duke of Cambridge had called her 'an English institution'. Inheriting a fabulous fortune, great common sense, and lofty ideals, she had sought the advice of the Duke of Wellington and Charles Dickens on how to put her money to the best use. She founded schools, replaced slums with model housing, even helped feed, clothe, and revive whole districts in south-west Ireland during the famine.

As the wife of the new Secretary of State for India, Jennie went to work for the National Association for Supplying Medical Aid to the Women of India. The Association built dispensaries, provided medical treatment for the poor, and spurred the medical careers of many Indian women. In those days, even in England, the woman doctor was a rarity.[23]

Taking his third vacation that year, Randolph went to Scotland and Ireland with his secretary Cecil Wolff. He wrote Jennie concerning the Medical Association for India, advising her that the best means of promoting more publicity for the fund-raising was to 'get hold of Mr Buckle [editor of *The Times*], and fascinate him and make him write you up'. She fascinated Buckle, and many others, so well that the Association's finances became brighter than they had ever been.

Jennie was also involved with determining policy for the Primrose League. The League proved so successful that Jennie got letters from her friend, the elegant Comtesse de Paris, asking advice on forming a similar group in France, aimed at restoring the monarchy. The Comtesse, who was the sister of the Queen of Spain and the mother of the Queen of Portugal, did start the 'White Rose League' with gilt badges shaped as roses—but it never grew out of the seedling stage.

Jennie's most crucial problem, however, was not the Primrose League but Randolph. Despite his repeated and prolonged vacations, his disease was sapping his strength. 'I have no longer any energy or ideas,' he told a friend in August of 1885, 'and I am no more good except to make disturbance.' One such disturbance was his threat to resign because the Queen appointed her younger son to an office in India without consulting him. 'However, he has returned to reason "having taken calomel",' Salisbury wrote Queen Victoria, 'and is not going to resign.' The Queen then expressed the hope that Lord Salisbury 'would restrain Lord Randolph as much as he can,' and Salisbury warned Randolph, 'If you once go a step too far—if you once break the spring—you may take years to get over it.'

Caring for a sick, temperamental husband left Jennie little time for her sons. Five-year-old Jack was still under a nanny's care, but eleven-year-old Winston needed more special attention. Jennie's theory about children was that they should be given as much responsibility as they could handle. George Smalley remembered Winston inviting him and Jennie and Jack to go boating. 'He took command of the party,' wrote Smalley, 'first on land and then on water. But nobody thought of disputing his claim. I'd lived enough in boats to see that Winston, though with no great skill in waterman-

168

ship, knew what he was about; and though he ran some needless risks, it was never necessary to interfere.'[24] Jennie realized how important it was to let Winston take command without her interference or suggestions. For part of the summer, though, she sent him to Chesterfield Lodge on the east coast of England. He wrote her unhappy letters, wanting to come home, asking 'Do you miss me much?' and despairing, 'The governess is very unkind, so strict and stiff, I cannot enjoy myself at all. I am counting the days until Saturday. Then I shall be able to tell you all my troubles . . . .'

While Winston had to fight for attention in his mother's crowded schedule, he knew he could always reach her and that she would always listen. When St. George's School was too hateful to him, she was the one who transferred him to another school. When he begged to go to Europe on vacation with them, it was she who insisted on taking him. When he had a special request or needed more money, it was she who attended to it. She wrote to him regularly, visited him when she could, brought him home when there was time. Winston always felt sure of her love. His father, however, was merely a famous person to Winston, someone he could boast of to his classmates, whose autograph was a valuable commodity to swop or sell, but not someone he could talk to or touch.

Grandfather Jerome always proved to be a refreshing change for Winston. His was a love and pride shown openly and freely. Jerome had come to England for a visit late in the summer of 1885, in time to observe some of Jennie's political campaigning.

Everyone had realized that the Salisbury government was simply filling a caretaker role until the general election. The Voting Reform Bill had expanded the electorate by some two million voters and no one could predict whom they would want. Randolph's Woodstock constituency had been abolished, so he now challenged the highly popular John Bright in the Radical stronghold of Birmingham. In a not-very-anonymous article in the popular *Fortnightly Review*, Randolph had disclosed his own radical attitude toward the leadership of the Tory Party:

Unfortunately for Conservatism, its leaders belong solely to one class; they are a clique composed of members of the aristocracy, land owners and adherents whose chief merit is subserviency. The party chiefs live in an atmosphere in which a sense of their own importance and the importance of their class interests and privileges is exaggerated and which the opinions of the common people can scarcely penetrate. They are surrounded by sycophants who continually offer up the incense of personal flattery under the pretext of conveying political information. They half fear and half despise the common people. . . .

Churchill offered the British people an alternative. His banner was 'Tory Democracy', a phrase he coined. ('Tory Democracy', he later confided to a friend, 'is a democracy which supports the Tories.') His slogan was 'Trust the people and they will trust you.'

Randolph trusted them so much that he did not campaign and again let Jennie take charge. This time, however, Jennie's mother-in-law, the Dowager Duchess, joined her. During the campaign, the two women grew as close as they would ever be, and each somewhat revised her opinions of the other. Afterward, the Duchess for a while even defended Jennie to some of her society friends, emphasizing how much Jennie had 'matured' since she had entered politics.

'It was the first time that women had ever indulged in any personal canvassing in Birmingham,' wrote Jennie,

and we did it thoroughly. Every house in the constituency was visited. The Duchess would go in one direction, and I in another; the constituency was a large one and the work arduous. The voters were much more enlightened than the agricultural laborers of Oxfordshire; the men particularly were very argumentative and were well up on the questions of the day. . . . The wives of the Radicals were also admirably informed, and on more than one occasion routed me completely.

She told of an incident which occurred when she visited a factory to talk to the men during their lunch hour.

'I was received in sullen silence. When I inquired why, one, speaking for the rest, said they did not like being asked for their vote.'

'But you have something I want,' she told them, and added, 'How am I to get it if I do not ask for it?'

'This struck them as quite reasonable, and when I left they cheered me.'

Not all her receptions became as friendly. Visiting a pub, Jennie talked to the wife of the landlord, who called to her husband in the cellar, 'Lady Churchill wants to see you.'

'Well, tell Mrs Churchill to go to—'

'At which time,' said Jennie, 'I beat a hasty retreat.'

She had greater success with a butcher to whom she gave a flower.

He not only gave her his vote, but afterward sent her half a sheep.[25]

The excitement of politics had infected Winston—his father fighting a vital election, his mother hot on the campaign trail. And even his grandmother, the highly proper Dowager Duchess, ringing doorbells and soliciting votes. Winston found a classmate whose father was also a parliamentary candidate. If both fathers won, Winston wrote, he and his friend were going to have a victory supper.

But there was no victory supper. Bright beat Randolph Churchill by 773 votes. Randolph took his defeat gracefully. 'Gentlemen,' he said, 'the man who can't stand a knockdown blow isn't worth a damn.' The blow was quickly countered. A Churchill admirer in South Paddington, a safe Conservative district, withdrew in Churchill's favour, and Randolph was promptly elected there the next day.

The over-all election result, however, was that the Salisbury Conservatives were out and the Gladstone Liberals were in again, with 335 seats to 249. Randolph's opposition friend, John Morley, met Randolph in St. James Park after the election.

'You look a little pensive,' said Morley.

'Yes, I was thinking—I have plenty to think of. Well, we're out—you're in.'

'Yes, we're in for three months; then we dissolve and you're in for six years.'

Shortly after that, another friend asked Randolph:

'What will happen now?'

'I shall lead the Opposition for five years,' answered Randolph. 'Then I shall be Prime Minister for five years. Then I shall die.'[26] Randolph's prediction was to be less accurate than Morley's.

Windsor Castle, November 30, 1885

Dear Lord Randolph:

The Queen wishes to personally confer the Insignia of the Order of the Crown of India on Lady Randolph Churchill on Friday next the fourth of December at three o'clock.

Will she come back here to luncheon?

The 1:10 train from Paddington is the most convenient one, and if Lady Randolph will let me hear whether she comes by that or another train, I will send the carriage to meet her here.

Yours very truly,
Henry Ponsonby.

Jennie then received a note from the Queen's lady-in-waiting, advising her of correct attire and procedure:

LADY RANDOLPH CHURCHILL:

Bonnet and morning dress, grey gloves.

To kiss the Queen's hand after receiving the decoration, like the gentlemen to-day. A room will be prepared for her.

For any woman of the time an audience with the Queen was a highlight in her life. The curtsey and a kiss of the Queen's hand were considered by some as second in importance only to their marriage. The main test was of grace, and any awkwardness became a badge of shame.

The Queen, with one of her daughters and a lady-in-waiting, received Jennie in a small room:

She stood with her back to the window, wearing a long white veil which made an aureole around her against the light. Addressing a few kind words to me, to which in my embarrassment I made some inaudible answer, she proceeded to pin the order on my left shoulder. I remember that my black velvet dress was thickly embroidered with jet, so much so that the pin could find no hold, and unwittingly the Queen stuck it straight into me. Although like the Spartan boy, I tried to hide what I felt, I suppose I gave a start, and the Queen realizing what she had done was much concerned. Eventually the pin was put right and I curtsied myself out of the Royal Presence. As I reached the door, her majesty suddenly stepped forward saying with a smile, 'Oh! You have forgotten the case,' holding it out to me at the same time. This little touch of nature relieved an otherwise somewhat formal ceremony. Remarking afterward to the lady-in-waiting that I was afraid that I had been awkward, and nervous, she answered, 'You need not be troubled. I know the Queen felt more shy than you did.'[1]

The pin was a pearl and turquoise cipher attached to a pale blue ribbon bordered with white. The next day Jennie received a note from the Queen's lady-in-waiting:

My dear Lady Randolph,
I hope you got home quite comfortably yesterday, and took no cold. The Queen told me she thought you so handsome, and that it had all gone off so well.

Believe me ever,
Yours truly,
Jane Ely.

The Queen remarked in her Journal, 'Lady Randolph (an American) is very handsome and very dark.'[2]

Within a few months, the Randolph Churchills were invited to dine with the Queen at Windsor and spend the night. Jennie remembered the dinner as being in a small room surrounded by family portraits on the wall, the conversation carried out in hushed whispers almost oppressively quiet. 'I tried to keep my tongue under control,' she said later.

You know how I tend to rattle on, and I was terrified of saying a word too much, and arousing that dread 'We are not amused.' . . .
When the Queen spoke, even the whispers ceased. If she addressed a remark to you, the answer was given while the whole company listened.

The Queen's first impression of Randolph was 'his extraordinary likeness to darling Leopold, which quite startled me'. Both had an arrogant moustache and protruding eyes. Prince Leopold's sculpted figure in Oxford Cathedral indeed bears a considerable resemblance to Storey's marble of Randolph at Blenheim. Another time, she noted in her diary after a conversation with Randolph, 'We remained talking in the corridor until half past ten. . . . He said some strange things to me which I will refer to later.' The strange things concerned the Government's conduct in India and his strong feelings against Lord Hartington. 'The Queen thought it looked as if he [Randolph] was likely to be disagreeable, and wanted the Queen to agree with him.' She also commented, 'Lord Randolph was looking very ill.'[3]

Of that evening, Jennie wrote her mother on Windsor Castle stationery that 'dinner was a very solemn, ghastly affair. . . . I was the only "strange lady".' But if the Queen was concerned about Randolph, she was obviously pleased with Jennie. 'The Queen was most amiable last night and talked to me for some time.'

During the following spring, eleven-year-old Winston suddenly became critically ill with pneumonia—a disease whose recurrence would plague him all his life. Jennie rushed to her son's bedside, and Dr Roose sent reports to Randolph. 'We are still fighting the battle for your boy. His temperature is 103 now, but he is taking his nourishment better. . . .' The doctor advised that the right lung was infected and the left lung strained from the overwork.

This report may appear grave, yet it merely indicates the approach of the crisis which, please God, will result in an improved condition, should the left lung remain free. . . . I am in the next room and shall watch the patient during the night, for I am most anxious.

Three days later the delirium ceased and the fever subsided. 'Winston has had six hours of quiet sleep.' The crisis had passed, but Roose warned Jennie. 'I am so fearful of relapse, knowing we are not quite out of the woods yet.' Winston, he said, must have absolute quiet, and even Mrs Everest should not be allowed in the sickroom the first days because 'the excitement and pleasure of seeing her might do harm!'

Jennie's mother-in-law sent a note of sympathy: 'Such hours make one years older, and one feels how one's happiness in this world hangs on a thread. . . . I am so thankful for God's goodness for preserving your dear child. . . .'⁴ Moreton Frewen wrote, 'Poor, dear Winnie, and I hope it will leave no troublesome after-effects, but even if it leaves him delicate for a long time to come, you will make the more of him after being given back to you on the very threshold of the unknown. . . .'⁵

But during that year of 1886 Jennie was not able to concentrate love and attention on her son. That was the critical year that shattered all hopes for her husband and herself. Randolph's syphilis seemed in a recessive stage, but Jennie was always aware of its spectre. Dr Roose did not hold out excessive hope for Randolph. Perhaps to insure that Roose would maintain professional silence, Randolph kept their relationship close and friendly. Roose was deeply appreciative:

When I realize, as I do daily, that through *you*, I have opportunities, introductions and a kindly sympathy . . . I feel I cannot do too much for you and yours. And with this feeling of deep gratitude, I accept your cheque, almost with pain! ... Please do not be offended with me for saying again and again that I have no desire nor anticipation of fees from you, and that no amount of work I can do for you will redeem the immense service you have and do render to me by your mention of my name to so many.[6]

A member of the Royal College of Surgeons in England, Robson Roose had studied at Quebec and Edinburgh Universities, had served as physician to the Ottoman Embassy as well as the St. Andrews Home for Boys in Brighton.[7] A prolific writer on medical subjects, he wrote one book entitled *Nerve Prostration* and another on *The Waste and Repair in Modern Life*. In the latter work, Roose noted the different capacities of individual men for hard mental work.

Previous training, constitution and temperament are potent factors in determining the amount which each is capable of doing. Some men can stand an enormous amount of mental strain without any apparent injury; others, from what may be called, for want of a better term, 'weakness of the brain', are incapable of anything requiring mental tension.

The fact, however, remains that not a little of the brainwork of the world is done by men whose standard of health is extremely low; and the weak and ailing condition of body has been proved to be quite compatible with great ability for severe mental exertion. Such cases are, however, the exception.[8]

Lord Randolph at this time had his own concept of the ideal life: 'to lie in bed all day, dozing over a book, to dine in one's dressing gown, and then with all convenient speed to find one's way back to bed again.'[9] But Jennie's persistence kept him from idling.

Returning as Prime Minister with a narrow majority, Gladstone promptly announced that his Liberal government would propose a Home Rule Bill to give Ireland its own Parliament. The House of Commons immediately became a setting of high drama, the chamber so packed that Members of Parliament sat on the steps leading up from the floor, even on the arms of benches and on each other's knees. Side by side in the jammed galleries were the famous of the world, from English bishops to Indian princes. Frank Harris sat between two of Jennie's intimates, the Marquis de Breteuil and Herbert von Bismarck. Harris described Gladstone:

His head was like that of an old eagle—luminous eyes, rapacious beak and bony jaws; his high white collar seemed to cut off his head of a bird of prey from the thin, small figure in conventional, black evening dress. His voice was a high, clear tenor; his gestures rare, but well chosen; his utterance as fluid as water; but now and then he became strangely impressive through some dramatic pause and slower enunciation, which emphasized, so to say, the choice and music of the rhythmic words.[10]

The predominant mood of Parliament was hostile when he started, and Gladstone was tired. He began speaking slowly:

I do not deny that many are against us whom we should have expected to be for us. . . . You have power, you have wealth, you have rank, you have station, you have organization, you have the place of power. What have we? We think that we have the people's heart; we believe and we know we have the promise of the harvest of the future. . . . I believe that there is in the breast of many a man who means to vote against us tonight a profound misgiving, approaching even to a deep conviction, that the end will be as we foresee, and not as you—that the ebbing tide is with you, and the flowing tide is with us. Ireland stands at your bar, expectant, hopeful, almost suppliant. . . . She asks a blessed oblivion of the past, and in that oblivion our interest is even deeper than hers. . . . She asks also a boon for the future; and that boon for the future, unless we are much mistaken, will be a boon to us in respect of honour no less than a boon to her in respect of happiness, prosperity and peace. . . .'

The theme was one he would return to again and again: 'It is liberty alone which fits men for liberty.'[11]

The House cheered for five minutes. Bismarck told Harris it was the greatest speech he had ever heard.

The Home Rule Bill split Gladstone's Liberal Party. Churchill saw it as the political opportunity of his lifetime. 'Let him defeat us [the Conservatives] with the aid of the Parnellites, and then let us dissolve and go to the country with the cry of, "The Empire is in danger!"' Randolph even queried Frank Harris for more details on Parnell's affair with Mrs O'Shea—for possible use as political ammunition. His friendly association with Parnell was automatically dissolved in the expediencies of politics. Ambition was the key and the Prime Ministership was the prize.

Randolph admired Gladstone personally and afterward called him 'the wisest, cleverest and most experienced parliamentarian that ever lived'. But now his invective against the Prime Minister was almost savage. He referred to the Home Rule Bill for Ireland as 'a conspiracy against the honour of Britain . . . startlingly base and nefarious . . . to gratify the ambition of an old man in a hurry. . . .' In his biography of his father, Winston Churchill said of that speech, 'If the address was vulgar, it was also popular.'[12]

'The moment the very name of Ireland is mentioned,' said critic Sidney Smith, 'the English seem to bid adieu to common feeling, common prudence, and common sense, and to act with the barbarity of tyrants and fatuity of idiots.'

Gladstone had gone out on a precarious political limb for the benefit of a people he had hardly seen—he had been to Ireland only once on a short visit. The issue to him, however, was one of practicality as well as principle.

Randolph called the speech 'a piece of premature gush', and to an ally predicted, 'we shall roll the old man over.'

Manchester proved to be the barometer of the country's mood. 'Among the many political meetings I attended with Randolph during those two years,' Jennie recounted,

I think the biggest and most imposing was that held in the Manchester Drill Hall. Eighteen thousand people filled the place to suffocation—no singer that ever lived can command the audience of a popular politician. If the building had held 40,000 or 50,000, it would still have been crowded. Most of the people had been standing two hours before we arrived. Manchester gave Randolph a magnificent reception; thousands lined the streets and covered the roofs of the houses as we slowly drove through the town in a carriage drawn by four horses. Over 200,000 people were said to have turned out that day. I felt very proud. Randolph's speech lasted for over two hours. The heat was great and on leaving the building the crowd pressed round the carriage to such an extent that two men were killed.

Because Manchester was a traditional Liberal stronghold, Jennie opened a new Primrose Habitation there, and spoke before the large crowd that had met:

When Mr. Gladstone appears in his new role of undertaker, let us hope, with the exception of a few hypocritical mourners, he may be left to bury his doomed Bill alone. When that melancholy rite is accomplished, and he appeals to the country, I trust with all my heart that it will answer with one voice in favor of that party which is pledged to support all that is dear to England—religion, law, order, and the unity of the Empire.

Posters advertising the meeting had billed Arthur Balfour as the star speaker. Newspaper reports, however, treated the meeting differently. One gave a glowing account of Jennie's speech, adding the postscript, 'Lady Randolph was ably supported by Lord Salisbury's nephew, Mr Balfour, M.P.' That was a considerable compliment for her, since John Buchan later called the future Prime Minister 'the best talker I have ever known'.[13]

177

Commenting on the speech, a reporter noted the strong resemblance in style and tone between Jennie's public addresses and Randolph's.[14] London society wondered again whether Jennie wrote Randolph's speeches, just as she ran his campaigns. They also wondered about Randolph's remarkable reversal on the Irish issue, and whether Jennie had played any part in that.

It was true, as later events proved, that Jennie had the greater talent as a writer and editor, and it is quite possible that she helped him with his speeches more than other people knew. But if she did pressure him on the issue of Ireland, ambition would have been her motive. If her husband could ever become Prime Minister, as she felt he could, she knew that it must be soon. Immersed in politics as deeply as she now was, it was obvious to her that the Home Rule issue stirred so much public sentiment in England that it could quickly kill the Gladstone government.

Of course Randolph was subject to many other pressures concerning this issue, and he had his own ambition, his own timetable. But it does not seem unreasonable to assume that if he trusted his wife enough to let her run his campaigns, he would also seek out her judgment on political questions. If that was so, who and what most influenced Jennie?

First was Balfour. A tall, elegant figure of a man, Arthur Balfour had all the silken, deprecatory manners of the Court. He was not a man to carry bold standards. Detached and philosophical, he was highly impersonal in his dealings with most people. Ramsay MacDonald later said of him, 'He saw a great deal of life from afar,' and Winston Churchill remarked, 'Arthur Balfour did not mingle in the hurley-burley. He glided upon its surface.' Jennie admired Balfour's intellect, his political philosophy, his considerable charm for people he liked. Margot Asquith had called him 'irresistible' and Lady Battersea had said, 'What a gulf between him and most men!' Balfour's admiration for Jennie was probably more platonic than romantic. (He reputedly had concentrated his emotional fire on Gladstone's niece, May Lyttleton, some years before, and was said to have 'exhausted his powers in that direction'. Closer friends claimed it was not so much that Balfour was cold to women as that he was warm to his freedom.) In any event, Jennie respected Balfour's judgment highly, and Balfour was the policy pipeline from his uncle Lord Salisbury. Salisbury realized, better than most, that the Irish issue was the pivot that could return him as Prime Minister.

In addition to Balfour, Jennie was friendly with many respected politicians who were in revolt against Gladstone on the issue. Among them was Joseph Chamberlain, who some said was tired of waiting for Gladstone's retirement and felt he could rise faster with the newly formed Liberal-Unionists, a faction split from the Liberal Party. Salisbury, always suspecting Chamberlain's convictions, once told a friend, 'Mr Gladstone was hated but he was very much loved. Does anyone love Mr Chamberlain?' Chamberlain thought cool and hit hard, and he and Jennie each admired the other's strength. Jennie's energy made such an impression on Chamberlain that he ultimately went to America to seek a wife.

Then there was the aristocratic Lord Hartington, dedicated to government service rather than ambition. 'How can we have a more honest guide?' Balfour had said of him. Hartington's split with Gladstone on Home Rule caused an explosive political reaction. Moreover, Jennie not only respected Lord Hartington but was a good friend of his wife, who provided the drive for her own husband.

Jennie's affection for Ireland and the Irish people was fervent, but her commitment to Britain and Empire and to her husband's political future was more so. Conducting Randolph's campaign for re-election in South Paddington, Jennie now operated with the panache of a professional. As one critic noted, the 'American wife flashed hither and thither—not a butterfly, but a comet, influencing the orbits of even the greater planets.'[15] It went so well that Randolph contented himself with sending a written manifesto to his electorate, and they swept him into office by a majority of better than three to one.

Winston wrote his mother a congratulatory note, 'I'm very glad Papa got in for South Paddington by so great a majority. I think that was a victory.' He also wanted her professional opinion on whether the Conservatives would win the General Election scheduled to take place within a couple of weeks. And he added, 'I should like you to come and see me very much.'

But Jennie still had no time. As a leading official of the Primrose League, she had a major role to play in the national election, and she plunged into it. Not Randolph.[16] He was on a fishing trip in Norway with Tom Trafford, and money seemed much more on his mind than election results. 'It seems to me,' he wrote Jennie, 'we want the £5,000 a year badly. But really we must retrench. I cannot understand how we got through so much money.' (A letter from his bank some months earlier confirmed a six months loan for a thousand pounds, based on a note he and Jennie had signed. His secretary that month also noted the payment of some racing bets, including £25 to Count Kinsky.)

Parliament was dissolved on June 27, 1886, after only four months of Gladstone's stewardship. The general election in July brought back the Conservatives, now united with the Unionist faction.

Randolph had predicted both the cause and shape of the victory, and the public question was what would be his prize? Gladstone's comment was a bitter one: 'If I were in a dying condition, I confess I should have one great apprehension in my mind—what I conceive to be the great danger to my country. . . . It is the men of the future —personalities of the stamp of Randolph Churchill.' Queen Victoria expressed similar concern. 'Lord Salisbury came to me again at four,' the Queen's Journal reads for July 25th, 'and we talked about everything. He feared Lord Randolph Churchill must be Chancellor of the Exchequer and Leader, which I did not like. He is so mad and odd,[17] and also in bad health. . . .'

Randolph was given both appointments. Lady Jeune described the Dowager Duchess's reaction:

I shall never forget the bright ecstasy and joy with which she welcomed his being made Leader of the House of Commons. I . . . shall always remember the passionate delight with which she spoke it. He had reached the height of his ambition, and she was content.[18]

Randolph felt otherwise. Asked by a friend, 'How long will your leadership last?' Randolph smiled and said, 'Six months.'

'And after that?' asked the friend.

'Westminster Abbey,' answered Randolph.[19] He was then thirty-seven years old.

'So Lord Randolph has secured the object of his ambition,' a friend wrote to Curzon, who had been elected to Parliament in the Conservative sweep. 'I hope he will use his great position wisely. I must confess to being a wee bit anxious as to how he will lead. A leader requires angelic temper—this, I fear, Lord Randolph has not.'[20] More than ever, Randolph was sensitive, impulsive, moody, impatient, petulant. Much later, Jennie wrote:

Personality exercises a vast influence, and it is not the prerogative of great people. Without it, it is true, the front rank can never be reached, but, on the other hand, its complete fulfillment is only possible where it combines with the power to achieve.[21]

Randolph's health flagged. If he still had the skills for leadership, he often no longer had the will. Of the duties of Members of Parliament then, Dr Roose wrote:

Work begins in the committee-rooms at noon; the House assembles at four, and the sittings are often prolonged till midnight. Before the adoption of the 12-o'Clock Rule, readers of the debates became quite familiar with the announcement, 'The House was still sitting when we went to the press!'
. . . Besides his duties at Westminster, he must attend to his constituents, show himself among them from time to time, and must be ever-ready to listen to complaints, suggestions or even dictates . . . a Cabinet Minister . . . begins the day by making himself acquainted with the contents of the daily papers, and perhaps by giving a few minutes to his private correspondence. The study of official papers . . . will occupy him till eleven o'clock, the ordinary time of attendance at his office, where he remains until the meetings of the House to which he belongs. . . . In addition to official work, not a few hours are required for preparing parliamentary speeches and extra parliamentary discussions of various kinds. . . . If in charge of any important measure in Parliament, he must be present during any debates on it, and often make speeches in its support. Replies to questions have to be carefully prepared. . . . Attendance is at Cabinet councils and meetings of the Privy Council, at state balls and concerts, at dinners and meetings of every conceivable kind, . . . and if to these items be added the multifarious duties of a private character, which almost necessarily devolve upon him, it will be readily admitted that the work of a Cabinet Minister at the present day is such as to tax to the utmost even the highest degrees of mental and physical vigour. The diversified character of his work would appear to be its redeeming feature.

Many a man enters upon parliamentary life under the idea that he has an important mission to fulfil; but session after session passes, and he finds himself no nearer to the goal. Meanwhile, he has had to listen, night after night, to an incessant flow of talk, the larger portion of which is unattended by any practical result. . . . There are, at times, other reasons for disappointment and disgust. Speeches made and votes given for party purposes, in support of measures believed to be mischievous, must, in some cases at least, be productive of no ordinary amount of self-contempt. A certain amount of anxiety—the sensation which Dr. Hughlings Jackson has happily described as 'fright spread out thin,' is of course unavoidable. . . . Many a man might ask himself whether the game he is playing is really worth the candle, and whether less bustle and hurry, or even one of the quieter walks of life would not, after all, be much more conducive to happiness than the constant whirl of excitement and anxiety. Mr. Greg remarked, 'A life without leisure and without pause—a life of haste and excitement—a life so full that we have no time to reflect where we have been and where we intend to go, what we have done and what we plan to do, can scarcely be deemed an adequate or worthy life.'[22]

When his mood was good, Randolph still demonstrated a contagious gaiety and exercised a facile, audacious control of conversation. Except from his close friends, however, he resented any attempts at familiarity. While he usually maintained an Old World courtesy and manner, his rudeness increased—more against his seniors than his juniors. He could be so abusive that Jennie once made him apologize to a hostess whose food and drink he had criticized excessively. If he disliked a person at a dinner, he was apt to take his knife and fork and move to another place at the table. A few timorous hostesses even sent him their guest lists for his approval because they wanted to suffer no scene.[23] High society, however, loved social 'lions', and Randolph Churchill was a prize lion. His rudeness was part of the price a hostess paid, for the quintessence of a successful dinner was the quality of conversation. Conversation did not mean chatter or flippancy, and there was seldom anything casual about it. Conversation meant pertinent politics interlaced with wit and the subjects that moved the world.

Of course, cuisine of the highest quality was requisite. The Churchills knew many people who had worked their way into society through the accomplishments of a gifted chef.

Rosa Ovenden, the Churchills' cook, had been a pretty kitchen maid for the cigar-smoking Comtesse de Paris before being hired by Jennie as an occasional cook, to fill in for the busy chef. Rosa soon ruled the kitchen with a choice set of Cockney expletives which quickly circulated among the Churchills' friends. Still, Rosa was a perfectionist in her own way, as was Jennie. 'Lady Randolph Churchill only wanted a few things, but those things she wanted the most perfect, and perfect things to eat,' Rosa explained. 'She was one of the most perfect women herself that I have ever met. She always put all her money in a few things.'

Jennie regularly checked the menus with Rosa before a party. Mrs Hofa-Williams, for example, could not eat lobster patties because 'it always brings her out in spots'. As for Randolph, Rosa wrote that he 'would rather eat a perfect dish of his favourite *oeufs brouillés aux truffes* than have a seat in the Cabinet'. A favourite dish of the Prince of Wales, who had become portly enough to be known as 'Prince Tum-Tum', was plain broiled truffles 'served like little ebony apples on a silver dish wrapped around with a white linen napkin'.[24]

The Prince also liked Rosa. In the course of time, he gave her many little gifts of brooches and bracelets in appreciation of her affections. Years later, Rosa even maintained a suite of rooms for the Prince in the Cavendish Hotel, which she then owned. In the course of time, too, Rosa became the model for characters in several novels, including one by Evelyn Waugh, who always remembered her commanding him, 'Take your arse out of my chair.'

Rosa remembered the Churchills' Connaught House as 'a social merry-go-round' but their marriage as 'not a very happy one'. It pained her to see her mistress 'treated badly by Lord Randolph', and she was shocked to see Randolph 'running up such huge gambling debts'. Rosebery once quoted Randolph as saying, 'I have a great horror of gambling in any form.' But the gossip columns often reported Randolph as participating in baccarat games, either with the Prince of Wales or 'a group of gilded youths'. And no one better enjoyed betting on horses. Rosa summed up the Churchills by saying that 'although he was a very clever man, he would never have been half the man he was if it had not been for her'.

Rosa's earliest memory of Winston was the time he came home for a short vacation and wandered into her busy kitchen, surprised to find so many people at work. He asked her whether the Prince was coming for lunch, and she chased out the little red-haired boy, saying, 'What the devil are you messing about here for? Hop it, copper-nob.'[25]

Winston was a lonely boy then, with few friends. His brother Jack was six years old, too young for Winston to play with more than occasionally (though Jack once told a guest that his brother was teaching him to be naughty). Leonie noticed that Winston roamed about the house with a kind of aimlessness and wrote her father that the boy 'flitted in the background'.

His health better now, Winston reassuringly wrote his mother from the Brighton school, 'We had gymnastic examination on Monday, and I find, in addition to gaining back my strength, I have gained more than I possessed before. . . . It is superfluous to add that I am happy. . . .' Other news included his learning *Paradise Lost* for elocution, his having had a lecture on astronomy, the fact that he could now swim the length of the pool—some sixty feet, that he wanted to learn to play the violoncello instead of the piano, that he planned to have 'some fine barricades' with Jack the next time home, and that 'I am very sorry to say that I am bankrupt, and a little cash would be welcome'.

His mother had criticized the slangy language in some of his letters, and he answered, 'I intend to correspond in the best language which my small vocabulary can muster.'[26]

Winston later wrote of more formidable problems he had begun encountering that year of 1886.

I had scarcely passed my 12th birthday when I entered the inhospitable regions of examinations, through which, for the next seven years, I was destined to journey. These examinations were a great trial to me. The subjects which were dearest to the examiners, were almost invariably those I fancied least. I would have liked to have been examined in History, Poetry, and writing essays. The examiners, on the other hand, were partial to Latin and Mathematics. And their will prevailed. Moreover, the questions which they asked on both these subjects were almost invariably those to which I was unable to suggest the satisfactory answer. I should have liked to be asked to say what I knew. They always tried to ask what I did not know. When I would willingly have displayed my knowledge, they sought to expose my ignorance. This sort of treatment had only one result: I did not do well in examinations.[27]

Winston continued his pleading for affection and attention. In one letter, he begged his mother to give up a dinner party at her home and come to Brighton School to see an 'English play, French play, Latin and Greek, Recitations, Supper, Dancing. Commencing 4:30 P.M., ending 12:00 P.M.' He particularly wanted her to see him act in one of the plays at which he was 'working hard', and also asked if she would possibly play the piano, in which case the teacher promised to double the admission prices. Or, at least, he said, she could distribute the prizes. 'It would give me tremendous pleasure, do come, please.' Then he made a final appeal: 'Now you know I was always your darling, and you can't find it in your heart to give me a denial. . . .' The dinner, however, was important and she could not cancel it.[28]

Winston wrote a note to his father, too, tinged with sadness and bitterness: 'You never came to see me on Sunday when you were in Brighton.'

But the son's problems seemed of less consequence than his father's. At first flush, Randolph appeared firmly entrenched politically. *The Times*, in fact, editorialized that it could 'not think there is much chance of turning out Randolph for a long time to come'. And Queen Victoria, who had been so reluctant to accept him as a Cabinet member, wrote him a note of thanks:

Now that the session is just over, the Queen wishes to write and thank Lord Randolph Churchill for his regular and full and interesting reports of the debates in the House of Commons, which must have been most trying.

Lord Randolph has shown much skill and judgment in his leadership during this exceptional session of Parliament.[29]

But the Exchequer was a post of intricate difficulty for Randolph. He was unable to cope with all the statistics. Commenting on the columns of decimals he had to struggle with, he once said, 'I could never make out what those damned dots meant.' Holding that same Cabinet position, Winston Churchill would one day have similar trouble.[30]

Randolph often quarrelled with his fellow Cabinet members on budget economies, and found himself increasingly alone in his opinions. He outlined some of his new financial proposals to George Smalley, the New York *Tribune* correspondent in England. 'You break with all tradition,' said Smalley, himself a great Bohemian and individualist. 'What do you suppose I am here for?' Randolph answered. 'Have you ever known me to adopt an opinion because somebody else had adopted it?'[31]

He further isolated himself from his colleagues with ever more critical speeches, even against some of his friends. To one of his closest friends, Lord Rosebery, who had given him an icy stare after an irritating remark, Randolph roared out in the House of Commons, 'Don't think you are going to terrify me with that poached-egg eye of yours.' (The simile, however, was apt. Rosebery, who later became Prime Minister, had the classic poker face, a remarkable control that enabled him to maintain a bored, blank look to great effect). Lord Rosebery thought Randolph was broaching disaster, and privately predicted that 'Randolph will be out of the Cabinet or smashed up before Christmas'.

Even his most loyal adherent, Louis Jennings, a Conservative member of the House from Stockport, often found it impossible to follow the sudden zigzags of Randolph's tactics. Jennings, who had been an editor of both *The New York Times* and *The Times of India*, was the man Randolph later named in his will as the co-executor of his private papers. It was Jennings who had edited a book of Randolph's speeches and to whom Randolph had confided the full story of how he had contracted syphilis. But not even Jennings could persuade him to guard his political power and wait for a more propitious time to move.

With his continued arrogance and belligerence, Churchill soon painted himself into a political corner. 'No man is so entirely alone and solitary as I am,' he told Thomas Escott.[32] Curzon, himself a snob, said of Lord Randolph then, 'I used to know him well, and to be on familiar terms with him. But since he became a swell, he will scarcely look at his subordinates, and the barest civility is all that one can expect.'[33]

Not only did Randolph constantly quarrel with his political colleagues, but he openly and strongly disagreed with his Party boss, Prime Minister Salisbury, on most foreign policy issues. Salisbury wanted to ally England with France against Russia, and Churchill loudly urged an alliance with Germany. In a revealing letter, Salisbury described his difficulty in 'leading an orchestra in which the first fiddle plays one tune, and everybody else, including myself, wishes to play another.'

Arthur Balfour, who still played the part of Randolph's friend, wrote his uncle:

My idea is that at present we ought to do *nothing* but let Randolph hammer away. . . . I am inclined that we should avoid, as far as possible, all 'rows' until R. puts himself entirely and flagrantly in the wrong by some act of Party disloyalty which everybody can understand and nobody can deny. . . .

The conflict with Salisbury was heightened in that autumn of 1886. Randolph went abroad with Tom Trafford and received enormous publicity on the continent. 'I am hopelessly discovered,' he wrote Jennie. 'At the station yesterday I found a whole army of reporters at whom I scowled in my most effective manner. Really it is almost intolerable that one cannot travel about without this publicity.'

He soon was forced to realize the division within the Party was heavily weighted against him—he, almost alone, poised on one side, the full strength of the Salisbury Government on the other. 'I can't go on at this rate,' he wrote W. H. Smith, the War Minister.

186

'Whether on foreign policy or home policy or expenditure, I have no influence at all. The Government are proceeding headlong to a smash and I could be connected with it. . . .' Insisting on certain economies in the War Office Randolph added, '. . . nothing will induce me to give way on this matter and if I cannot get my way, I shall go.' Analysing his father's position, Winston Churchill would write, 'It is no doubt that he rated his own power and subsequent responsibility too high.'

Salisbury made it plain that he sided with Smith and told the Queen, 'We are not a happy family.' The Queen answered that Churchill 'must not be given way to'.

During the growing tempest, Jennie was outside her husband's confidence. He had drawn everything more and more into himself, everything into his weakened brain with its fitful fevers and delusions, into his enervated body, into his depressed and irresolute personality. As love is akin to hate, Jennie had said, so perhaps is success akin to failure. She and Randolph were never more far apart.

'How often in matrimonial difficulties,' Jennie later wrote, 'the more culpable of the two is given all the sympathy. . . .' In this case, the rumour-mongers noted Lady Randolph and her assorted escorts and gave Lord Randolph the sympathy.

With the increased political pressures, the chaos in Randolph's mind finally had shaped a decision. One afternoon he stopped off at Connaught Place for his bag, as the Queen had invited him to spend the night at Windsor Castle. En route to the station, he saw his fellow Cabinet member Lord George Hamilton, who was also going to Windsor. Randolph invited Hamilton to share a train compartment. Hamilton later remembered that Randolph had an almost spectral air about him, his mood artificially gay, almost cheerful.

'I am going to resign,' Churchill said.

'What are you going to resign about?' asked the thunderstruck Hamilton.

'Smith's and your estimates.'

'But we have practically settled everything.'

'No,' said Churchill. 'I cannot go on any longer.'

He wrote his letter of resignation to Salisbury at Windsor Castle and even read it aloud to Hamilton. In it he detailed some controversial budget items for the Admiralty and War Office and added:

I know that on this subject I cannot look for any sympathy or effective support from you. I am certain I shall find non-supporters in the Cabinet. I do not want to be wrangling and quarrelling in the Cabinet; and therefore must request to be allowed to give up my office and retire from the Government. . . .

Lord Randolph had his audience with Queen Victoria after dinner, telling her nothing of his intentions. She noted that he was 'gloomy' and 'tired'.

At a luncheon in town the next day, Randolph was in fine form. Afterward, he confided to Wolff what he had done, but to nobody else. Randolph already had received word from Smith that Salisbury would accept his resignation were it offered. He soon received a letter from Salisbury himself, saying, 'In presence of your very strong and decisive language I can only again express my profound regret.' There was no hint of a further meeting to discuss the situation.[34]

Jennie was later to write:

. . . So little did I realize the grave step Randolph was contemplating, that I was at that moment occupied with the details of a reception we were going to give at the Foreign Office which was to be lent to us for the occasion. Already the cards had been printed. The night before his resignation, we went to a play with Sir Henry Wolff. Questioning Randolph as to the list of guests for the party, I remember being puzzled at his saying: 'Oh! I shouldn't worry about it if I were you; it probably will never take place.' I could get none of his meaning and shortly after the first act he left us, ostensibly to go to the club, but in reality to go to *The Times* office and give them the letter he had written at Windsor Castle three nights before. In it he resigned all he had worked for for years, and, if he had but known it, signed his political death warrant.[35]

Appropriately enough, the play at the Strand Theatre was *The School for Scandal*.

There are two versions of Randolph's interview with G. E. Buckle, the editor of *The Times*: one insists that Buckle tried to persuade him not to send the letter and that Randolph replied, 'It is gone.' The other version claims that Randolph tried to persuade Buckle to support him in a leading editorial and that Buckle refused. 'There is not another paper in England that would not show some gratitude for such a piece of news,' Randolph is alleged to have said, with Buckle answering, 'You cannot bribe *The Times*.'[36]

Randolph's letter of resignation was delivered by messenger to Salisbury at Hatfield, where the Prime Minister was host at a ball.

Among his guests were Randolph's mother and sister. The letter arrived at 1:30 A.M. in a red despatch box. Salisbury read it without altering his composure, then resumed his conversation with the Duchess of Teck. Later he simply went to bed without telling anyone of the letter. The Dowager Duchess of Marlborough spent the night with the Salisburys.

Early the following morning, Salisbury was awakened early by his wife and reminded that he had to see the Duchess off. 'Send for *The Times* first,' was his sleepy response. 'Randolph resigned in the middle of the night, and if I know my man, it will be in *The Times* this morning.'[37] Lady Charles Beresford described the morning scene at Hatfield to Lady Leslie:

Can you picture to yourself the bomb that exploded.... Fanny [the Dowager Duchess of Marlborough]... wept large tears of fury and mortification... and was conveyed to London speechless.... I travelled up by later train with the Premier, who seems as much astonished as anyone, and declares he cannot account for it. Liver or madness? Charles said it must be a woman!! (Of course.)

'Liver or madness?' answered Lady Leslie. 'Let us hope the latter, and that he will be shut up before he can do further mischief. It is a cruel blow just before Christmastime.'

'When I came down to breakfast,' wrote Jennie,

the fatal paper in my hand, I found him calm and smiling. 'Quite a surprise for you,' he said. He went into no explanation, and I felt too utterly crushed and miserable to ask for any, or even to remonstrate. Mr. Moore [the Permanent Under Secretary at the Treasury], who was devoted to Randolph, rushed in, pale and anxious, and with a faltering voice said to me, 'He has thrown himself from the top of the ladder, and will never reach it again!' Alas! he proved too true a prophet.

Jennie's reaction was one of horrified shock, almost as if a loved one had suddenly died. What had died was her dream of someday being the wife of the Prime Minister of Great Britain and providing the support he needed to rule an Empire. She would then have been one of the most important women in the world. And how hard she had worked for it, how much she had endured. Now, in a single stroke, it was made futile. Not only had he never discussed his decision with her, but he had planned it as a brutal surprise.

The general response to Churchill's resignation was steeped in bitterness and outrage. Wrote *The Times* leader:

Lord Randolph Churchill declared not long ago that the whole basis of the government to which he belonged was to maintain the union of the party. . . . We may well ask what has become of that conviction concerning the paramount duty of unity, when he himself drives a wedge into the very centre of the party at the most critical moment of its existence. . . .[38]

The Vienna *Tagblatt* was more scornful:

Lord Salisbury's patronage did a great deal for Lord Randolph Churchill, who, if he stood alone, would have small weight. Lord Randolph has played the frog, blowing himself out to look like the bull. It may surprise him, however, when he joins the Radical Party, to find that he is received simply as a frog, and not as a bull. . . . He has not the stuff of a leader in him. . . .

Queen Victoria was incensed. Writing to a friend on Christmas Eve, she said:

The resignation of Lord Randolph Churchill has placed Lord Salisbury in considerable difficulty; and its abruptness and, I am bound to add, the want of respect shown to me and to his colleagues have added to the bad effect which it has produced. Lord Randolph dined at my table on Monday evening and talked to me about the Session about to commence, and about the *procedure*, offering to *send me* the proposed rules for me to see! And that *very night at the castle*, he wrote to Lord Salisbury, resigning his office! It is unprecedented![39]

Assessing his father's action years later, Winston Churchill wrote that Randolph undoubtedly 'had chosen bad ground at the worst time', that he had acted with 'the highest imprudence'.

If he had put away for a season his pledges and his pride, both might have been recovered with interest later on. As it was, he delivered himself unarmed, unattended, fettered even, to his enemies; and therefrom ensued not only his own political ruin, but grave injuries to the causes he sustained.[40]

Reginald Brett visited Randolph at Connaught Place the day after the public announcement in *The Times*. He found Randolph sprawled on the sofa in his library looking 'completely prostrated'. Randolph told Brett he had been 'shunned like a pest' and visited by almost nobody, 'not even those who owe everything to me.' Brett noted that Randolph not only looked drawn and ill, but also seemed doubtful that he had done the right thing.

More courteous than candid, Salisbury wrote to the Dowager Duchess of Marlborough, who had made a personal and passionate appeal to him.

Do not think I gave up the hope of converting Randolph to views in which his colleagues could go with him at once. I had a very long correspondence with him as you recommended, before he wrote those final letters, and I did all in my power to persuade him. I am afraid that he was, as you say, suspicious that my sentiments toward him were changed, that made him assume so inflexible an attitude. He is very amiable, very fascinating, very agreeable to work with, as long as his mind is not poisoned by any suspicion, but men inferior to himself are able to invest suspicions which seem to madden him. Nothing has happened seriously to injure or damage a career of which you are so justly proud, or to deprive the country of the value of his services in the future.

But to a friend inquiring of Randolph's possible return to the Cabinet, Salisbury said, 'Did you ever know of a man, having got rid of a boil on the back of his neck, wants another?'

In a desperate attempt to search for a way to alter the situation, Jennie soon afterward attended a dinner and dance, just to see Salisbury and talk with him about it. 'But he was very nervous,' Jennie wrote Leonie in Ireland, 'and I had the greatest difficulty to get him to speak of Randolph. I rather had the impression that they could never come together again.' And then she sadly added, 'Snippy, I feel very sick at heart.'

At the age of thirty-seven, Randolph Spencer-Churchill had killed himself politically with one brief letter. The Salisbury Government shook for eleven days, but did not crack. G. J. Goschen, a frequent house guest of the Churchills, an old admirer of Jennies, and a strong critic of Randolphs, was asked to take the position at Exchequer. 'I forgot Goschen,' Randolph told Lady Jeune.[41]

On January 14, 1887, several weeks after Randolph's resignation, Jennie received a letter from Arthur Brisbane, London correspondent of the New York *Sun*, who later became a prominent editor:

My Lady,
An article furnished me this week for enclosure in my Saturday cable to the New York *Sun* deals with the details of a separation which the writer alleges to be pending between yourself and Lord Randolph.

Unwilling to publish so grave a statement without having first made every effort to verify its exactness, I called twice, hoping to see either Lord Randolph or yourself, in order to be guided in correcting or entirely withholding the article in question, by what you might wish to say. If you will make an appointment for me before noon tomorrow, when my dispatch is sent, I shall be pleased to wait upon yourself or Lord Randolph. I endeavored to see your father, Mr. Jerome whom I have met, but could not learn whether he had gone from the Langharn. I may add that a cable received today informs me that rumors are current there of the story, of which the article sent to me purports to be a confirmation.

Believe me, my lady, very truly yours.

Jennie passed the letter on to Randolph, who promptly wrote a blistering reply to Brisbane. Whatever his matrimonial problems, he had no intention of resolving them publicly, particularly at that time. Brisbane answered that he had simply tried 'to save a lady and a compatriot from the uncontradicted publication of scandalous gossip'.

'Scandalous gossip' increased when Randolph decided to go off on holiday to the Mediterranean, again without his wife—this time with Harry Tyrwhitt, 'a most amiable companion.' More rumours of separation or divorce reached public print. The American magazine *Town Topics* ran a leading article, flatly declaring that the real reason Randolph had resigned was his alleged involvement with Lady Brooke, who was suing her husband for divorce, and predicting the affair would cause a more explosive scandal than the Dilke case. All kinds of other ill-founded rumours kept cropping up.[42]

In *Savrola*, Lucille's husband plans to abdicate leadership in his government and she asks herself: 'Can I do nothing, nothing? Have I played my part? Is the best of life over?' And then, with a hot wave of resolve, 'I will do it—but what?'

When a messenger from Parliament came to collect the official robes Randolph had worn as Chancellor of the Exchequer, Jennie refused to surrender them, saying, 'I am saving them for my son'.

# 13

'How dark those days seemed!' Jennie wrote:

In vain I tried to console myself with the thought that happiness does not depend so much on circumstances as on one's inner self. But I have always found in practice that theories are of little comfort. The vicissitudes of life resemble one of those gilded balls seen in a fountain. Thrown up by the force of the water, it flies up and down; now at the top catching the rays of the sun, now cast into the depths, then again shooting up, sometimes so high that it escapes altogether, and falls to the ground.[1]

Randolph saw it quite differently. 'It is certainly very pleasant to get away from the cold and worry of London,' he wrote his wife from Algiers. And from Palermo, 'In any case, I am in no hurry to come home—and, am, too, thankful I went away.' His tour of the Mediterranean lasted two months. It apparently mattered little to him that he had left Jennie behind to face the gaggle of gleeful enemies, the smirks of society, to conduct herself with grace under pressure.

Let us not paint the picture of the sad, mournful wife. Jennie was not that. She had as many friends as her husband had enemies; London society was full of people who would say: hate him, love her. Her friends swarmed around her, her admirers assumed an almost belligerent stand in her defence, her family closed ranks. Soon there were more invitations than ever. She almost became a cause.

'We are sorry Randy is in the muck, less for his own account than for that of the gallant American girl he had the luck to marry,' wrote *Town Topics*. 'She had worked so hard to popularize him and forward his ends. . . .'[2]

Not that she was dependent on any of that—she had her own strength and courage, her own ability to be flauntingly defiant. She reserved her sadness for letters, revealed her sorrow to her sisters. Everyone else knew only the gay, witty, lovely woman. And she never gave up searching for the slimmest rays of political hope.

In his private diaries, Sir Algernon West recounted his meeting Jennie coming away from Devonshire House and the two of them discussing the Gladstone government. He told her he doubted the rumours of Gladstone's immediate retirement, but said it was inevitable 'that a man whose eyes were gradually getting worse . . . could not last . . . very long'.[3] Jennie asked what he thought of the possibility of a dissolution of Parliament. 'I said there would be none, unless unforeseen circumstances, such as a defeat, were to happen.'

Politics were still on Randolph's mind, much as he tried to blot them out in the hot Mediterranean sun. 'When a politician dwells upon the fact that he is thankful to be rid of public cares, and finds serene contentment in private life, it may usually be concluded that he is extremely unhappy,' remarked Winston Churchill years later. Tyrwhitt wrote Jennie that Randolph sat brooding and silent for hours, smoking cigarettes incessantly. 'What a fool Lord S. was to let me go so easily,' Randolph wrote.[4] To Lord Rosebery, who met him in Rome, Randolph confessed, 'There is only one place, that is Prime Minister. I like to be boss. I like to hold the reins.' Churchill's political tragedy was that when he had the strength to be Prime Minister, he did not have the opportunity; when he had the opportunity, he did not have the strength.

After a short time, the Randolph Churchill affair was overshadowed by the accelerating excitement of the Jubilee Years, Victoria's fiftieth anniversary as Queen of Britain and the Empire. 'Everything that year was dubbed "Jubilee",' wrote Jennie,

from knights and babies to hats and coats. 'God Save the Queen' was heard *ad nauseam* until the tune became an obsession. This led to a practical joke at the Castle which caused much amusement. One morning, speaking of the Jubilee craze, I pretended that I had received as an advertisement a 'Jubilee bustle' which would play 'God Save the Queen' when the wearer sat down. This, of course, created much curiosity and laughter. Having promised to put it on, I took my hosts into my confidence. An aide-de-camp was pressed into the service, and armed with a small musical box was made to hide under a particular armchair. While the company was at luncheon I retired to don the so-called 'Jubilee wonder,' and when they were all assembled I marched in solemnly and slowly sat down on the arm-chair where the poor aide-de-camp was hiding his cramped limbs. To the delight and astonishment of everyone the National Anthem was heard gently tinkling forth. Every time I rose it stopped; every time I sat down, it began again. I still laugh when I think of it and of the astonished faces about me.

This musical bustle quickly became a London craze, almost 'a perfect nuisance'.

Winston wanted to come home and share the fun. His Brighton teacher did not want to let him go, because, she said, his parents would be too busy to be with him. More, Buffalo Bill had brought his circus to London, and Winston was desperate to meet this celebrated friend of his Uncle Moreton. 'I shall be very disappointed,' he wrote his mother. 'Disappointed is not the word, I shall be miserable, after you have promised me, and all, I shall never trust your promises again.' He was 'in torment' and had many things 'pleasant and unpleasant' to tell her. 'I must come home, I feel I must. . . . I love you so much dear Mummy and I know you love me too much to disappoint me.' He even enclosed the draft of a letter she should write to his teacher. Then in a final postscript, 'For Heavens' sake Remember!!!'

She let him come. June 21, 1887, was a memorable day. Jennie described it:

London was crowded to its utmost, and people came from all parts of the world to see the pageant and the crowded ceremony in Westminster Abbey. The day was blessed with the proverbial 'Queen's weather.' Rarely had I seen London look so festive—blue sky and bright sunshine, flags everywhere and an excited yet patient crowd filling the thoroughfares and the route of the procession. As the wife of an ex-Cabinet Minister, I was given a good place in the Abbey. The magnificent sight impressed me greatly. Gorgeous uniforms and beautiful dresses were enhanced by the 'dim religious light', pierced here and there by the rays of the summer sun as it streamed through the ancient stained-glass windows. The Queen, representing the glory and continuity of England's history, sat alone in the middle of the great nave, a small, pathetic figure surrounded by that vast assembly, whose gaze was riveted upon her.

Instead of a black bonnet, which she had worn for twenty-six years of mourning, the Queen wore a coronet-shaped bonnet of white lace covered with diamonds, making her look many years younger. Royalty and the leaders of the world were there, from Queen Emma of Hawaii to the Imperial Prince of Japan.

Gentlemen wore cocked hats and black velvet Court attire, admirals wore uniforms of blue, white, and gold, generals came dressed in brilliant scarlet, judges wore their wigs and robes. Sheriffs were there from the counties of Britain, mayors from the main cities and boroughs, representatives from the twelve million square miles of the British Empire. 'I think that for once the English were not taking their pleasure sadly,' said a writer in the *Monthly Packet*.

O

Except the Queen. 'A wave of emotion passed over the crowd,' Jennie wrote, 'as silent tears were seen to be dropping one by one upon the Queen's folded hands.' Victoria later explained her tears to her Journal:

The day is come, and I am alone, though surrounded by many dear children. . . . Fifty years today since I came to the throne! God has mercifully sustained me through many trials and sorrow . . . I sat *alone* (Oh, Without my beloved husband, for whom this would have been such a proud day!)[5]

Winston saw his Queen and Buffalo Bill and was taken with Jennie and the Prince of Wales on the royal yacht, where he met a young man whom he would later know better as King George V. His Uncle John also took him to the circus to see the strong man and 'the boneless wonder'. But Winston was obviously not on his best behaviour that holiday because he later felt impelled to write a note of apology to his mother: 'I hope you will soon forget my bad behaviour while at home, and not make it alter any pleasure in my summer holidays.'

He asked his mother to send him a book by Rider Haggard,[6] his favourite author, and notified her that he liked literature 'tremendously', was getting along in Euclid 'capitally', and enjoyed collecting butterflies 'immensely'. Proudly he informed her, too, that he had learned to dive off the top springboard and was getting along very well in his role as Robin Hood, but ruefully admitted he was still weak in Greek and added how much he would like five shillings 'as I am absolutely bankrupt'. He also asked his mother if he and his friends could join her chapter of the Primrose League. 'I want to belong to yours most tremendously.' A further request was for six autographs from his father and six from his mother. (He apparently did a brisk business in these autographs, as he constantly asked his parents for more of them.)

Jennie and Randolph decided that Winston must have a tutor for the summer to prepare for the entrance examinations to Harrow. When Winston was told of this, he quickly replied that he would be happy to go to Harrow and would tolerate a tutor, but only under one condition, 'Not to do any work.' It was 'against my principles. . . . I have never done work in my holidays and I will not begin now. . . . Even if it is only one hour a day . . . it would hang like a dark shadow over my pleasure. . . .' Then he asked his mother to please visit him, as he had not seen her for three weeks 'and I want to see you very very much'.

Increasingly bored with politics and himself, Randolph again turned his attention to horses. Jennie gladly joined him. Randolph bought horses in partnership with Lord Dunraven, the only member of the Salisbury Government who had resigned when he did. (Rumour alleged that their partnership extended beyond horses and included Jennie, whom Dunraven openly admired and frequently escorted.)

The shining light of their shared stable was a beautiful black mare for which they had paid three hundred guineas. Jennie described her as 'a gallant little thing with a heart bigger than her body'. She had been one of five yearlings up for sale at Doncaster, and one of the reasons Randolph had chosen her was that she was the cheapest of the five. Jennie had been reading a French book by Renan entitled *L'Abbesse de Jouarre* and named the horse after the book. The public, however, nicknamed it 'Abcess of the Jaw'. But the Abbess soon proved a startling moneymaker, winning the Prince of Wales Handicap (£1,000), the Portland Plate (£775), and the coveted Manchester Cup (£2,202). The Churchills, though, did not see the Abbess win her biggest victory, the Oaks at Epsom (£2,600), because Randolph was on another fishing trip and Jennie was away visiting with friends. What made it worse was that they had not bet on the Abbess, and the odds against her were twenty to one.[7]

Usually Randolph sat for hours prior to a race, checking his calculations in Ruff's Guide before making his bet. But once he had a dream about a race in which he saw a number hoisted on the board. Checking his race card the next morning, he saw only one horse with that high a number, bet on it heavily, and won. When word of this dream leaked to the press, Lord Hartington was quoted as saying that Lord Randolph 'had better give up politics and stick to dreaming'.

Of all the courses, Newmarket was the Churchills' favourite. Ascot was more social and stilted, with its elaborate garden parties and its pageantry of fashion. Goodwood, equally picturesque, with a short racing season during July, was even more famous for its deer, pheasants, kennels and tennis courts. Epsom Downs, of course, had the Derby and the Oaks, and the Prince of Wales always made them social events, taking a crowd down on his 'Royal Special' train.

But Newmarket was the home of horses. Here on the Heath more than a thousand racehorses always seemed to be in some stage of training. Here was the home of the Jockey Club. The racing tradition at Newmarket was more than two hundred years old, and there was always more talk of animals than of people. It was not the place for Duchesses to come and do their needlework. In fact, of the racing habitués, there were hardly a dozen women like Jennie, and all of them wore country clothes instead of velvets and feathers.

'We would ride out in the early morning from six to seven to see the horses do their gallops,' wrote Jennie. 'It was a most healthy and invigorating life.' It was a good time for both of them. Away from parties and people, away from the friction of politics and the responsibilities of their position, they shared the peace of a country home, the daily conversation that centred on the horses they loved. Riding was so exhilarating that it buoyed them, perhaps brought them closer together than they had been for a long time. 'Very pleasant and very fresh it was,' Randolph wrote his mother from Newmarket. He also told her that he and Jennie were going to Cowes.

Perhaps they reminisced at Cowes about their first meeting aboard H.M.S. *Ariadne* there and wondered about the guests of honour at the party—now the Czar and Czarina—for they decided to travel together to Russia the coming winter. But the plan probably did not illustrate the cliché of romance born afresh at the site of a first meeting, as they decided to take along with them two more people. It was an odd ménage—almost as if they had chosen a companion for him and one for her: Tom Trafford and the Marquis de Breteuil.

Like most of Jennie's admirers, Henri Charles Joseph le Tonnelie, the Marquis de Breteuil, was a man of great distinction. Six years older than Jennie, dashing, handsome, brilliant, he had been a much decorated captain in the cavalry during the Franco-Prussian War, a prominent member of the Chamber of Deputies,[8] a strong spokesman for the restoration of the monarchy. Son of a family of distinguished French diplomats, one of Breteuil's ancestors had been the French Ambassador to the Imperial Court of the Empress Catherine of Russia. Had the monarchy returned to power in France, Breteuil would have become Foreign Minister. He was a dynamic speaker, extremely popular, and a spectacular horseman.

Marcel Proust later knew Breteuil, as well as Jennie, and modelled

198

the 'Marquis de Bréauté' in *Remembrance of Things Past* after him. Portraying Bréauté wearing 'pearl-grey gloves, his crush hat and white tie', Proust further remarked that the Marquis looked through his monocle with 'an infinitesimal gaze that swarmed with friendly feeling and never ceased to twinkle at the loftiness of ceilings, the delightfulness of parties, the interestingness of programmes and the excellence of refreshments'. But the charming Bréauté was also a 'would-be connoisseur of art who loved to give advice with an air of expert knowledge on things he knew nothing whatever about, recommended marriages which always failed, suggested interior decorations which looked hideous and urged investments which usually slumped.'

Queen Victoria was uneasy about the proposed trip to Russia. She wrote Lord Salisbury, on December 7, 1887, 'Think it of great importance that the Foreign Governments and the country should know that Lord Randolph is going simply on a private journey, in no way charged with any message or mission from the Government, nor is likely to return it. . . .'

Reports of the Queen's concern reached Randolph, who wrote to the Prince of Wales repeating that the trip had no political connotations. The Prince forwarded Churchill's letter to the Queen and also expressed his own opinions:

I know that Lord Randolph's visit has no political object of any kind, as I saw him, the day before he started, at Ashridge. . . . I know he wanted to be out of England till Parliament met, so as to avoid making speeches at meetings, though he entirely supports Lord Salisbury's Government, and I own, I regret that he is not asked to rejoin it, because in spite of his many faults and constant errors of judgment, he is very clever and undoubtedly a power in the country. . . . My impression is that he will be careful, and I expect shortly to hear from him.

The Queen answered:

I cannot, I own, quite understand *your* high opinion of a man who is clever, undoubtedly, but who is devoid of all principle, who holds the most insular and dangerous doctrines on foreign affairs, who is very impulsive, and utterly unreliable. . . .

*Pray don't* correspond with him, for he really is *not* to be trusted and is very indiscreet, and his power and talents are greatly overrated. Sir R. Morier agreed with me as to the danger of his visit to Russia and his total unreliableness. I don't state all this from any personal enmity toward Lord Randolph; but I *must* say what I *know from experience* to be the case. Let the subject drop now.

The Prince, however, asked Princess Alexandra to give Randolph and Jennie a letter of introduction to her sister, the Czarina. Upon their arrival in Russia, that letter opened wide every Imperial door and so swept up the Churchills in the orbit of Russian society that they saw only the glitter of the country and none of its sordidness. Jennie was fascinated with Russia:

Everything was new and attractive to us. The people were charming and hospitable, and seemed full of *bonhomie*, and we saw no signs of that grinding despotism and tyranny which is supposed to be synonomous with Russian life. My first impression of the scenery was one of disappointment, the country between Berlin and St. Petersburg, or rather, the part beyond the Russian frontier, being flat and uninteresting. The waste and dreary expanse, when covered with snow, inspires a feeling of deep melancholy. To live for months every year, buried in that cold, monotonous silence, is quite enough, I should imagine, to account for the vein of sadness which seems to be the basis of the Russian character, and which betrays itself in all Russian music and painting. As our snow-laden train crawled into the station in St. Petersburg, we stepped out joyfully, and stretched our cramped and tired limbs. The broad streets, full of life and animation, and as bright as day with electricity, seemed a delightful contrast. I do not know what I expected to see, but the city disappointed me with its modern appearance. Looking at the houses of rather mean exterior, with their small double windows and tiny doors, little did I dream of the splendor within. Space, however, seemed to be immaterial, and this struck me the more forcibly, accustomed as I was to London, with its narrow streets and considered inches. . . .
I thoroughly enjoyed the outdoor life of sleighing and skating. Comfortably seated in the sleigh, behind the good fat coachman to keep the wind off, I never wearied of driving about. The rapidity with which one dashes noiselessly along is most exhilarating, notwithstanding a biting wind or blinding snow.

She also admired the coachman, with his fur-lined coat gathered in at the waist, his bright red or blue octagonal cap with gold braid, and the way he did the driving with his arms extended forward in order to preserve his circulation.

I was much impressed with the fact that the coachmen hardly ever seemed to use their short, thick whips, which they kept carefully hidden. A footman stands on a small step behind, his tall hat and ordinary greatcoat looking a little incongruous, I confess, and marring an otherwise picturesque sight. The horses are so beautifully broken that a word will stop them. The whole time I was in Russia, I never saw a horse ill-used.

Jennie wrote long descriptive letters about all this to her sisters and her sons. Those letters became the basis of a magazine article which she later wrote about Russia and which afterward she developed as part of a book.

The Randolph Churchills had an audience with the Czar and the Czarina in the Winter Palace at Gatchina, about an hour's train-ride from St Petersburg and approached from the station through a series of small parks. The Czarina took Jennie on a tour of the palace:

Among many rooms, I remember a large hall, worthy of an old English country-house, full of comfortable armchairs and writing tables, games and toys. In that room, their Majesties often dined, I was told, even when they had guests; and after dinner, the table would be removed, and they would spend the remainder of the evening there. This seemed strange to me, when I thought of the many hundred rooms in the enormous building. But their tastes were the simplest, and the Czar particularly affected tiny rooms, though they were much at variance with his towering frame and majestic bearing. His manner impressed me with a conviction of sincerity and earnestness.

In his interview with the Czar, Randolph advised the Czar not to take any notice of the English national press, since 'no public man in England ever cared a rap for anything they said'. Randolph later reported that 'the conversation began in French, which was a great disappointment to me, for he can speak English perfectly; and sometimes he talked rather low and in his beard, so that I, who do not hear very well, missed some of his remarks'. Balfour once had described the Czar as 'an immense, big fellow, with a good-humoured countenance, but not much mind in it'. Randolph, however, found much more mind than he expected.

The Czar told him:

With regard to the Black Sea and the Dardanelles, if you desire peace and friendship with Russia, you must not mix yourselves up there against us. We will never suffer any other power to hold the Dardanelles, except the Turks or ourselves; and if the Turks ultimately go out, it is by Russians that they will be succeeded.

... You have a great task before you on your return to England—to improve the relations between Russia and England.

Randolph reported that to the Prince of Wales, adding, 'I feel certain that they not only do not desire war, but will do much to avoid it.' The Queen heard of the correspondence and complained to her son, saying it was dangerous for him to write to Lord Randolph, much less support him. In that, too, the Prince ignored his mother.

Jennie and Randolph, meanwhile, received disturbing news from the Dowager Duchess. Mrs Everest had contracted diphtheria, and the Duchess had whisked the boys away to Blenheim. 'I hope neither of you worry about the children,' she wrote.

Do not mind if you hear I am strict and discourage going out and keep Winston in order. . . . I only do as if they were my own. I do not like Winston going out. . . . I really think he goes out too much and I do object to late parties for him. He is so excitable. . . . He is a dear boy but wants a firm hand.[9]

Winston's letters were unhappy. 'I feel very dull—worse than school. It is very dull without you. I do so long to kiss you, my darling Mummy. How I do wish I was with you in the land of "pink, green and blue Russe".'

When Winston returned to school, the Duchess wrote Randolph:

I do not feel sorry for he is certainly a handful. Not that he does anything seriously naughty except to use bad language which is bad for Jack. I am sure Harrow will do wonders for him for I fancy he was too clever and too much the boss at that Brighton school. He seems quite well and strong and very happy—Jack is a good little boy and not a bit of trouble. . . .

Before leaving St Petersburg, the Churchills were again invited to Gatchina. They travelled on a special train with about 150 other guests. Entertainment at the palace featured three short plays, each in a different language, after which supper was served. 'I had been given a seat in the third row,' Jennie wrote, 'but when the Royalties came in, I was bidden to sit behind the Empress, who every now and then would turn round and make some pleasant remark.'

A woman with a graceful figure and a small head, the Czarina resembled her sister, Princess Alexandra, 'though not so beautiful.' She asked Jennie 'endless questions about England', and Jennie remembered the Czarina from Cowes as a wholesome, normal girl with a love of laughter.[10] Jennie noted the mass of attendants, some with black, white, and orange feathers in their caps, 'giving a slightly barbaric appearance to the scene'. Outside the Czarina's audience chamber were two Nubians dressed in white, with turbans and scimitars, making the scene even more bizarre.

A New Year's reception was held at eleven in the morning at the Winter Palace and attended by the whole Court. The procession began as the Czar, dressed in the uniform of the Gardes du Corps, gave his arm to the Czarina, who wore a magnificent tiara and a blue velvet and ermine train. The couple were followed by the Imperial Family. Four young officers carried the train of each Grand Duchess. 'I remember that of the young Grand Duchess Vladimir's was of silver brocade, with a sable border, half-a-yard in depth,' Jennie wrote.

These were followed by long files of ladies-in-waiting, dressed in green and gold, and maids-of-honor in red and gold. The procession ended when all the court officials, resplendent in gorgeous uniforms and covered with decorations, walked with measured steps through the long suite of rooms, and lined up on each side with officers in the red, white, or blue of their regiments. To these, the Czar spoke as he passed, saying, 'Good morning, my children,' to which they replied in unison, 'We are happy to salute you.'

Jennie observed that most Russian ladies smoked cigarettes, and one of the reception rooms at a party was always set apart for this purpose, 'which caused a continual movement to and fro — taking off the stiffness of a formal party and enabling people to circulate more freely . . .' She also noted that Russians had enormous appetites, and were very fond of good living, good eating, and hard drinking.

Drinking in Russian society is not considered a heinous offense. The night we went to Gatchina, the officer in charge, the Colonel of the Probejensky Guards, the smartest regiment in Russia, who was responsible that night for the safety of the Czar, was so drunk that he fell heavily on my shoulder when presented to me. Those nearer laughingly propped him up, evidently thinking nothing of it.

She found Moscow more striking than St Petersburg.

Everything was a source of interest, from the narrow streets filled with a motley crowd of fur-clad people, the markets with their frozen fish or blocks of milk, from which slabs would be chopped off, and carcasses or beasts propped up in rows against the stalls, to the Kremlin, with its palaces and churches. . . . We visited the Trichiakoff Picture Gallery, belonging to a retired merchant, where I was amazed to see depicted all the grimmest and most gruesome incidents of Russian tyranny and cruelty: Ivan the Terrible murdering his son, or receiving on a red staircase of the Kremlin, a hapless envoy, whose foot he transfixed to the floor with a spike ferrule of his walking-stick, while he read some unwelcome passage; Siberian prisoners; horrible deeds perpetrated in the Fortress of Peter and Paul; and many other atrocities.[11]

All their visits were fully covered in the *Moscow Gazette*, which paid high compliments to Lord and Lady Randolph. It reported that they visited Prince Dolgoroukoff, Governor-General of Moscow and attended the opera with him, after which the Prince gave a grand dinner in honour of his guests. Dolgoroukoff was a charming old man of 80; a *'Grand Seigneur* of the old school, he looked very smart and upright in the uniform of the Chevalier Gardes. He told me that he had been 22 years Governor of Moscow, and had served 56 in the Army under three Czars.'

The Prince had issued an order requiring all beggars to be off the streets so that the Churchills would not be annoyed by them. And the couple were also followed throughout Moscow by two detectives,

not, as we at first imagined, to spy upon us, but to see that, as distinguished strangers, we were not molested in any way.

Before leaving, we attended the 'Bal de la Noblesse', in the Assembly Room. It was a fine sight, the floor excellent, and the music most en-spiriting. . . . Officers would be brought up to me, clicking their spurs together and saluting; then they would seize my waist without a word, and whisk me around the enormous room at a furious pace, my feet scarcely touching the ground. Before I had recovered, breathless and bewildered, I would be handed over to the next, until I had to stop from sheer exhaustion.

Just before the Churchills' departure, there was a last round of gala parties in their honour, including one at the British Embassy for six hundred people.[12] 'It would bore me dreadfully to go to all these dinners and parties and things,' Lord Randolph wrote to his mother, 'but here it amuses me. I wonder why it is.' The day they left Moscow, the Governor came to see them off, and presented Jennie with a lovely bouquet of orchids. The temperature, however, was twenty-two degrees below zero and the flowers shrivelled before she had time to sit down.

While the men of Russia had impressed her, so had the women:

Not indulging in any sport and taking little or no exercise, they stay a great deal indoors, and in consequence, have much time to educate themselves, to read, and to cultivate the fine arts. Speaking many languages, and reading widely, they form a most attractive society. . . . It was, however, a matter of surprise to me that women so eminently fitted by nature and education to influence and help those struggling in the higher vocations of life, should have seemingly but one ambition, to efface themselves, to attract no attention, to rouse no jealousies. Yet I doubt not that their influence is felt, though it may not be open and fearless, as in England or America.

One woman of influence was the Dowager Duchess of Saxe-

Coburg-Gotha, the only daughter of the previous Czar, Alexander II. She had married the Duke of Edinburgh and had lived in England until his death. As the Czar's daughter, it had been her duty for two hours daily to read her father's correspondence and the secret news of the world. She and Jennie were close friends, and Jennie maintained an extensive correspondence with her throughout the years.

On their way home, the Churchills spent five days in Berlin. It was perhaps not a coincidence that Count Kinsky was there. He had been transferred to the Berlin Embassy in September 1887, after having been recalled to the Foreign Office in Vienna some months earlier. He would become the Secretary of the Berlin Embassy by March 1888 and would again be transferred to London. For Jennie and Kinsky their time in Berlin allowed a brief reunion.

Randolph wrote his mother that upon seeing Otto von Bismarck he had noticed that the 'old Emperor was looking very brisk'. In 1886 Prince Otto von Bismarck had made his son Count Herbert von Bismarck-Schonhausen Secretary of State, putting him in full charge of foreign affairs. Discussing Herbert von Bismarck, Randolph wrote, 'We talked very freely for a long time and drank a great deal of beer, champagne, claret, sherry and brandy! H. B. is delightful, so frank and honest. . . .'

Jennie wrote of a private dinner the Count gave in Berlin for the Churchills: 'I remember that at this dinner he had an argument on the subject of Mr Gladstone, whom he cordially hated.' Herbert quoted his father as saying, 'Gladstone would drag England to the lowest ground of Hell.' In later years, Herbert would change his mind about Gladstone and yet become increasingly anti-British, favouring an alliance instead with Russia. But at that time the Bismarcks were friends of Great Britain.

Herbert von Bismarck was a giant of a man with a long, blond moustache and blue eyes. He and Jennie were quickly attracted to each other, and the attraction grew over the years into a long-lasting affair. It was typical of Jennie that she found herself in Berlin ardently surrounded by three suitors—Bismarck, Breteuil, and Count Kinsky. Bismarck's reputation for women-chasing was as celebrated as Kinsky's and Breteuil's—he had just been involved in a divorce scandal with a popular singer. The jealousy and competition of the three men for Jennie was natural, but what was not natural was

Randolph's obvious friendships with all three men, friendships he maintained throughout his lifetime.[13] It was almost as if there were an unspoken arrangement: Jennie could have her suitors and Randolph had his friends[14]

Jennie and Randolph visited the palaces, galleries, and museums of Berlin. In one of the galleries, they saw three paintings which had been at Blenheim, one of them the famous 'Bacchanalia' by Rubens, which had covered one wall of the dining room.

On the gala performance night at the opera, the Churchills were taken into a small room where the Emperor William stood surrounded by the Royal Family, Court officials, and the Diplomatic Corps.

The Emperor, looking most upright in a smart uniform, welcomed me in a few well-chosen words, also referring to our tea party at Gastein and the jokes we had had with the children. Little did I or anyone else present think that this was to be his last entertainment, and that in a few weeks, the kind and noble old monarch would be no more. Suddenly, a side door opened; the Empress Augusta, sitting in a small bath-chair, was wheeled in. Dressed in pale blue satin, with jewels to her waist, her venerable head crowned with a magnificent tiara, she made a brave, if somewhat pathetic, figure. She asked me many questions in excellent English, addressing me as 'Lady Churchill', and inquiring after the Czarina, whom she understood I had just seen. She also asked so much after her 'dear Queen Victoria', that I came to the conclusion that she was mistaking me for Queen Victoria's lady-in-waiting, Jane, Lady Churchill. Her remarks were almost inaudible; and I had to answer in a very loud voice, as she did not hear well. I do not recollect ever having felt more embarrassed or uncomfortable than during this conversation at cross-purposes, carried on before the whole Court, which was listening in respectful silence.

In a letter to Leonie, Jennie described the Emperor and Empress as

both half alive only and their ancient bodies covered with Orders. The Empress a thin mummy with her whole breast removed from cancer, yet it was covered with jewels, her head tied on! And she jerked out her orders like an automaton, and was then carried off and put to bed! And the Emperor was not allowed to dine.

After leaving Berlin, Randolph and Jennie stopped off in Paris to meet General Boulanger, the French 'man on horseback', who intended to return royalty to power in France. Boulanger impressed Randolph but not Jennie. He was a handsome man with a fierce moustache, immensely popular, particularly with rich French widows, but Jennie sensed that he was 'a man not quite sure of himself'. He later came to dine several times at their home in London, but only confirmed Jennie's original impression. She proved to be right. Boulanger had a single moment in the French plebiscite of 1889 when he could have swept himself into power, but prolonged his hesitation until it was too late. A French critic described him as 'a comet crossing the skies—an empty-headed thing with a fiery tail'.

Upon the Churchills' return to London, Randolph dutifully reported his observations of Russia to Lord Salisbury. A few short years earlier, Salisbury would have been respectful of Lord Randolph's opinion, but now he passed them on to the Queen with the curt comment, 'It seems odd that so clever a man should attach the slightest value to such a promise on the part of Russia.'[1]

Salisbury had moved up his nephew, Arthur Balfour, to fill the vacuum left by Randolph. The appointment was not mere nepotism; Balfour had served as Chief Secretary in Ireland, made a record of clear accomplishment, and revealed a tough core beneath his genteel features. 'The Conservative Party are evidently tired of Lord Randolph,' wrote Henry Lucy in *Punch*, 'and turn with favour to welcome a rising young man, who, they say, at least, has never betrayed them.'

Balfour was also the central sun of an intellectual group called 'The Souls'. The Earl of Ronaldshay, Curzon's official biographer, credits Jennie with inventing the name. British Society had split off into three main streams, and only a handful, like Jennie, swam in all of them. First, there was the Queen's Set, also called the Court Set or The Incorruptibles—old Tory families, the quiet, class-conscious crowd of form and tradition. Then there was the Smart Set, the group that clustered around the Prince of Wales, also known as the Marlborough House Set, the Party Set, or the Horsey Set. And finally there were The Souls. Instead of playing bridge or baccarat, this small, select group preferred to meet regularly to 'talk about each other's souls'.[2]

Lady Warwick, who was more body than soul, described them this way:

This little coterie of Souls loved literature and art and were perhaps more pagan than soulful. They were decidedly ambitious, clever and well-read, and exercised great influence on London society for five or six years. I think they sent us all back to reading more than we otherwise should have done, and this was an excellent thing for us.[3]

The world of the intellectual had increasingly become Jennie's world. Most of the men in her life had intellectual qualities of the first rank. She could talk to them on their own terms, just as she could to jockeys at Newmarket on theirs, and just as she could discuss Society with Lady Nevill or music with Paderewski or clothes with the Countess of Warwick or the theatre with Sir Henry Irving.

She already had created something of a small literary stir with her magazine article about her Russian trip. A British publisher later thought enough of her French and her literary style to contract her to translate a French book into English. But her real literary prominence would come after the turn of the century, when she would be best known as an author, playwright, editor and publisher of *The Anglo-Saxon Review*.

Describing a Souls dinner party at the Bachelors Club, the *World* wrote: 'This highest and most aristocratic cult comprises only the youngest, most beautiful and most exclusive of married women in London. . . .' Asked to sum up these Souls, Sir William Harcourt said, 'All I know about The Souls is that some of them have very beautiful bodies.' The fact was that women Souls were supposed to be different from 'all those people who have lovers', but the main difference was their discretion, not their abstinence.

One of the pastimes of the Souls was for each participant to write a parody at half an hour's notice. Curzon wrote one of Edgar Allan Poe's 'The Bells':

> I sing the attraction of the Belles,
>> London Belles,
>> Society Belles.
> Of the manifold allurement of the Belles.
> Oh what rhapsodies their charm deserves;
> How delicious and delirious are the curves
>> With which their figure swells—
> Voluptuously and voluminously swells—
> To what deed the thought impels.

Curzon had an opinion on everything, and it was always an absolute opinion. Debating with Curzon in Parliament, a Thomas Bowles dissolved the House into laughter when he pointed to Curzon and said, 'That is my difficulty which I am sure you all share. He has been everywhere; he has seen everything; he has read all the books—he has written most of 'em.'[4] Years later, Winston Churchill said of Curzon:

Commons found something lacking in him. It was certainly not information nor application, nor power of speech nor attractiveness of manner and appearance. Everything was in his equipment . . . yet somehow or other the total was incomplete. . . . The House considered him from the earliest day of his membership a lightweight. He aroused both admiration and envy but neither much love nor much hatred.

Oscar Wilde would be even more devastating, calling Curzon a 'plodding mediocrity'. Though he may often have been more hardworking than brilliant, more fluent than witty, Curzon's later record as Viceroy of India was largely a distinguished one. There is small question that he was one of the most popular Souls.

Jennie Churchill could attend a meeting of The Souls—at The Clouds, the home of Sir Percy Wyndham, for example—settle back in a sofa, and count a whole cluster of men there who had courted her, including their leaders, Balfour and Curzon. Among the more interesting men for her was the handsome, six-foot-four future Ambassador to Berlin, Lord D'Abernon.[5] Freshly returned from a visit to the United States, D'Abernon had received red-carpet treatment from a horde of social matrons eager to capture him. His abilities as linguist, horseman, and fencer were celebrated. He had recently served as financial adviser to the Khedive, refused to touch liquor, and abhorred ice.

Soul-member Margot Asquith wrote later of D'Abernon, 'His face was even more conspicuous than his height and the beauty of his countenance can never be forgotten.'

Another of Jennie's conquests, one who lingered longer than most, was Henry John Cockayne Cust, whom his Soul-mates called Harry. Sir Ronald Storrs, his nephew, years later referred to an Eton professor who had taught in succession Rosebery, Curzon, and Cust and who, of the three, had chosen Cust as the future Prime Minister. Cust was not only 'irresistibly fascinating' to women,[6] but in many ways the most brilliant and enthusiastic of all the Souls. A sensitive poet, an athlete, a scholar, a fastidious critic, a handsome man with a flowing moustache, he was also reckless and self-indulgent and the heir to the Brownlow barony.

Cust wrote considerable love poetry, most of it privately published, and each of his women friends felt each poem was privately for her. It was thought that 'To a Portrait', was for Jennie:

> Beautiful Face!
> Is your heart broken that you look so sad?

Is there no heart of earth that once made glad
Your heart, to hearten yet your flower of grace?
Is God untender toward you?
Or can Man,
Loving such dear eyes. Or, save despairing
For too much caring,
Grudge his uncrownedness in the race he ran,
And squandered life and loved, and lost the prize?
They pay the worthiest cost,
Whose lives for you were lost.

And 'Amictus Amoris':

About the perfect body of my love
A Vesture clings, wherefrom no force may free her. . . .

And 'Immortal End':

It matters not what life we spend,
What anguish we inspire,
So there be one immortal end
To one immense desire.

Cust once gave a dinner for some twenty guests, including Balfour and probably Jennie. The talk was so absorbing that when a fire broke out upstairs, both the dinner and the conversation continued. While the firemen were fighting the blaze, the footmen passed out bath towels to the dinner guests to protect them from the water of the hoses.

Little towels could not protect the Souls, however, from the steady stream of criticism. A satire by W. H. Mallock was representative of the kind of attack generally made on them:

You keep talking of faith, of devotion and purity,
Things deep and things high are your favourite themes;
We have dreamed of them, too; but our song, in maturity,
Has sunk to one burden, 'Goodbye to our dreams.'
Oh sons and Oh daughters of art and of culture!
Forget for a moment your play and your parts;
And take pity upon us, for whom time is a vulture,
Which leaves us our livers and feeds on our hearts.

The criticism was well taken. The world of Jennie's Souls was the world of the abstract and the intellectual and had little to do with the livers and hearts of London.[7] Although Jennie moved easily among the varied levels of society, and although she had penetrated to the level of the working people during her political campaigning, her understanding of their living conditions was superficial. Times were changing. Among the English masses there was restlessness as well as fear. The poet and essayist Matthew Arnold feared that England was 'on the verge of anarchy'.[8] When the London dockers asked for an additional sixpence an hour, most employers considered this a 'monstrous wage increase'. Many of Jennie's friends thought that labourers must be kept in their place, for 'the more you give them, the more they will ask'. But the dockers won public sympathy when they paraded the London streets carrying samples of the horrible food their pitiful pay forced them to eat.[9]

This was a time when the poverty line for a family of five was put at £55 a year, and almost 16 million English workers (including postmen and policemen) earned less than £50 a year. Most of the white-collar class (about 3 million) earned an average of £75 a year. Farm workers still used the scythe and the sickle, working from 5 A.M. until dark.

If Jennie knew little of this, Randolph knew less. What they did know was there were 115 persons in England who each owned more than fifty thousand acres, half of these landowners with an annual income of £50,000. Of the forty-five who owned 100,000 acres, half of them had an annual income of £100,000. Of the 30 million people then in Great Britain, there were 2,500 landowners who owned more than 3,000 acres.

Randolph had talked of 'Tory democracy', criticizing the inbred rule of the aristocracy, and Jennie had sympathized with and encouraged his view, but both nonetheless had gravitated toward the powerful rather than the weak. The Reverend Benjamin Jowett had said, 'We must study the arts of uniting Society as a whole, not clinging to any one class of it.' Jennie was still a snob and would remain so the rest of her life, but more and more now she and Randolph chose their friends on the basis of intelligence, talent, accomplishment, charm, but not social class.

Lord Randolph was still a Member of the House of Commons for the safe Paddington seat, but he was a quiet Member, most often absent from the House and from his constituency. Despite the depth of his political dive, however, there were still many who expected him to bounce back to the surface. But Randolph himself seemed disgusted with the interplay of politics and found himself in opposition to the Salisbury government on a growing number of issues. When a friend told him he hoped to live to see Randolph back again in the Cabinet, Randolph answered swiftly, 'I sincerely hope you will not.'

He now limited his horizons. The Prime Ministership was a dead dream, but what about the position of Viceroy of India? He knew India and had many friends there. It would restore glitter to his name, fame to his family, and provide an end to his increasing financial worries. Salisbury heard about Randolph's great expectations and wrote to the Queen:

I understand he [Randolph] has told two of his friends that the post above all others he desires is that of Viceroy of India. Of course it is impossible; his reputation for rashness is too pronounced, but it is odd that he should desire it. It is said that his pecuniary position is very bad.[10]

Salisbury was right about the Churchills' 'pecuniary position'. Their Russian trip had been expensive and they had borrowed from banks to make it possible. Randolph even felt impelled to borrow money from his sister Cornelia's husband.

Whatever the deterioration of his mind and personality and the bleakness of his future, Randolph maintained a sense of the fitness of things. At any time he could have lent his renowned name to the Board of Directors of a number of companies and lived well from them. Many of his friends had done so, but he would have none of it. His dignity and his code and his heritage were immutable.

They thankfully had Jennie's annual income from the rental of the Madison Square house, as well as frequent 'tips' from her father. Of all the Jerome women, Jennie received the most money and love from their father. From the content of his letters, however, it is clear that Jerome did not know of Randolph's fatal disease. He realistically evaluated the futures of two of his sons-in-law—seeing John Leslie's clear road to respectability, Moreton Frewen's cloudy road to despair—but Randolph's road he supposed full of great promise of political achievement. So if he financially coddled Jennie and Randolph whenever he could, if he catered to their needs more than the others', it was not only because of his special relationship with Jennie but also because he regarded the Churchills' future as greater than the others'.

Jerome came to visit them that year, as he often did, and more carefully inspected his grandson Winston, whom Mrs Jerome had described as 'a naughty, sandy-haired little bulldog'. Mrs Jerome preferred Jack, who was much quieter, more polite, more predictable.

Winston was thirteen years old, working hard to prepare himself for the entrance examination to Harrow, scheduled for March 1888. 'You will be pleased to hear,' he wrote his mother, 'that we are learning the geography of the U.S. When I come home, you must question me.'

Miss Charlotte Thomson of the Brighton School, who escorted him to the examinations for Harrow, wrote Jennie afterward that Winston had a 'severe attack of sickness' after the exam, due 'to the nervous excitement'.

In his reminiscences, Winston Churchill remembered that he had not answered a single question on the Latin paper. 'I wrote my name at the top of the page,' he noted.

I wrote down the number of the question, 'I'. After much reflection I put a bracket round it thus, '(I)'. But thereafter I could not think of anything connected with it that was either relevant or true. Incidentally, there arrived from nowhere in particular a blot and several smudges. I gazed for two whole hours at this sad spectacle: and then merciful ushers carried it up to the Headmaster's table. It was from these slender indications of scholarship that Mr. Welldon drew the conclusion that I was worthy to pass into Harrow.[11]

As headmaster, Welldon had considerable latitude in evaluating the candidates. While Winston had blanked out in the Latin exam, his marks in arithmetic had been 'the best'. The thirty-four-year-old Reverend J. E. C. Welldon was new at Harrow, but he was not so new that he was unaware Winston Churchill was the son of one of the most important men in England who still, conceivably, might one day be Prime Minister. Before the examinations, in fact, Welldon had received a letter from one of the Marlboroughs, informing him about Winston's application. Welldon had answered that it would be a pleasure for him to find room at Harrow for the son of Lord Randolph Churchill.

'I have passed,' Winston wrote his mother, 'but it was far harder than I expected.'

Winston Churchill later liked to exaggerate his schoolboy stupidity, perhaps to make his eventual metamorphosis seem all the more astonishing. But his dullness was a fiction. Like most boys, Winston did well in some subjects, poorly in others. Latin and

Greek he had never liked, but at Brighton School he had won prizes in English and in Scripture, and he had always come out high in History. Welldon wrote Jennie that Winston was not 'in any way wilfully troublesome', and 'I do not think he is idle, only his energy is fitful, and when he gets to his work, it is generally too late for him to do it well.' The headmaster described Winston as 'a remarkable boy in many ways . . . as far as ability goes, he ought to be at the top of his form, whereas he is at the bottom'.

Later the headmaster also reported to Jennie that Winston's slovenliness was 'phenomenal', and added, 'if he is unable to conquer this slovenliness . . . he will never make a success of public school.' Furthermore, Winston's

forgetfulness, carelessness, unpunctuality and irregularity in every way have really become so serious, that I write to ask you, when he is at home, to speak very gravely to him on the subject. . . . He is so regular in his irregularity that I really don't know what to do.

Jennie's letters to Winston at Harrow usually accentuated the positive but not always. She knew when to prod and when to approve, just as she understood the need for absolute sternness. She was, after all, not only the mother of her two sons but had to take the role of father as well. Randolph at best was indifferent to them. Winston's letters to his father were usually either pleading or apologetic. 'I have written a very long letter and have taken up a lot of your time,' he once respectfully wrote, adding, 'When do you think you'll be able to come and see me?'

Discussing his father with Frank Harris years later, Winston Churchill said, 'He wouldn't listen to me or consider anything I said. There was no companionship with him possible to me and I tried so hard and so often. He was so self-centred no one else existed for him.' And then he added quietly, 'My mother was everything to me.'[12]

While Jennie did try to help organize Winston's mind and discipline his behaviour, she never tried to stifle his spirit. Lady Warwick noted this during one of Winston's weekends at home: 'True to her American training, she did not check Winston when he asked questions or argued with her.'[13] When he felt that he was being treated unfairly at school, he begged his mother to come to Harrow and argue with Welldon about it. 'You must stick up for me, because if you don't, nobody else will. . . . Now you know

Mama you told me to rely on you and tell you everything so I am taking your advice.'

He had no one else. He loved Mrs Everest deeply, but she was a simple, uneducated woman. As a child, he had been able to confide in her fully, but he could not as a growing young man full of new ideas. Both grandmothers were stiff martinets. He loved his American grandfather, but saw him only seldom. He saw his own father hardly more. His aunts were lovely and interested, but busy with their own broods. His mother was the only one he could always reach. She often kept her own distance and she did not always fall in with his wishes, but he knew how to focus on her guilt feelings, knew how much he could persist. But most of all, he was sure of her love. More than just a mother's love, her devotion was part of another love she was gradually transferring from her husband to her sons.

Jennie did go to Harrow to defend her son against the headmaster's severity, but she still maintained a severity of her own with him. When she considered his letters too slangy, she tried to stir in him a greater readiness of expression, a greater concern for language. When his reports were poor, it was she who wrote the letter that his father should have written: 'You know darling how I hate to find fault with you, but I can't help myself this time.' His report was 'a *very* bad one'. His work was fitful and 'inharmonious'. If only he were a little more methodical, she said, she would *try* to find an excuse for him.

You make me very unhappy. I had built up such hopes about you and felt so proud of you—and now all is gone. My only consolation is that your conduct is good, and that you are an affectionate son—but your work is an insult to your intelligence. If you would only trace out a plan of action for yourself and be determined to do so—I am sure you could accomplish anything you wished.

His thoughtlessness was his biggest enemy, she wrote. He was old enough to understand the seriousness of this and realize that what he did in the next year or two could affect his whole life. 'Stop and think it out for yourself and take a good pull before it is too late. You know dearest boy that I will always help you all I can.'

Winston's reply was contrite: 'My own Mummy I can tell you your letter cut me up very much.' He admitted he had been 'rather lazy' and promised to 'do my *very best* in what remains'.[14]

Randolph was more concerned about his horses. His references to Jennie in his letters at this time concerned her coming from somewhere or going to somewhere else, but he mentioned very little about their going anywhere together. He was soon off to Tarbes, France, where he was a guest of the Marquis de Breteuil. 'Here we are, peaceable and comfortable,' he wrote Jennie. 'Beautiful weather, splendid mountains, nothing to worry about.' He told of the arrival of a Parisian actress travelling with two men—one who was 'her first and original lover, who is now only her friend, and with another young man, who is the present lover. These three travel about together. So French!'

It is difficult to imagine that Randolph's remarks were simply innocent gossip, rather than at least an oblique reference to the parallel in his own life. Jennie was never blatant about her relationship with Breteuil or anyone else, but neither was she furtive. Whenever Randolph was away, which was often, there were men who escorted her everywhere. The names of all of them were linked with hers in the press, in society living rooms, in family letters. News of all this certainly reached Randolph from a dozen directions.

Why, then, would he pay a prolonged visit to Breteuil? For the same reasons, perhaps, that he had invited the Marquis to join them on their trip through Russia. The simple, strange fact was that, despite their obvious relationship with Jennie, he liked Breteuil, Kinsky, the Prince of Wales, Herbert von Bismarck—and they all liked him and honestly admired the qualities in him that could have made him greater than they. It is true that Randolph had occasional rows with some of them, open clashes that reached public print. The Prince of Wales acted as mediator in one heated argument between Randolph and Count Kinsky, and again intervened when Randolph threatened to thrash the Prince's 23-year-old son for too open and too ardent courting of Jennie. The Prince packed his son off to Malta. And Jennie's nephew, Shane Leslie, remembered the evening that Randolph ordered the 48-year-old Prince of Wales out of his house for paying similar attention to Jennie.[15]

But all these were quarrels soon repaired. Randolph had long ago resigned himself to the status of cuckold, and he surfaced in anger only when the gossip became too blatant and unbearable or when his strained nerves tore him apart. Most important, he wanted to preserve a proper social face on his marriage for the few remaining years of his life. He was too tired for scandal, too drained to face divorce, and ever-aware of the demands of his heritage.

He did have one platonic female friend, who also became one of Jennie's closest friends—Pearl Mary Teresa Richards, daughter of a New York merchant who had settled in England. She was a dozen years younger than Jennie, but they shared a passion for music and had known unhappiness in marriage. She had married Reginald Craigie in 1887, borne him a son in 1890, and divorced him the same year. Later she became a prominent novelist under the pseudonym John Oliver Hobbes.

Randolph's brother Marlborough, on the other hand, wanted more than platonic female friends. During that summer of 1888, he went to New York, where Leonard Jerome had lined up a prospective new bride, a good-natured, very wealthy widow named Lily Hammersley. She had gained some notoriety by covering the walls and ceiling behind her opera-box with orchids. 'I hope the marriage will come off,' Jerome wrote his wife, 'as there is no doubt she has lots of tin.'

The New York press gave the Duke a mixed greeting. One of the more gossipy journals wrote, 'Where the great Marlborough conquered campaigns, the little Marlborough conquers courtesans; the man of the past won battles, the man of the present wins bawds.' Another magazine, noting his thirty-five pieces of luggage, remarked, 'Everything His Grace of Marlborough brought with him was clean, except his reputation.'[16]

The Duke's visit was not confined to bride-hunting and 'boozy' parties. He met Thomas Alva Edison and talked of his plans for a scientific laboratory at Blenheim. Edison wrote of him to Moreton, 'I thought the English Duke was a fool with a crown on his head. But this man knows a great deal which I do not intend inventing till next fall.'[17]

Before the month was out, Jerome reported, 'Well, Blandford is married! I went with him to the Mayor's office in the City Hall at one o'clock today and witnessed the ceremony. I took charge of his cable to the Duchess. Also sent one of my own to Jennie.'

The new Duchess of Marlborough came in for much critical comment. Snidely observing that the Duke had obviously been smitten 'by her manifold charms and her multifarious millions', one magazine noted that the 'Duchess Lily' weighed some 160 pounds, was 'a common looking and badly dressed woman with a moustache, but yet a pleasant face'. It then pointed out that she also had an annual income of 150,000 dollars a year and a personal fortune of some five million dollars. 'And ready cash buys Norman blood.' Another report proclaimed that her spaniels dined on chicken fricassee, cream, and macaroons, and slept on silk sheets under satin blankets.

The press also observed that the Duke's first wife had been a god-daughter of Queen Victoria, and as the Queen was still incensed about the scandalous divorce, it seemed quite unlikely that Duchess Lily would be presented at Court. 'The Lord Chamberlain must rue the day when the Queen consented to receive American women at Court,' added *Society Magazine*. 'The poor man has been so besieged with applications.' Discussing 'the successful raids made by our American sisters-in-law on the English marriage market', *Society* further commented: 'The American republic was founded, it has been said, by housemaids out of place, and mechanics out of employment. It is being solidified by English aristocrats out of elbows.'

'I like the Americans very well,' said Lady Dorothy Nevill, 'but there are two things I wish they would keep to themselves—their girls and their tinned lobster.'[18]

Marlborough, however, had no complaints. His wife's money enabled him to make many badly-needed repairs at Blenheim and to convert the palace's top floor into a giant laboratory for his experiments in chemistry and metallurgy. Randolph described the improvements to his mother:

Well! Have seen everything here, and am not very much impressed. All the electric-lighting and heating in stables have been well-done, and are no doubt great improvements. Although there may have been heaps of money spent on the drawing-rooms, I cannot see much, if any, improvement; they might just as well have been left alone. I have been rather bored here. The Duchess Lily talks about Blandford and to Blandford all day long, flatters him and exalts him to his heart's content. He believes himself to be a beneficent genius. . . . I never knew anything like the unpunctuality here; yesterday, we did not get breakfast till eleven, lunch until three, and dinner till nine; most tiresome. I don't think the Duchess Lily looking at all well in health, and the moustache and beard are becoming serious. . . .[19]

But Jennie moved quickly to ease Duchess Lily's entry into

British social life. In the course of years, Jennie had become a kind of bridge between the new American brides and the old British. She recognized that a new arrival must manœuvre to make an entry. In the case of the visiting Mrs Cornelius Vanderbilt, Jennie simply arranged for a small dinner party with the Prince and Princess of Wales. In the case of Duchess Lily, it was not so simple. It took all of Jennie's assets to help launch the Duchess. Jennie realized better than most that it mattered little to most Englishmen whether an American woman's father was a landowner or a streetcleaner—as long as the American woman was bright, beautiful, witty, and rich. In Duchess Lily's case, her money had to make up for her other obvious deficiencies, although Jennie did manage to persuade her to diet twenty pounds from her heavy figure and remove some of the excessive hair from her face. In all this, Jennie had the determined help of her five sisters-in-law—Lady Wimborne, Lady De Ramsey, Lady Marjoribanks, Lady Curzon, and the Duchess of Roxburghe—as well as the Dowager Duchess, all of whom pressured their friends to accept the new Duchess of Marlborough.

Jennie was soon concerned with other family problems—news of her father was discouraging. He had been forced to give up Jerome Park, had witnessed the deterioration of the American Jockey Club, and was searching fruitlessly for funds to build a new racecourse. Past seventy, Jerome was often rakishly called 'The Squire', but his letters had begun to show him as a beaten and bitter man. He complained to his wife that he had just paid the year's 'ugly bill' for taxes of $4,551.90 and that he had mailed Leonie £100. To Leonie he had felt impelled to write:

I think you must give up your Newport excursion. It would be very charming, but unavoidably expensive. It's the first time I refused any of you girls anything on the ground of expense. I must really know how some things are going to turn out before spending any more than we can reasonably help.

Leonie and John Leslie made a dramatic decision. John resigned from the Guards and he and Leonie moved to Paris so that he could study art at Julien's Academy. But John Leslie's painting would never be as successful as his marriage. Even years later, Leonie's letters to her husband were always full of her love, as when she wrote him, 'The more I think of you, the more adorable do you appear. I mentally kiss you from head to foot.'[20]

And enduring passion also kept Clara married to her ever-wandering Moreton. He could write her:

Lovers we are always ... so often, half awakening, I feel for the soft fair beauties that were my own, and I find them not. But sometimes a dear dream of love comes to me and once again I hold you in my arms and press long lingering kisses on your lips, your neck, your glowing bosom ... when I return—I pray late very late—may I wanton with the lovely masses of that bright hair, may I kiss you anywhere everywhere at my own dearest will. May I sink all my life and strength in fervent passion. ...[21]

Leonard Jerome was particularly fond of Frewen. 'I don't wonder you are in love with him,' he told Clara. 'I am in love with him myself.' As for Moreton's failure to make a fortune, Jerome wrote, 'It is nothing here. It is a common saying that one must fail once or twice here before he learns how to make or keep a fortune.'

Moreton had a new hope now. Randolph had recommended him as financial adviser to Sir Salar Jung to help clear up the mess in his Indian state of Hyderabad. The elder Jung had allied his Mohammedan subjects to the British, and his son had shot tigers with Randolph. Sir Salar was a huge man, six feet four and weighing over twenty-three stones at the age of twenty-four. He was also charming, intelligent, ambitious. But he drank too much, and the Nizam of Hyderabad had displaced him as Prime Minister and sent him into exile. Frewen had to try to arrange a rapprochement between Sir Salar and the Nizam, and then worry about improving the state's finances, as well as his own.[22]

Upon joining Sir Salar in Cairo, one of Frewen's first assignments was to bargain in a Turkish harem for a bride for Sir Salar. And when Sir Salar wanted to go to England to see a big horse race, Moreton had Leonie rent Cardinal Manning's large house near Goodwood and collect a cheerful party. Among the guests were the Duke of Marlborough, who spoke Urdu, Jennie, and Count Kinsky. Kinsky brought along an Hungarian band, whose discordant notes caused two Indians to hurry away from the party.[23]

After returning to India with Sir Salar, several of Moreton's letters to Leonie contained urgent messages:

Ask Jennie to write Sir Salar how sorry she was not to see him to say goodbye and a little civil regret that she and Randolph were out of town. If R. would write a form of letter of this sort, it would do heaps of good. ...
... I hope Jennie has written to thank Sir Salar for that silver work, if

not please remind her and ask her to write an exceptionally friendly letter. . . . I am feeling grateful even to Randolph, and if I make a million here in railroads, I will send Jane a 'bit'. [Moreton often called Jennie 'Jane'.]

Sir Salar never was reinstated as Prime Minister, even though he kissed the Nizam's boot. So Moreton, without a fortune, headed for America to work on his project to create a new town out of a natural harbour in Canada, a project in which he had persuaded Count Kinsky to invest.

Moreton's first letter home carried sad news about Lawrence Jerome. 'Dear, kind Uncle Larry . . . is sinking fast. Everyone feels that a great friend is going from the world.' When Lawrence died, the New York *Tribune* obituary said, 'The merriest spirit in all the world goes when Lawrence Jerome crosses the dark river.'[24] Leonard Jerome was heart-broken over the death of his favourite brother. The two had married sisters, lived in adjoining houses, made, lost, and risked fortunes together; they were not only men of the same blood but of kindred natures.

Lawrence Jerome was buried in the family mausoleum in Greenwood Cemetery, Brooklyn, in a massive vault overlooking the water. Nearby rested Jennie's seven-year-old sister Camille.

Lawrence left his wife, the vinegary Catherine Hall, and two sons. When Alderman Murphy of the Bronx renamed Jerome Avenue after himself, Catherine ordered new signs made and hired a crew of workmen to change all the 'Murphy' signposts back to 'Jerome'— and so they stayed. Lovell Jerome, the elder son, had been in the Army unit that arrived too late at Little Big Horn and became a burial party for the massacred victims of Custer's Last Stand. For his charge against Chief Lame Deer in the Battle of the Big Muddy, Lovell had received the Congressional Medal of Honor. William Travers Jerome later so distinguished himself as New York District Attorney[25] in his fight against Boss Tweed's Tammany Hall that he was prominently mentioned as a presidential possibility. Jennie would tell Travers it was her ambition to see her son as Prime Minister of Britain and William Travers Jerome as President of the United States.

Moreton Frewen's trip to the United States was prolonged and typical of his dozens of trips all over the world, on which he almost always went alone. Clara had been particularly jealous of the fact that Moreton had gone to America on the same ship with his former flame, Lily Langtry, and was reportedly seeing her in New York.

Oh Lord what a creature you are—I don't see any nice women out here—and I fear I am getting . . . a little beyond that game! But if it were otherwise, and some nice creature took care of me while I am 5,000 miles away—you ought to be rather pleased than otherwise. On the other hand, if someone looks after you while I am that distance off, well . . . that is quite another pair of shoes.

But the beautiful Clara had acquired one of Jennie's suitors, King Milan of Serbia. A striking looking man, King Milan was thick-set with bulging black eyes, inky black hair and heavy moustache. A newspaper of the time described him as 'a man of many faults and some virtues'. Among his virtues were intelligence and an agreeable personality. Jennie had encouraged his courtship, partly perhaps to make Kinsky jealous, for he and Milan were close friends.

Although she liked him, Jennie described Milan as 'certainly one of the most uncivilized beings I have ever encountered'. At one of Jennie's many small dinner parties, King Milan told of his early years as a goatherd, barefoot, clad in rags, often starving, fighting wild beasts. 'He became so excited that, suddenly forgetting he was not in his native wilds, he began to eat with his fingers, tearing the meat on his plate.' But Jennie also remembered dining with him at the Amphitryon in a private room he had ordered covered with orchids. Milan was separated from his Queen, and for that reason was not welcomed by Queen Victoria. 'His life on the whole was a sad one,' wrote Jennie.[20]

For Jennie, King Milan was in the same category as such men as Ernest Cassel and William Waldorf Astor, dynamic men whom she admired, who could challenge and help her, but whom she could not love. The men she wanted were the few who combined strength and sensitivity, body and brain. But these others—Milan, Cassel, Astor, and a host like them—fit into only a small part of her life.

'Personally, I feel my acquaintance can never be too large,' Jennie wrote, 'when I reflect that there are thousands of delightful and interesting people one may be missing, no opportunity ought to be lost in cultivating as many as possible. Friends are in another category. Time alone can prove friendships.'

King Milan, perhaps wanting more than friendship, turned his attentions to Clara. One advantage in this was that Kinsky was not competing for Clara. Another was that Clara's husband was on another continent, while Jennie's husband did make occasional appearances. Besides, the blonde Clara may have been even more attractive to him than Jennie.

Milan arrived daily at Clara's doorstep with a box of gardenias for her and presents always for her children. Among the surviving gifts is an exquisite tortoiseshell musical box with a tiny golden bird that pops out and sings. In Serbian, Milan's surname meant 'bird'. But he was hardly bird-like; Clara referred to his 'over-powering ways'.[27]

Jennie, meanwhile, had had a distant, exotic admirer in the Shah of Persia. He had heard of Jennie's beauty and specifically asked that she be presented to him during the Court Ball in his honour. Later she was informed, however, that she did not meet the Shah's expectations—she was not fat enough.

Clara often felt alone, increasingly dependent on Jennie for affection and money. With her creditors growing more insistent, Clara also was sent some money by her mother, who took the opportunity to warn, '. . . Be sure that Moreton knows nothing about it, as he would leave it all for us to do and his money would go to someone else. *Write urgently* to him for money to *live on*.'

The financial scene began to change again for Leonard Jerome. Years ago, he could have had millions for the asking, but it had become a local joke to ask Jerome if he had found $400 to build a new track. Finally, he was able to answer, 'No, I have not found the $400; but I have found 40 millions.' He had met John A. Morris and persuaded him to build the new racecourse they would call Morris Park Course. The *Tribune* later described it as 'an immensity. . . . The enclosure seems to have no bounds, the stables may be measured in miles. The betting ring would hold all the bookmakers in the United States.' That winter of 1888 Jerome was in funds enough to make a proposal to his wife:

How would it do for you and Clara to go over to Paris and establish yourselves alongside Leonie and Jack? I would come over by the French Line and spend Christmas and a week or two or more with you. Besides, I will pay all extra expenses, whatever more it may cost you to live three months in Paris. . . . For Christmas week, Jennie and Randolph might come over and visit us. The scheme strikes me as very sensible, very possible and very jolly. What do you say?

Hearing the news, Moreton promptly wrote his wife urging her to accept her father's offer and leave London. He also asked her to send his stuffed buffalo head and his stuffed eagle, among other trophies, to Jennie's house for safekeeping. 'I'd like her to have them,' he said; besides, 'it will more likely be six [years] before we can "show our head" in London.'

When they agreed to go, Leonard wrote Leonie in Paris to tell her about it and advise her, 'Don't try to live together. You have done it several times heretofore, and successfully, but it is not good policy.' He then mentioned that Jennie and Randolph were also expected to come, and added, 'Tell me how you propose to live, how to amuse yourselves in Paris. It is the place of all others for young people capable of enjoying the world's pleasures without running to excess. A hundred pound bill enclosed.'

The three Jerome sisters did live together, however, in Avenue Kléber, and it made quite a ménage—Grandmother Clara, Leonie with her four boys, Clara with her two boys and a girl, Jennie occasionally bringing over her two boys. The three Jerome sisters were at their social peak in Paris. Theirs was the lively life—theatres, parties, restaurants, seldom eating meals in their apartment. The Marquis de Breteuil was in constant attendance; Count Kinsky,[28] too, of course; and the Prince of Wales dropped in.

By that time, Prince Edward was very stout, and his tight clothes emphasized his girth. He had cut down on his drinking, but not on his eating. One critic had started calling him 'Spuds', insisting that his head looked an enormous potato ready for the pot. His tremendous hands, his outsize nose and ears, and his large grey codfish eyes hardly helped dispel the Spuds impression. But he was nonetheless an impressive man, whose full beard and moustache and slightly accented English lent him a continental distinction. He still lived the sensuous life of a *bon vivant* and still set the style. They called him 'Collars and Cuffs' because he always showed more linen than any other Englishman. If H.R.H. arrived at a party one evening wearing three shirt studs instead of two, as he once did, men automatically scurried to search for another stud. A serious kidney disease was said to have slowed down his dalliances with the ladies, but the decrease was barely discernible.

Two new admirers for the sisters, particularly for Clara and Jennie, were Widor, the famous French organist, and Alexandre

Eiffel. Eiffel escorted Clara to the uppermost part of the tower he was building for the Paris Exhibition (his 'construction of amazement'), telling her she was the first woman in the world to have been so high. Widor often gave private recitals for each of the Jerome sisters in his organ loft at St. Sulpice.

Always available for escort duties was Count Kinsky's friend, the 60-year-old Baron Maurice de Hirsch, a financier and philanthropist who had made his fortune in Balkan railways.[29] The rumour of the time was that Baron Hirsch was an illegitimate son of the Emperor of Austria. In addition to his charming house on the rue d'Elysée, Hirsch also had a vast estate in Hungary, where the Prince of Wales often went to shoot partridges and the Jerome sisters were frequent guests. Just the year before, the Marquis de Breteuil, then treasurer of the Orleanist Party, had gone to Hirsch for a campaign contribution. Hirsch pulled at his Napoleonic moustache and then wrote out a cheque. 'My knees shook under me,' said Breteuil. 'It was for six million francs.' Hirsch came often to the Jerome parties, and Jennie said that he 'was one of the few millionaires I have met who knew thoroughly how to enjoy life'.

# 15

By early November, 1888, the Churchills were back in London and Randolph introduced to Jennie a Colonel John North, also known as 'The Nitrate King', intimating that North was a man with the Midas touch who would help them accumulate their own fortune. Though his nitrate mines were in Chile, Colonel North kept a large London house where he entertained lavishly. He was a vulgar man, however, boisterous and ostentatious. When he told Jennie he had paid £8,000 for a painting, she asked him the name of the artist. North could not remember; nor could he remember the subject of the painting, but he did know that 'it is twelve feet by eight'.

For a time, Randolph planned a series of trips to South America, and the Churchills arranged a number of parties at which North was their guest of honour. A gossip sheet[1] reported that the grateful Colonel North 'put Lord Randolph into some snug little schemes to enable him to realize quite a handsome fortune'. If so, it was not the oversize fortune that Randolph had so rosily expected.

Another friend of Randolph, among the richest men in the world, was former American Minister to Italy William Waldorf Astor, impolitely known as 'Wealthy Willie'.[2] Gossip writers coupled his name with Jennie's almost regularly throughout the years. After the death of Astor's wife and Jennie's husband, it was even reported that Astor and Jennie were engaged to marry. He was a big, blue-eyed, handsome man with a blond moustache, a rugged build, and an overpowering personality, aided and abetted by eighty million dollars. They called him 'Walled-Off Astor', because he had built high walls topped with glass around his 300-acre Cliveden Estate on the Thames, had barred his windows, and actually used the drawbridge at Hever Castle to keep people out.[3] The real wall, though, was around his soul.

Addicted to timetables, minutes mattered more to him than people. For weekend guests, Astor would arrange a schedule that suffered no possible deviation. When it was letter-writing time and one guest chose to roam the garden, she was approached by a nervous servant who timidly suggested that perhaps the lady had forgotten that it was letter-writing time and Mr Astor would be displeased to know that she was not following the schedule. When the angry guest told the servant she would not stay in such a house and asked him to call her carriage, the unhappy servant said he would not dare to do so before Mr Astor's scheduled time for guests to leave.

Such a formalized man hardly fitted in with Jennie's free-moving ways. Nor did she like his views on the America he had left. After his unsuccessful campaign for Congress Astor had been quoted as saying, 'America is good enough for any man who has to make a livelihood, though why travelled people of independent means should remain there more than a week is not readily to be comprehended. . . . America is not a fit place for a gentleman to live.'[4]

Astor's main attraction for Jennie was his power and money, and she introduced him into the orbit of the Prince of Wales, who was attracted by the same things. Jennie and Astor were, however, friends, and they remained so. It may have been coincidence, but when Astor bought the *Pall Mall Gazette* in 1892, he offered the editorship to Harry Cust; and when he bought *The Observer*, he said it was mainly to retain the services of its editor, James Garvin. In addition to Cust, Garvin was another of Jennie's conquests. How much Jennie influenced Astor's choices is not known.

Suddenly an unexpected opportunity for the Churchills loomed large and ripe. John Bright, the grand old man of Birmingham, died in March 1889, and a Birmingham delegation invited Randolph to run for Bright's seat. Randolph was safely settled in his Paddington seat, but a victory in Birmingham, the heart of the Liberal stronghold, would be spectacular. It would mean for him a political revival of the first order, catapulting him into the forefront of the Conservative Party where the Prime Minister's job would again be within reach. To make it more attractive, Randolph's friends guaranteed him a safe seat elsewhere in the event that he lost Birmingham.

Jennie was exultant. Everything was possible again. Certainly Randolph was often ill, but she would always be there to help him. She could not speak for him, but she could write and manœuvre for him even more than she had before. She knew the most important men of her times; she had travelled throughout Europe and met the royal rulers, and she understood the intricacies of continental diplomacy. She had conducted political campaigns throughout England and was familiar with the vital issues that confronted the country. She could be her husband's right hand, his common sense, his strongest supporter and adviser. After all, he was only forty years old. His disease had been quiescent for some time, and perhaps it would stay that way long enough for him to become Prime Minister. Jennie recruited all their closest friends to pressure Randolph into accepting the candidacy. Even Colonel North cabled from Santiago, 'BE SURE CONTEST BIRMINGHAM.'

Randolph was stirred by the possibilities. He asked Louis Jennings[5] to write him a farewell speech for the voters of Paddington South and a campaign speech for Birmingham.

'When do you want them?' asked Jennings.

'This afternoon,' answered Randolph.

While Jennings was busy with the speeches and arrangements, Churchill was caving in under the pressure of Joseph Chamberlain. A sometime friend and occasional rival of Randolph, Chamberlain was still the undisputed king-pin of Birmingham. During his three terms as Mayor, he had cleared city slums and vastly improved the water and gas services. As an M.P., he had broken with Gladstone on the Home Rule issue, quitting his Cabinet post as President of the Board of Trade, yet Balfour said of him that he 'does not completely mix, does not form a chemical combination with us'. Twelve years younger than Chamberlain, Balfour also commented, 'The difference between Joe and me is the difference between youth and age; I am age.'[6]

Chamberlain was a man of firm intellectual control who seldom deceived himself. He knew the complications that would ensue if Randolph Churchill moved into his arena of Birmingham. He liked Randolph personally, but he did not want to share political prominence in Birmingham with anyone.

Once firm and fierce, Randolph's mind was now weak and malleable, and after their second meeting he succumbed to Chamberlain's arguments. 'It's all over,' Randolph told his supporters. 'I cannot stand for the seat.'[7] In another time, in another Britain, Joseph Chamberlain's son Neville would count on the loyalty of Winston Churchill.

'It was a great blow to his friends and supporters in Birmingham who felt that they had been offered up on the altar of Mr Chamberlain's ambitions,' Jennie confided in her memoirs.

Bearing in mind the political campaign of 1885, and the hard work in which I had taken part and which now seemed a waste of time and energy, I felt very incensed. On the day when Randolph returned from the House of Commons and informed me of the pressure brought to bear on him, and how he had given in, I accused him of showing the white feather for the first time in his life. He had, he said, 'made up his mind to abide by the opinion of the leaders of the party'. 'But not when those leaders are your political enemies,' I cried. Arguments, however, were useless. If he was right, he got no thanks for it, and a great opportunity was lost for him to show his strength and power.[8]

Writing to Salisbury on June 2, 1889, about the situation, Balfour said:

He [Chamberlain] now goes the length of saying that the Conservative Party are not so strong in the central ward of Birmingham as they were when Randolph Churchill fought the seat in 1885. At that time, the Conservatives were far better organized than they are now, and there was a very active Primrose League, under the direction of the Duchess of Marlborough and of Lady Randolph, which did great service in the most radical ward of the constituency. All this, according to him, is now at an end, and the Conservative organization is, for all practical purposes, worthless.

The Birmingham incident marked a milestone in Randolph's decline, much more than the speeches and articles that attacked and insulted him. Here was the great opportunity for which his supporters had worked so hard, and he had missed it—his followers felt he had been betrayed by Chamberlain. 'After Randolph left the Government, our relations with Lord and Lady Salisbury became gradually more and more strained,' Jennie said.

Outward appearances were kept up, such as our still being invited to the political parties given in Arlington Street, but all real cordiality ceased. Mutual friends indeed tried to bring about a rapprochement, and eventually we were asked to dine. Much against his inclination, Randolph was persuaded to accept. The dinner, which was a large one, was a fiasco, so far as the object of our being there was concerned. For beyond a bare greeting, neither Lord nor Lady Salisbury exchanged a word with Randolph. This he resented very much, and regretted having gone. I do not think this was intended as a slight.

Shortly after, Jennie received a very friendly letter of invitation from Lady Salisbury to a garden party which was to feature speeches by Chamberlain and Lord Randolph.

Great was to be the gathering of Unionists, and a solid front was much desired. At the last moment, however, Randolph flatly refused to go. No arguments moved him; he insisted that I should keep the engagement alone. As I drove up to the historical Elizabethan house [Hatfield House], an ideal residence for the Prime Minister of England, my feelings were anything but enviable. I shall never forget the look of blank dismay and the ominous silence with which my feeble excuses for Randolph's absence were greeted. That night at dinner, in the splendid banqueting-hall, I sat next to Lord Salisbury. Courteous as ever, he talked pleasantly to me, but made no allusion to the subject uppermost in my mind. The next day was fine, and masses of people, brought by special trains from London, filled the beautiful gardens, crowding round the various speakers. Cries for Randolph were heard on every side, many had come expressly to hear him, and bitter was the disappointment when they realized that he was not there. No adequate reason could be given for his absence, and the 'rift within the loot' [sic] was made more apparent than ever. I confess I was very glad when I could slip away, for rarely had I felt so uncomfortable or experienced anything more disagreeable.[9]

So much had Randolph alienated himself from his party's policy, that when he asked for a glass of water during one of his speeches in the House of Commons, no one stirred. Thinking that he had not been heard, he repeated the request. No one moved. After a prolonged silence, a young Tory M.P. went out for the water. Taking the glass from him, Randolph said solemnly, 'I hope this will not compromise you with your party.'

'Many of those who witnessed this incident,' wrote Robert Rhodes James, 'could not help but remember the gay evening in the palmy days of the Fourth Party, when Randolph demanded a drink in the middle of a speech, and called out cheerfully after the departing Gorst, "Remember, Gorst, brandy and seltzer."'[10]

Randolph lost his last loyal friend, Jennings, when he unexpectedly switched his position on a forthcoming bill—without telling Jennings, who had made a preliminary speech in favour of it. Jennings considered it a 'stab in the back'.

Jennie spent a great deal of time in Paris in 1889, visiting her mother and sisters and Count Kinsky. She was also a regular guest at the popular literary salons of Mrs Ferdinand Bischoffsheim, an American. 'It was there that I first met Monsieur Bourget, then unmarried,' she wrote later. Paul Bourget, who wrote mainly about intellectuals and aristocrats, was then an important and popular literary figure. He and Jennie developed a close friendship that grew more intimate in the coming years. They exchanged an extensive correspondence, and in one letter Bourget wrote her, 'Arrived at a certain point in life, one knows too much about it, wishes to do too much, and is not able to express what one has to say. Do you know that Turgenev has summed it all up when he said, "Life is a brutal affair."'[11]

Jennie was thirty-six years old, reaching for younger men and more excitement. There seemed nothing now to hold her back except hypocrisy, and she had little of that. *Town Topics* reported that a footman saw Jennie dancing the Can-Can at a party given in Dublin by the Viceroy. 'She suddenly touched the mantelpiece with her foot, making a dreadful exposé,' the magazine wrote, and added, 'This is only one of her many freaks which have caused much scandal.'

Randolph, in the meanwhile, had his own routine, his own private friends. In the autumn of 1890, he and Harry Tyrwhitt leased a houseboat on the Nile for several months. 'The days slip by as if they were hours, . . . life on the Nile is ideal,' he wrote Jennie. It was a life of 'good food, hock, champagne, Pilsener beer, Marquis chocolate, ripe bananas, fresh dates and literally hundreds of French novels.'

'These few months were decisive to his fortune,' wrote Robert Rhodes James. In the strange way of politics, Randolph's political fortune was tied to the strength of Charles Stewart Parnell and his pivotal group of M.P.s in the House of Commons. Together they held a balance of power. Faced with that fact, Salisbury needed unity within his own party, and this meant a cagey treatment of the popular Randolph Churchill.

Ten-year-old Jack wrote his father about a story in the *Graphic*: 'It said you had a hot temper, and yet everyone was willing to hear what you had to say. It said you were going to be in office again, and that the office suited you very well. What it all means, I do not know.' It meant that Randolph's disease was still largely a family secret and that in the public's view his political power was inevitable and growing. But the power crashed finally and utterly with the fall of Parnell.

Parnell had survived the smear of a highly publicized facsimile reprinted in the *Times* in 1887, supposed to have been a letter he had written approving the Phoenix Park murders. He denied he had written the letter, but it took him two years to win public vindication.[12] Then in 1890 Captain O'Shea, the husband of Parnell's mistress, sued his wife Kitty for divorce, naming Parnell as corespondent. O'Shea, who had long known of his wife's association with Parnell and had lived well off it, had finally offered a divorce for £20,000. When Parnell was unable to raise the money to buy him off, the Captain filed his suit.[13]

Parnell refused to defend himself,[14] refused to resign the leadership of his group of Home Rulers, and consequently split both his party and his country into bitter factions. 'Don't throw me to the wolves,' pleaded Parnell, the 'Uncrowned King of Ireland', to his Irish Parliamentary Party. 'The Irish did not throw him to the English wolves,' James Joyce later wrote, 'they tore him to pieces themselves.' Even Gladstone felt forced to turn against Parnell, though he once remarked that he had known eleven former Prime Ministers, every one an adulterer. Parnell's sin, later wrote Mrs O'Shea, was that he had violated the Eleventh Commandment, 'Thou shalt not be found out.'

Parnell married Kitty O'Shea in June 1891. He died in October that same year, at the age of forty-five.

The scandal set back any possibility of passing the Home Rule Bill for many years. Gladstone said of it sadly, 'For five years, I have rolled this stone patiently uphill. And now it has rolled to the bottom again and I am 81 years old.'[15]

With Parnell's fall and the collapse of Irish unity in the House, Salisbury no longer thought it necessary to consider any future impact of Randolph Churchill on the Conservative Party. Realizing what had happened, Randolph wrote Jennie from Egypt of

my decision to have done with politics and try to make a little money for the boys and for ourselves. I hope you do not all intend to worry me on this matter and dispute with me and contradict me. More than two-thirds, in all probability, of my life is over, and I will not spend the remainder of my years in beating my head against a stone wall. I expect I have made great mistakes; but there has been no consideration, no indulgence, no memory or gratitude—nothing but spite, malice and abuse. I am quite tired and dead sick of it all, and will not continue political life any longer.... It is so pleasant getting near home again. I have had a good time, but now reproach myself for having left you all for so long....

Of this, Lord Rosebery wrote:

233

Surely a tragic letter. The revelation of a sore and stricken soul. He was sick of heart and body when he uttered this burst of melancholy candour ... and all that may be written about the tragedy of Randolph's life, there will be nothing so sad as this letter of his.[16]

It was some time in 1891 that Lord Randolph had copied out some famous lines by Dryden:[17]

> Happy the man, and happy he alone,
> He, who can call today his own;
> He who, secure within, can say:
> 'Tomorrow do thy worst, for I have lived today.
> Be fair, or foul, or rain, or shine,
> The joys I have possessed, in spite of fate, are mine.
> Not Heaven itself upon the past has power;
> But what has been, has been, and I have had my hour.'

For all his many and varied faults, for all the injury and disappointment he had heaped on her life, Randolph had given Jennie her 'hour', too. He had opened the door of a new world for her. His name and his title had given her access to the finest minds and most fascinating personalities of her time. His prominence in politics had given her a position of clear visibility at the hub that moved the wheels of the British Empire. But if he had provided the entrée, she had made the friends—and she had kept those friends when he could not. If his political position had revealed the hub to her, she had supplied to him the drive to help turn the wheel.

Now his letter from Egypt struck a responsive chord. He had found himself in an enormous, lonely void, and he was reaching out to her for a point of purpose. Jennie brightened her letters with cheer and encouragement. She wrote good news about Jack, then at Elstree School. Ten years old, he was a model student, always near the top of his class, despite poor vision in one eye. Jack himself wrote his father, 'I wish I'd come to Egypt with you, and roam and see all the world. I wish a good many things which do not occur.'

There was good news about Winston, too. He had written his mother that he was 'working very well', and 'very hard'. 'Arithmetic and Algebra are the dangerous subjects.' He also reported to her that there was a good chance of his winning a chess tournament, and 'I have been drawing little landscapes and bridges, and those sort of things'. In addition, he had passed the test for corporals in the school Corps.[18]

Winston's focus on an Army career had begun one day in his

room when he and Jack had their opposing armies of toy soldiers arrayed against each other, ready for war. Randolph came into the room and surveyed the impressive scene.

At the end he asked me if I would like to go into the Army. I thought it would be splendid to command an Army, so I said 'Yes' at once: and immediately I was taken at my word. For years I thought my father with his experience and flair had discerned in me the qualities of military genius. But I was told later that he had only come to the conclusion that I was not clever enough to go to the Bar.[19]

After that incident Winston's education was geared toward entrance into Sandhurst. Jennie went to Harrow and then reported to Randolph that Welldon thought Winston was working as hard as possible and perhaps now might pass the preliminary examination for Sandhurst in the autumn. Winston, she wrote, was 'looking pale, but he was very nice and full of good resolutions which I trust will last'.

Winston did take the preliminary examination. In commenting on the tests, Winston thought his mother might be pleased that with a choice of subjects for the essay test, he had chosen the one on The American Civil War.[20] Then he added his customary footnote, 'A remittance would not be altogether misplaced.'

Shortly afterward, Jennie was able to write her husband:

I am sure you will be delighted to hear that Winston has passed his P.E. [Preliminary Examinations for entrance into Sandhurst] in *everything* one of the only four boys of Harrow who got in. . . . I think you ought to make him a present of a gun as a reward. He is pining for one and ought to have a little encouragement.

Randolph returned from Egypt in February 1891 wearing a beard but with little else changed. His loneliness and his yearning for home and family seemed to have disappeared with the sea voyage. His life with Jennie did not improve.

Winston wrote his father, pleading with him to visit Harrow. 'You have never been to see me and so everything will be new to you.' He even told him of a fast train that only took half an hour from Baker Street. 'P.S. I shall be awfully disappointed if you don't come.' He was awfully disappointed.

If Randolph had changed his mind about his need for family closeness, he had not changed his mind about his need for money. The magic word was 'gold', and the magic place was South Africa.

235

Within a short time, he announced his intention to leave for South Africa at the end of April, the trip to last some nine months.[21] The *Daily Graphic* had agreed to pay him two thousand guineas for twenty articles of four thousand words each. His good friend Lord Rothschild loaned him £5,000 and sent along his best mining engineer, a Mr Perkins, to help in the gold hunt.

Randolph originally intended to take his brother-in-law Moreton with him. Frewen's latest prospective fortune-maker was a gold-crushing machine he had patented and in which the Churchills had bought some stock. The *Western Daily Mercury* scathingly deemed the invention most appropriate to Frewen, 'seeing that he is a prominent bi-metallist and therefore anxious to crush gold as far as possible out of existence.' But Randolph had good advice and second thoughts on the crusher, and wrote Moreton that he could not continue investing in the machine:

All my available resources are taken up with my journey to Mashonaland. ... On reflection I am of opinion that you and I had better not go to South Africa together. ... We shall not agree on business matters and ... we might quarrel and separate out there which is a result to be avoided.

Realizing the Frewens' financial straits, Jennie refused to accept back any money she and Randolph had given Moreton for their goldcrusher stocks. Moreton wrote Randolph, 'Jane threatened to return this second cheque to Clara, which was very kind of her, very; but it would hurt my feelings if she did.'

Randolph, however, had no such qualms about accepting the money. 'I have had so many accounts to settle and payments to make before leaving that I am rather short and racing has been distinctly adverse. ... If you will pay the £200, I will be much obliged. ...'[22]

As Randolph was making his final preparations for departure, Leonard Jerome came to England for his final visit. Here was a man who had packed his life full: the loveliest women had loved him, the finest minds had listened to him, and a whole generation of Americans were richer in spirit because of him. His was the kind of remarkable energy and imagination that was so much a part of the growth of the American republic. When his health had begun to fail, his wife had urged him to hire a servant. 'I have no use whatever for a servant,' Jerome answered. 'He would only be a nuisance. When one has been in the habit of putting on one's own shoes and stockings for 60 or 70 years, it would become rather awkward to have another do it.'

Now he was seventy-three, tired and dispirited, and he had come to die among his family. As his nephew Eugene Jerome had written to Moreton from New York, 'It must have been something of a shock to you to see how much he has failed and how helpless he has become. From all I have learned of his doctor here, he will never recover the use of his leg.'

Leonard moved into Clara's house in Aldford Street. The street opened onto Park Lane, and from Clara's windows one could see the trees and the nearby Grosvenor Chapel. Jerome sat in a big, black velvet chair behind a screen, tended by his wife, nursed by his daughters, observed by many grandchildren. The children were told that their American grandfather had 'galloping consumption'.

'It is thawing today, and we hope Papa has a good day,' Leonie wrote her mother-in-law in January. 'If Papa is well enough, Jennie wants to go and meet Randolph at Marseille, but I doubt her getting away.'

Leonard grew worse and the family decided to move him to Brighton for the sea air. He and his wife stayed at Lyon Mansions and the daughters were there almost daily. Shane Leslie wrote that in his last days Jerome lived on champagne and oysters. He died in a big brass bed, surrounded by his wife and daughters. His final words were, 'I have given you all I have. Pass it on.'

Of all his daughters, Jennie had been closest to him. He had given her most—not only of money, but of himself. She had the most of his drive, imagination, and courage—and she would pass it on.

But at that moment, she felt drained and lonely. For one of the few times in their marriage, Jennie needed Randolph more than he needed her. Her needs, however, were no longer his.

In addition to the family at the funeral in Grosvenor Chapel, were the United States Minister, the Hon. Robert T. Lincoln (son of President Lincoln), the German Ambassador, and some thirty friends. The New York *Daily Tribune* carried a large headline, 'LEONARD JEROME DEAD', and the New York *Herald* noted, 'At Leonard Jerome's death, a warm feeling of sorrow awakened in English social circles.'

Moreton Frewen agreed to take the body back to the family mausoleum in Greenwood Cemetery, Brooklyn.

Instead of a fortune, Leonard Jerome left behind only debts. Among his effects was a diamond necklace he had bought for his wife during the days of the Imperial Court of Napoleon. Moreton, however, persuaded his mother-in-law to part with it, along with other heirlooms, as a sure investment in his goldcrusher, which would make millions for everyone. 'When I return, I will build a big yacht for you,' he wrote Clara, 'and you shall take a year's holiday!'

Jerome's death did not deter Randolph from sailing the next month, but Jennie would not be alone. She would have her sons and her sisters and her friends. As her husband had become more and more a shadow in her life, she would have to find the substance elsewhere.

The months that followed her father's death in 1891 were months of anguish for Jennie. 'I feel as though I were living in an atmosphere of disease, funerals, graves!' she wrote Randolph. 'It is too much for me—the black fog on top of it makes me feel too depressed for words. . . . I am making myself too melancholy. . . .'

'It is wet and cold here,' she said in another letter, 'and I fight against depressions the whole time . . . I am always saying to myself that life is too short for the blues.'

She was troubled, too, about Winston, who at sixteen was seriously in need of a man with whom he could walk and ride and talk, someone he could use as a model. Later that year, Jennie wrote Randolph of Winston, '. . . Honestly he is getting a bit too old for a woman to manage. . . . He really requires to be with a man. . . .' While his father was distant and dim, Count Kinsky was visible and available.[1] Kinsky's nephew, Prince Clary[2] remembers him as a man of charm and kindness, handsome and bright, the kind of man a boy quickly accepts as a hero. His outstanding characteristic was an absolute fearlessness, a quality he demonstrated many times in his life—hunting, racing, and during war. For a boy whose only adventures were lived through the imaginary actions of 1,500 toy soldiers, Kinsky was a model larger than life. Winston vividly described the day that Kinsky took him to the Crystal Palace and someone tried to stop them as they moved past a waiting queue: 'The Count whom you know is immensely strong grew furious and caught hold of the blackguard's hand crushing the fingers in his grasp,' Winston wrote his brother. Kinsky also took him to the zoo, fire brigade drill, and to dinner. Winston delightedly reported that at the restaurant the head waiter said there were no tables 'but Count K. spoke German to him and it had a wonderful effect'. Kinsky even decided that Winston was old enough to share some champagne.[3]

Winston and Count Kinsky developed a close friendship. 'What a wonderful stepfather Kinsky could have made for Winston,' remarked Winston's cousin Shane Leslie, who knew Kinsky. 'Kinsky could have given Winston so much that he badly needed.' Kinsky would have been able to provide Winston an earlier sense of self-confidence, a greater emphasis on manliness. Jennie could advise and influence her son, but she could not transform his softness into steel. Without a father's love, Winston wanted more of his mother, and even into early maturity his letters to her were gushing, as if he were still a child pleading for her kisses. He was a mama's boy, and Jennie knew it and worried about it. She could give him a great deal but she could not give him his manhood.

Jennie, her mother, her sisters, and all the children spent the summer of 1891 at the Churchills' home at Banstead. For part of the summer, Kinsky was at his country estate adjacent to the Churchills'. All the sisters' husbands were elsewhere: John Leslie with his family in Ireland, Moreton Frewen in America en route to Australia ('I don't ask their plans as they change every week,' wrote Jennie), Randolph in South Africa.

Winston and Jack, their visiting cousins, Shane Leslie and Hugh Frewen, and the gardener's son worked together to construct a large two-room hut of mud and wood which they called The Den. They also built a moat and filled it with water, a drawbridge that actually pulled up and down, and a catapult that used unripe apples as ammunition. Not quite seventeen, Winston was the general who drilled his soldiers and organized the battles.[4]

The boys also looked after their chickens. 'My hens have had one brood of four chickens and laid eighty eggs,' Winston wrote his father. He also had two hens sitting on some turkey eggs, but the guinea pig died, as did two of the captured rabbits. Jennie supplemented the Banstead news somewhat in her own letters to Randolph. 'The boys are very happy. Kinsky has gone out with them to put up a target. I am going to try to buy a gun for Winston.'

Kinsky occasionally roamed elsewhere. Lady Warwick happily mentioned in her memoirs that Count Kinsky had shared many 'of my horsey adventures'. Even Jennie's cook Rosa later reminisced, 'Kinsky had a great time of it in London.'[5] But at this time, he seemed to concentrate completely on Jennie.

Randolph's letters home were longer now and more frequent. He was a wasting and disappointed man. In a letter to Winston, he tried to make his South African adventure sound gay, describing it as 'a regular gypsy life' which included sleeping on a mattress in a tent, dressing and washing in the open air, eating round a campfire, shooting a variety of wild game, examining gold mines, travelling in 'a spider'—a wagonette with eight mules, capable of doing about fifty miles a day. He then added a rare fatherly footnote: 'Take care of yourself, don't give Mama any trouble.'

But in fact, Winston was causing her some trouble. Jennie described him in a letter as being 'just at the "ugly" age—touchy and tiresome'. He often seemed to be working himself up to a bilious attack. 'I fear his blood is out of order.'

Welldon at Harrow wrote Jennie that he thought Winston should spend some of his holidays abroad and live with a French family to improve his skill at the language. Winston reacted violently to the idea, and Jennie wrote to Randolph, 'I am going to try to find a little governess (ugly) who wants a holiday. . . . Just to talk and read with him. . . . If I can't I will have to send him away.' Finally she did find a young man from Cambridge ('rather nice') who came at the end of August to tutor Winston for several weeks.

But Jennie was quite concerned about their dwindling finances. The horses which had often brought in much-needed cash were not doing well, either. 'The stable seems to have been very unlucky at the Derby. Three horses beaten. . . . Old Sherwood is rather disgusted.' Furthermore, she had to pay £200 for forage, stables, trainers, and so forth. 'I thought it best to settle all I could as it is better to owe money to the bank than to a man like Slater.' She also wanted to buy a pony for Jack from a certain 'Billy' for fifteen pounds. 'He says he won't send it until I send him the money.' Jack ultimately got his pony, however. Lack of money occasionally slowed down Jennie, but seldom stopped her. She wrote her husband that she thought she could manage until November. 'I have been obliged to pay a few bills, one big one, and of course, the boys' school bill and the tutors will have to be paid. . . .' And later, 'I'm afraid you must feel that our future is in a bad way, as regards money. . . . But we must not despair. . . .' At a recent party where everyone had to make a wish, she also told him, 'I wished that you might make a lot of money.'[6]

While Jennie had her annual income, however inadequate, Clara never seemed able to keep clear of creditors. 'Cannot your mother help you?' Moreton wrote. '. . . Your mother seems to think R and

Jenny's future is alone of any consequence, that whether we sink or swim is nothing!'[7]

Mrs Jerome, in fact, was rapidly becoming a niggardly recluse. Her grandchildren later remembered her as a sad, silent, and lonely woman who looked increasingly like an Indian squaw they had seen in picture books. Hugh Frewen described her as an old lady

severe and exacting to my young mind. She laid down the law, and did not seem kindly disposed to us children. She was a great disciplinarian. One day I said to her, 'Grandmama, when are you going to your *own* home?' My mother thought this was a great joke.

Though Clara Jerome still had her own fund of money, she kept it mostly to herself, except for paying her daughter Clara's critical expenses. Finally she settled into a cheap boarding-house at Tunbridge Wells and economized to the point where she refused to have fires in the fireplace, even during some of the coldest days of the winter. She had long ago left the Society to which she had so snobbishly clung. The real sadness was that this woman—who had never been able to talk the same language or live in the same world as her husband—now was incapable of reaching into the lives of her children and grandchildren. Jennie's shared confidences were with her sisters, not with her mother, but she always remained loyal and affectionate toward her.

With the summer's end, Jennie wrote her husband that she was seeing the boys off to school. 'They have been as happy as kings, riding and shooting.' Winston was 'in tearing spirits. . . . I know Jack was quite worn out rushing after Winston . . . the difference in their ages is beginning to tell. . . . I shall be very dull without the boys. . . .' Her loneliness wasn't helped by the fact that Kinsky had gone to Austria on a shooting trip.

While in Africa Randolph also did considerable shooting, but his most telling shots were in the *Graphic*. His columns hit at all kinds of people, traditions, institutions, and soon stirred up considerable public reaction.[8] Jennie quoted Salisbury as saying, 'Since when has Randolph become the correspondent of a penny-paper!' Arthur Balfour complained to Jennie that Randolph's critical column on the Land Bill had caused him to have 'a tiresome time with mutual friends in Parliament'.

Jennie herself offered some personal comments on his columns: 'It was very interesting to me,' she wrote of one of them, 'but perhaps not very to the general public. I marvelled at your writing so much with so little to go upon.' Another time she observed, 'I am afraid people think your letters a bit prosy—but I don't see how you can write differently.'[9]

Caricaturists lampooned Randolph daily, a moustache-twirler among the lions. At their annual conference, delegates of the National Union Convention booed his name. Editorials poked fun with barbed jabs. The Gaiety Theatre so burlesqued him that the Lord Chamberlain forbade one of their more satirical songs. 'Everyone is much amused,' wrote Jennie.

The Dowager Duchess was not amused. A comic paper called *Funny Folks*, she informed her son, 'has a stupid thing every week about "Randy on the Rampage".' And she was sending him 'some poisonous remarks of the *Pall Mall* which I feel to be utter lies and therefore you should see. . . .' She also mentioned that some had praised his first letters in the *Graphic* but 'people laughed at your botany'. The Duchess herself disapproved of the *Graphic* columns because 'they seem to bring them out so as to help the sale of the papers'.

The Duchess felt that 'there is a great desire to get you back. I must own, however, that your name is not always well received.' The Salisburys were guests at a party she had attended, but 'I never went near them'. Even months later, she would write, 'I cannot make up my mind to go to any of Lord S's parties.' Her grudge was deep. 'I fear a trap was laid for you into which you fell, and I know you must get out and confound your enemies. God help you . . . I long to get you back again, dearest, and think of nothing else.'

Winston was also disturbed by the criticism of his father. 'The papers are exceedingly spiteful and vicious. . . . You cannot imagine what biles of wrath you have uncorked. All the papers simply rave. But oh! I will not bore you with the yappings of these curs. . . .' He did tell him, though, that '*Punch* has got a very stupid article in which they announce that Capt. Gwynydd writes the letters and reads them to you for approval.'[10] But Winston was more worried about something else. He knew a Harrow boy, he said, who had been to Kimberley for the summer holidays 'and he told me the people out there said you were looking ill'.

In one letter, Winston drew a picture of a man with a rifle, facing a mean-looking lion, with the heading, 'I imagine you.' Under another heading, 'Don't forget my—' he drew an antelope head. He then explained to his father that he didn't expect him to bring home a live antelope, just a stuffed head for his room. At the end of that letter, he wrote, 'Wishing luck, sport, amusement and health.' And in another, 'Mama has got a big map of S.A. on which she follows your route. I wish you had taken me. What fun I should have had.' Then, in printed capital letters: 'HAVE YOU FOUND A GOLD MINE? HAVE YOU SHOT A LION YET?'

Jennie had other questions for Randolph: Was there really going to be a war in Mashonaland? Was it true that a friend of theirs had had his body mutilated by tribesmen before having a bullet put into his head? Could he tell her more about the Dutch Parliament? 'What creatures those Boers must be!' His column on the Boers, she commented, was the best he had written. 'I hope they won't make it too hard for you.'

She passed on whatever political news she could garner. Gladstone had told a mutual friend that he felt certain to be returned to office in the next general election. (Jennie added she could not see what he would do when he got there.) The press was starting to pick on Balfour for some of the bills he proposed. The Irish seemed to have no 'go' left after the Parnell–O'Shea scandal. Everybody she talked to seemed 'so bored with the government'. Lord Hartington had been quite pleased with himself for telling the Queen that all the government had done was 'Thanks to Mrs O'Shea'.

Interviewed by a reporter somewhere in South Africa, Randolph was asked, 'What quality do you consider most necessary for success in an English politician?'

'Nimbleness,' he replied.[11]

His most interesting letters home still were written to his mother. Jennie complained, 'I have not seen your letter about the lions, so am rather in the vague as to your encounter.' And then she added that it seemed 'such ages since I had heard from you'. Again Jennie remarked that Randolph failed to mention her, even in some of his longest letters to his mother.

Despite the occasional adventures with wild animals and the potential excitement of finding gold, time often dragged for Randolph in the monotony of so many months of camp life. 'It is rather tiresome here,' he wrote his mother once. The coffee was very bad, the water dirty, the food 'piggy', the meat rationed, the flies ubiquitous.

Jennie seemed little happier. 'London does not seem to be very gay. Hardly anything going on—even the Opera is a failure.'

She had moved into her mother-in-law's house in Grosvenor Square, to save expenses, and let their Connaught Place house. It was a galling situation for Jennie. She and her mother-in-law had settled into a quiet rapprochement, but within each of them was an uneasiness toward the other, a lingering resentment. 'I know beggars can't be choosers but I feel very old for this sort of thing,' Jennie wrote Randolph. 'I shall be so glad to get you back,' she offered in another letter. 'I feel rather low and lonely at times.' Randolph had used most of their funds and had borrowed money to finance his trip to South Africa. Yet, whether from guilt or sympathy, he did respond to Jennie's unhappiness by sending her a diamond, which she had made into a pin and later into a ring. 'It is quite lovely,' she wrote him. 'Everyone admires it immensely. . . . I never dreamed of it. . . .'

One of the activities that kept Jennie busy was music. She and Leonie organized 'a pilgrimage' to Bayreuth for the Wagner Festival. To help familiarize everyone with the Wagner scores, Jennie had a noted German musician and a Wagnerian singer perform for their small group. She also arranged for a series of lectures on Wagner, but the professor's English was so limited and his accent so thick that an unexpected note of hilarity was added to the meetings.

Only half-a-dozen finally made the trip to Bayreuth, including her sisters and Lady de Grey.

Our little party was settled to meet between the acts and exchange opinions, but so great were our emotions that we all fled in different directions, avoiding one another, until the performance was over, when we should be more calm.

Parsifal's wig fell off in the third act, but the audience was such a serious one that there was not a titter.[12]

Jennie afterward helped lay the groundwork for the first performance of *The Ring* in London and later met Siegfried Wagner, the composer's son, at a small dinner in his honour. Guests were asked to select their two favourite composers. 'I was the only one who did not name Wagner,' said Jennie. 'Partly out of contradiction and partly because I think so, I mentioned Bach and Beethoven.' Amid the room's embarrassed confusion, Siegfried Wagner smiled and proclaimed, 'My father would also have chosen them.'

Ignace Paderewski was Jennie's personal pride.[13] Shane Leslie remembered being in a carriage with his mother Leonie, Jennie, and 'Paddy'. They were all excited about the prospect of launching him in London.

I was lying on the seat, but everytime I woke I could see Jennie and my mother trying to guess the tunes that Paderewski played in the air with his fingers. It was a curious game but they were all in high, tearing spirits and Paddy's fingers never seemed to stop....[14]

Jennie arranged Paderewski's first London performance.

I invited to meet him a select few whom I knew to be capable of appreciating and judging him. Needless to say, their admiration and enthusiasm was unbounded. A few days later, he gave his first concert in St. James's Hall. The place was only half-full, and behind me were two musical critics, taking notes for their papers. 'There's not much in this fellow,' said one. 'He would be all right,' said the other, 'if he would leave Chopin alone, which he plays against all traditions.'

Jennie would like to have informed them that Chopin's friend Stephen Heller had told her the great composer never played his works twice in the same way. 'The following year, Paderewski, having had a gigantic success in Paris and elsewhere, returned to London, where he received an ovation from an excited and enthusiastic audience, who stormed the platform to kiss his hands!'

Paderewski particularly enjoyed playing duets with Jennie, said Shane Leslie, but was musically in love with all the Jerome sisters and told them that whenever any of their children got married, he would be happy to come and play at the wedding.

Jennie also met Liszt at the Russian Embassy in London:

I sat next to the great man, whose strong, characteristic face, so often delineated both by brush and chisel, seemed strangely familiar. He was so blind that he ate his asparagus by the wrong end, until I pointed out his error.... After luncheon, notwithstanding his gouty fingers, he was prevailed upon to play.... I never heard him at his best.

Anton Rubinstein I well recollect, with his long hair tossed about, the perspiration pouring down his face, as his big hands tore up and down the piano. Full of tricks—to which so many artists become addicted—when he reached the culminating *fortissimo,* wild with excitement, he would hit with his palms or his forearm as many notes as he possibly could, until he seemed positively to get to the end of the instrument, making the strings snap and the wood sound.[15]

Several months earlier, Jennie's mother-in-law had asked her to undertake a concert for one of her favourite charities, the Padding-

246

ton Recreation Centre. 'It will be a great trouble and care,' Jennie wrote Randolph, 'but I suppose I must.'

Soon she was swept up in its excitement. Princess Alexandra sent her a note offering help. The famous actor-manager Sir Henry Irving offered her the use of his Lyceum Theatre. Artist Julian Story set to work designing three tableaux—one Venetian, one French, and one in which the figures moved.[16] Following a small notice in the paper, Jennie began receiving 'an avalanche of mail from tiresome people all wanting to act or recite'. After the Prince of Wales agreed to sponsor the performance, many of the lovely ladies of London started to compete for the right to appear in the tableaux. 'H.R.H. was very kind and has fussed greatly about it all,' Jennie wrote. 'It *must* be a success. It is no use doing anything unless one is sure of success.'

It was a great success, some nine hundred people packing the theatre, the platform covered with palms and flowers. Even Nellie Melba was one of the performers. 'The Paddingtonians seemed very pleased,' Jennie wrote of the evening.

I had an awful moment when two of the performers who had to begin the concert did not appear. I had to take the place of one of them. . . . Thank goodness it is over. . . .[17]

Personally, I have never been able to surmount the nervousness one feels in playing before the public, whether in concerted pieces or alone. What musical performers, good, bad or indifferent, have not at some time felt their nerve giving way as they approach the difficult passage? Only to think of it is fatal! Once, at some concert for charity, I was playing a classical piece, the first movement of which had a few bars of some difficulty. The first time for the *da capo*, I got over it all right, but to lead for the next movement, it had to be repeated with variations in another key. To my consternation, I found myself embarking on the same one, which, of course, led me to repeating the first movement. Again, as I came to the fatal passage, I trembled and did the same thing. Three times did I repeat that movement, until the audience were becoming quite familiar with the tune. As for me, I felt in a hideous nightmare, and was on the verge of jumping up from the piano and rushing off the stage, when oh! joy! the fourth time, I mechanically played the right bars and was able, eventually, to bring the piece to its conclusion. Hans von Bülow is supposed to have done the same thing once, with a sonata of Beethoven, until, in desperation, he had to send for the music.

Something equally embarrassing happened to her at a concert before a large audience at the Mansion House. She and another woman were to play a Chopin Polonaise on two pianos.

247

As our turn came, the mademoiselle, who was the professional of some experience in execution, said hurriedly to me, 'At the 11th bar on the 6th page, when I make you a sign, stop, as I mean to put in a little cadenza of my own.' Before I could remonstrate, or point out that it would be unnecessary addition to one of Chopin's masterpieces, the lady had seated herself at the piano, and perforce I had to follow suit. When she arrived at the 11th bar of the 6th page, she nodded violently to me, and then proceeded to dazzle the company with arpeggios, runs and trills, until I began to wonder if I should ever find a propitious moment to re-enter. I finally did, and had the pleasure of hearing from the occupants of the front row as I went out, 'Poor Lady Randolph, what a pity she lost her place for so long.'[18]

Randolph's prolonged stay in South Africa stirred up rumours. 'With such a charming wife and so many political and social inducements to remain in England,' a magazine reporter remarked, '. . . and as he has been out of England a great deal of late, . . . I sincerely hope that nothing has gone wrong in the Churchill household.' At the same time Jennie was linked in the press with more and more men of reputation, although many of them were of no real meaning to her.

She and the Prince of Wales had often been guests of the Baron Hirsch at his home in Paris, and he invited them now to attend an international shooting party at St Johann, his Hungarian estate. It was a chance for Jennie to get away from the gossip and from the dismal Grosvenor Square home of her mother-in-law.

'Life at St Johann was simple and healthy,' she wrote.

Shortly after breakfast, a parade of victorias appeared, the horses in gay harness and the postilions in hussar-like blue jackets, Hessian boots and shiny high-crowned hats. The guests then drove to the rendezvous. There an army of 600 beaters were waiting. The guests started off at the sound of a bugle, advanced in line, walked for miles over the sanded, stubbled plains, saw enormous blue hares and the plentiful partridges, roe-deer, blackcock and pheasants. Luncheon was always out-of-doors, regardless of weather.

Jennie particularly remembered one guest: 'As the huge coveys flew over him, seemingly from every point of the compass, he kept calling out to them in his excitement, "For heaven's sake, stop! Oh, do wait one moment!" ' The total bag of partridges for one day reached three thousand.

As she passed through Paris on her return home Jennie had an unpleasant but exciting experience. She was standing by the midday train, in one of the busy archways in the Gare du Nord, when I suddenly heard a shot fired, followed by two or three more in rapid succession, and a man with a hand to his hip and an agonized expression on his face, ran, or rather hobbled, past me from behind one of the pillars of the archway. He was closely followed by another man who held a revolver, which he again fired off, this time so close to me that I fled in terror, seeing, as I ran, the victim fall to the ground, the murderer still firing at him. A large crowd, which had scattered in every direction at the first shots, now rushed to the spot. Meanwhile, fearing that the man was running amok, and that I might be the next recipient of his wild firing, I ran down the platform as fast as the heavy fur coat and various encumbrances permitted me. Unfortunately, I dropped my muff, which happened to be a sable one, adorned with tails, containing my purse and ticket. Before I could pick it up, a man pounced on it and made off at top speed toward the swinging glass doors leading out of the station. As I followed, calling out, I saw him vanish through one of the doors and reappear by another like a clown in a pantomime. Calm and unconcerned, he was swinging a cane, and no muff was visible. While I stared at him in utter amazement, I spied one of the tails of the muff sticking out from his coat, which he was endeavoring to keep closed. At that moment, the bell, which announced the departure of the train, began to ring. There was no time for words; it was a case of 'do or die.' I rushed at the thief, seized the tail of the muff, and jumped into the train which I just managed to catch, leaving the man with his mouth wide open, still staring as we crawled out of the station. As to the wretched victim of the shooting, I heard afterward that the assassin had shot him seven times before he was overpowered, and then tried to beat out his brains with the butt-end of the revolver, so great was his determination to kill him. A passenger received a stray shot in his leg, and altogether it was a scene of wild excitement and confusion. From the paper which gave an account of the fray, it appeared that both men were Americans, the murderer having stalked his prey for more than a year, and caught him as he was leaving France for America. It was proved at the trial that love and money were the motives of the crime.[19]

After returning to London, Jennie was apparently quite upset to learn that the Marquis de Breteuil had found an American heiress named Miss Garner and was going to be married. The wedding ceremony was at Pau, and Jennie did not attend. Writing to Randolph of the Marquis's marriage, she commented, 'I hope Breteuil's wife will keep sane.' Back from a visit to the United States with his bride, Breteuil wrote Jennie an enigmatic letter. 'I am happier every day and I will never forget that you had pushed me. . . . What I miss is not seeing you any more . . . believe me again of my attachment. . . .' This letter somehow fell into Randolph's possession and was found among his papers.

Jennie now moved back to her home in Connaught Place and was hardly bereft of male companions. John Strange Jocelyn, 'the delightful Strange', had come from Ireland and called. The King of Greece took her to a concert. The Prince of Wales came to tea, 'but not the Princess'. She and the Prince went to the Fitzwilliams' for a weekend. After she and Kinsky had been out for an evening, Winston arrived unexpectedly to find them breakfasting together. George Curzon took her to dinner. She spent an evening with Arthur Balfour. 'A.B. sends you his love,' she wrote Randolph.

*Town Topics*, which gobbled up all the gossip, reported: 'Society has invented a new name for Lady R. Her fondness for the exciting sport of husband-hunting and fiancé-fishing, when the husbands and fiancés belong to other women, has earned her the title of "Lady Jane Snatcher".'

The rounds of pleasure were soon replaced by pain. 'Those pains I used to think were in my "mind" were really the thing beginning. I've got lots of pain,' she wrote Randolph. The doctors found that she had a growth in the rectal area, 'a lump about the size of a pullet's egg.' They were unable to tell if it would grow or not, she reported, but if it did, it would have to be cut out and that would be a serious operation.

I can't remember anything else he said—but I am not to give way to nerves and depression. Thank goodness I have done with doctors for the present. I was going down to see the boys today, but Clara has gone. . . . Recommend me some good books, will you? I feel better than I did, though somewhat bruised by those doctors.

Jennie's illness did not cause Randolph to hurry his return. Nor did he attend the wedding of sister Sarah (for whom Jennie had acted as matchmaker). He would return only after he found gold.

Randolph travelled from Kimberley and Johannesburg to Bechuanaland and Mashonaland. Depressed that the gold remained at the end of the rainbow, he wrote to Salisbury and to Balfour asking for appointment to the vacant Ambassadorship at Paris. Balfour, certainly pressed by Jennie, urged his uncle to give Randolph the post: 'It would take him out of a sphere where, in these days of reckless electioneering promises, he is really dangerous and put him in one where he would be relatively powerless from mischief.' The Prime Minister refused.

'I have been horribly low ever since,' Jennie wrote when she heard of the refusal. 'I have not breathed it to anyone, not even your mother. You can tell her when you get home. . . . The idea is too galling that the only thing you ever asked for should be refused!'

Randolph was also bitter at the parade of events. In November, Balfour had been made First Lord of the Treasury and Leader of the House. Randolph wrote to Jennie:

So Arthur Balfour is really the Leader—and Tory Democracy, the genuine article, at an end. Well I've had quite enough of it all. I've waited with great patience for the tide to turn, but it has not turned, and will not now turn in time.

Jennie's problems with Winston also had multiplied by the winter of 1891. He was approaching his seventeenth birthday, and he seemed to have reached the age of indecision. 'Really I feel less keen about the Army every day,' he wrote his mother. 'I think the church would suit me much better.' He then decided to be confirmed in the Church of England. 'Perhaps it will steady him,' Jennie wrote her husband. However, she added that she suspected the main reason he wanted to be confirmed was 'only because it will get him off other work!' She knew her son well. His interest in the Church gradually became remote. (As an adult he liked to quote Disraeli: 'All sensible men are of the same religion.')

Winston had a persistent way of converting an invisible crisis into an imagined catastrophe. 'I can't tell you what trouble I have had with Winston this last fortnight. He has bombarded me with letters, cursing his fate and everyone,' Jennie wrote Randolph. The crisis concerned Welldon's renewed suggestion that he spend the coming Christmas holidays with a family in France, in order to better prepare himself for the French examination for Sandhurst admissions. Winston objected vehemently: 'I beg and pray that you will not send me to a vile, nasty, fusty, beastly French "Family".' Jennie partly surrendered and persuaded Welldon instead to make arrangements at the Paris home of one of Harrow's French teachers. Winston now attacked from another angle.

Darling Mummy, I shall think it will be very unkind and unnatural if you allow him to do me out of my Christmas. . . . Please don't *you* put any pressure on me. . . . Mummy, don't be unkind and make me unhappy . . . I have firmly made up my mind not to go abroad until after the 27th.

Jennie answered firmly, 'You can be quite certain my darling that I will decide for what is best, but I tell you frankly that *I* am going to decide and not *you*.'[20]

Winston enjoyed Paris much more than he had imagined he

would. The Marquis de Breteuil invited him to lunch and Baron Hirsch took him on a visit to the morgue, then a favourite Parisian pastime. 'I was much interested,' Winston wrote, except that he was disappointed at finding only three bodies there that day—'not a good bag.'

As was her custom, Mrs Everest wrote long, solicitous, loving letters. In one she told him she was sending his big tweed coat, 'some fine flannel shirts to sleep in', and his new suit. 'Winny dear do try and keep the new suit expressly for visiting, the brown one will do for everyday wear, please do this to please me. I hope you will not take cold my darling take care not to get wet or damp.'

In another she described her Christmas supper at Connaught Place with the house help.

After supper they all sang songs and then we went into the kitchen and they put aside the table and danced for dear life. Edney whistled and I played the comb like we used to do in our good old nursery days . . . and we drank to the health and happiness of Mama and Papa, Mr. Winston and Mr. Jack which of course I heartily joined in you may be sure.

She continued, 'Cheer up old Boy enjoy yourself try and feel contented you have very much to be thankful for if you only consider and fancy how nice it will be to *parlez vous francais*. . . .'[21]

Jennie had kept Jack with her in London. 'Jack's holidays are so much shorter, I must have him with me,' she had written Randolph. A studious boy, Jack continued to do well at school, and his admission to Harrow appeared certain.[22]

Randolph was finally returning with gold. 'Pa' Perkins, the American engineer representing Rothschild, had found the gold-bearing reefs and determined the direction and depth necessary for Rand Gold-Mining Company shafts to reach the area. Before the news caused a price rise, Rothschild had lent Randolph £5,000 to buy Rand shares. Even after selling two-fifths of his shares to pay debts, within three years Randolph's remaining stock was still worth more than £70,000.

Just before the discovery, Esme Howard reported how drastically changed Randolph was when she saw him there. 'He seemed to be a man who knew he was finished.' Afterward, Lord Winchester saw Randolph crossing a river in Mashonaland in a litter laden with champagne.

'Papa arrived yesterday morning looking very well but with a

252

horrid beard,' Jack wrote his brother in Paris on January 9, 1892. He and his mother had missed the train to the ship by six minutes and had to wait two hours for the next one. The *Globe* had noted, 'Lady R. Churchill nimbly ran across the dock.'

Randolph's beard was a 'terror', Jennie wrote Winston; 'I think I shall have to bribe him to shave it off.' But Randolph kept his ragged beard. Shane Leslie later wrote:

To a child, Randolph was then a grizzled and bearded hunter returned from South Africa. . . . I ventured once to offer him the fruits of my own hunting in the local bush; an empty bird's nest. He stared at me long and sadly, perhaps madly, without uttering a word. It looked a harassed and haunted face; and when he came into the room, everyone started whispering, as in a church.[23]

Randolph did write Winston a reasoned letter, however, although the handwriting revealed a severe tremble. Winston had asked that his father visit him in Paris or get him an extra week's vacation so that he could come home and hear the stories of lions and tigers and gold. Randolph answered that it was much more important for Winston to get back to school and start studying again for the Sandhurst examinations. 'After you have got into the Army you will have many weeks for amusement and idleness should your inclinations go in that direction.'

Answering another money request from Winston, Randolph was more caustic: 'If you were a millionaire, you could not be more extravagant. . . . If you are not more careful . . . it will see you in the Bankruptcy Court.'[24]

Randolph extended his bitterness to Jennie, and Clara must have witnessed some angry scenes between them, for she described them in a flow of detailed letters to her husband. Moreton answered:

. . . What a fright you must have had. That of itself was enough to make you ill. . . . I am so sorry for dear Jane; very sorry; but good times are at hand and when they come in full measure we shall be able to make things much more comfortable for her also. She is a great dear, and with all her faults, I am devoted to her. . . . Poor dear kind Jennie, I shall so long to know things are tolerable with her again. She, of all people, must be fretting under such circumstances. He is a very hateful creature in many ways.
. . . Dear sweet Jenny, I am so sorry for her worries; worries too, not like ours to be got over; he is an impossible man that; a bad-natured man essentially; but the sense of the mistakes he had made would embitter a much better disposition than he has.[25]

253

Even Jennie's mother was now aware of the situation. 'I have just seen Randolph in the park,' she wrote Leonie hurriedly. 'He is in a frantic state of mind about the state of affairs. . . . I must see you, I am so worried. Randolph is going out of town. . . .' But Jennie left town first, together with Clara, for an extended trip to southern France.

Anything disagreeable or disruptive within an upper-class British family of the time was always submerged and kept from the children. Winston knew nothing of his family's continual financial and personal crises and continued writing requests for money and for visits. He had become an expert fencer, with a 'quick and dashing attack which took his opponents by surprise', and which made him the school's fencing champion. It was one of the few times he had ever won anything, but his father's congratulation was curt, 'I only hope fencing will not too much divert you from the army class.' Nor would his father come to see him compete for the Public School Fencing Championship, because he said he had to attend the Sandown Races that day. Winston won that championship, too, against 'much taller and more formidable' opponents.

It was at this time, too, that his first words reached print—in an anonymous letter to the *Harrovian,* signed 'Junius Junior', urging more student participation in gymnasium activities.

Winston was less successful with the final entrance examination for Sandhurst. His tutor thought it was a creditable first try, and noted that Winston would have another chance at it within six months. But Randolph, highly sceptical, wrote his mother, 'If he fails again, I shall think about putting him in business.'

Jack seemed to be everything Winston was not, conscientious, responsible and placid. He was also far more popular with his older relatives. But he, too, was lonely. He wrote his father, 'I waited all afternoon for you. . . . You might come down and see me. You have been here only once, the whole time I have been down here [three years].' Jennie tried to make up for Randolph's obvious lack of affection for his sons. Still in France, she remembered to send Jack a box of tangerines and a dispatch case for his twelfth birthday. She also wrote him how delighted she was when he was admitted to Harrow. Jack and Winston were reunited at Harrow in 1892 and shared a room.

The many who did not know of Lord Randolph's disease still

considered him a potential political force. Salisbury asked him to dinner: 'We shall be very glad to see you.' Arthur Balfour invited him to sit with him on the front bench in the House: '*Everyone* desires that you should do so, and *most of all* yours ever, A.J.B.' Party leaders invited him to attend their meeting on parliamentary tactics. Joseph Chamberlain could not have been kinder. And even the press adopted a friendlier tone. Requests for him to speak publicly came from everywhere again. Randolph, however, confided to an associate, 'Politics interests me less and less.'

Despite his apparent disinterest in politics, Randolph was plainly delighted when the Gladstone Liberals defeated Salisbury's Conservative government in the General Election of July 1892, by a bare parliamentary margin of forty. Randolph never forgave Salisbury for so quietly accepting his resignation and refusing to appoint him as either Viceroy of India or Ambassador to France. As for the Conservative Party, Randolph wrote that it had 'boycotted and slandered me . . . for five years'.

His health was failing again. 'I have been very seedy . . . with giddiness,' he told Rosebery. Jennie had returned from France, and she also was ill. 'Her condition is so full of serious possibilities,' Dr Roose wrote Randolph, 'that I felt it my duty to advise her Ladyship seeing at once Dr Keith.'

Jennie made light of it. She journeyed to Scotland for a short visit with friends, while Randolph stayed close to his horses at Newcastle. But her pain suddenly increased, and she went to Dr Keith for a more detailed examination.

A tall, gentle man with a full beard, long hair, intense eyes, and a musical voice, Dr Thomas Keith not only became Jennie's physician but later advised on Randolph's case in its final stages. He was a prominent surgeon, educated in Boston and Edinburgh, a specialist in the genital and ovarian areas, and widely known for his use of electricity in treating uterine tumours.[26] His examination of Jennie revealed a swelling in the right groin near the uterus, a pelvic peritonitis and cellulitis. Operations for such a condition were rare and dangerous. There was, however, hope that the whole thing might quieten down, Keith pointed out. 'Rest is essential in order to avoid the risk of an acute attack. . . . In moving about, she must keep within the limits of pain.'

'We have to face many months of terrible anxiety . . . and there is no margin for mistake,' Roose wrote Randolph at Newcastle. 'Her Ladyship is holding her own, but has a great deal of suffering.'

'He said if I wished to avoid an operation, I must be very quiet,' Jennie wrote her husband. 'By that he meant no mental worry or physical exertion. It is rather gloomy here and I miss you much.'

Randolph, who knew all about suffering and gloom, suddenly realized that Jennie might die. Despite the drift of their marriage, he had always been certain that she was there and that she would always be there when he truly needed her. That knowledge had buoyed him through his steady series of crises. But with her gone, there would be no one but his mother; there would be emptiness. No matter how self-centred he was, this was a time to turn away from self-pity in concern and care for his wife. He must have been moved, torn by the fact that despite everything, she still wanted her husband near her.

Jennie's crisis also converted Randolph into a father again. He promptly returned to London and wrote his sons.

Your dear mother was extremely ill yesterday and we were rather alarmed. But thank God today there is an improvement and the doctors are very hopeful. I only got up to town this evening. I will keep you informed as to how your dear mother progresses.

Since Winston was busy preparing for his repeat examination for Sandhurst, Randolph added, 'Your mother would be in such good spirits if she thought you were going to do well in your examination.' Then in an affectionate, paternal note, 'Kiss Jack for me.'

Winston replied immediately, 'I am awful sorry to hear that Mama is so bad. I hope that she will soon be better, and that you will let us know every day how she is. Is it very good writing to her?'

It was a time of trouble and death. The eighth Duke of Marlborough, died unexpectedly in 1892 at the age of forty-eight. It was a shock and hurried Randolph's own physical disintegration. Troubles piled upon troubles. Shortly after his brother's death, Randolph received a desperate note from his widow. Some time before, she said, the Duke had written an article on 'The Art of Living' for the *Fortnightly*. 'I am anxious to get it back,' she wrote. 'I could not have it appear in print. See Mr Frank Harris, and get this article from him at any price.'

The Duke had done the piece for the *Fortnightly* in order to get Frank Harris to publish a dull article by his mistress, Lady Colin

Campbell, the unorthodox lady who had decided to become an actress. In his will, the Duke had left Lady Campbell the sum of £20,000 'as a proof of my friendship and esteem'. The article was full of personal revelation in which he wrote, among other things, that he thought women were the only things in life worth winning.

Randolph sent for Harris. 'When he came across the room to shake hands with me,' said Harris,

I was appalled by his appearance. In a couple of years he had changed out of character, had become an old man instead of a young one. [Randolph was then forty-three years old]. His face was haggard; his hair greyish and very thin on top; his thick beard, also half-grey, changed him completely. He held himself well, which added dignity, but the old boyish smile was gone.

Randolph asked Harris not to publish his brother's article. Harris protested, but Randolph answered, 'You won't refuse an old friend's last request,' and held out his hand.

'As I took his hand,' said Harris, 'and looked at him I felt sick: the deep lines on his face, the heavy gummy bags under his miserable eyes, the shaking hand—it might well be his *last* request!'

'It shall be as you wish,' promised Harris.

Before Harris left, he told Randolph to get well and strong. 'I fear the dice are loaded against me,' Randolph replied.[27]

Randolph had vertigo, numbness of the hands, palpitations, increasing deafness, and a growing difficulty in articulating. His letters, once clear and concise, now rambled on in all directions and were written in a tremulous script. His behaviour was increasingly erratic and moody. On one occasion he had a most congenial dinner with his old friend and political enemy, Joseph Chamberlain; then at another dinner in the same week, for no apparent reason, he snarled at Chamberlain and ordered the waiter to put a bowl of flowers between them.

He was equally unpredictable with his family. When his sons put on an amateur theatrical at Banstead for a small family audience, Randolph said frostily, 'I shall preserve a strong and acid silence.' Then again, he might show a much softer side of himself. Late in 1892 when his boys were on holiday, the family was at Banstead for a weekend. Winston fired a double-barrelled shotgun at a rabbit that appeared on the lawn, and the sound startled Randolph.

'He had been very angry and disturbed,' Winston wrote later.

Understanding at once that I was distressed, he took occasion to reassure me. I then had one of the three or four intimate conversations with him which are all I can boast. He explained how old people were not always very considerate towards young people, that they were absorbed in their own affairs and might well speak roughly in sudden annoyance.

In a quiet, fatherly, almost affectionate tone, Randolph told Winston how glad he was that he liked to shoot, and that he would arrange for him to shoot partridges on their small property.

Then he proceeded to talk to me in the most wonderful and captivating manner about school and going into the army and the grown-up life which lay beyond. I listened spellbound to this sudden departure from his usual reserve, amazed at his intimate comprehension of my affairs. Then at the end, he said, 'Do remember things do not always go right with me. My every action is misjudged, and every word distorted . . . so make some allowances.'[28]

Perhaps Jennie was making more allowances, too. She had been very dangerously ill, and her recovery was slow. Deeper than ever now, she understood the mood and the mind of her husband, whose suffering and closeness to death was so intense and shameful and predictable. And in her time of real danger, he was the one she had wanted to be with her. She was thirty-eight. Her beauty was still rich but no longer fresh. The young men she had known were now no longer young and most of them were married. Though her husband was only a remnant of the man she had married, he was still her husband.

'My dear sweet old Jane,' her brother-in-law Moreton wrote from America:

Troublous times at least do this—they turn us back upon those really near and dear with a feeling of gentle reliance and that is why I am writing to you. . . . I am anxious that you have these worries, not only these abominable money troubles, vile and vulgar as they are. Please God, good times are near and I will take a house in Leicestershire, and a lot of horses for you, and we will renew youth and health also at the dear old game.[29]

A dream, to be sure, but this was a time when she needed such dreams. Count Kinsky was not available to console her, as he had been summoned by the Archduke Franz Ferdinand, the heir to the Austro-Hungarian throne, to accompany him for three months travel in India and Ceylon as part of a world tour. The two men formed a fast friendship, and the Archduke would again ask for Kinsky to come with him on future tours.[30]

Jennie, however, did receive sympathy from an unexpected

source—her mother-in-law, the Dowager Duchess. Their conflict had lost its sharp edge, and although there was still a large reservoir of resentment left, it did not prevent the Dowager Duchess from offering Jennie the Marlborough home at 50 Grosvenor Square whenever Randolph was away nor Jennie from accepting the offer. Now, with Jennie's illness and Randolph's worsening health, the Duchess suggested that they both move in with her because 'it might be much more comfortable and economical.' And so they did.

No sooner did Jennie begin slowly improving than things started happening again to Winston. Late in January 1893, she was informed that he had failed his final examination for Sandhurst for the second time. He wrote that he was 'awfully depressed'. Randolph asked Welldon for further advice about his son and Welldon recommended a 'crammer', a Captain Walter James. Winston later wrote that with the crammer's help 'no one who was not a congenital idiot could avoid passing thence into the Army'.

But before Winston could begin the cram course, he had a serious accident in which he was almost killed. The Churchills had given up Banstead, but Randolph's adoring sister Cornelia, Lady Wimborne, had lent Jennie and the boys her comfortable estate in Bournemouth for January. The estate had some fifty acres of pine forest ending in sandy cliffs and smooth beach. Playing a game of chase with his twelve-year-old brother and fourteen-year-old cousin, Winston found himself trapped in the middle of a bridge, so he climbed the balustrade and tried to jump onto the top of a nearby fir tree. He missed and fell almost thirty feet to the ground. It was three days before he regained consciousness and two months before he was back at school.

Randolph had gone to Dublin for a reunion with friends, when Jennie summoned him home with the news. Among other injuries, Winston had a ruptured kidney. As he put it, 'I looked at life round the corner.' The Harley Street specialist whom Dr Roose had brought told Jennie that her son 'should not return to hard study any more than he should take vigorous exercise.'

This suited Winston perfectly. He was brought to the home of the Dowager Duchess on Grosvenor Square, and it turned out to be a truly happy time for him. Jennie gave her son solicitous attention and kept his mind stirred with the excitement of parliamentary politics.

My mother gave me full accounts of what she heard, and Mr. Edward Marjoribanks, afterwards Lord Tweedmouth, Mr. Gladstone's Chief Whip, was married to my father's sister, Fanny. We thus shared, in a detached way, the satisfaction of the Liberals at coming back to power after their long banishment. We heard some, at least, of their hopes and fears. Politics seemed very important and vivid to my eyes, in those days. They were directed by statesmen of commanding intellect and personality.

It seemed a very great world in which these men lived; a world where high rules reigned and every trifle in public conduct counted; a duelling ground where although the business might be ruthless, and the weapons loaded with ball, there was ceremonious personal courtesy and mutual respect.[31]

Jennie invited most of these 'statesmen of commanding intellect' for dinner, and Winston listened in awe as they discussed 'the burning topics of the hour'. Among the guests were three future Prime Ministers—Rosebery, Balfour, and Asquith—all of whom, in one way or another, would help shape Winston's future. Jennie encouraged Winston not simply to listen, but to ask questions, and even politely argue.

'In those days, people could not see any definite principle behind Jennie Churchill's upbringing of her sons,' wrote Lady Warwick:

They did not realize that she was developing in them qualities, which, in the ordinary course, take years to show themselves. She always found time to encourage her boys to express themselves.... I still chuckle when I remember how, as a schoolboy, he [Winston] would comment to his face upon the views of such a politician as Lord Hartington.[32]

In addition to filling her house with important political figures and encouraging Winston to involve himself in the discussions, Jennie explained at length all the intricacies of political manœuvre which so fascinated him. She supplemented that with her own estimates of the political leaders of both parties. So vividly and excitingly was the way of politics described that it enveloped him enough to help pattern the direction of his life.

As soon as Winston was allowed to go out, Jennie encouraged him to visit the House of Commons to listen to the debates and watch the great men he had observed in private conversation now acting their parts in public. One thing immediately struck him as remarkable: political opponents did not allow even their most violent parliamentary clashes to hurt their friendly social relations. Winston particularly remembered one interchange between his father and Sir William Harcourt in Parliament.

Sir William seemed to be quite furious and most unfair in his reply, and I was astonished when only a few minutes later, he made his way up to where I sat, and with a beaming smile, introduced himself to me and asked me what I thought of it all.[33]

Frank Harris once asked Winston Churchill about his father.

'Did you never talk politics with him?'
'I tried, but he only looked with contempt on me and would not answer.'
'But didn't he see you had something in you?'
'He thought of no one but himself. No one else seemed to him worth thinking about.'
'You didn't like him?'
'How could I? I was ready enough to as a boy, but he wouldn't let me. He treated me as if I had been a fool; barked at me whenever I questioned him. I owe everything to my mother; to my father, nothing.'[34]

During those early months of 1893, Winston could see the effects of his father's condition. 'As time wore on, I could not help feeling that my father's speeches were not as good as they used to be. There were some brilliant successes; yet, on the whole, he seemed to be hardly holding his own.' Henry Lucy reported one painful episode:

He had, at the proper moment, taken some drug to 'buck up' his frail body through the hour he intended to speak. But someone raised the question of privilege, discussed for a full hour, through which Lord Randolph sat, fuming. When the hour had sped, the tonic effects of medicine were exhausted. It was a decrepit man who, with bowed figure, and occasionally inarticulate voice, at length stood at the table—a painful spectacle, from contemplation of which Members gradually withdrew. The chamber which once filled at the signal, 'Churchill is up', was almost empty when he sat down.[35]

At Jennie's urging, Edward Carson had a private dinner with Winston at Harrow and explained to him at length how the Liberals, of whom he was one, planned to overcome the opposition of the House of Lords to the Home Rule Bill (which they did not do). Carson also invited Winston to dine with him at the House of Commons. 'If you would rather I would not go, please send me a wire,' Winston wrote his father.[36]

Jack wrote Jennie from school that Welldon had told him 'if I worked like Winny did his first three years here, it would turn his hairs white.' When she visited him at Harrow, she learned that Jack was 'the youngest boy in the school', but was happily settled. Welldon's report was excellent.

Winston, however, still was not a serious student, and Captain James complained that he was 'casual', 'inattentive', and 'rather too much inclined up to the present to teach his instructors instead of endeavouring to learn from them. . . .' Furthermore, Winston had developed other distractions. At eighteen, he was a good-looking young man with a ruddy face, an aggressive manner, and an eye-catching crop of red hair. He had caught the eye of Mabel Love, a young actress at the Lyric Theatre, who sent him some pictures and notes—much to the envy of his Harrow friends.

Finally, on his third try, Winston passed the entrance examination into Sandhurst, but barely. He later said of that:

If this aged, weary-souled Civil Service Commissioner had not asked this particular question about these cosines or tangents in their squared or even cubed condition, which I happened to have learned scarcely a week before, I might have gone into the church and preached orthodox sermons in a spirit of anxious contradiction to the age.

I might have gone into the City and made a fortune. I might have gravitated to the Bar, and persons might have been hanged to my defence. Anyhow, the whole of my life would have been altered and I suppose would have altered a great many other lives.

His marks, however, were not high enough to qualify him for an infantry cadetship, so he was assigned to the cavalry.

I had already formed a definite opinion at the relative advantages of riding and walking. What fun it would be, having a horse! I say to parents, and especially wealthy parents, 'Don't give your son money. As far as you can afford it, give him horses.' No one ever came to grief—except honourable grief—through riding horses. No hour of life is lost that is spent in the saddle. Young men have often been ruined through owning horses, or through backing horses, but never through riding them; unless, of course, they break their necks, which, taken at a gallop, is a very good death to die.[37]

Winston wrote his father a letter of youthful exuberance about his success in entering Sandhurst, and he got this caustic response:

The first extremely discreditable feature of your performance was missing the infantry, for in that failure is demonstrated beyond refutation your slovenly happy-go-lucky harum scarum style of work for which you have always been distinguished at your different schools. Never have I received a really good report of your conduct in your work. . . .

With all the advantages you had, with all the abilities which you foolishly think yourself to possess . . . with all the efforts that have been made to make your life easy and agreeable . . . this is the grand result. . . .

262

Randolph went on to say that if Winston kept up his past performance, 'you will become a mere social wastrel, one of the hundreds of the public school failures, and you will degenerate into a shabby, unhappy and futile existence.'

How much of that bitterness was a reflection of his own frustrations and failures? How much resulted from his having asked the Duke of Cambridge to reserve a place for Winston in his regiment, the 60th Rifles, and now having to face the embarrassment of rescinding the request? But part of his resentment was based on the fact that the cavalry meant an expense of two hundred pounds a year, plus the cost of several horses and possibly a string of polo ponies.

Randolph ended his diatribe to Winston with, 'Your mother sends her love.' It was a venomous letter, and Winston never forgot the pain it caused him.

Randolph also wrote to the Duchess his views of Winston:

I have told you often and you never would believe me that he has little [claim] to cleverness, to knowledge or any capacity for settled work. He had great talent for show-off exaggeration and make believe. The whole result of this either at Harrow or at Eton [was] to prove his total worthlessness as a scholar or a conscientious worker. He need not expect much from me.

Just as Winston had not known at thirteen whether his father had gone to Harrow or Eton, neither did Randolph seem to know now that his son had never been to Eton.

Jennie had small illusions about any hope of a cure for her husband, but she did think the mineral baths at Kissingen might quiet his nerves and give him some needed rest. Most of all, though, she wanted to get him away from London, where he was making more and more a pitiful spectacle of himself at public and social affairs.

For her sons that summer of 1893, Jennie arranged a walking tour of Switzerland with a young Eton tutor. Of the Matterhorn Winston wrote, 'I don't wonder that people want to go up in spite of the numerous graves in the churchyard.'

At Kissingen, Jennie and Randolph were visited by Prince Otto von Bismarck, who by then was out of power. 'He came up to our rooms—which luckily are on the first floor—and sat down and we began to converse,' Randolph wrote to his mother.

I had sent off a message to Jennie, who had gone to the Kurhaus to see a friend, so I had about a quarter of an hour in which to talk to the Prince. . . . He is 78—so he told me afterwards—but he looks so much younger than Mr. Gladstone. . . . He struck me as being very nervous. Perhaps it was meeting with a total stranger, because he had never seen me before. However, he was most gracious and seemed very anxious to please. You may imagine that I did my very best to please him, for I thought it a great honour for this old Prince to come and see us. . . . He further in conversation said that he should be very alarmed and anxious if such a man as Mr. Gladstone governed 'my country'. Then Jennie arrived, and he talked mainly to her for a few minutes, when he announced that his son Herbert and his recently-married wife arrived that afternoon to stay a few days with them, and that he hoped we should see something of them.[38]

They later had dinner together, Prince Otto and the Princess, Jennie and Randolph, Count Herbert and his new wife. The new Countess was the former Marguerite Hoyes. Herbert had earlier intended to marry Princess Elisabeth of Carolath-Beuthen, but the scandal of their affair and the Princess's divorce of her husband had forced the Count to give her up. The social stigma remained so acute, however, that the Count and Countess would be snubbed by Berlin Court Society for some time.[39] Jennie described the dinner in detail:

We dined with him at the old *Schloss*, where he was living, its picturesque red roof making a landmark in the flat Bavarian scenery. . . . At dinner, I sat on one side of the Prince, and Randolph on the other, the huge boar-hound, our host's constant companion, lying on the ground between us. Conversation was animated. Bismarck spoke excellent English, but very slowly; and if he could not find a word he wanted, he would pause and think until he did.

His family looked up to him with awe and admiration, and listened with the greatest attention to every word he uttered. The old Princess, who seemed very feeble, did not take much part in the conversation. After dinner, we adjourned to another part of the room, where we sat round a long table covered with books and newspapers. There were a great many illustrated papers, full of caricatures of Bismarck, which in answer to a question, he assured me he did not mind in the least. Later, however, Count Herbert contradicted this, saying that his father was really very sensitive, and disliked being caricatured.

Speaking of the country and the long walks he took daily, Bismarck said he loved nature, but the amount of life he saw awed him, and that it took a great deal of faith to believe that an 'all-seeing Eye' could notice every living atom, when one realized what that meant. 'Have you ever sat on the grass and examined it closely? There is enough life in one square yard to appal you,' he said. When we were about to leave, his great dog fixed his fierce eyes on mine in so persistent a manner that I became alarmed and thought that he was going to spring upon me; but the Prince reassured me, saying, 'He is looking at your eyes, because he has not seen any like them.'[40]

During the two months the Churchills were at Kissingen, Winston entered Sandhurst and Jennie kept in close touch with him. Things went very well for Winston from the start. Gone were the 'discomfort, restriction and purposeless monotony. . . . One could feel oneself growing up almost every week.' He was given an infantry cadetship, after all, which pleased his father. His marks were consistently good. 'It shows that I could learn quickly enough the things that mattered,' he said.

Randolph still seemed sceptical of Winston, however, and pointedly criticized both the content and style of his son's letters. Almost in retaliation, Winston let his mother know how happy he was to be able to write to her 'unreservedly instead of having to pick and choose my words and information'. He closed with, 'Do come back as soon as you can as I am longing to see you. . . . Goodbye dear darling Mummy. Ever so much love and more kisses from your ever loving son.' The sentiment seems overripe for a young man nearing nineteen. The emotion more properly belongs to a boy lonely for his mother, or to a young man pining for his sweetheart. Seen in the context of his father's constant rejection of him, however, Winston's longing for love reflected a continuing need.

Jack shared his brother's need. Jennie did not return to London with Randolph but went to Paris to visit Leonie, and Jack asked his father repeatedly, 'When is Mama coming home?' And with repressed anger he said, 'I suppose that you are too busy to come and see me one day this term. Even a Sunday would do.' Randolph promised he would go, but then Jack wrote his mother, 'Papa changed his mind or something and did not come to see me although he sent me one pound but I would rather he would come down.'

Randolph finally did visit Jack at Harrow and brought along his friend General Lord Roberts, V.C. The three had dinner with Welldon. ('Such an honour,' Winston wrote his mother about the hero's visit. 'I can never remember a lower boy going before.')

When Jennie wired Randolph for money so she could stay in Paris longer, he simply answered that their bank balance was overdrawn. She returned home. Jack's letter was waiting for her, telling her about his father's visit and declaring that he needed 'a little money', a new silk hat, and was tired of wearing Winny's 'shabby' coat which was 'awful'.

But Jennie's more serious worries concerned Winston. During the past year she had continually made mention to Randolph of Winston's need to be made a man, to have the advantage of fatherly advice and male companionship. Finally her campaign had effect. Winston's new status as a gentleman cadet improved his position with his father. Examining his son in this new light, Randolph informed the Dowager Duchess, 'He has much smartened up.' In the coming months, Winston's relationship with his father reached its peak. Conversations were minimal and there was still no sign of emotional feeling, but there was more contact.

Randolph began taking his son to the theatre, a few racing parties, and some political gatherings. He even sent Winston two boxes of his favourite cigars, advising him though, 'Keep down the smoking, keep down the drink and go to bed as early as you can.' Winston answered, 'I shall take your advice about the cigars, and I don't think I shall often smoke more than one or two a day—and very rarely that.'[41]

Winston's letters now had a more worldly air. He thought his father's remarks on the coal strike 'were splendid'. Had his father read a new novel called *Euthanasia*? 'It seems well written.' Would his father please put his name down for a good club? And also, 'Am now in tails according to your instructions.'

There was going to be a ball at Sandhurst, he wrote. 'If Mama is home, I shall ask her to come.' Both boys were proud of their mother's beauty, talents, social position, and striking personality. 'She didn't seem to be like other women at all,' said Shane Leslie. 'I think her sons and I looked on her as something far more beautiful than any of the actresses we were called on to admire.'

But Winston was not so awed by his mother that he could not raise his voice in indignation toward her. The reason now was that the Dowager Duchess had dispensed with the services of Mrs Everest, who was, he wrote, 'In my mind associated—more than anything else—with *home*. . . . She is an old woman who has been your devoted servant for nearly twenty years—she is more fond of Jack and I than of any other people in the world.' She had fed them, clothed them, nursed them, kissed them, played with them, cried with them, fought for them, loved them. ('I am going to make

Winnie's box cover tomorrow. . . . I am longing to see my darling Jackie to have some kisses. . . .') They were, in a sense, her cubs more than Jennie's.

The Dowager Duchess had sent Mrs Everest on holiday, and while she was away had stopped her wages and sacked her. The Duchess never had liked Mrs Everest, considering her a barrier between herself and her grandsons. With Jennie and Randolph living with her, she used the excuse of inadequate space to fire Mrs Everest. Winston called it 'cruel and mean'.

'I know you have no choice in the matter and that the Duchess has every right to discharge a servant for whom she has "no further use",' he wrote his mother. But 'it is in your power to explain to the Duchess that she *cannot* be sent away until she has got a good place.' He was not asking his mother, he was insisting. If she did not see that Mrs Everest was provided for, he said, he would go directly to his father.

Jennie, of course, was in no position to ask for anything. She and Randolph were in the Duchess's home on pure sufferance. She tried to find Mrs Everest a place, and finally did, at the home of a Bishop in Essex, 'an outlandish part of the world', and also continued to send her a small, separate cheque.

Mrs Everest was most unhappy away from her boys and away from the lively circle of the Churchills. For the short remainder of her life, Elizabeth Ann Everest maintained a constant and motherly correspondence with Winston and Jack and saw them whenever she could. (She had visited both her boys at Harrow when their parents could not come. Jack's son Peregrine insists that it was his father, not Winston, who met her at the station, kissed her, and openly escorted her through the school.[42] One of his classmates commented, 'I wish I had the courage to do that with my nanny.')

With Mrs Everest in Essex and their parents so often either travelling or socializing, Winston and Jack still had a host of homes they could visit for weekends or short holidays. Their family was large and quite closely-knit. The aunts were the anchors, the grandmothers the bedrock, and the horde of cousins provided a ready intermingling of companionship and love. They were always welcome at Blenheim, in Ireland, Paris, and the town and country homes of a dozen close relatives.

After his flurry of concerned fatherhood, Randolph retired again

267

to his racehorses, which were having an excellent year. For the previous four years, in fact, Randolph and his partner, Lord Dunraven, had been among the biggest winners of the British turf. Jennie again substituted for him in visits to Sandhurst and her letters to Winston were longer now.[43] But it was soon time to be more wife than mother.

'In the spring of 1894, it became clear to all of us that my father was gravely ill,' Winston Churchill wrote.

He still persisted in his political work. Almost every week, he delivered a speech at some important centre. No one could fail to see that these efforts were increasingly unsuccessful. The verbatim reports dropped from 3 to 2 columns, and to 1½. On one occasion, the *Times* mentioned that the hall was not filled.[44]

Just before he was scheduled to address Parliament in March 1894, his friends John Morley and Arthur Balfour talked about it. 'He told me that Randolph was going to make a speech two hours long,' Morley said afterward.

'What about?' Morley asked.

'Heaven only knows,' answered Balfour.[45]

When Randolph got up on that occasion to speak, his face prematurely aged, his hands shaking, his speech so garbled that it became unintelligible after the first sentence, Members fled into the lobby. To check their onrush, there were cries of 'Order, order!' A friend described the speech as a waking nightmare. Randolph's face had a terrible, mad look, and he even screamed, 'You damned fools! You're playing the devil with the Tory Party and making hell of the House of Commons.' But it was he who was making the hell, and Arthur Balfour sat next to him, his head bowed, his hands over his face in pity and shame.

'There was no curtain, no retirement,' wrote his dear friend, the Liberal Lord Rosebery. 'He died by inches in public.'[46]

Rosebery replaced Gladstone as Prime Minister in March 1894. The Queen had coolly accepted the resignation of the proud old eagle—she had never liked Gladstone. Silver-tongued Rosebery was more to her taste. Even Gladstone had once called him the cleverest man in politics. Rosebery possessed a remarkable voice with natural authority, and he could be as terrible to his enemies as he was irresistible to his friends. His smile could be playful, his silence freezing. He could also discuss Greek poets or racehorses with equal skill (his horses would win the Derby three times). He seemed to have everything, except ambition. But Rosebery had come into power when Liberal fortunes were at their lowest. It was the end of an age, and he was not the man to begin a new one.

Randolph was Rosebery's personal sadness. 'Why recall those last days except to recall the pity of them,' Rosebery wrote. He begged Jennie to keep Randolph away from the House of Commons, stop his public appearances, prevent any further speeches. Jennie tried. Winston Churchill later wrote:

I heard my mother and the old Duchess, who so often disagreed—both urging him to take a rest, while he persisted that he was all right and that everything was going well. I knew that these two, who were so near and devoted to him, would never have pressed him thus without the gravest need.

'I don't think any wife could have played a greater part than Jennie did,' Shane Leslie said. 'She had tremendous powers; she had a touch of Cleopatra in her and she never lost heart.'[47] There were numberless times when she almost did. To maintain her own equilibrium, Jennie took frequent trips to Paris to be with Leonie. Clara was often there, too.

Randolph's public conduct was completely unpredictable. After sitting alongside him at a dinner, Lord Carnarvon had written that Randolph's conversation was 'as mad a one as I ever listened to from mortal lips'. Attending another dinner at Sir Henry Thompson's, Frank Harris sat opposite Randolph. Harris had seen him only a couple of months before, but now Randolph was far worse. His face was drawn and his skin leaden grey; there were gleams of hate, anger, and fear in his eyes, 'the dreadful fear of those who have learned how close madness is.'

All through the next course Lord Randolph didn't speak a word. As the game was being taken round, the footman noticed that it was not properly cut, so he passed Lord Randolph quickly to get it dispieced at the sideboard. At once Randolph pointing with outstretched hand, squealed out as if in pain, 'E-e-e-e-e-e!'
'What is it, Lord Randolph?' asked the host in utter solicitude.
'E-e-e-e!' He repeated the high squeal, while pointing with his finger after the footman. 'I want that—e-e-e! Some of that—!'
'It shall be brought back,' said Sir Henry. 'I'm very glad you like it.'
The grouse was brought back: Randolph helped himself and began to eat greedily. Suddenly he stopped, put down his knife and fork and glared at each face round the table, apparently suspecting that his strange behaviour

had been remarked. He was insane, that was clear. From that moment on I could drink but not eat. Randolph Churchill mad! Like Maupassant![48]

On May 27, Wilfrid Scawen Blunt visited Churchill at Grosvenor Square and then described his condition:

He is terribly altered, poor fellow, having some disease, paralysis, I suppose, which affects his speech, so that it is painful to listen to him. He makes prodigious efforts to express himself clearly, but these are only too visible. He talked of his election prospects at Bradford, and the desire of the Conservatives to delay the turning out of the Rosebery government.

About Egypt, Randolph said, 'You know my opinion is unchanged, but my tongue is tied.' He walked his friend Blunt to the door, trying to say something about Egypt, but finally broke down, almost in tears. 'I know what to say, but damn it, I can't say it.'[49]

Randolph was still saddened by the death of his closest friend Louis Jennings, who had succumbed to cancer at the age of fifty-six. Jennings had been his constant support in Parliament, and had made his own reputation as an editor of the London edition of the New York *Herald*, as a crusading editor of *The New York Times* during the Tweed Ring exposé, and as the author of a three-volume novel, *The Philadelphian*. In his will, Randolph had named Jennings as one of his literary executors, and never changed the designation, even after Jennings's death.

The doctors decided that Randolph should go with Jennie on a world tour, then changed their minds,[1] worried that he would need a doctor's attention, and finally agreed that Dr Keith[2] would accompany him. Randolph had sold his Connaught Place house plus some of his gold stocks to pay his bills and provide funds for the trip. He had also sold his share of the Abbess to Lord Dunraven for some £8,000.

Down to the dregs of his life, Randolph still had the stamp of the patrician, a sense of fitness and dignity. His had been a life of pleasure, sport, and fashion, but he had left his mark as a stormy statesman with a record of sporadic brilliance. His temper was imperious, his disdain overbearing, his rudeness vicious. No man had made more enemies. Yet he demonstrated—when he chose— gifts of grace and charm. He showed vestiges of those graces at a dinner for some of his oldest friends just before leaving on the tour. He talked little and worried excessively about the comfort of his guests. But 'one noticed how nervously his hand beat on the table, as he gazed round.'

'I cannot even now make up my mind whether I wish that I had dined or stayed away,' Lord Rosebery later wrote. 'It was all pain, and yet one would not have liked to have missed his good-bye. I still cannot think of it without distress.'

Before leaving, Randolph contracted to write a series of columns for a Paris journal describing his world tour, but they were columns he would never write.

It was not a trip Jennie wanted to make—a whole year away from the world she loved, a year with a husband nearly insane. In addition, she had had a showdown with Count Kinsky. He could not and would not lose her for a whole year. He had waited too long, and a year out of their lives now was more than he could tolerate. The whole world would understand if she were to leave Randolph, a virtual madman. Kinsky had already requested and received permission to transfer to the legation in Brussels. From there they could transfer together to any embassy in the world, a new world, their own. They were entitled to the rest of their lives together. But Jennie turned away. Randolph was the man she had once loved. He was her husband and he was dying, and he needed her because he had no one else. She could not leave him now.

They started their world tour on the S.S. *Majestic* on June 27, 1894. A few old friends came to see them off, among them Rosebery aud Goschen and Lady Jeune, as well as their sons.

'I was making a road-map . . . when a cyclist messenger brought me the College Adjutant's order to proceed at once to London,' Winston Churchill later wrote.

My father was setting out the next day on a journey round the world. An ordinary application to the college authorities for my being granted special leave of absence had been refused, as a matter of routine. He had tele-graphed to the Secretary of State for War . . . and no time had been lost in setting me on my way to London.

We drove to the station the next morning—my mother, my younger brother and I. In spite of the great beard, which he had grown during his South African journey four years before, his face looked terribly haggard and worn with mental pain. He patted me on the knee in a gesture which, however simple, was perfectly informing.[3]

Leonie later talked about Randolph with Frank Harris:

Randolph was quite mad when my sister took him on that last trip round the world. We all knew it. No one but Jennie would have trusted herself to go with him, but she's afraid of nothing and very strong. Yet from things she has let drop, she must have had a trying time with him. Why once, she told me, he drew out a loaded revolver in the cabin and threatened her, but she snatched it from him at once, pushed him back in his berth, and left the cabin, locking the door behind her. Jennie is the bravest woman I ever knew.

Harris reported that Jennie herself told him, 'At first, when he was practically a maniac and very strong it was bad enough, but as soon as he became weak and idiotic, I didn't mind.'[4]

Perhaps her words were actually less harsh, but even if not, they can be understood with sympathy. He was mad and she knew it, yet she went with him—and she did not have to. The decision was hers and the strength was hers. And so was the final horror.

Jennie's cousin William Travers Jerome, then an assistant district attorney in New York City, met her for the first time when the Churchills arrived in New York. 'Shall I call you Aunt Jennie or Cousin Jennie?' Jerome asked her. She answered, 'Why don't you just call me Jennie. It will make you feel older and make me feel younger.'[5]

What might have made Jennie feel older in New York was to note that there was a new Madison Square Garden, designed by Stanford White, directly across the street from the old Jerome house on Madison and 26th Street. Even newer was the Metropolitan Life Insurance headquarters only three blocks away, foreshadowing the change of the Madison Square area from a residential to a commercial centre.[6]

The weather was hot in the city, and the Churchills stayed only two days. Perhaps they were speeded on their way by the pressure of the social invitations they could not face. A local magazine reported:

His Lordship is much changed from the gay, clever and vivacious young man who gained wide popularity here and at Newport, 10 or 11 years ago, when he came to visit the family of Mr. Leonard Jerome. He is restless, nervous and irritable, and walks feebly, with jerky steps, like a man uncertain of where he is putting his feet. His whole manner indicates a painful nervousness and mental irritation, from the querulous tones of his voice to his compressed lips, which he keeps drawn over his teeth in an apparent effort to control their trembling.[7]

Chauncey Depew, one of the few people they saw, put his private railroad car at their disposal for their journey to Bar Harbor. After the dust and heat of New York, Bar Harbor was a haven of fresh sea breezes, lovely drives and mountain walks. But Jennie commented, 'As far as I could gather, life there was very much a second edition of Newport, and consisted in perpetual dressing, dinner, and dances, and that horror of horrors, the leaving of cards.'

The Churchills and their party then travelled across Canada by train.[8]

On an average, our train stopped every half-hour, with much whistling, ringing of bells, and exchange of greetings between the engine-driver and the inhabitants. Every log-cabin was the station, and every platform the club of these poor people whose only excitement was the daily arrival of the train. . . . Life on one of these prairies, although probably monotonous, must have the compensations which come with peace and the close study of nature. . . . At Banff, we had our car put into a siding, and passed two days there, which well repaid us. For the first time, we saw the Rockies and all their grandeur. We could not resist the 'call of the wild', and drove about all day in uncomfortable buckboards and 'cutunders'.[9]

During one of those drives, Jennie insisted on getting down and touching some 'hoodoos' for luck. These were curious natural monuments, half earth, half stone, some seventy feet high, looking like the half-formed figure of a man seated on a pedestal. Indians treated them with great superstition and awe.

During the trip through Canada, they also saw great forest fires,

and at times we would wend our way through burning trees on every side. It was a melancholy sight to see the miles of black stumps and leafless skeletons, their twisted and tortured branches standing out against the background of snow, while the bright-green ferns and variegated flowers made a carpet at our feet. . . . In some places we saw trees burning down close to the stations on the railway track, but no one attempted to put the fires out.

At Victoria she found an excellent Steinway piano in the hotel and played it frequently, to the evident delight of some old ladies who congregated to hear her.

On one occasion, however, I scattered them like frightened wood-pigeons when, to the inquiry, what was the 'sweetly-pretty' tune I was playing, I answered, 'Gotterdammerung!' with an emphasis on the third syllable. With one look of pained surprise, they gathered up their skirts and fled.

They arrived at San Francisco on a windy and sunless day, amazed at the innumerable electric tramways, 'which seem to come upon one from every direction.' They visited Chinatown with a detective, finding the joss-houses, opium dens, and gambling places very stuffy and astonishingly small. 'The opium smokers lie on bare boards, and in such uncomfortable attitudes that it is a mystery to me how they can find enjoyment in the pernicious practice.'

Jennie was awed by the gardens of Monterey.

I was never tired of walking about and admiring the splendid trees, shrubs, and plants of all kinds, while the flowers were in a profusion I have never seen equalled anywhere. . . . After several miles of forest, the ocean suddenly came into view, and a quantity of seals were seen disporting themselves on the rocks, while an exciting fight was going on between two. We watched them for a long while—sometimes they would tumble off into the water, but quickly scrambled up again, to have a few more rounds. I proposed to wait and see the end, but our driver informed us they might go on for a couple of hours. On our way back, we passed through the celebrated Cypress Grove, a very entrancing spot, full of mystery and charm. These ancient trees, so old that generations have lost count of them, twist their gnarled trunks away from the sea, their dark green heads embellished by long, pale strands of the feathery moss which eventually strangles them.

274

She smiled when the driver pointed out several buildings and seriously said that they were very ancient, dating from 1850.

The Churchills and their party went on to Japan. They were fascinated by the country, particularly the theatres in Yokohama, with their plays of fourteen or fifteen acts that lasted all day, and sometimes two.

Occasionally Randolph would go berserk, buying up whole shopfuls of goods. Jennie would patiently and quietly make explanations and then cancel all the orders. She described an incident of another kind that occurred in a shop evidently not frequented by Europeans:

As the little maids who waited on us hovered about me with the greatest curiosity, and before I could stop them, one had put on my gloves, another had seized my hat, which I'd taken off . . . and a third was strutting about with my parasol.

Jennie also told about peasant women in some of the small villages.

The married ones were easily recognized by their shaved eyebrows and blackened teeth, in which hideous custom they indulge, in order to remain faithful to their husbands, but which conceivably might produce the reverse effect on the husbands themselves. Among them were a number of girls, their shiny hair stiff with camelia-oil, and adorned with combs, tiny chrysanthemums and coral beads, their painted faces breaking into a smile, if you looked at them.

They travelled quite extensively through Japan.

I never tired of the mountains, with their changing shadows, deep gorges, and rushing streams and cascades, with here and there a peep of the sea in the distance. The vegetation was a great source of interest and pleasure, it was all so new and so attractive: On our journey up, I counted 55 different kinds of agricultural products and shrubs.

Randolph suddenly worsened at Yokohama. Dr Keith reported 'a transient paralysis of the left arm'. The doctor and Jennie wanted to take him home, but Randolph insisted on continuing the trip.

Jennie did not write her sons about their father, but Winston was now a young man of twenty with a mind of his own. 'I persuaded Dr Roose to tell exactly how Papa was. . . . He told me everything and showed me the medical reports. I have told no one. . . . I need not tell you how anxious I am.'[10] The ugly reality was a shock for Winston. The psychological impact of the word 'syphilis' might explain much of Winston's future way of life, his own relations with women, and his strengthened relationship with his mother, whom he now saw in terms of the innocent woman.

Winston wrote constantly after speaking to Roose, and Jennie found in his letters a renewed tenderness and concern:

Darling Mummy, I do hope that you are feeling well and that the fatigues of travelling as well as the anxiety you must feel about Papa—are not telling on you. I can't tell you how I long to see you again and how I look forward to your return.

He wanted to go there himself to help her handle his father, and he wanted her to confide everything in him.

Do, my darling Mama, when you write let me know *exactly* what you think. . . . You know you told *me* to write to *you* on *every subject* freely.

I fear that much worry will tell on you—and that the continual anxiety added to the fatigues of travelling will deprive you of any interest and pleasure in the strange things you see. If I were you I would always try to look on the bright side of things. . . . Above all, don't get ill yourself. . . .

She tried hard to follow his advice and filled her letters with colourful description of all she saw. 'Your letters are a treat,' he wrote encouragingly.

We made a flying visit to Canton, going up the Pearl River in a large steamer which had an English captain. As I entered the ship, I caught sight of stacks of rifles in the saloon, with printed instructions to the passengers to use them, if necessary. This did not make me feel at all safe, these river-steamers having been known to be attacked by pirates. At Hong Kong, we were advised not to go to Canton, since owing to the war and their defeat, the Chinese were in rather a turbulent state. We thought, however, as we meant to spend only the day there, we should be safe enough. The steamer was obliged to anchor at the mouth of the river, as there were torpedoes laid across it, and the Chinese pilots were rather vague as to their locality. It was a lovely, moonlight night, and I remember the ghostly effect of a searchlight from a fort nearby, which was constantly being turned on us, lighting up strange crafts and great, lumbering Chinese junks with square sails, which hovered near.

. . . The streets were full of open shops, banners, Chinese lanterns and gaudy signs. A continuous stream of people hurrying along made it a most animated scene. They scowled and glared at us as we passed, calling us 'Frankwei' ('foreign devils'); and they spat at one of our party and hit another, who luckily did not retaliate. Otherwise, we might have been made into mincemeat. The shops were very attractive; and Randolph bought me one of the green jade bangles, which have since become fashionable. It is supposed to keep the devil away.

A visit to the execution ground was not so attractive. Eight men had been decapitated a few days before, and the blood was still on the ground.

We were asked if we would like to see the heads, which had been placed in jars, an offer we declined with thanks.

They next went to Singapore, where the heat 'was like a vapor bath and so enervating that one felt absolutely incapable of doing anything.'

The Sultan of Johore gave them a sumptuous luncheon, and showed them through his palace. In one room, the tables and chairs were made of cut glass, upholstered in bright blue velvet with glass buttons.

After luncheon, the Sultan, who's a charming and courteous old man, sent for his Sultana to come and see us. She was a very pretty Circassian of about 25, a present from the Sultan of Turkey. Enormously fat, we were told that she was fed every two hours, the Sultan admiring large proportions. Her costume was most peculiar, to say the least—a Malay sarong of silk; a blouse with huge diamond buttons; round her neck a rivière of diamonds and one of sapphires; and on her short black curls, cocked over one ear, a velvet glengarry cap with an eagle's feather and a diamond aigret. The Sultan, thinking, I suppose, that she had been seen enough, suddenly pointed with a stern gesture to the door. Casting a frightened glance at him, she fled as fast as her fat little feet could take her.[11]

Jennie and Dr Keith again tried to persuade Randolph to end the trip and return home. The heat had intensified and they were afraid he would not last much longer. But he had been the man in the British Cabinet most responsible for annexing Burma to the British Crown and 'he would have gone alone', said Jennie. The sea was rough and very hot, the ship full of beetles, ants, and rats.

'I have met very few people one could talk to since we left England,' Jennie wrote Clara.

I can't tell you how I pine for a little society. It is so hard to get away from one's thoughts when one is always alone. And yet the worst of it is I dread the chance even of seeing people for his sake. He is quite unfit for society . . . one never knows what he may do. At Government House Singapore he was very bad for two days and it was dreadful being with strangers. Since then he has become much quieter and sometimes it is quite pathetic but Keith thinks it is a bad sign. . . .[12]

It was so bad a sign that they added to their luggage a lead-lined coffin.[13]

It was at Rangoon that one of the major lights went out of Jennie's life. She received a telegram from Count Charles Kinsky. He had given up the long wait for her and was now engaged to be married.[14]

Jennie wrote of it to Clara: 'I *hate* it! I shall return without a friend in the world and too old to make any more now.' She would not then have appreciated an epigram by her friend Oscar Wilde, who said, 'Women spoil every romance by trying to make it last forever.'

Randolph had deteriorated. His disease had reached the final stage in which walking becomes stumbling and the feet move sideways, hitting the ground with a stamp. Sores break out all over the body and refuse to heal. The victim loses control of his bladder; the joints in his legs and feet swell into painful masses of deformed bone. The brain is mostly imbecilic. With Randolph, the syphilitic germs seemed highly unselective—they attacked everywhere. 'You cannot imagine anything *more* distracting and desperate, than to watch it and see him as he is and think of him as he was,' Jennie wrote.

Winston sent her a gay letter about his first public-speaking experience at the Empire Theatre. A crowd of several hundred people had started tearing down the barricades put up to separate the bars of the Empire from the nearby promenade where women liked to walk. Winston then jumped on top of the broken barricade and shouted to the crowd, 'You have seen us tear down these barricades tonight; see that you pull down those who are responsible for them at the coming election.'[15] The Countess of Aberconway was there and quoted Winston as saying, 'Ladies of the Empire! I stand for Liberty!'

*The Westminster Gazette* printed Winston's letter on the subject. 'It was I who led the rioters—and made a speech to the crowd,' Winston wrote, enclosing a newspaper clipping to prove it.

Winston celebrated his twentieth birthday at Hindlip Hall near Worcester as Lord Hindlip's guest at the local Hunt Ball. In the post office the following morning, he was handed a letter with the news that his father was dying.

'The collapse of an airplane in mid-air is always more terrible than the overturning of a hackney cab in the street,' said Shane Leslie. 'Randolph fell from meteoric heights.'

Yet Churchill's mind and body had been tearing apart for too long to allow for any surprise. His family and friends had seen the final collapse coming for many years—only the vast public were unaware of what was happening to him. To them his was a magic name. The anonymous contributor to the *Dictionary of National Biography* would say of Lord Randolph Churchill:

His personality had fascinated the masses, who admired his courage, his ready wit, and the brilliant audacity with which he dealt his blows at the loftiest crests, whether those of friends or adversaries. Moreover, it was perceived by this time that there was a fund of intellectual power and a genuine depth of conviction behind his erratic insolence and reckless rhetoric.

The small, sad group arrived back in London just in time for Christmas. Winston saw that his father was 'as weak and helpless in mind and body as a little child'. For a month Randolph lingered. Clara Frewen wrote Leonie of the misery of the final days, of how Randolph 'groaned and screamed with pain and instead of the dose of morphia they gave him acting in five minutes it took 20 before he got relief and went into a sleep which lasted 4 hours. Jennie never left him . . . she hasn't eaten or slept since she arrived. . . .'

The hope had died long before. The hope of living. The hope of a good marriage. The hope of being Prime Minister and of shaking the world. His had been an agony protracted, a genius long misguided, a promise unfulfilled.

In *Savrola*, Winston Churchill has his leading male character say to his wife just before dying,

And you—will you forget? . . . do not allow yourself to mourn. I do not care to be remembered for what I was. If I have done anything that may make the world more happy and more cheerful and more comfortable, let them recall the action. If I have spoken a thought which, rising above the vicissitudes of our existence, may make life brighter or death less gloomy, then let them say: 'He did this, or he did that.' Forget the man; remember, perhaps, his work.

Sir Richard Temple remembered an elderly Tory saying of Randolph, 'He made the people believe in us.'[16] The whole of his spectacular political life had lasted less than six years, the brilliance of an exploding rocket leaving nothing. Dante Gabriel Rossetti, who had died a dozen years before, had summed up one such as Randolph Churchill in the couplet:

> My name is Might-have-been;
> I am also called No-more, Too-late, Farewell.

The press gave prominent coverage to Randolph's daily health bulletins. There were many callers. On January 23, 1895, he sank into a coma. In the early hours of the next morning, Winston was summoned from a nearby house where he was sleeping. 'I ran in the darkness across Grosvenor Square, then lapped in snow.' At 6:15

279

the next morning, January 24, Randolph died in his sleep at the age of forty-five. On that very day, seventy years later, Winston Churchill would die.

Moreton Frewen wrote Leonie:

So poor R. has flickered out; dear sweet little Jane my mind runs on her very much. I wish I could hear that she is left comfortably off, and that life might look smilingly on her after many days. . . . Love and luck sweet Kali. . . . Oh! To have got rid of that hair shirt—poor fellow—for ever. . . . There was much nice about him, but he was mad always. . . .[17]

When Lord Salisbury sent a letter of condolence to the Duchess of Marlborough, she answered bitterly. Within a period of eighteen months, she had lost both her sons:

Dear Lord Salisbury: I thank you for your sympathy with this terrible sorrow. But oh, it is too late, too late. There was a day, years ago, when in my dire distress, I went to you and asked you, as a father, to help me—for my Darling had no father. He had but *me*, and I could do nothing, though I would have given my life for him. I went to you—I would have fallen at your feet if you could have helped me, and sympathized with me. He knew not what I did, but I was desperate, and I knew he had been misled and made a fatal mistake; and yet I knew all his real cleverness and real goodness and what he had been and could be to his Party. . . . Your heart was hardened against him. I suppose he had tried you, and worry and anxiety beset you for it was Fate.

But from that Hour, the Iron entered into his soul. . . . He never gave a sign, even to me, of disappointment, but for Days and Days, and Months, and Years, even it told on him and he sat in Connaught Place, brooding and eating his Heart out and the Tory Press reviled him, and the Tory Party, whom he had saved, abused and misrepresented him, and he was never the same. The illness which has killed him is due, they tell me, to overwork and acute mental strain, and now he is gone and I am left alone to mourn him and the Grace. . . .

It's all over now. My Darling has come Home to die, and oh, it seems such bitter mockery that *now* it is too late, he seems to be understood and appreciated.[18]

They did not bury Randolph in the Marlborough family vaults in Blenheim but in the small cemetery behind the tiny church in nearby Bladon. There, too, his wife and sons would be buried.

Shane Leslie described his uncle's funeral:

I was due to go to school for the first time, but I was kept for the funeral in Westminster Abbey. It was immensely solemn; and the great roof stretched over us in icy space. It was like a cathedral of the arctic. I heard the lugubrious choir and the voice of Dean Farrar, and then the Dead March from 'Saul' crept into our shivering souls. When it was over, I caught sight of Parliamentary heroes only known through their caricatures in *Punch*. Down the aisle passed Arthur Balfour, and a grizzly 'Black Michael' Hicks-Beach. Both had been Irish Secretaries; and there was a certain queer look which distinguished English statesmen who had ever held that office. Sir William Harcourt, looking like Jumbo, and Lord Rosebery followed. There was a flag half-mast at St. Margaret's; and in Parliament Square, we were told to rise and bow from the carriage to a grey-bearded gentleman of prophetic appearance who returned our bows solemnly. It was Lord Salisbury, who no doubt mistook us for Randolph's brood. It was well known that he was one of those who could not tell a hawk from a handsaw. The haggard Sir Henry Irving also passed down the aisle. In youth, Randolph was said to have asked Irving in Dublin how the play of 'Hamlet' finished! Randolph was finishing like Hamlet, himself. There were four captains to bear him to his grave. 'For he was likely, had he lived, to have proved most royal.' The funeral procession passed through Paddington, followed by Walden, the faithful valet, and thence under the shadow of Blenheim, into the endless Nirvana which swallows the short and agitated lives of statesmen, if they could only realize it.

It was the first death I had ever heard announced. I was swung off my hinges. I did not believe grown-ups could die. This was a fate I believed reserved for the heathen, for pirates, and enemies of the Queen. . . . It was my first funeral; and as godson to the deceased, I thought myself bound to observe the strictest mourning. I became susceptible to the grief of my elders. In hushed whispers, they mentioned Randolph's last miseries and madnesses; and I recorded the event in my first diary, January 24, 1895: 'Uncle Randolph became a saint in Heaven.[19]

As Jennie lay in her widow's bed, her face pale, her eyes burning, the inevitable death of her mad husband perhaps seemed in part a vast relief.[20]

Only two weeks before, however, on January 7, Count Charles Andreas Kinsky had married Countess Elisabeth Wolff Metternich zur Gracht, a lovely woman twenty years younger than Jennie. After Kinsky's marriage, Jennie had written Leonie:

The bitterness, if there was any, has absolutely left me. He and I have parted the best of friends and in a truly *fin de siècle* manner. So darling don't worry about me on that score. . . . Pity or mere sympathy even from *you* is wasted on me. No one can do me *any* good. He has not behaved particularly well and I can't find much to admire in him but I care for him as some people like opium or drink although they would like not to. . . .

Thus did the hope seem dead for her, too. She had given of herself to her world without reservation. She had offered her best to a husband who could not accept it, so she had scattered among others her wit, her charm, her drive, her imagination, her love. But Charles

Kinsky had been the romantic drama of her life; the many other men had merely filled the intermissions. He would not forget the love she had given him, and she would not forgive his relinquishing it. It was a concentrated, fiery love, a love accumulated from many neglected sources. If not for Kinsky she might have had more for her sons.

Now she was forty, and what was there left? Ardent admirers all married, sons at school, house empty.

'Why do you always wear black?' asks Medvedenko in Chekhov's *The Sea Gull*.

'I am in mourning for my life.'

The clouds surrounding her were dark. She could not know that the world was just beginning to open for her.

# Bibliography

of books, journals, newspapers, etc., referred to in the text and in the Critical
References and Notes (see page 289).

BOOKS
Abels, Jules: *The Parnell Tragedy* (Bodley Head, 1966).
Airlie, Mabell, Countess of: *With the Guards We Shall Go* (Hodder & Stoughton,
1933).
Andrews, Allen: *The Splendid Pauper* (Philadelphia, Lippincott, 1968).
Anon: *Blenheim* (Henry Slatter, n.d.).
Anon: *Kings, Courts and Society* (Jarrolds, 1930).
Anon: *Reminiscences of an Oxogenarian* (London, n.d.).
Anon: *Uncensored Recollections* (Philadelphia, Lippincott, 1924)
Arnold, Matthew: *Culture and Anarchy* (London, 1869).
Aronson, Theo: *The Golden Bees: The Story of the Fabulous Bonapartes* (Old-
bourne, 1965).
Arthur, Sir George: *Concerning Winston Spencer Churchill* (Heinemann, 1940).
Asquith, Margot: *The Autobiography of Margot Asquith* (Thornton Butter-
worth, 1920).
Baldick, Robert: *The Siege of Paris* (Batsford, 1964).
Balfour, A. J.: *Chapters of Autobiography* (Cassell, 1930).
Balfour, Lady Frances: *Ne Obliviscaris* (Hodder & Stoughton, 1930).
Balsan, Consuelo Vanderbilt [Duchess of Marlborough]: *The Glitter and the
Gold* (Heinemann, 1953).
Baron, A. L.: *Man Against Germs* (New York, Dutton, 1957).
Beerbohm, Max: *Things New and Old* (Heinemann, 1923).
Berger, Mayer: *The Story of the New York Times* (New York, Simon & Schuster,
1951).
Birmingham, Stephen: *Our Crowd* (New York, Harper, 1967).
von Bismarck, Otto: *Reminiscences* (New York, Harper, 1899).
Blake, Robert: *Disraeli* (Eyre & Spottiswoode, 1966).
Blunt, Wilfred Scawen: *My Diaries: Being a Personal Narrative of Events*
(Martin Secker, 1921).
Bolton, Reginald Pelham: *Washington Heights, Manhattan: Its Eventful Past*
(New York, Dyckman Institute, 1924).
Bott, Alan, and Clephane, Irene: *Our Mothers* (Gollancz, 1932).
Bromage, Mary C.: *Churchill and Ireland* (South Bend, Indiana, University of
Notre Dame Press, 1964).
Buckley, Jerome Hamilton: *The Victorian Temper* (Allen & Unwin, 1952).
Caffyn, Gladys E.: *Fragments in the Life of Ambrose Hall* (Palmyra, New York,
1956).
Callender, James H.: *Yesterdays on Brooklyn Heights* (New York, Dorland
Press, 1927).

Carter, Lady Violet Bonham: *Winston Churchill as I Knew Him* (Collins, 1965).

Castelot, André: *The Turbulent City: Paris* (Barrie & Rockliffe, 1963).

Cecil, Lady Gwendolen: *The Third Marquis of Salisbury* (Hodder & Stoughton, 1931–2).

Chanler, Julie: *From Gaslight to Dawn* (New York, Pacific Printing Co., 1956).

Churchill, Lord Randolph: *Mines and Animals in South Africa* (1892).

Churchill, Lady Randolph (Mrs George Cornwallis-West): *Reminiscences of Lady Randolph Churchill* (1908).

*Small Talks on Big Subjects* (Pearson, 1916).

Churchill, Randolph S.: *Fifteen Famous English Homes* (Verschoyle, 1954).

*Winston S. Churchill* (Heinemann, 1966–).

Churchill, Winston S.: *A History of the English-Speaking Peoples* (Cassell 1956–8).

*Lord Randolph Churchill* (Macmillan, 1906).

*Marlborough: His Life and Times* (Harrap, 1934).

*My Early Life* (Odhams, 1958).

*Savrola* (1900).

*Thoughts and Adventures* (Thornton Butterworth, 1932).

Clarke, Sir Edward: *The Story of My Life* (Murray, 1918).

Comyns Carr, Mrs J.: *Reminiscences* (Hutchinson, 1926).

Corley, T. A. B.: *Democratic Despot: A Life of Napoleon III* (Muller, 1958).

Corti, Count Egon: *Elizabeth, Empress of Austria* (Thornton Butterworth, 1936).

Cowles, Virginia: *Edward VII and His Circle* (Hamish Hamilton, 1956).

Crewe, Quentin: *The Frontiers of Privilege* (Stevens Press, 1961).

D'Abernon, Viscount: *Portraits and Appreciations* (Hodder & Stoughton, 1931).

*Debrett's Peerage, Baronetage, Knightage & Companionage.*

*Dictionary of National Biography, The.*

Duby, Georges, and Mandron, Robert: *The History of French Civilization* (Weidenfeld & Nicolson, 1964).

Eliot, Elizabeth: *They All Married Well* (Cassell, 1960).

*Encyclopaedia Britannica* (1960).

Ensor, R. C. K.: *England: 1870–1914* (Oxford University Press, 1936).

Escott, T. H. S.: *Randolph Spencer-Churchill* (Hutchinson, 1895).

Fielding, Daphne: *The Duchess of Jermyn Street* (Eyre & Spottiswoode, 1964).

Fiske, Stephen: *Offhand Portraits of Prominent New Yorkers* (New York, Lockwood & Sons, 1884).

Forbes, A.: *Life of Napoleon III* (New York, Dodd, Mead, 1897).

Franz Ferdinand, Archduke: *Tagebuch Meiner Reise um die Erde* (Vienna, 1895).

*From Punch: Society Pictures* (Bradbury, Agnew, n.d.).

Frewen, Moreton: *Melton Mowbray & Other Memories* (Herbert Jenkins, 1924).

Gardiner, A. G.: *The Life of Sir William Harcourt* (Constable, 1923).

Gifford, M. J., ed.: *Pages from the Diary of an Oxford Lady* (London, n.d.).

Gilbert, Judson Bennett: *Disease and Destiny* (Los Angeles, Dawson's, 1962).

Gooch, G. P.: *The Second Empire* (Longmans, 1960).

Guedella, Philip: *The Hundred Days* (New York, Doubleday, 1936).

*Mr. Churchill: A Portrait* (Hodder & Stoughton, 1941).

*The Second Empire* (Hodder & Stoughton, 1922).

Gwynn, Stephen (and Tuckwell, Gertrude M.): *The Life of the Rt. Hon. Sir Charles Dilke, Bart., M.P.* (Murray, 1917).

Hadfield, John, ed.: *The Saturday Book—25* (Hutchinson, 1965).
Hardinge, Sir Arthur: *The Fourth Earl of Carnarvon* (Oxford University Press, 1925).
Harris, Frank: *Contemporary Portraits* (New York, Brentanos, 1920).
  *My Life and Loves* (W. H. Allen, 1964).
Haslip, Joan: *The Lonely Empress: Life of Elizabeth, Empress of Austria* (Weidenfeld & Nicolson, 1965).
Hauk, Minnie: *Memories of a Singer* (New York, M. Philpot & Co., 1925).
Hazen, Charles Downer: *Europe Since 1815* (New York, Henry Holt, 1910).
James, Robert Rhodes: *Lord Randolph Churchill* (Weidenfeld & Nicolson, 1959).
Kelley, Frank Bergen: *The Historical Guide to the City of New York* (New York, Frederick Stokes, 1909).
Kranzberg, Melvin: *The Siege of Paris* (Oxford University Press, 1950).
Kraus, René: *Young Lady Randolph* (1944).
Kurtz, Harold: *The Empress Eugénie* (Hamish Hamilton, 1964).
Lambton, George: *Men and Horses I Have Known* (Thornton Butterworth, 1924).
Lang, Theo: *My Darling Daisy* (Michael Joseph, 1966).
Langley, Marjorie, ed.: *America's Taste* (New York, Simon & Schuster, 1960).
Latimer, Elizabeth: *France in the 19th Century* (Chicago, A. C. McClurg, 1892).
Leslie, Seymour: *The Jerome Connexion* (Murray, 1964).
Leslie, Anita: *The Fabulous Leonard Jerome* (Hutchinson, 1954).
Leslie, Sir Shane: *American Wonderland* (Michael Joseph, 1936).
  *The End of a Chapter* (Heinemann, 1917).
  *Long Shadows* (Murray, 1966).
  *Men Were Different* (Michael Joseph, 1937).
  *The Passing Chapter* (Cassell, 1934).
  *Salutation to Five* (Hollis & Carter, 1951).
  *Studies in Sublime Failure* (Benn, 1932).
'Lettres de Napoléon III' (*Revue des Deux-Mondes*, September 1, 1930).
Longford, Elizabeth: *Victoria R.I.* (Weidenfeld & Nicolson, 1964).
Lucy, Sir Henry: *Diary of a Journalist* (Murray, 1920).
  *Later Peeps at Parliament* (Newnes, 1905).
  *Speeches of the Rt. Hon. Lord Randolph Churchill with a sketch of his life* (Longmans, 1885).
Mann, Cornelius: 'Two Famous Descendants of John Cooke and Sarah Warren' (in *The New York Genealogical and Biographical Record*, LXXIII, No. 3, July, 1942).
Marlborough, Duchess of: *See* Balsan.
Martin, Ralph G., and Harrity, R.: *Man of the Century: Churchill* (New York, Duell, Sloan and Pearce, 1962).
Maurois, Simone André: *Miss Howard and the Emperor* (Collins, 1957).
Monypenny, W. F., and Buckle, G. E.: *Life of Benjamin Disraeli* (Murray, 1929).
Morley, John, Viscount: *Life of William Ewart Gladstone* (Macmillan, 1932).
  *Recollections* (Macmillan, 1917).
Morris, Lloyd: *Incredible New York* (New York, Random House, 1951).
McAllister, Ward: *Society as I Have Found It* (Cassell, 1890).
McCullough, Ed.: *Good Old Coney Island* (New York, Scribner's, 1957).

McKelvey, Dr Blake: *Rochester, the Waterpower City* (Cambridge, Mass., Harvard University Press, 1945).

'Winston Churchill's Grandparents in Rochester' (in *Genessee Country Scrapbook*, III, No. 1. Spring 1952. The Rochester Historical Society).

Nevill, Lady Dorothy (ed. Ralph Nevill): *Leaves from the Notebooks of Lady Dorothy Nevill* (Macmillan, 1907).

*Under Five Reigns* (Methuen, 1910).

Nevins, Allen, and Halsey, Milton, eds.: *The Diary of George Templeton Strong* (New York, Macmillan, 1952).

New York City Landmarks Preservation Commission, November 23, 1965, Calendar No. 2, LP-0015.

Norris, A. G. S.: *A Very Great Soul* (International, 1957).

O'Brien, R. Barry: *The Life of Charles Stewart Parnell* (Smith, Elder, 1898).

O'Connor, Richard: *Courtroom Warrior* (Boston, Little, Brown, 1963).

Ostrander, Stephen M.: *History of the City of Brooklyn* (Brooklyn, 1894).

Peacock, Virginia: *Famous American Belles of the Nineteenth Century* (Philadelphia, Lippincott, 1901).

Proust, Marcel: *Remembrance of Things Past* (Chatto & Windus).

*Punch*. See *From Punch*.

Raymond, E. T.: *Uncensored Celebrities* (T. Fisher Unwin, 1918).

Reader, W. J.: *Life in Victorian England* (Batsford, 1964).

Richter, Werner: *Bismarck* (Macdonald, 1964).

Ronaldshay, Earl of: *The Life of Lord Curzon* (Benn, 1927).

Roose, Dr Robson: *The Waste and Repair in Modern Life* (Murray, 1897).

Rosebery, Lord: *Lord Randolph Churchill* (1906).

*Miscellanies* (Hodder & Stoughton, 1921).

Rowse, A. L.: *The Early Churchills* (Macmillan, 1956).

*The Later Churchills* (Macmillan, 1958).

Russell, Rt. Hon. G. W. E.: *Portraits of the Seventies* (T. Fisher Unwin, 1906).

St. Hélier, Lady: *Memories of Fifty Years* (Arnold, 1909).

Sheridan, Clare: *Nuda Veritas* [Naked Truth] (Thornton Butterworth, 1928).

Sichel, Pierre: *The Jersey Lily* (W. H. Allen, 1958).

Smalley, George: *Anglo-American Memories* (Duckworth, 1911).

Smalley, Virginia Jeffrey: 'Reminiscences of the Ruffled Shirt Ward' (Genessee Country Scrapbook, III, No. 1, Spring 1952. The Rochester Historical Society).

Smith, D. H.: *Life of Commodore Vanderbilt* (New York, McBride, 1927).

Spender, J. A., and Asquith, Cyril: *Life of Herbert Henry Asquith, Lord Oxford and Asquith* (Hutchinson, 1932).

Stiles, Henry R.: *The Civil, Political, Professional and Ecclesiastical History and Commercial and Industrial Record of the County of Kings and City of Brooklyn* (New York, W. W. Munsell, 1884).

Storrs, Sir Ronald: *The Memoirs of Sir Ronald Storrs* (1937).

Taylor, A. J. P.: *Bismarck* (Hamish Hamilton, 1955).

Thompson, R. W.: *The Yankee Marlborough* (Allen & Unwin, 1953).

*Times, The* (27 contributors to): *Fifty Years: 1882–1930* (Thornton Butterworth, 1932).

Trevelyan, G. M.: *English Social History* (Longmans, 1943).

Tschuppik, Carl: *Empress Elizabeth of Austria* (Constable, 1930).

Tuchman, Barbara: *The Proud Tower* (Hamish Hamilton, 1966).

Vanderbilt, Cornelius Jr.: *The Vanderbilt Feud* (Hutchinson, 1957).

Victoria, Queen: *Letters and Journals of Queen Victoria* (Series I, 1907; II, 1926–8; III, 1930–2; Murray/Longmans).

Von Folkmann, Josef Erwin: *Die Gefurstete Linie des Uralten und Etlen Geschlechtes Kinsky* (Prague, 1861).

Ward, Mrs E. M. (Elliott O'Donnell, ed.): *Mrs E. M. Ward's Reminiscences* (New York, Pitman, 1911).

Warshow, Robert Irving: *The Story of Wall Street* (New York, Greenburg, 1929).

Warwick, Frances, Countess of: *Afterthoughts* (Cassell, 1931).
   *Discretions* (New York, Scribner's, 1931).
   *Life's Ebb and Flow* (Hutchinson, 1929).

Washburne, E.B.: *Recollections of a Minister to France* (New York, 1887).

West, Sir Algernon: *Private Diaries* (Murray, 1922).

Williams-Ellis, Amabel, and Fisher, F. J.: *The Story of English Life* (New York, Coward-McCann, 1936).

Wolff, Sir Henry Drummond: *Rambling Recollections* (Macmillan, 1908).

*Newspapers, journals etc.*
   Cardiff *Mail*
   *Current Literature*
   *The Daily Telegraph*
   *The Evening News*
   *Fortnightly Review*
   *Genessee Country Scrapbook*
   *The Graphic Magazine*
   *The Lancet*
   New York *Herald*
   *The New York Times*
   New York *Tribune*
   Palmyra *Courier-Journal*
   *Princeton Alumni Weekly*
   *Punch*
   *Review of Reviews*
   Sheffield *Telegraph*
   *The Spectator*
   *Town Topics*
   *The Times*
   *Tit Bits*

*Papers, official records, etc.*
   Blenheim Palace, Muniments Room.
   Buzzard, Dr Thomas: The Buzzard Papers.
   Marsh, Sir Edward: Unpublished papers (in the possession of the Marquis of Bath).
   Consular Dispatches, Trieste.
   *Medical Annual of the District of Columbia* (1955).
   *New York Genealogical and Biographical Record.*
   *Princeton Faculty Minutes.*

# Critical References and Notes

## Prologue

[1] This was the title of a magazine article in *Current Literature* (December 1908).

[2] In Spain, *criadores* breed the courage of a bull not from the bull, but from the cow. In Ireland, the spirit of a foal is traced from its mare. And when Winston Churchill was born, a racing friend of the family commented to Mrs Clara Jerome, 'Interesting breeding, stamina goes through the dam and pace through the sire.' Anita Leslie quotes this in *The Fabulous Leonard Jerome*.

[3] Jennie was fifty-four when Winston Churchill was married in 1908, and in its December issue that year, *Current Literature* commented, 'It seems cruel to say that, at the recent marriage of her illustrious son, his mother seemed the junior of the bride by at least two years.'

[4] From *The Autobiography of Margot Asquith*. Her husband Herbert Asquith became Prime Minister in 1908.

## Chapter 1

The most definitive source material on the origins of the Jerome family is the New York Genealogical Library and the Genealogical Room of the New York Public Library. *The New York Genealogical and Biographical Record*, LXXIII, No. 3 (July 1942), 159–66, has an excellent genealogical summary of the family in an article called 'Two Famous Descendants of John Cooke and Sarah Warren' by Cornelius Mann. Another valuable reference is *Fragments in the Life of Ambrose Hall* by Gladys E. Caffyn. Vera Curtis has an interesting article about the Jerome family in the Palmyra *Courier-Journal*, December 25, 1947, but unfortunately it has some serious errors. The best book on the subject of Leonard Jerome is Anita Leslie's *The Fabulous Leonard Jerome*, but unfortunately, it is also subject to errors of fact. Randolph S. Churchill's excellent biography of his father, *Winston S. Churchill*, concentrates on his father's British background, and gives only short space to his American heritage.

Mrs John Sloane of New York City has possession of the Jerome family Bible, as well as an excellent family scrapbook, both of which are invaluable.

The most rewarding intimate material on the family came from interviews with Sir Shane Leslie, Leonard Jerome's grandson, whose book *American Wonderland* has warm and colourful material.

The Jerome family in Rochester is best treated by Dr Blake McKelvey, city historian of Rochester, in his article 'Winston Churchill's Grandparents in Rochester' in the *Genessee Country Scrapbook*, III, No. 1 (Spring 1952), published by the Rochester Historical Society. In that same issue there is a good article on Rochester society of that era by Virginia Jeffrey Smith, 'Reminiscences of the Ruffled Shirt Ward.' Dr McKelvey also has dealt with Rochester history and society most ably in his book *Rochester, the Waterpower City*.

The Brooklyn background of the family is everywhere skimpy and inaccurate. The story of Brooklyn itself at that time is generally disappointing. *Yesterdays on Brooklyn Heights* by James H. Callender has captured little of the flavour of the place; *The Historical Guide to the City of New York* by Frank Bergen Kelley even less. *The Civil, Political, Professional and Ecclesiastical History, and Commercial and Industrial Record of the County of Kings and the City of Brooklyn* by Henry R. Stiles is heavy going and not worth much. The same may be said for *History of the City of Brooklyn* by Stephen M. Ostrander. Indeed, the best material on Brooklyn has come from interviews with James Kelly, city historian of Brooklyn.

The material on New York City is vastly better. *Incredible New York* by Lloyd Morris is most valuable. *The Diary of George Templeton Strong*, ed. Allen Nevins and Milton Halsey, has some pertinent colour and anecdotes worth searching for. *Courtroom Warrior* by Richard O'Connor focuses on Leonard Jerome's nephew, William Travers Jerome, but nevertheless provides some fine background on the family and the time. In contrast, *The Yankee Marlborough* by R. W. Thompson adds nothing new. Of less value is *Young Lady Randolph* by René Kraus, which has more fiction than fact.

A good vignette of Leonard Jerome can be found in *Offhand Portraits of Prominent New Yorkers* by Stephen Fiske, even though it is not entirely accurate. Some sidelights into Leonard Jerome's Wall Street manipulations are dealt with briefly in *The Story of Wall Street* by Robert Irving Warshow. *Good Old Coney Island* by Ed McCullough deals slightly with some of Jerome's racing record and *The Jersey Lily* by Pierre Sichel details some of his involvement with Lily Langtry. *Washington Heights, Manhattan: Its Eventful Past*, by Reginald Pelham Bolton, is hardly worth examining. But Ward McAllister's *Society As I Have Found It* has excellent glimpses into the society of the time. So has *The Vanderbilt Feud* by Cornelius Vanderbilt, Jr., which has a particularly fine description of life at Newport.

*From Gaslight to Dawn* by Julie Chanler has only a few scattered references to young Jennie. *Reminiscences of Lady Randolph Churchill* is unfortunately skimpy on the early years, devoting only three pages to her early life in the United States; and some of her statements are based on faulty memory. The book, however, is excellent with regard to her later years, except that she herself has said, 'There may be some to whom these Reminiscences will be interesting chiefly in virtue of what is left unsaid.'

[1] Jerome maintained a financial interest in The New York Times Newspaper Establishment from 1858. During the Civil War period, he had fifteen to twenty of the hundred shares, each of $1,000 par value. Meyer Berger, *The Story of The New York Times*.

[2] Jerome family scrapbook of Mrs John Sloane, New York.

[3] Mrs Sloane's Jerome family records estimate his total estate value at £7,000, a fortune in those days.

[4] A copy of the inventory, filed with the county clerk in Wallingford, Connecticut, appears in Ralph G. Martin and Richard Harrity, *Man of the Century: Churchill*.

[5] Leonard Jerome wrote a letter to his wife, May 6, 1889, in which he explained: 'My grandfather, Aaron Jerome, in 1786, married Betsy Ball, daughter of Major Stebbings Ball, of the Army of the Revolution, and grand-daughter of Rev Eliphalet Ball, of Ballstown Spa, Saratoga County, who was an own cousin of Mary Ball, Washington's mother. Washington had no lineal descendant. Consequently, we are the nearest of kin!!'

[6] The activity of his American ancestors in the Revolutionary War made Sir Winston Churchill an honorary member of the Sons of the American Revolution. Martin and Harrity, *op. cit.*

[7] The Isaac Jeromes lived to celebrate their Golden Wedding in 1857, three years after Jennie was born.

[8] Professor T. J. Wertenbaker, historian of Princeton University, has written the full story of the incident in the *Princeton Alumni Weekly* (November 19, 1943).

[9] From *Princeton Faculty Minutes* (July 10, 1838).

[10] In a letter to Princeton, Jerome amplified his offer, 'I think that the most pressing necessity of young America just now is, we have plenty of science and are pretty well up . . . in art, but our manners, I must say, are rather rough. The character of a gentleman I consider within the capacity of all—at least, it requires no extraordinary intellect. A due regard for the feelings of others is, in my judgment, its foundation.'

[11] Cornelius Mann, in 'Two Famous Descendants of John Cooke and Sarah Warren', *New York Genealogical and Biographical Record*, LXXIII, No. 3 (July 1942), 159–66, details the fact that Winston Churchill and Franklin Delano Roosevelt were eighth cousins, once removed.

[12] There are no facts to support any story of Indian ancestry in the Jerome family. Most of the genealogical lines of the Jeromes are carried back to the seventeenth century, with the exception of the Anna Baker line. She was Jennie's maternal grandmother. In his biography of his father, *Winston S. Churchill*, I, 15–16, Randolph S. Churchill notes that Anna Baker's mother's maiden name is not recorded in the genealogies and 'is believed to have been an Iroquois Indian'. However, Anna Baker and her mother came from Nova Scotia, and there were then no Iroquois Indians in Nova Scotia. Furthermore, intermarriage between whites and Indians were then very rare. Gladys E. Caffyn, in *Fragments in the Life of Ambrose Hall*, pp. 135–36, discounts the whole Indian claim as a myth. However, the physical fact of the marked Indian features of Clara Jerome and her sisters and their children could be held to lend credence to the possibility that Anna Baker may have been raped by an Indian, and that Clarissa Willcox may have been a half-caste. Certainly it was a Jerome family legend. Anita Leslie, in *The Fabulous Leonard Jerome*, quotes her grandmother, Leonie Leslie, remarking on her energy as saying, 'That's my Indian blood—only don't let Mama know I told you.'

[13] These descriptions come from Moreton Frewen's letters in Allen Andrews, ed., *The Splendid Pauper*, from Shane Leslie's *American Wonderland*, and from Mrs John Sloane's Jerome family scrapbook.

[14] The daughter of Samuel Wilder. Dr Blake McKelvey, in *Genessee Country Scrapbook*, III: I (Spring 1952), notes that the Jerome brothers published a sprightly pamphlet called *The Fancy Party*, about an elaborate costume party at the home of Mrs William H. Greenough.

V

[15] Abraham Lincoln said this of *Uncle Tom's Cabin.*

[16] Stephen Fiske, *Offhand Portraits of Prominent New Yorkers.*

[17] Reported in the New York *Herald,* March 5, 1891, a story of reminiscence on Jerome's death.

[18] The family joke was that Clara was the only woman Leonard Jerome had ever dated more than once who couldn't sing a single note.

[19] One of Clara's most persistent courtiers was Baron William Teggethoff, of whom she wrote, 'he seemed to be, though one should not say it, rather taken.' Jerome family letters.

[20] Twenty thousand New Yorkers waited until midnight outside Jenny Lind's apartment while three hundred red-shirted volunteer firemen, with flaming torches, came to serenade her. Seats to her concerts sold at auction for as high as $225.

[21] Jennie's actual birthdate has long been in question. Brooklyn kept no birth records at that time. The city eventually set a plaque on the house on Henry Street indicating that Jennie Jerome was born there in January 1850 (no day given). This corresponds to Jennie's own imagined recollection in her memoirs of being in Trieste when her father was Consul. But Jennie was never there. Leonard Jerome's first letter to the State Department from Trieste on May 1, 1852 (filed in the *Consular Dispatches,* Trieste, Vol. IV), mentions his wife 'and child'—not 'children'. This is further substantiated by the Manifest of Passengers of *Baltic,* preserved in the National Archives in Washington D.C. (Roll 133, List 1146, November 13, 1853, lists Clara Jerome, aged two years, six months, as the only child of Mr and Mrs Jerome to arrive with them in New York.)

This also clearly indicates that Jennie was born after that date. The date recorded in the family Bible, although put in some years later, was made by Leonard Jerome's cousin, Margaret Middleton, an historian for the Daughters of the American Revolution and an accomplished genealogist. She unquestionably checked her facts with the immediate family. Further confirmation of the 1854 birthdate comes from a letter Jennie wrote to her husband on January 8, 1883, thanking him for a present: 'Just in time for my birthday tomorrow—29 my dear! but I shall not acknowledge it to the world, 26 is quite enough.'

Randolph S. Churchill, in *Winston S. Churchill,* I, adds the further evidence of Jennie's christening mug which was engraved '*Jennie Jerome 1854*'.

For a time there was even confusion as to whether Jennie was born in Brooklyn or Rochester. In 1941, in a speech at the University of Rochester, Winston Churchill said, 'As you tell me, my mother was born in Rochester.' And, later, touring the Henry Street home in Brooklyn, Churchill was overheard by his accompanying guide, James Kelly, historian of Brooklyn, to mumble, 'But I thought it was Rochester?' However, even Dr Blake McKelvey, city historian of Rochester, has firmly eliminated Rochester as Jennie's birthplace.

[22] Cornelius Vanderbilt Jr., in *The Vanderbilt Feud,* also adds that the top floors contained rooms for thirty-three servants. Vanderbilt noted that his grandparents spent five million dollars to build The Breakers at a time when a dollar represented a daily wage for an average worker.

[23] During a hectic period of partnership, Jerome told Vanderbilt, 'My God, Commodore, if we keep on, we'll break every house on The Street!'

'My God, Commodore,' became a Wall Street watchword. This anecdote appears in D. H. Smith, *Life of Commodore Vanderbilt.*

[24] *Ibid.*

[25] Napoleon III was the third son of Louis Bonaparte, King of Holland and brother of Napoleon I. The two other sons had died leaving no children.

[26] Lloyd Morris, *Incredible New York*, adds that the seven-story Fifth Avenue Hotel, built by Amos Eno, was called 'Eno's Folly' because it was said to be too far uptown to be profitable, and that its main business would be as a summer resort.

[27] New York City Landmarks Preservation Commission (November 23, 1965, Calendar No. 2, LP-0015) lists the Jerome house as the 'first of New York City's "private palaces".' It added that it 'represented one of the finest manifestations of that carefree architecture which transcended the miles of timid brick and correct but gloomy brownstones with a new gaiety.' Its architect was Thomas R. Jackson.

[28] From Morris, *op. cit.*; also, Allen Nevins and Milton Halsey, eds., *The Diary of George Templeton Strong, 1835–1875*. Both note that Jerome built the stables first.

[29] Stephen Birmingham, *Our Crowd*. Belmont later became financial adviser to the Democratic Party. His wife's father, Commodore Matthew Perry, lived for a while with the Belmonts.

[30] Louise Chanler (whose mother was married to an Astor), lived nearby and was a childhood friend of Jennie's, remembering her as 'a madcap', who caused her no end of trouble. Another mutual friend and neighbour was Consuelo Yznaga, who later became the Duchess of Manchester: Julie Chanler, *From Gaslight to Dawn*. Several blocks away from Jennie lived a distant cousin of hers, four years younger, a boy named Theodore Roosevelt. He later became a close friend of Jennie's brother-in-law, Moreton Frewen.

[31] All of Jennie's comments in this chapter come from her *Reminiscences of Lady Randolph Churchill*.

[32] In 1865, when the Atlantic cable was reported broken, Jerome offered his yacht to take the engineer Everett to repair the break. A New York newspaper reported, 'This liberality on the part of Mr Jerome will not only prevent any delay in the transmission of cable messages but will enable the Telegraph Company to meet the expedition with a vessel of which not only the American yachtsmen but every man in the country may be proud.' Anita Leslie, *op. cit.*

[33] Anita Leslie, *op. cit.*

[34] Minnie Hauk, *Memories of a Singer*. Miss Hauk also remembered how Mr Jerome would take her and his daughters on dog-cart rides almost every Saturday.

[35] On December 31, 1862, President Lincoln approved a contract to resettle these 5,000 Negroes on Haiti, at the cost of fifty dollars apiece. Jerome's original involvement was to handle 450 of them.

[36] Sir Shane Leslie had an old Princeton College magazine clipping (no date) which said, 'The United States owe more than is generally known to such men as . . . Leonard Jerome. Mr Jerome gave at this period literally many hundreds of thousands of dollars for the preservation of the Union. . . .'

[37] Best sources of this are the files of the newspapers, particularly *The New York Times*, the New York *Tribune*, and the New York *Herald*.

[38] Lloyd Morris, *op. cit.* Morris notes that Wall Street speculator Jim Fisk later outshone Jerome with a coach; using three pairs of black and white horses,

gold-plated harnesses, two Negro postillions in white livery on the leaders, and two white footmen in black livery on the back. Upholstery was of gold cloth.

[39] Widely quoted was Travers's remark to his wife, after returning late from carousing with the Jerome brothers:

'Is that you, Bill?' his wife asked.

'Ye-yes. Wh-why—yes,' he stammered. 'Who-who did you expect?'

It was also Travers, attending a yacht race with fellow stockbrokers, who asked, 'B-but, wh-where are the customers' yachts?'

[40] From Shane Leslie, *op. cit*. Leslie records that his grandfather used some of his betting profits from that race to build a magnificent six-horse sleigh, painted in red, blue, and gold.

[41] Jerome had arranged for a competition of dinners between him, Belmont and Travers. The goal was the most perfect dinner ever achieved in Society. Lorenzo Delmonico, who made them all, called them 'The Silver, Gold and Diamond Dinners.' The competition was generally regarded as a tie. The menu for Jerome's dinner included 'Aspic de Canvasback, salad of stringbeans with truffles and a truffled ice cream.' (*Incredible New York*, Lloyd Morris.)

[42] Anita Leslie, *op. cit*., quoting a member of the Belmont family.


Chapter 2

There is a large library of material on the Franco-Prussian War period in France. Two of the best books I found were both called *The Second Empire*, one by Philip Guedalla and the other by G. P. Gooch. Even more important as an eyewitness account of the time was *France in the 19th Century* by Mrs Elizabeth Latimer. *Democratic Despot* by T. A. B. Corley is also solid and useful. *The Golden Bees* by Theo Aronson is interesting because it concentrates on individuals rather than events. *A History of the English-Speaking Peoples*, Vol. IV, by Winston S. Churchill concentrates on events. *The Empress Eugénie* by Harold Kurtz has much of interest, as has *Miss Howard and the Emperor* by Simone André Maurois. Of little value is *A History of French Civilization* by Georges Duby and Robert Mandrou.

The literature on Bismarck is equally large. *Bismarck* by Werner Richter is worthwhile, but *Bismarck* by A. J. P. Taylor is much better.

[1] From A. Forbes, *Life of Napoleon III*; Encyclopedia Britannica (Chicago, 1960).

[2] G. P. Gooch, in *The Second Empire*, describes the features of the exhibition: the steam locomotive, the first aluminium, the new American rocking chair. The prize-winner, however, was a huge gun exhibited by Herr Friedrich Krupp of Essen. Gooch also wrote, 'Paris has gone quite mad for the divine Patti when she sang "Lucia. . . ." '

[3] Jennie's comments in this chapter are quoted from her *Reminiscences of Lady Randolph Churchill*, unless specifically attributed to letters.

[4] From Anita Leslie, *The Fabulous Leonard Jerome*.

[5] March 14, 1891.

[6] Stephen Fiske, in *Offhand Portraits of Prominent New Yorkers*, describes Jerome's status just before this time: 'He led the street now to the exclusion of

everyone ... was the pet as well as the king ... almost worshipped as well as watched and imitated.'

[7] His fortune has been estimated at $10 million, but it was probably never more than half of that.

[8] From Anita Leslie, *op. cit.*

[9] From Philip Guedalla, *The Second Empire.*

[10] Guedalla quotes the British Ambassador, Lord Cowley: 'To hear the way men and women talk of their future Empress is astounding. . . . She has played her game so well that he can get her in no other way but marriage, and it is to gratify his passions that he married her. People are already speculating on their divorce.'

[11] Empress Eugénie's doctors informed her that a second pregnancy might be fatal. After that she told a friend, 'There is no longer any Eugénie. There is only the Empress.' Simone André Maurois, *Miss Howard and the Emperor.*

[12] *Ibid.*

[13] Gooch, *op. cit.* Gooch also quoted Princess Mathilde as saying, 'He is never angry. His strongest expression is "Absurd".'

[14] From Theo Aronson, *The Golden Bees.* Aronson quotes Carolyn Murat, 'Oh, the boredom of these gatherings which lacked gaiety and life, which were absolutely devoid of witty conversation. There was no thought, save as to who should have precedence—a struggle which was renewed every Monday during the 52 weeks of the year!'

[15] *Ibid.* Aronson reports that at the age of seventy, Princess Mathilde discovered that her young lover Claude Popelin had been deceiving her. Mathilde and Popelin had been lovers for twenty years.

[16] Harold Kurtz, *The Empress Eugénie.* Pauline's husband, Prince Richard Metternich, was the son of the famous Chancellor. Pauline was not only his wife, but his niece. Dr Bartens, who recorded the singing incident, later noted that he afterward had met the Princess in her home, where she seemed 'the most accomplished great lady, serious in her manner, and wrapped up in her home and children.'

[17] T. A. B. Corley, *Democratic Despot.*

[18] July 30, 1892. A. J. P. Taylor, *Bismarck.* Bismarck's general, Moltke, said years before the war: 'Nothing could be more welcome to us than to have *now* the war we must have.'

[19] From Philip Guedalla, *op. cit.* Empress Eugénie, however, denied that she had said 'It is only a little war.'

[20] Winston S. Churchill, *A History of the English-Speaking Peoples.*

[21] From Mrs Elizabeth Latimer, *France in the 19th Century.*

[22] *The Spectator* published this poem about the incident:

> How jolly, Papa! How funny!
> How the blue men tumble about!
> Huzza! There's a fellow's head off—
> How the dark red blood spouts out!
> And look, what a jolly bonfire!
> Wants nothing but coloured light!
> Oh, Papa, burn a lot of cities,
> And burn the next one at night!

[23] On reading the news, Empress Eugénie was described as saying, 'No, the

Emperor has not capitulated. A Napoleon never capitulates. He is dead!...
Listen to me: I say he is dead and they are trying to keep it from me!' Afterward
she said, 'Why didn't he get himself killed? Why isn't he buried under the walls
of Sedan?... Had he no feeling that he was dishonouring himself? What a
name to leave to his son!' 'Lettres de Napoleon III,' *Revue des Deux-Mondes*
(September 1, 1930), p. 8.

[24] Henri Rochefort in *La Lanterne* at the time wrote his celebrated *bon mot*,
'France has thirty-six million subjects, not counting the subjects of discontent.'
T. A. B. Corley, *op. cit.*

[25] The yacht belonged to Sir John Burgoyne, grandson of the General
Burgoyne who surrendered his British Army to the Americans at Saratoga. It
was only a small yacht with a crew of six.

Chapter 3

There is a whole series of fascinating books on the siege of Paris, but perhaps
the best is the two-volume *Recollections of a Minister to France* by E. B. Washburne. The Washburne volumes are excellent source books. Mrs Elizabeth
Latimer's *France in the 19th Century* also has some vivid first-hand descriptions
and anecdotes. Other good books on the subject include *The Siege of Paris* by
Robert Baldick; *The Siege of Paris* by Melvin Kranzberg; and *The Turbulent City:
Paris* by André Castelot. *Europe Since 1815* by Charles Downer Hazen has some
amplifying material, but not much. The *Reminiscences* of Otto von Bismarck are
very much worth reading. A. J. P. Taylor does not deal with this siege in his
*Bismarck*. Philip Guedalla's book *The Hundred Days* has a short but excellent
section on Bismarck and the siege. Guedalla's *The Second Empire* has some good
material on Napoleon's final days in England. So does Mme. Maurois' book,
*Miss Howard and the Emperor*.

The best sources of Jennie's life in Paris and England at this time are *Reminiscences of Lady Randolph Churchill* and Anita Leslie's *The Fabulous Leonard
Jerome*. There are also some family letters.

There is, of course, a vast library of material on English life at this time. A
standard source, and a very good one, is *England: 1870–1914* by R. C. K. Ensor.
More valuable for social history is *Our Mothers* by Alan Bott and Irene Clephane. *Life in Victorian England* by W. J. Reader and *The Victorian Temper* by
Jerome Hamilton Buckley were both of minimal value for my purpose. *Edward
VII and His Circle* by Virginia Cowles offers a good, personal biography of the
Prince of Wales. Frances, Countess of Warwick, wrote several books, all of them
revealing of that social strata: *Life's Ebb and Flow; Discretions;* and *Afterthoughts*. A more royal view comes from the invaluable three-volume *Letters
and Journals of Queen Victoria*.

G. M. Trevelyan has some interesting material in his *English Social History*
and so does Quentin Crewe in *The Frontiers of Privilege*. The Crewe book is
illustrated. But one of the best sources of the mood of the times is a book of
*Punch* cartoons, *Society Pictures*.

The files of *Graphic Magazines* also have some excellent material. *The Story of English Life* by Amabel Williams-Ellis and F. J. Fisher was not very useful.

¹ Dec. 31, 1870. From Philip Guedalla, *The Second Empire*.

² Brown's was a fashionable hotel, 'a dingy looking building on a narrow street, frowsy-looking rooms with a bewildering variety of the "rubbish of centuries". Rigid armchairs had lace antimacassars; comfortless couches stood stiffly against the wall.... A chandelier with gas flares hung over a large round table on which was spread *The Times,* the *Morning Post,* a copy of *Punch* and the fashionable weekly, *The World*. Over the window hung heavy plush curtains, and the meagre light was still further dimmed by the heavy lace window curtains.' Consuelo Vanderbilt Balsan (a former Duchess of Marlborough), *The Glitter and the Gold*.

³ There was also a pigeon postal service. From Elizabeth Latimer, *France in the 19th Century*.

⁴ From Simone André Maurois, *Miss Howard and the Emperor*. It later became the clubhouse of the Chislehurst Golf Club.

⁵ *Ibid.*

⁶ From Latimer, *op. cit.*

⁷ Theo Aronson, *The Golden Bees*. Charles Joseph Bonaparte was a grandson of Jerome Bonaparte and his American wife, Elizabeth Patterson of Baltimore. The young Bonaparte was then only twenty; he later graduated Harvard Law School and afterward became U.S. Attorney General in President Theodore Roosevelt's Administration.

⁸ From Robert Baldick, *The Siege of Paris*.

⁹ From Werner Richter, *Bismarck*.

¹⁰ From Latimer, *op. cit.*

¹¹ E. B. Washburne, *Recollections of a Minister to France*. 'Amid all these sad scenes, the French will have their fun,' wrote Washburne. 'One of the illustrated papers exhibits the danger of eating rats, by the picture of a cat which has jumped down a man's throat after the rat, leaving only the hind legs and tail sticking out of his throat.'

¹² Many Frenchmen directed their emotions toward villifying Napoleon and Empress Eugénie. Obscene caricatures of Eugénie were sold in the streets showing her in the nude being fondled by several men. Melvin Kranzberg, *The Siege of Paris*.

¹³ From Philip Guedalla, *The Hundred Days*.

¹⁴ From Anita Leslie, *The Fabulous Leonard Jerome*.

¹⁵ From Elizabeth Longford, *Queen Victoria*.

¹⁶ From Alan Bott and Irene Clephane, *Our Mothers*. Bott and Clephane add that Queen Victoria served no refreshments at Palace receptions, and permitted no smoking.

¹⁷ From R. C. K. Ensor, *England: 1870–1914*. Ensor also quotes a poem from a play *Dipsychus* (Scene V) by Arthur Hugh Clough, which typified the Victorian Age:

> Staid Englishmen, who toil and slave
> From your first childhood to your grave
> And seldom spend and always save—
> And do your duty all your life
> By your young family and wife.

[18] From Bott and Clephane, *op. cit.*

[19] From George Du Maurier, *From Punch: Society Pictures.*

[20] From Bott and Clephane, *op. cit.*

[21] From Frances, Countess of Warwick, *Life's Ebb and Flow.*

[22] From Virginia Cowles, *Edward VII and His Circle.*

[23] Max Beerbohm, *Things New and Old.* The caption under the cartoon reads, 'The rare, the rather awful visits of Albert Edward, Prince of Wales, to Windsor Castle.'

[24] From Cowles, *op. cit.*

[25] From Frances, Countess of Warwick, *Discretions.* The Countess also added, 'We considered the heads of historic houses who read serious works, encouraged scientists and the like, very, very dull. . . . We wished to know as little of them as possible, and our wishes were law.'

[26] From Cowles, *op. cit.*

[27] From Jerome Hamilton Buckley, *The Victorian Temper.*

[28] From Guedalla, *The Second Empire.* Guedalla quotes Napoleon III as saying that armies do not follow ill men in carriages.

[29] From *Reminiscences of Lady Randolph Churchill.*

[30] From Bott and Clephane, *op. cit.*

[31] From Anita Leslie, *op. cit.*

[32] *Ibid.*

Chapter 4

The bulk of the basic reference material in this chapter came from a big black metal box of family archives in the Muniments Room of Blenheim Palace. It contains everything from letters to the oversize marriage contract. It is invaluable.

Sir Shane Leslie has another large supply of letters, particularly from Leonard Jerome and from the Jerome sisters, which is equally invaluable. So are Sir Shane's books, particularly *Studies in Sublime Failure* and *Men Were Different*, which deal so perceptively with Sir Shane's uncle and godfather, Randolph Churchill; also *The Passing Chapter* and *The End of a Chapter*, which focus so sharply on the society of the time. His *American Wonderland* is richly rewarding for its material on Leonard Jerome.

The best single book on Randolph Churchill is by Robert Rhodes James, *Lord Randolph Churchill.* There have, of course, been many other books on Randolph Churchill, including a two-volume biography by his son, Winston S. Churchill, *Lord Randolph Churchill.* The Winston Churchill biography is beautifully written and detailed, particularly in the political areas, but it is much less a personal biography.

*Reminiscences of Lady Randolph Churchill* is surprisingly skimpy concerning this period of courtship, and Anita Leslie's *The Fabulous Leonard Jerome* remains the best source book on the Jerome sisters at this time. Of the courtship, however, Jennie has written a short but revealing memoir, which is among the family papers at Blenheim.

A. L. Rowse, *The Early Churchills*, has creditably detailed the early Marlborough history and Winston S. Churchill's great two-volume *Marlborough: His Life and Times* is a superb description of his ancestors. The account in Randolph S. Churchill's biography, *Winston S. Churchill*, is also excellent.

*The Dictionary of National Biography* and *Debrett's Peerage* are indispensable reference books for this period. The files of *The Times* and *The Graphic* were of important use.

Sir Edward Clarke's *The Story of My Life* has a single anecdote on Randolph Churchill at this time that is highly pertinent. The first volume of *Life of Herbert Henry Asquith, Lord Oxford and Asquith* by J. A. Spender and Cyril Asquith has an even briefer sidelight. *Leaves from the Notebooks of Lady Dorothy Nevill*, ed. Ralph Nevill has some fascinating anecdotes of the time. *Offhand Portraits of Prominent New Yorkers* by Stephen Fiske has a fine anecdote concerning Leonard Jerome at this time. But, again, all this is peripheral material—the heart of the chapter comes from the letters in the family archives.

¹ Jennie's own account of her first meeting with Lord Randolph and his subsequent proposal is in a private memorandum in the family archives in the Muniments Room at Blenheim Palace.

² Anita Leslie, *The Fabulous Leonard Jerome*.

³ *Leaves from the Notebooks of Lady Dorothy Nevill*, ed. Ralph Nevill. Lady Nevill afterward commented that, 'I think the influx of the American element into English society has done good, rather than harm, whilst there are many old families which, in mind and pocket, have been completely revivified by prudent marriages with American brides.'

⁴ *Reminiscences of Lady Randolph Churchill*.

⁵ Anon., *Kings, Courts and Society*.

⁶ Winston S. Churchill, *Lord Randolph Churchill*.

⁷ Merton College at the time had about seventy students, tutors, etc. The best rooms went to the students who had the most money because one paid rent for the rooms. Randolph's room later became part of the college library, but before it did, it was used by Max Beerbohm, who found the name 'Lord Randolph Churchill' carved on the table.

⁸ He was also a member of the Debating Club.

⁹ Anonymous, *Reminiscences of an Oxogenarian* describes the author's memory of his first day at Oxford, seeing young Randolph Churchill throwing oranges at a fellow classmate's open window, and saying to his companion, 'More oranges.'

¹⁰ Frank Harris, *My Life and Loves*.

¹¹ Robert Rhodes James, *Lord Randolph Churchill*. Rhodes James notes that parliamentary critic H. W. Lucy tested Churchill's ability to memorize a page of Gibbon in the 1880's, and Randolph recited it perfectly.

¹² Most of the letters referred to in this chapter are in the family archives at Blenheim Palace.

¹³ Winston S. Churchill, *Marlborough: His Life and Times*.

¹⁴ Duchess Sarah and Jennie were much of a kind. Both were beautiful women who loved love, and yet both would have made mighty men. Each was exciting, furiously outspoken, and always conscious of her power. Much could be made of the parallel of their lives. Sarah was almost nineteen when she married John Churchill. If she loved him, he wrote her, 'it would make me immortal.' John Churchill had strength and ambition, but it was Sarah who did help make him

immortal. She and Jennie were both tempestuous women of courage and common sense.

[15] A. L. Rowse, *The Early Churchills,* also noted that the fourth Duke of Marlborough had a passion for astronomy, while the fifth Duke preferred botany.

[16] The *Dictionary of National Biography,* which also describes him as 'a sensible, honourable and industrious public man'.

[17] Stephen Fiske, *Offhand Portraits of Prominent New Yorkers.*

[18] Brodrick also wrote leaders for *The Times,* and later served as Warden of Merton College. He ran three times for Woodstock, and lost each time.

[19] Sir Edward Clarke, *The Story of My Life.*

[20] Herbert Asquith later became Prime Minister. J. A. Spender and Cyril Asquith, *Life of Herbert Henry Asquith, Lord Oxford and Asquith,* Vol. I, note that Asquith 'spent two or three hours a day sailing on the upper river and some of the residue of his time in speaking for Mr Brodrick against Lord Randolph Churchill at the Woodstock election.'

[21] Anita Leslie, *op. cit.*

[22] Rowse, *op. cit.*

[23] Jerome, in that same letter, also added, 'My daughter, although not a Russian princess, is an American and ranks precisely the same. And you have no doubt seen that the Russian settlement recently published claims *everything* for the bride.' Jerome was referring to Czar Alexander II's daughter, who had been married earlier that year to Queen Victoria's son, the Duke of Edinburgh. The bride was given about £200,000, the income from it for her 'exclusive use and enjoyment'.

[24] A letter from the British Ambassador in Paris, Lord Lyons, to British Foreign Secretary Lord Derby, dated April 15, 1874 (Public Record Office, F.O. 146, Book No. 1745, No. 380), reads: 'My Lord: I have the honour to transmit herewith, under flying seal, a letterhead which I have addressed to the Secretary of the Bishop of London's Registry Office, containing the certificate of a marriage solemnized at this Embassy, between Lord Randolph Henry Spencer Churchill, bachelor, and Jennie Jerome, spinster.

'Together with the usual declaration and customary fee of one pound for the due registry of the same.'

[25] Anita Leslie, *op. cit.*

## Chapter 5

Blenheim is best described by Winston Churchill in his two-volume biography of *Marlborough,* but there is also an excellent description by Randolph S. Churchill in *Fifteen Famous English Homes* and in a slim, anonymous and undated volume called *Blenheim.* Consuelo Vanderbilt Balsan, who became Duchess of Marlborough, gives an intimate account of the palace in *The Glitter and the Gold. Reminiscences of Lady Randolph Churchill* gives an intimate account from another point of view.

The files of *Punch* and *The Graphic* are still superb in picturing the times and the society, but the most revealing insights come from the family archives of Churchill and Jerome letters. The letters of the Jerome sisters to each other are particularly invaluable. Lady St. Hélier's *Memories of Fifty Years* and Ralph Nevill's *Leaves from the Notebooks of Lady Dorothy Nevill* are the memories of the two outstanding hostesses of the time.

Of Randolph Churchill, the biographies by Robert Rhodes James and Winston S. Churchill are still basic for this period, as they are for the whole of his life. Sir Henry Lucy's profile of Randolph Churchill in *Speeches of the Rt. Hon. Lord Randolph Churchill, with a sketch of his life,* is also well worth reading. *Randolph Spencer-Churchill* by T. H. S. Escott is better on the later portions of his life. Sir Shane Leslie, *Men Were Different,* has a fine chapter concerning him. Also worth looking at for important anecdotes and background are *Disraeli* by Robert Blake; *Life of Benjamin Disraeli* by W. F. Monypenny and G. E. Buckle, Vol. II; *Miscellanies* by Lord Rosebery, Vol. I; and *The Story of My Life* by Sir Edward Clarke.

Virginia Peacock, *Famous American Belles of the Nineteenth Century* has an excellent chapter on Jennie, giving the background to much of the feeling about Anglo-American marriages. *They All Married Well* by Elizabeth Eliot has more of the same. *The Fabulous Leonard Jerome* by Anita Leslie remains an important source book until Jerome's death.

*Winston S. Churchill* by Randolph S. Churchill, Vol. I and Companion Vol. I, Part I, are indispensable books. The short biographies in them are equally excellent.

The sources on syphilis come from the files of *The Lancet,* in the Wellcome British Medical Library in London and the files in the New York Academy of Medicine. An excellent book of detailed background is *Man Against Germs* by A. L. Baron, and another fine one is *Disease and Destiny* by Judson Bennett Gilbert. *The Medical Annual* of the District of Columbia, 1955, was also valuable.

It should also be mentioned that Winston S. Churchill's novel *Savrola* should be read for his many revealing descriptions not only of Mrs Everest, but of his relationship with mother and father.

For background on the Prince of Wales and his society, Virginia Cowles's book, *Edward VII and His Circle,* has good anecdotes and details. A book entitled *Kings, Courts and Society* has intimate detail which presumes a knowledge, but it unfortunately is anonymous. *My Darling Daisy* by Theo Lang, is equally intimate. A. L. Rowse, *The Churchills,* is well worth examining.

[1] Letter from Winston Churchill to Edward Marsh, April 30, 1937. (The Papers of Sir Edward Marsh, in the possession of the Marquess of Bath, unpublished.)

[2] Jennie wrote her mother on July 1, 1874, that the Duke of Marlborough paid £10,000 for the lease. 'Randolph had no settlements made on him when he married,' Jennie added, 'and this, of course, makes a settlement. If anything was to happen to him, this house comes to me.'

[3] During an election campaign, Winston Churchill spoke at Blenheim before a huge crowd. Before his speech, he walked through the palace with Gerald O'Brien, and then suddenly asked, 'O'Brien, has this old ruin got bathroom facilities for all these people?' (Ralph G. Martin and Richard Harrity, *Man of the Century: Churchill*).

[4] Consuelo Vanderbilt Balsan, *The Glitter and the Gold.*

[5] Part of the epitaph for Blenheim's architect, Sir John Vanbrugh, was:

> Lie heavy on him, earth, for he
> Laid many a heavy loan on thee.

[6] A different view comes from *Blenheim* (Oxford, Henry Slatter, n.d.) quoting the *Travels of Mirza Abu Taleb Khan, 1799–1803*: 'This place is without comparison superior to any thing I ever beheld. The beauties of Windsor Park faded before it, and every other place I had visited was effaced from my collection, on viewing its magnificence.'

[7] *Reminiscences of Lady Randolph Churchill.*

[8] M. J. Gifford, ed., *Pages from the Diary of an Oxford Lady.*

[9] Earl of Ronaldshay, *Life of Lord Curzon.*

[10] Jennie remembered how the blood from the wounded pigeons often stained the gowns of the watching women. Lady Warwick noted in *Discretions*: 'I saw two birds, one with a broken wing and one with a broken leg, come painfully to rest on the green. That was enough! I vowed I would never go there again. . . .'

[11] Anon., *Kings, Courts and Society.*

[12] Virginia Cowles, *Edward VII and His Circle.*

[13] Margot Tennant, who later became Margot Asquith, the wife of the Prime Minister, described the Prince of Wales as 'a professional lovemaker'. After but a single meeting, the Prince sent her a gold sharkskin cigarette case with a diamond and sapphire clasp. Virginia Cowles, *op. cit.* Rudyard Kipling called Prince Edward 'that corpulent voluptuary'. A cartoon of the time showed a pretty girl getting dressed for an evening out. Beside her looking glass was an invitation to Buckingham Palace; the cartoon caption said, 'She Stoops To Conquer' (Theo Lang, *The Darling Daisy Affair*).

[14] Interview with Sir Shane Leslie.

[15] Consuelo's marriage had the greatest social prestige, since there were only twenty-seven Dukes in the United Kingdom. When the Duke arrived in the United States to court Consuelo, the New York *World* ran a headline, 'Attention American Heiresses, What Will You Bid?' and then went on to say, 'Manchester is the poorest Duke in Burke's Peerage, financially and in morals.' Consuelo's father was a Cuban who had settled in Louisiana and become a rich cotton plantation owner. Consuelo, like Jennie, was beautiful and witty, but she was soon very unhappy. Elizabeth Eliot, *They All Married Well.*

[16] Sir George Arthur, *Concerning Winston Spencer Churchill.*

[17] Anita Leslie, *The Fabulous Leonard Jerome.*

[18] Lady St. Hélier, *Memories of Fifty Years.*

[19] Quoted in Robert Rhodes James, *Lord Randolph Churchill.*

[20] H. W. Lucy, *Speeches of the Rt. Hon. Lord Randolph Churchill, with a sketch of his life.* Lucy described him then as 'a well-groomed young man with protuberant eyes, pale face and a ponderous moustache.' Lucy himself was described as 'absolutely unique . . . the only individual in the world who can amusingly describe the proceedings of that dismal, make-believe assemblage, the modern House of Commons.'

[21] Rhodes James, *op. cit.*

[22] W. F. Monypenny and G. E. Buckle, *The Life of Benjamin Disraeli*, Vol. II.

[23] Shane Leslie, *Men Were Different.* Sir Shane also reminds that the Churchill family shield is inscribed with the Spanish words, 'Fiel Pero Desdicado' ('Faithful but Unfortunate').

[24] Lady St. Hélier, *op. cit.*

[25] *Reminiscences of Lady Randolph Churchill.* Lady Randolph regarded Gladstone and Lord Salisbury as two of the pleasantest companions at dinner 'of all the statesmen I have met. Both had the happy knack of seeming vastly interested in one's conversation, no matter what the subject . . . there was no condescension or "Tempering of the wind to the shorn lamb" about it. . . .'

[26] Anita Leslie, *op. cit.*

[27] *Leaves from the Notebooks of Lady Dorothy Nevill,* ed. Ralph Nevill. Lady Nevill revealed her formula as a successful Charles Street hostess: To make a ball successful, three men should always be asked to every lady—one to dance, one to eat and one to stare—that makes everything go off well.'

[28] Randolph S. Churchill, *Winston S. Churchill,* I, 5.

[29] Winston S. Churchill, *Savrola,* pp. 32–33.

[30] Virginia Peacock, *Famous American Belles of the Nineteenth Century.* Peacock adds, 'One of the first American women before whom these latter-day barriers of social prejudice gave way, was Jennie Jerome of New York. She penetrated the innermost recesses of British society, opening the way more than any other woman to the position her countrywomen occupy there at the end of the century, and holding herself a place second to no other American woman in Europe.'

[31] A. L. Baron, *Man Against Germs;* Judson Bennett Gilbert, *Disease and Destiny. Medical Annual* (District of Columbia, 1955) also lists a number of other prominent people who supposedly had syphilis: King Francis I, Ivan the Terrible, Pope Alexander VI, Pope Julius II, Guy de Maupassant, Frederick the Great, Benvenuto Cellini, Beethoven, Schubert, and Heinrich Heine. The researcher at the Wellcome British Medical Library adds Goya, Lenin, Rabelais, Oscar Wilde, Edouard Manet, and Woodrow Wilson.

## Chapter 6

The most complete account of the origins of the quarrel between the Prince of Wales and Randolph Churchill is in *Winston S. Churchill* by Randolph S. Churchill, Vol. I. Robert Rhodes James has a shorter but fine account in *Lord Randolph Churchill.* Anita Leslie's *The Fabulous Leonard Jerome* is intimate on this, but much more sketchy. The letters themselves, particularly those between Jennie and Randolph, are the most revealing source. Winston S. Churchill barely touches the matter in *Lord Randolph Churchill.* George Smalley's *Anglo-American Memories* does not deal with the cause of the quarrel, but with its solution, which differs from that in Randolph Churchill's version. It is possible that both versions are parts of the same piece.

For a general background on the Queen and her relations with the Prince, there are many books: *Victoria R.I.* by Elizabeth Longford is good and so is Churchill's *History of the English-Speaking Peoples.* Monypenny and Buckle's *Life of Benjamin Disraeli* and John Morley's *Life of William Ewart Gladstone* are both valuable sources. Rowse's *The Early Churchills* has a good summary.

Atmospheric descriptions of the United States at that time can be found in Lloyd Morris's *Incredible New York* and in the files of *The New York Times,* the New York *Tribune,* and the New York *Herald.*

[1] Philip Guedalla, *The Hundred Years*.

[2] *Ibid.*

[3] James Truslow Adams, in *Empire on the Seven Seas*, adds that the Queen objected to conversation with the respectful but blunt Gladstone 'as tho she were a public meeting', but that she enjoyed talking to Disraeli. Winston S. Churchill, in *A History of the English-Speaking Peoples*, Vol. IV, quotes Gladstone as saying, 'The Queen is enough to kill any man.' The Queen's preference for Disraeli was based on his flattery of her as much as on the fact that he bought control of the Suez Canal, and also made the Queen the Empress of India.

[4] W. F. Monypenny and G. E. Buckle, *The Life of Benjamin Disraeli*, Vol. II. The letter was addressed to Lady Bradford and dated April 4, 1876.

[5] A. L. Rowse, *The Early Churchills*.

[6] Randolph S. Churchill, *Winston S. Churchill*, I, 29.

[7] *Ibid.*, Supplement Number II (April 21, 1876).

[8] Anita Leslie, *The Fabulous Leonard Jerome*.

[9] Extract from letter dated March 10, 1876, the Royal Archives, published in Randolph S. Churchill, *op. cit.*, I, 29.

[10] George W. Smalley, *Anglo-American Memories*. Smalley was a noted American editor and a good friend of the Churchills, Lady Jeune, and Lady Nevill. However, it seems that these were not the only copies of the letters. See Randolph Churchill, *op. cit.*

For an excellent description of Hartington, see Barbara Tuchman, *The Proud Tower*.

[11] Robert Rhodes James, *Lord Randolph Churchill*. Randolph S. Churchill gives the most complete account of the whole incident in the first volume of his *Winston S. Churchill*, although he does not have the details of Lord Hartington's intervention, as described by G. W. Smalley.

[8][2] *Reminiscences of Lady Randolph Churchill*.

[13] Winston S. Churchill, *Lord Randolph Churchill*.

[14] Randolph S. Churchill, *op. cit.* Letter dated April 20, 1876.

[15] Harry Tyrwhitt-Wilson was better known to his close friends as 'The Smiler'. He was the eldest son of Sir Henry Thomas Tyrwhitt and the Baroness Berners, and assumed the name of Wilson by royal licence in 1876. He was also a good friend of Lord Rosebery's and an equerry to the Prince of Wales.

[16] Lloyd Morris, *Incredible New York*.

[17] Lawrence Jerome was the sixth of eight sons of Isaac Jerome, and younger than Leonard. He and Leonard had married the Hall sisters, Clara and Catherine. This made Lawrence's son, William Travers Jerome, a double first cousin of Jennie. Jennie wrote of the Philadelphia trip with her Uncle Larry, 'He kept us in transports of laughter.'

Chapter 7

The only good source of reference for Jennie's life in Ireland is her own *Reminiscences* and the family letters. Rowse's book *The Later Churchills* is skimpy here, and Robert Rhodes James and Winston Churchill, in their biographies of Lord Randolph Churchill, both concentrate on the political focus.

*The Life of Charles Stewart Parnell* by R. Barry O'Brien, in two volumes, is essential for another political view of this time and for a discussion of Parnell's relationship with Randolph Churchill.

The family archives at Blenheim Palace, supplemented by Randolph S. Churchill's biography of his father, provides vital personal news of the family. The British Museum newspaper library at Colindale and the newspaper library of the New York Public Library both have files of assorted Irish newspapers which offer some general background.

There have been a number of books about the Empress of Austria, but no one of them is truly good. Some of the better ones: *The Lonely Empress* by Joan Haslip; *Elizabeth, Empress of Austria* by Count Egon Corti, and *Empress of Austria* by Carl Tschuppik.

*Churchill and Ireland* by Mary C. Bromage deals mainly with Winston Churchill and completely neglects any real description of Ireland in Randolph's time.

[1] *Reminiscences of Lady Randolph Churchill.*

[2] Winston S. Churchill, *My Early Life.*

[3] Viscount D'Abernon, *Portraits and Appreciations.*

[4] Randolph S. Churchill, *Winston S. Churchill*, I, 35.

[5] R. Barry O'Brien, *The Life of Charles Stewart Parnell.* O'Brien noted, 'Parnell liked few men; above all, he liked few Englishmen. Yet he regarded Lord Randolph Churchill with no unfriendly feelings. He thought that the young Tory Democrat possessed generous instincts, entertained kindly feelings toward the Irish, and was full of originality, resource and courage.'

[6] Louis J. Jennings, ed., *Speeches of Lord Randolph Churchill.*

[7] Winston S. Churchill, *Lord Randolph Churchill.* Churchill also quotes the rest of the Duke's letter, which expressed amazement and annoyance and encouraged a public rebuke of his son's views.

[8] Randolph S. Churchill, *op. cit.*, I, 35-36.

[9] Winston S. Churchill, *My Early Life.*

[10] This, of course, may also explain Jennie's supposed paucity of maternal feeling for Winston in his early years.

[11] Joan Haslip, *The Lonely Empress,* and Count Egon Corti, *Elizabeth, Empress of Austria.* Haslip also quotes the Empress as saying of Ireland: 'The great advantage of Ireland is that it has no Royal Highnesses. . . . Here at last I feel free and at my ease. . . .'

[12] Winston S. Churchill, *My Early Life.*

[13] Airlie, Mabell, Countess of, *With the Guards We Shall Go.* In 1880 Strange Jocelyn succeeded to the Earldom.

[14] John Spencer-Churchill.

## Chapter 8

All the previously mentioned biographies of Lord Randolph Churchill are important here, particularly Winston Churchill's biography of his father, the Robert Rhodes James biography, and the books by Henry Lucy. Morley's biography of Gladstone, Blake's *Disraeli*, the Monypenny and Buckle *Disraeli*, and O'Brien's *Parnell*, all have supplementary information.

*Reminiscences of Lady Randolph Churchill* is particularly good here, as are Lady Warwick's *Discretions* and Lady St. Hélier's *Memories of Fifty Years.* Another interesting book of background is *Fifty Years: 1882–1930*, written by twenty-seven contributors to *The Times.* Sir Shane Leslie in *Long Shadows* has some charming anecdotes about young Winston and his mother, and Winston has even more in *My Early Life.* G. W. E. Russell, *Portraits of the Seventies*, has some material on Randolph, but not much.

Barbara Tuchman, *The Proud Tower*, is excellent on Balfour and Gladstone, and Cowles's *Edward VII and His Circle* is good on the Lily Langtry craze.

On Frewen in the United States, Moreton Frewen has written *Melton Mowbray & Other Memories*, and Allen Andrews, *The Splendid Pauper*, reveals him even more intimately in his letters. Again, the best resource are the letters in the family archives at Blenheim Palace.

[1] From W. J. Reader, *Life in Victorian England*: 'Authority, except in the special case of the Queen, nearly always meant male authority. . . . women, because they were weaker, should be protected rather than exploited.'

[2] From R. C. K. Ensor, *England: 1870–1914.*

[3] Frances, Countess of Warwick, *Discretions.* She added, 'Nobody felt quite safe—How could we, recognizing that, in the feverish search for pleasure, any woman might lose her lover, any man's mistress might be lured away!'

[4] Anon., *Uncensored Recollections*: 'The illness that first seized him during his Oxford days, began ere long to cause trouble, and although he was always willing, nay glad enough to consult any specialist, he never would follow the treatment recommended.' He would say, 'All right,' and do nothing. The author told of taking Randolph to see a famous specialist in Paris. 'When we got to the doctor's, he wanted to back out and I had to take him to the Hotel Chatham bar and refresh him with a brandy cocktail before he would go any farther.' The author tells of tipping the manservant to get immediate access to the doctor without waiting. 'When I returned triumphant . . . I found that Randolph had bolted down the *escalier de service*! I rushed after him, dragged him back; the doctor saw him at once, prescribed for him and warned him. But all in vain. . . .'

[5] They had sublet their Charles Street home while in Ireland.

[6] Winston S. Churchill, *My Early Life.*

[7] Winston S. Churchill, *Lord Randolph Churchill.*

[8] Shane Leslie, *Long Shadows.* Other games Leslie remembers Jennie playing that night with Winston included 'Hunt the Thimble' and 'Hunt the Slipper'. By 2 A.M., Shane Leslie quotes Jennie as saying, 'Winston, you are impossible.' Leslie notes that this occasion marked the first time Mrs Everest had gone on holiday in five years.

[9] This letter is reproduced, without a date, in Anita Leslie, *The Fabulous Leonard Jerome.* Randolph S. Churchill in *Winston S. Churchill*, I, reproduces another letter dated Jan. 4, 1882, which he regards as Winston's first letter.

[10] Winston S. Churchill, *My Early Life.*

[11] Shane Leslie, *op. cit.*

[12] *Reminiscences of Lady Randolph Churchill.*

[13] G. W. E. Russell, *Portraits of the Seventies.*

[14] Sir Henry Lucy, *Diary of a Journalist.* Lucy suggests the origin of the Fourth Party name came when a Member of the House said in debate that there were

two great political parties in the State. Parnell then called out, 'Three,' and Randolph stood up and yelled, 'Four'. But Lucy also says that Frank Hugh O'Donnell already had referred to the Irish Nationalists as the Third Party.

[15] *Reminiscences of Lady Randolph Churchill.*

[16] Barbara Tuchman, *The Proud Tower*, quotes Lord Hartington as saying of Balfour, 'Of all the statesmen I have known [he was] the most persuasive speaker.'

[17] John Morley, *Life of William Ewart Gladstone.*

[18] R. Barry O'Brien, *The Life of Charles Stewart Parnell.* O'Brien adds that Parnell 'also had the shrewd suspicion that there was nothing which this rattling young Tory would relish more keenly than "dishing" the Whigs—except perhaps "dishing" the Tories.'

[19] *Ibid.*

[20] *Reminiscences of Lady Randolph Churchill.*

[21] Robert Rhodes James, *Lord Randolph Churchill.*

[22] Winston S. Churchill, *My Early Life.*

[23] Rhodes James, *op. cit.*

[24] Moreton Frewen, *Melton Mowbray & Other Memories.* Frewen described his father-in-law's conversational dinners: 'I doubt if, on the earth's surface, did such a far-flung group of men ever collect round a single table. What a poem was the table itself! It was a slab of Honduras mahogany, lacquered with age and care.'

[25] *Ibid.* Frewen later listed Jennie as one of three 'really beautiful Americans' in England.

[26] Virginia Cowles, *Edward VII and His Circle.* Cowles writes that Frewen was one of Langtry's earliest admirers.

[27] Lady St Hélier (Mary Jeune), *Memories of Fifty Years.* Lady Jeune notes that the one unchanging quality in his unpredictable nature was his deep feeling for his mother.

[28] Jerome family letters.

[29] *Ibid.*

[30] Lloyd Morris, *Incredible New York.*

[31] *Ibid.*

[32] *Reminiscences of Lady Randolph Churchill.*

Chapter 9

The files of *The Times* of London become increasingly important about this time because the Churchills have become increasingly important, and the accounts of the couple are fuller. This is similarly true of the periodicals of the time, from *Punch* to *Fortnightly Review*. The previously mentioned memoirs of women such as Lady Nevill are almost invaluable now for the intimate flavour of the time.

The Kinsky material comes from contact with Prince Clary in Venice, who knows the basic background of the man and has the visual memory, and from the Countess Kinsky in London who passed on family stories and memories of her husband. George Lambton's *Men and Horses I Have Known* has a few

W

interesting anecdotes, but little more. The family letters, particularly those of Jennie to her sisters, tell more about Kinsky than any other source. There are also a few scattered and most discreet references in Jennie's *Reminiscences*. According to Prince Clary, Jennie's letters to Kinsky no longer exist.

The social life at Sandringham is excellently described in Jennie's *Reminiscences*. The Curzon material comes largely from *The Life of Lord Curzon* by the Earl of Ronaldshay and from *Discretions* by Frances, Countess of Warwick.

[1] Jennie also noted in her *Reminiscences* that the dynamo in her basement which generated the electricity made so much noise that 'it greatly excited all the horses as they approached our door'.

[2] But a slogan was 'Have nothing in your house except what you know to be useful or believe to be beautiful.' R. C. K. Ensor, *England: 1870–1914.*

[3] An article in the *Evening News*, October 15, 1921, describing a sale of Lady Randolph Churchill's furniture and belongings, mentioned a catalogue of objects and art from at least five countries. The anonymous author also noted, 'I remember once seeing in one of her houses, a tall, slender cupboard, lined with silk, and glass-fronted, which contained nothing but brocaded evening shoes, shelf upon shelf of them, with their old paste buckles glistening through the glass. I remember her saying that she never threw away her evening shoes, and that some of them, she had had for twenty years. . . . Lady Randolph's feet were exceptionally small and beautifully formed, so that her shoes kept their shape and always looked nice, to the end of their days. Consequently, this array of tiny shoes was most effective and pretty.'

[4] 'My father was over five feet nine and a half inches—quite a passable stature,' wrote Winston Churchill in *Thoughts and Adventures*, 'but because he was pictured in conflict with Mr Gladstone, he was always represented as a midget.' Churchill added that he continually got letters from people asking of his father, 'Is it really true he was no more than five feet high?'

[5] Robert Rhodes James, *Lord Randolph Churchill.*

[6] Colonel Burnaby of the Royal Horse Guards served as a war correspondent for *The Times*, took a solo balloon flight from Dover to Normandy, and captured national attention in 1875 with his ride from London to Khiva—Russian protests stopped his riding on to Samarkand in Central Asia. He was killed in 1885, 'sword in hand, while resisting the desperate charge of the Arabs at the battle of Abu Klea.'

[7] *Leaves from the Notebooks of Lady Dorothy Nevill,* ed. Ralph Nevill. In *Under Five Reigns,* also edited by her son, Lady Nevill quoted the comment, often repeated, 'I have seen women so delicate that they were afraid to ride, for fear of the horse running away; afraid to sail, for fear the boat might upset; afraid to walk, for fear that the dew might fall; but I never saw one afraid to be married!'

[8] *The Daily Telegraph* in London, July 3, 1963, quoted the New York State Supreme Court ruling that it was 'an inalienable right' to have one's body tattooed, regardless of the contention that it might cause hepatitis. The article said, 'Lady Randolph Churchill, mother of Sir Winston Churchill, was tattooed for ornamental purposes as were King Frederick IX of Denmark, King George V, Edward VII, Alfonso XII of Spain, Viscount Montgomery, and countless other distinguished members of society.'

308

[9] In Randolph Churchill's biography of his father, and in the supplemental volumes, which is the definitive collection of Churchill letters, there are very few letters from Randolph to Winston.

[10] George Lambton, *Men and Horses I Have Known*, relates the story of Kinsky's first experience in London society, a dinner by Sir Horace Farquhar. A drunken cabman had taken Kinsky all over London before bringing him to the Farquhar home, at which time the dinner there was half over. Kinsky was explaining all this to his host with such furious gestures that he knocked a plate of soup into Lady Castlereagh's lap. Kinsky was so handsome and such a hero that Lady Castlereagh 'continued her conversation with him as if nothing had happened'.

[11] Von Folkmann, Josef Erwin, *Die Gefürstete Linie des Uralten und Etlen Geschlechtes Kinsky* (Prague, 1861), traces the Kinsky family back to the year 1209.

[12] Blandford was quoted as saying, 'Mistress, yes; but future Duchess of Marlborough, *never*!'

[13] Curzon was five years younger than Jennie. There is a family story that Jennie once loaned Curzon her nightgown when he unexpectedly decided to spend the night at Blenheim and had no pyjamas.

## Chapter 10

A short but excellent review of the tone of the times in this chapter comes from *The Saturday Book—25*, ed. John Hadfield. Again, the files of *Fortnightly Review*, *The Spectator*, *Punch*, and *The Times* are all indispensable for a proper study of the period.

Lady Warwick's several books of memoirs, previously mentioned, are particularly good for this, but perhaps the best books that connect the Churchills with doings of British society then are the first and second series of *Anglo-American Memories* by George W. Smalley. Smalley was not only a trained correspondent and editor in England for the New York *Tribune*, but also a *bon vivant*, an intimate of all levels of British society and his house served as a salon for everybody from royalty to Sarah Bernhardt. Mrs J. Comyns Carr, herself a celebrated society leader, noted in her *Reminiscences*: 'It was through my friends, the George Smalleys, that I met most of the Americans I knew.' Smalley's wife was the daughter of the celebrated American, Wendell Phillips. His memoirs are the works of a trained observer with a sharp facility for the pertinent anecdote.

Sir Shane Leslie's memories and private papers are invaluable for the description of his mother's marriage. The family letters are particularly important here.

Frank Harris's *My Life and Loves* has a most revealing anecdote in great detail typifying the relationship of Jennie and her husband at this time.

Jennie's own *Reminiscences* are excellent on the details of the Primrose League, and Robert Rhodes James's biography of her husband is even better. Winston Churchill's biography of his father has supplementary information well worth reading.

¹ Her membership card number was 12.

² John Hadfield, ed., *The Saturday Book—25.* Hadfield refers to this Victorian period as 'the Sober Eighties', as compared with the oncoming 'Naughty Nineties'. He quotes William Butler Yeats as saying, 'Everybody got down off his stilts; henceforth, nobody drank absinthe with his black coffee; nobody went mad; nobody committed suicide . . . or if they did, I have forgotten.'

³ Shane Leslie, *The End of a Chapter.*

⁴ *Reminiscences of Lady Randolph Churchill.*

⁵ January 24, 1884. Winston S. Churchill, *Lord Randolph Churchill.*

⁶ George W. Smalley, *Anglo-American Memories.* Smalley adds, 'The Duchess of Marlborough was a woman who may always be adduced in support of the theory that qualities of mind and character descend from mother to son.'

⁷ *Ibid.*

⁸ Randolph later told Jennie, 'This is the sort of remark that overturns a coach.' Robert Rhodes James, *Lord Randolph Churchill.*

⁹ *Reminiscences of Lady Randolph Churchill.*

¹⁰ R. C. K. Ensor, *England: 1870–1914*; see also Stephen Gwynn, *The Life of the Rt. Hon. Sir Charles Dilke, Bart., M.P.,* completed and edited by Gertrude M. Tuckwell. Dilke's public downfall came when he refused to testify in the divorce case listing him as a co-respondent.

¹¹ Lady Randolph Churchill, *Small Talks on Big Subjects.* She also added, 'If people sufficiently prominent for one reason or another succeed in surrounding themselves with an atmosphere of mystery, the interest of the public is aroused, for the possibilities of the "dark horse" are always attractive.'

¹² Leonie, in a letter to Clara, commented on the rumour of Randolph and Lady de Grey, and said that 'Randolph is not in the least devoted to Gladys de Grey . . . only as she [Jennie] has no flirtation on hand, she suddenly notices his coldness. It has been like that for years. . . . *Chacun à son gout.*'

¹³ Rhodes James, *op. cit.*

¹⁴ Elliott O'Donnell, ed., *Mrs E. M. Ward's Reminiscences.* Mrs Ward added, 'Lady Randolph Churchill showed a decided talent for painting. . . . She brought her father to see my studio, and on more than one occasion, was accompanied by her son Winston, a delightful little boy in short trousers. It was at her house that I first saw cigarettes handed to a lady, a departure which seemed to me then a matter for wonder, rather, I think, than of annoyance.'

¹⁵ *Punch* ran a series of cartoons on Professional Beauties. The caption to one of them read:

Gwendolyn: 'Uncle George says every woman ought to have a profession, and I think he's quite right.'

Mama: 'Indeed! And what profession do you mean to choose?'

Gwendolyn: 'I mean to be a Professional Beauty.'

¹⁶ Frances, Countess of Warwick, *Discretions.* Virginia Cowles, in *Edward VII and His Circle,* records that Randolph Churchill, years before, had written Jennie, 'I dined with Lord Wharncliffe last night and took in to dinner a Mrs Langtry, a most beautiful creature, quite unknown, very poor, and they say she has but one black dress.' In her *Reminiscences,* Jennie commented, 'Mrs Langtry owned one dinner dress, not because of poverty, but because, until now, she had only needed one.'

¹⁷ Sir Shane Leslie's private papers. Sir Shane noted, 'Poor Leonard Jerome must have read those figures with an ashen heart.' The newspapers reported 'elegantly appointed equipages' blocking the streets near Grace Church, and that 'Solomon's concubines in their glory could hardly have equalled' the clothes of the attending society women. Sir Shane also remembered that the Leslie family in Ireland regarded the wedding day as a tragic day for fasting. The date was October 2, 1884.

¹⁸ Frank Harris, *My Life and Loves*. Harris noted after the incident that he remonstrated with Randolph that he should not have done that in front of him because 'your wife will always hate me for having been the witness of her humiliation'. Harris added, 'Ever afterwards Lady Randolph missed no opportunity of showing me that she disliked me cordially. . . . She showed her worst side to me almost always and was either imperious or indifferent.'

Chapter 11

The Kinsky material comes from a variety of sources: Jennie's own letters and the letters of her sisters, particularly Leonie; the letters and papers of Moreton Frewen; Prince Clary and Countess Kinsky; and some small references in a variety of memoirs, including Jennie's own—although the latter is the most sparing of them all.

Winston Churchill's novel *Savrola* provides through its heroine an excellent description of his mother. Jennie's friend and rival, Lady Warwick, has some anecdotal material in her several memoirs. Clare Sheridan, Frewen's daughter, describes well in *Nuda Veritas* their home and atmosphere, and so does Anita Leslie in *The Fabulous Leonard Jerome*. But the best material comes from the books and memory and papers of Sir Shane Leslie.

The clothes and style of women of that period are ably described in *Our Mothers,* by Alan Bott and Irene Clephane.

Again, Winston Churchill's biography of his father and Robert Rhodes James's biography ably supplement each other, particularly on the politics. Barbara Tuchman has a short but excellent profile of Lord Salisbury in *The Proud Tower*. The best account of Jennie's political campaigning is given by Jennie herself, supplemented by family letters and some newspaper reports.

¹ *Reminiscences of Lady Randolph Churchill.*

² Frances, Countess of Warwick, *Discretions*. Lady Warwick, also known to her friends and to the Prince as 'Daisy', was later to be involved in a scandal concerning a personal file of love letters sent to her by the Prince. She wanted a large sum of money from the Crown after Edward VII's death, or else, she threatened, she would print the letters in a book. The letters were never printed. Lady Warwick later became a Socialist.

³ Moreton Frewen, *Melton Mowbray & Other Memories*. Frewen also makes reference to the Hungarian band that Kinsky often brought along with him to entertain guests.

⁴ Leonie's letters that year are full of references to Jennie and Kinsky. Telling about a visit to the House of Lords on June 18, 1884, Leonie noted, 'Jennie, with Kinsky, came in after. . . .'

⁵ Lady Leslie had considered herself a good friend of both Dickens and Thackeray.

⁶ Clare Sheridan, *Nuda Veritas*. Clare Sheridan, the sculptress, was the daughter of Clara and Moreton Frewen. She tells the story of her father arriving home on one of his infrequent visits. 'I tried to get close to him by climbing onto the arm of his chair. Suddenly his smile faded. He turned to me severely: "Don't be clumsy, child! You've stepped on my varnished shoes".'

⁷ Interview with Sir Shane Leslie.

⁸ Despite an inheritance of some 30,000 acres, Lady Warwick also wore her mother's cast-off clothes.

⁹ Frances, Countess of Warwick, *op. cit.*

¹⁰ Alan Bott and Irene Clephane, *Our Mothers*. The bustle finally faded into oblivion by 1890.

¹¹ *Ibid.*

¹² Frances, Countess of Warwick, *Afterthoughts*.

¹³ Winston S. Churchill, *Lord Randolph Churchill*.

¹⁴ Lord Rosebery described Randolph's humour as 'burlesque conception, set off by an artificial pomp of style; a sort of bombastic irony, such as we occasionally taste with relish in an after-dinner speech.' Quoted in Philip Guedalla, *Mr Churchill: A Portrait*.

¹⁵ Barbara Tuchman, *The Proud Tower*. Mrs Tuchman also said of Salisbury that he cared nothing for sport and little for people, and added, 'His aloofness was enhanced by shortsightedness so intense that he once failed to recognize a member of his own Cabinet, and once his own butler.'

¹⁶ Robert Rhodes James, *Lord Randolph Churchill*.

¹⁷ Winston Churchill, *op. cit.*

¹⁸ *Ibid.*

¹⁹ *Reminiscences of Lady Randolph Churchill*.

²⁰ *Ibid.*

²¹ 'It was the tandem that did it,' wrote Sir Henry Drummond Wolff in *Rambling Recollections*.

²² The many suitors for the hand and fortune of the Baroness included King Leopold II of Belgium, but in 1880 she had married a 27-year-old American. She was then sixty-eight, and a smirking comment in a gossip magazine said: 'AN ARITHMETICAL PROBLEM: How many times does 27 go into 68 and what is there over?'

Campaigning for Coutts, Jennie was told by one male voter, 'If I could get the same price as was once paid by the Duchess of Devonshire for a vote, I think I could promise.' The Duchess had kissed him, he said. 'Thank you very much,' Jennie said, 'I'll let the Baroness Burdett-Coutts know at once.' The Baroness's young husband was later cut at the clubs because of his comments about his ageing wife. He was quoted as saying aloud at a charity bazaar, 'By Jove, I must go and look after my grandmother.'

²³ Across the street from where Jennie later lived in Great Cumberland Road, there is a plaque on a house which reads: 'Elizabeth Garrett Anderson, 1836–1917. The first woman to qualify as a doctor lived here.'

²⁴ George W. Smalley, *Anglo-American Memories*.

²⁵ Another Birmingham butcher asked her how late Lord Randolph slept in the morning. When she said he slept until eleven, the butcher said he would not

vote for any man 'what lies abed' that late. As she was walking out, he asked her name and she answered: 'I am Lady Randolph Churchill.' The butcher stared at her appreciatively, then said, 'I'll vote for him. He doesn't get up until eleven, eh? Well, by Gad, Mum, it's a wonder to me now he gets up at all!'

Jennie told her friends of knocking on another Birmingham door. A big strapping woman answered the door and Jennie asked, 'Is your husband home?'

The woman held her arms akimbo, stared, sneered, and said sarcastically, 'And what, in goodness' name, do *you* want with *my* husband?'

[26] John, Viscount Morley, *Recollections.*

## Chapter 12

The three volumes of *The Letters and Journals of Queen Victoria* are most valuable to supplement *Reminiscences of Lady Randolph Churchill* and the several biographies of Randolph Churchill. But best of all are the letters between the Jerome sisters.

Randolph Churchill's *Winston S. Churchill* has the best detailed description of his father's fight with pneumonia at the age of eleven. The strain of Randolph's own life, as well as his illness, are well described by Dr Robson Roose in his articles in *The Lancet,* and in his books, particularly *The Waste and Repair in Modern Life,* where he clearly uses Randolph's life as a case history. The articles and books are available at the Wellcome British Medical Library in London.

Frank Harris's *My Life and Loves* has a fine description of Gladstone's famous speech in Parliament on the Home Rule for Ireland. The clearest account of the 1886 election is still in Robert Rhodes James's biography of Randolph Churchill. Lady Randolph's *Reminiscences* is excellent on her own political campaigning experiences.

Barbara Tuchman in *The Proud Tower* has a concise but penetrating description of Balfour. Lady Warwick's memoirs add something to this, but not much. The same should be said of Margot Asquith's *Autobiography.*

Two books worth looking at for some interesting references to Randolph Churchill at this time are *Randolph Spencer-Churchill* by T. H. S. Escott, and Sir Arthur Hardinge's *The Fourth Earl of Carnarvon,* Vol. III. Only a few anecdotes or descriptions are offered, but they are choice. The same should be said for *The Life of Lord Curzon* by the Earl of Ronaldshay, and the three volumes of Morley's *Life of William Ewart Gladstone.*

The Blenheim Palace Papers are especially important as reference for this chapter. *A Very Great Soul* by A. G. S. Norris is not very good, but it does have a few interesting observations about Lady Randolph as a public speaker. Lady Randolph's book of essays, *Small Talks on Big Subjects* has some pertinent comment for this time. So do *They All Married Well* by Eliot, and Smalley's *Anglo-American Memories.*

Some warmly intimate material on Jennie comes from Rosa Lewis, in a biography of her by Daphne Fielding, *The Duchess of Jermyn Street.*

There are a number of accounts of Randolph Churchill's resignation as Chancellor of the Exchequer, and some of them are conflicting, but Robert Rhodes James makes the most effective case for his version.

[1] *Reminiscences of Lady Randolph Churchill.*

[2] G. E. Buckle, ed., *Letters and Journals of Queen Victoria.*

[3] *Ibid.*

[4] The illness is described in detail in Randolph S. Churchill's biography of his father, *Winston S. Churchill*, Vol. I and in Part II of the companion volume.

[5] Allen Andrews, *The Splendid Pauper*, 1968.

[6] Papers at Blenheim Palace.

[7] Medical records at the Wellcome British Medical Library in London.

[8] Robson Roose, *The Waste and Repair in Modern Life*, Chap. 1, 'The Wear and Tear of London Life.'

[9] T. H. S. Escott, *Randolph Spencer-Churchill.*

[10] Frank Harris, *My Life and Loves.*

[11] John Morley, *Life of William Ewart Gladstone.*

[12] Winston S. Churchill, *Lord Randolph Churchill.* In his speech, Randolph also referred to Gladstone's 'senile vanity'. Even Joseph Chamberlain called the speech 'rather strong'. The date of the speech was June 20, 1886.

[13] Buchan's added comment was that Balfour's gift was that he could pull the most out of other people and in conversation pull up the quality of discussion without monopolizing it. Barbara Tuchman, *The Proud Tower.*

[14] Jennie's style of speech was clear and concise. See Elizabeth Eliot, *They All Married Well.*

[15] The critic was Hugh Martin, quoted in A. G. S. Norris, *A Very Great Soul.*

[16] Randolph made only two speeches in that general election of 1886.

[17] A letter dated July 29, 1886, published in Sir Arthur Hardinge, *The Fourth Earl of Carnarvon*, Vol. III, quotes the Earl as saying, 'I cannot forget my last conversation with R. Churchill—which was, on his side, as mad a one as I ever listened to from mortal lips.'

[18] Lady St Hélier, *Memories of Fifty Years.*

[19] Winston S. Churchill, *op. cit.*

[20] The Rt. Hon. Earl of Ronaldshay, *The Life of Lord Curzon.*

[21] Lady Randolph Churchill, *Small Talks on Big Subjects.*

[22] Roose, *op. cit.*

[23] Ralph Nevill, ed., *Leaves from the Notebooks of Lady Dorothy Nevill.* Lady Nevill also said of Randolph Churchill that he 'would never allow the tone of the conversation to degenerate into familiarity, and would be quick to resent any approach to it. He always seemed to be, to me, a man who was secretly conscious that he must make his mark quickly. Who can tell that some foreboding of his premature end did not loom before him?'

[24] Daphne Fielding, *The Duchess of Jermyn Street.* Rosa Lewis, the subject of this biography, also noted that the Prince liked plain broad beans, ptarmigan game pie, and Carlsbad plums.

[25] *Ibid.*

[26] Winston would later write on the same subject to his younger brother Jack. Discussing the flowing style of letters of the past, and how much better they were, Winston wrote, 'In those times pains were taken to avoid slang, to write good English, to spell well and cultivate style. . . . I try to imitate their virtues.' Randolph S. Churchill, *op. cit.*, companion Volume I, part I.

[27] Winston S. Churchill, *My Early Life.*

²⁸ She did, however, send him a book for his twelfth birthday on November 30, 1886, 'To Winston S. Churchill, from his loving mother JSC.' The book was entitled *The Young Carthaginian.*

²⁹ *Letters and Journals of Queen Victoria.*

³⁰ It was in a speech to the House on some coal mining statistics that Winston Churchill said, 'Neither I nor my father was ever any good at figures.'

³¹ George W. Smalley, *Anglo-American Memories.*

³² Escott, *op. cit.*

³³ Earl of Ronaldshay, *op. cit.*

³⁴ Robert Rhodes James, *Lord Randolph Churchill.*

³⁵ *Reminiscences of Lady Randolph Churchill.*

³⁶ Robert Rhodes James reports both versions in *Lord Randolph Churchill.*

³⁷ In a letter to Sir A. Godley, January 31, 1901, Curzon wrote, 'I was at Hatfield that night; and I remember the thanksgivings and hosannas that went up. . . . He [Randolph] did not know that [Salisbury] would be only too pleased to get rid of him.' Curzon called it 'a thundercloud from the clear sky'.

³⁸ *The Times,* December 23, 1886. The editorial added, 'The resignation of Lord Randolph Churchill has, beyond all question, deprived the government of its ablest member, if we except the Prime Minister himself.'

³⁹ *Letters and Journals of Queen Victoria.*

⁴⁰ Hardinge, *op. cit.* Lord Carnarvon wrote of the resignation, 'The colour is taken out of the body; but I should fancy that there is no help for it, and that Randolph's temper was so imperious that they had little option.'

⁴¹ There has been a small argument as to whether Lord Randolph ever said that. However, Lady Dorothy Nevill wrote that Conservative Party leader Walter Long was with Randolph in the smoking-room of the Carlton Club when he was informed that Goschen, who was not a Member of Parliament, had accepted the Chancellorship of the Exchequer. Long quoted Randolph as saying, 'All great men make mistakes. Napoleon forgot Blücher, I forgot Goschen.'

In a letter to *The Times,* December 11, 1949, Sir Clive Morrison Bell remembered that when he was an Ensign of the Queen's Guard several years after Randolph's resignation, he was a dinner guest of Lord Annaly, as was Randolph Churchill. After dinner, during the coffee and cigars, Lord Randolph reminisced about the incident. 'It was then that he used those very words,' Bell wrote. 'The next day I wrote a long account of the evening to my father, including, of course, this historic sentence.'

⁴² A clipping from a New York magazine (source unclear), dated February 10, 1887, reported, 'Lady Randolph will accompany her father back to New York in April or May. Lord Randolph will not be in the party.'

Chapter 13

*Reminiscences of Lady Randolph Churchill* catches much of the love for horses and racing, but it is at its best in the author's penetrating and excellent description of the trip to Russia. *The Times* closely followed the Churchills on that trip, and *The Letters and Journals of Queen Victoria* adds still more to the political

315

aspects of the sojourn, as well as the Queen's personal criticism. Lady Gwendolen Cecil's biography, *Third Marquis of Salisbury*, Vols. III and IV, has a number of good references.

Sir Algernon West's *Private Diaries* has several excellent comments worth reading, and so does Margot Asquith's *Autobiography* and Lady Warwick's *Discretions*. Marcel Proust has some revealing description of the Marquis de Breteuil, whom he calls the Marquis de Breuté in *Remembrance of Things Past*. The Kinsky chronology comes from Prince Clary, and the description of Herbert von Bismarck comes from a variety of biographies of Otto von Bismarck.

[1] *Reminiscences of Lady Randolph Churchill.* Unless otherwise stated, all quotations attributed to Jennie in this chapter are from this source.

[2] The magazine went on to say, 'Jennie had converted Randolph Churchill from a *flaneur* into a hard-working man of affairs.'

[3] *Private Diaries of Sir Algernon West.* Sir Algernon also quoted Lady Randolph as saying, 'Instead of "the woman who hesitates is lost"—"the woman who does not hesitate is lost".'

[4] Margot Asquith in her *Autobiography* recorded that she later told Randolph Churchill at a dinner party, 'I am afraid you resigned more out of temper than conviction.' To this, he replied, 'Confound your cheek! What do you know about me and my convictions! I hate Salisbury! He jumped at my resignation like a dog at a bone! The Tories are ungrateful, shortsighted beasts!' And she also remembered his saying of Salisbury 'something I could not catch about Salisbury lying dead at his feet,' and then he added, 'I wish to God I had *never* known him!'

[5] Extract from Queen's Journal, Buckingham Palace, June 20, 1887, published in G. E. Buckle, ed., *Letters and Journals of Queen Victoria*. Of the day, Queen Victoria also recorded another feminine note: 'I wore a dress with the rose, thistle and shamrock embroidered in silver on it, and my large diamonds.'

[6] By the age of fourteen he supposedly had read Rider Haggard's *King Solomon's Mines* fourteen times.

[7] Abbess was by Trappist out of Festive, and Randolph Churchill bought her for three hundred guineas in September 1887. Between 1889 and 1891, Abbess won ten races valued at more than £10,050.

[8] Breteuil was a member of the Chamber of Deputies from 1877 to 1892.

[9] Blenheim Palace Papers.

[10] Lady Warwick, in *Discretions,* also remembered the Czarina as a girl, Princess Alix of Hesse, 'a wholesome, thoroughly normal person . . . loved to laugh and joke, and there were certainly no indications of any mystic leanings in her nature. . . . Court life had turned her into a nervous wreck. . . .'

[11] Jennie also visited a Russian museum where she recognized one of the furniture exhibits—an Italian cabinet that had once been at Blenheim.

[12] *The Times* reported on January 3, 1888, that the Russians hoped that they had convinced Randolph Churchill of the peaceful and harmless character of their people, so that he would try to convince other Cabinet members to resign as he did from a government which they regarded as the traditional enemy of Russia.

[13] When Kinsky was stationed at the Foreign Office in Vienna and returned to London for one of his many short trips, Leonie wrote a letter to her husband

noting that Randolph and Jennie were thinking of returning with Kinsky to Vienna for Whitsuntide.

[14] The strange note is that while there is frequent mention of Jennie's men friends being entertained at the Churchill home, there is rarely any mention of Trafford or Tyrwhitt as guests.

Chapter 14

The best descriptions of The Souls can be found in *Portraits and Appreciations* by Viscount (Edgar Vincent) D'Abernon, who writes as a Soul and, indeed, has written an amusing and revealing long poem about The Souls which can be found in the manuscript room of the British Museum. Lady Warwick deals briefly with The Souls in her memoirs, as does Lady Randolph Churchill in her *Reminiscences*, but Barbara Tuchman is even better in *The Proud Tower*.

The privately printed poetry of Harry Cust can be found in the main reading room of the British Museum. *The Memoirs of Sir Ronald Storrs* is excellent on Cust.

Mrs Tuchman and Lady Warwick ably describe both Balfour and Curzon, although there are a number of biographies of each man worth reading for background. The Earl of Ronaldshay's biography of Curzon is good, and Lady Frances Balfour's two-volume *Ne Obliviscaris* is worth looking into for more personal material. Margot Asquith's *Autobiography* is also good, with reference to both men, as well as to The Souls, of which she was a member.

On the Jerome and Frewen families, Moreton Frewen's *Melton Mowbray & Other Memories* is important and so is *Courtroom Warrior* by Richard O'Connor and Clare Sheridan's *Nuda Veritas*. The family letters of both the Jeromes and the Frewens, *The Splendid Pauper* by Allen Andrews, the Blenheim Palace Papers, and *Letters and Journals of Queen Victoria* are all vital for this chapter.

[1] Extract of letter from Marquis of Salisbury to Queen Victoria, February 13, 1888. G. E. Buckle, ed., *Letters and Journals of Queen Victoria*. An extract from the Queen's Journal on January 13, 1887, notes: 'Lord Salisbury considers Lord Randolph Churchill as a most selfish statesman, not caring for the good of the country. . . .'

[2] Barbara Tuchman, *The Proud Tower*, notes that the men of The Souls all followed political careers, and nearly all were Junior Ministers in Lord Salisbury's Government.

[3] Lady Warwick, *Discretions*. She called Curzon 'one of the most tragically misunderstood of men. . . . I never lost my affection for a personality that was both warm-hearted and lovable beneath a cold and rather hard surface.'

[4] *Op. cit.*

[5] There is an unpublished story passed on by a woman who knew Lord D'Abernon, and would rather not be named: she and Lord D'Abernon accompanied a friend of hers who had decided to buy a bed. In a shop on Bond Street they saw a magnificent bed with four posters which came together at the top in a cupola and crown. Her excited friend loved it and decided to buy it. But Lord D'Abernon paled. 'I would not buy it if I were you. It is very unlucky,' he said.

Her friend asked D'Abernon why he thought so. 'It belonged to Lady Randolph,' he said.

[6] Tuchman, *op. cit.*, writes that Cust's 'fatal self indulgence with regard to women' hurt his political career, which never fulfilled its promise.

[7] D'Abernon, *op. cit.*, described The Souls as being 'intellectual without being highbrow or pretentious; critical without envy; unprejudiced but not unprincipled; emancipated but not aggressive; literary but athletic; free from the narrowness of clique, yet bound together in reciprocal appreciation and affection.' He also admitted, however, that they were brilliant without being profound.

[8] From *Culture and Anarchy*.

[9] Lady Warwick, *op. cit.* Lady Warwick, who later became a Socialist, wrote that her friends felt it was necessary to 'keep servants in their place'. The dockers incidentally, won their fight for the 'dockers' tanner' with the help of the Australian dockers, who cabled £30,000 to support them. James Truslow Adams, *Empire on the Seven Seas*.

[10] *Letters and Journals of Queen Victoria*.

[11] Winston S. Churchill, *My Early Life*.

[12] Frank Harris, *My Life and Loves*.

[13] Frances, Countess Warwick, *Afterthoughts*.

[14] Randolph S. Churchill, *Winston S. Churchill*, I.

[15] In her book, *Small Talks on Big Subjects*, Lady Randolph Churchill later wrote: 'Indiscretion is not a crime. It is not even a vice. In the earlier Victorian days, the word had more meaning and more censure, wrecked plans and broke up homes. If a woman's behaviour was called indiscreet, it was "equivalent to social ruin". But in the changing times, the word applied in the same sense does not represent anything so serious.'

[16] A New York newspaper also reported how the Duke created a sensation by being arrested for 'scorching' (fast and reckless driving on his bicycle) on Riverside Drive.

[17] Moreton Frewen, *Melton Mowbray & Other Memories*.

[18] Lady Dorothy Nevill, *Under Five Reigns*. Lady Nevill said this to Joseph Chamberlain in 1888, before he married an American. Chamberlain answered, 'I am ready to give up the lobster, so you must be prepared to like the girl.'

[19] Blenheim Palace Papers.

[20] Leonie was the only one of the three Jerome sisters to celebrate a golden wedding anniversary. The Leslie family motto was 'Grip fast'. By family tradition, this was what Bartholomew, the Hungarian noble who escorted Queen Margaret to Scotland in 1067 and subsequently became the Queen's Chamberlain and founder of the Leslie family, said to the Queen when she was riding pillion to him as they forded a stream. The Queen's reply was 'Gin the buckle bide'—and two more buckles were added to the pillion and the charge upon Bartholomew's arms.

[21] Allen Andrews, *The Splendid Pauper*.

[22] Frewen mainly wanted to persuade Salar to 'an open mind whether all India might, in the fulness of time, drape her vast docile and elephantine bulk with those same Federal trappings, but subject to a white Mahout.' Shane Leslie, *Studies in Sublime Failure*.

[23] Frewen, *op. cit.*

318

<sup></sup>24 After his brother's three daughters married into aristocratic English families, Lawrence Jerome began a speech before the American Jockey Club by saying, 'Many years ago, before I had any blue blood in my veins. . . .'

<sup></sup>25 Leonard Jerome wrote his wife that Travers 'fought a great Tammany leader on a brutal assault, and got him convicted and sentenced to a one-year imprisonment and a $500 fine.' Richard O'Connor, *Courtroom Warrior*.

<sup></sup>26 King Milan, next to the last of the Obrenovitch dynasty, divorced his wife Queen Natalie in 1888 and abdicated his throne a year later in favour of his son.

<sup></sup>27 Clare Sheridan, *Nuda Veritas*. 'He was a big, gentle, tender "savage", and talked to me in a soft melodious voice. I loved him.'

<sup></sup>28 Count Kinsky had been transferred to the Austro-Hungarian Embassy in London from Berlin in March 1888 and then transferred to Paris less than a year later. Wherever he was, he made frequent trips to be with Jennie.

<sup></sup>29 Baron Hirsch's biggest project was building a railway from Vienna to Constantinople. He also shared the Churchills' love of horses and racing.

Chapter 15

The British Museum newspaper library at Colindale offers a variety of interesting comment on the Churchill activities at this time, not only in the London papers, but in such papers as the Sheffield *Telegraph* and the Cardiff *Mail*, which had no qualms about sharp editorial comment. In 1890, George Newnes started a small weekly journal called *Tit Bits*, which had more gossip than news, but offers some interesting leads in many areas. *The Review of Reviews* is also highly informative.

*Punch* Parliamentary critic Henry Lucy in his several books previously mentioned is particularly good on this period. So, as always, is Robert Rhodes James. The Parnell background comes from a variety of sources: James Adams, *Empire on the Seven Seas,* has a short but good account, and Jules Abels, *The Parnell Tragedy* goes into considerable detail. Shane Leslie in *The End of a Chapter* has a fascinating footnote on the tragedy.

Arthur Balfour's *Chapters of Autobiography* is well worth reading for his references to Randolph Churchill. So is Margot Asquith's *Autobiography* for her references to Joseph Chamberlain. The Birmingham fiasco is very well described in Lady Randolph Churchill's *Reminiscences* and also in Henry Lucy, *Later Peeps at Parliament*.

<sup></sup>1 *Town Topics.*

<sup></sup>2 In a retrospective article about Randolph Churchill, the *Review of Reviews* (March 1895), wrote, 'Lord Randolph made a special point of assembling round his table distinguished foreigners and eminent Americans. In this respect, his work was materially assisted by the fact that he married an American lady.'

<sup></sup>3 Lady Dorothy Nevill, *Under Five Reigns*. Lady Nevill added that 'nobody ever came to his estate unless they were invited, even his children'.

<sup></sup>4 *Ibid*. He also told Lady Nevill, 'I don't like your English aristocracy. They are not educated, they are not serious; but they do interest me. I want to find out all about them; I should like to be able to explain them to myself. I don't think anybody understands them and I want to do so.'

[5] On December 22, 1888, Randolph Churchill had added a codicil to his will bequeathing all his private papers, letters, and documents to his brother-in-law, Viscount Curzon, and his friend Louis Jennings, 'In trust to publish, retain all or any of them, as they in their absolute discretion think proper.'

[6] Margot Asquith, in her *Autobiography*, wrote of Chamberlain, 'He encouraged in himself such scrupulous economy of gesture, movement and colour that, after hearing him many times, I came to the definite conclusion that Chamberlain's opponents were snowed under by his accumulated moderation.'

[7] Henry Lucy remembered that day of decision and its physical effect on Randolph: 'He was so altered in personal appearance that for a moment I did not know him. Instead of his usual alert, swinging pace, with head erect and swift, glancing eyes, he walked with slow, weary tread, his head hanging down, and a look on his face as if tears had been coursing down it. No one who knew him only in public life would have imagined him capable of such emotion.' *Later Peeps at Parliament.*

[8] *Reminiscences of Lady Randolph Churchill.*

[9] *Reminiscences of Lady Randolph Churchill.*

[10] Robert Rhodes James, *Lord Randolph Churchill.*

[11] *Reminiscences of Lady Randolph Churchill.*

[12] The letter later turned out to be a forgery.

[13] Kitty O'Shea had inherited £144,000 from her aunt, but the will was contested, and none of the money was available.

[14] Parnell's lawyer, Sir George Lewis, urged Parnell to contest the divorce suit because he strongly believed it could not be pressed after cross-examination. Parnell refused, answering, 'My first duty is to the lady.' Shane Leslie was told this by Lady Lewis, and he reported it in *The End of a Chapter.*

[15] *Punch* showed Gladstone as an old pilgrim with a sword, advancing along a narrow ridge called Home Rule, with a bog of Irish nationalism on one side, and a last ditch of Orange Resistance on the other.

[16] Lord Rosebery, *Lord Randolph Churchill.*

[17] Arthur James Balfour, *Chapters of Autobiography,* ed. Mrs Edgar Dugdale, noted that Randolph Churchill had recited these lines to him. Six years before, Balfour also remembered, Randolph had recommended to him a new book entitled *Treasure Island.*

[18] But he was still embittered by his father's resignation. Shane Leslie, *op. cit.,* quotes him as replying to someone who noted a tear in the elbow of his jacket, 'How should I not be out of elbows when my father is out of office?'

[19] Winston S. Churchill, *My Early Life.*

[20] Lady Violet Bonham Carter, *Winston Churchill as I Knew Him,* quotes Churchill as saying of himself that he was 'a child of both worlds'.

[21] The Sheffield *Telegraph* on April 14, 1891, reports: 'Lord Randolph's high-flown reference to his going forth on a mission to seek homes for the overcrowded masses of the mother country has excited a titter among those who are acquainted with the real purpose of his journey. This is the plain truth. Fortune does not smile on Lord Randolph at home. He wants money, and like the bold adventurers who have planted the British flag all over the world he is going forth to search for it. If he can combine the acquisition of wealth for himself with the provision of homes for our surplus population, so much the better for all parties.'

[22] Allen Andrews, *The Splendid Pauper.*

# Chapter 16

The Churchill family letters at Blenheim Palace and the letters held by Peregrine Churchill, many of which have been included in Randolph S. Churchill's biography of his father, plus the letters of Mrs Oswald Frewen, all form the basic research of this chapter. All are invaluable.

Winston Churchill's *My Early Life* has special value here and his *Thoughts and Adventures* also has a few pertinent anecdotes. So has the *Recollections* of John, Viscount Morley, and Rosebery's *Lord Randolph Churchill*. Wilfred Scawen Blunt, *My Diaries: Being a Personal Narrative of Events*, Part One, 1888–90, has only a few observations on this subject, but they are worth having.

Daphne Fielding's *The Duchess of Jermyn Street*, the story of Rosa Lewis, is more revealing than one might imagine.

Randolph Churchill's newspaper columns, collected into *Men, Mines and Animals in South Africa* are well worth examining. The best account of Lady Randolph's concern for music at the Bayreuth Festival is her own *Reminiscences*.

Frank Harris has some fascinating anecdotes in *My Life and Loves* and Shane Leslie's books *Film of Memory* and *The End of a Chapter* are also excellent.

[1] Kinsky had been transferred from the Paris Embassy to London in June 1890.

[2] 'I have known Charles Kinsky all my life,' Prince Clary added, in a letter to the author, 'as he was not only a cousin, but also a very dear and close friend of my mother's, who was born Countess Thérèse Kinsky. When my father, who was an Austro-Hungarian diplomat, was sent to London in 1895 as Chancellor of the Embassy, my mother was received in the most friendly way by Lady Randolph and I remember having seen her several times in my parents' house in Lowndes Square. It was only much later, of course, that I heard of my uncle's great romance with Lady Randolph.'

[3] Count Kinsky also caught the measles from Winston.

[4] Shane Leslie, *The End of a Chapter,* and interviews with the author.

[5] Daphne Fielding, *The Duchess of Jermyn Street.*

[6] Jennie also wrote him, 'How I long for you to be back with sacks of gold.'

[7] Allen Andrews, *The Splendid Pauper.* Frewen also added that Mrs Jerome had managed her money so well that she had paid off most of the debt on the Madison Square house in New York, part rental of which still came to Jennie in quarterly payments.

[8] Randolph Churchill's columns were collected in a book called *Men, Mines and Animals in South Africa.*

[9] Blenheim Palace Papers.

[10] This printed rumour served as an interesting point for those who had previously claimed that Jennie had much more to do with the writing of Randolph's speeches than most people had imagined.

[11] The incident was reported by Rhys H. Price in a letter to the editor of *The Times* in London, August 6, 1926.

[12] Such was Jennie's love of music that even a severe toothache didn't prevent her attendance at all the Wagner performances.

[13] Paderewski arrived in London with a letter of introduction to Jennie from

a mutual friend. Her Connaught Place home, of course, was a haven for musicians arriving from all over Europe.

[14] Shane Leslie, interview with the author.

[15] *Reminiscences of Lady Randolph Churchill.*

[16] Count Kinsky had written Princess Metternich about Jennie's concert programme and she sent Jennie a long letter advising her about the setting of one of the scenes.

[17] A cartoon in *Punch* showed Jennie at the piano, with the caption, 'Her piano was forte.'

[18] *Reminiscences of Lady Randolph Churchill.*

[19] *Ibid.*

[20] Randolph S. Churchill, *Winston S. Churchill*, I.

[21] Peregrine Churchill collection.

[22] Jennie also wrote, 'I saw poor Harry Tyrwhitt at Ascot. He does look so ill, poor fellow, but seemed in fairly good spirits. He asked me much about you, and I told him how grateful you would be if he could find time to write you a line. I think he will do this.' Within a few months Tyrwhitt was dead.

[23] Shane Leslie, *Film of Memory.*

[24] Seymour Leslie, son of Leonie and John, in *The Jerome Connexion*, says of his uncle Randolph that he was 'rude and arrogant' to his servants and 'aloof in manner to his two boys—Leonie, it is clear, did not like her brother-in-law'.

[25] Andrews, *op. cit.*

[26] Dr Keith had written several books on the subject, including *Contributions to Surgical Treatment of Tumours in the Abdomen*. He was also a Honorary Fellow of Gynaecology in the United States. His son George Elphinstone Keith was a gynaecologist like his father, and the two had written several books together.

[27] Frank Harris, *My Life and Loves.*

[28] Winston Churchill, *My Early Life.*

[29] Andrews, *op. cit.*

[30] Kinsky's friendship with the Archduke, as well as his family position, accounted for the ease with which he managed to be transferred from one embassy to another. In his diaries, *Tagebuch meiner Reise um die Erde*, the Archduke describes Kinsky as 'an excellent travelling companion' who had 'helped make the journey such a success'.

[31] Winston Churchill, *op. cit.*

[32] Frances, Countess of Warwick; *Discretions.* Another frequent guest was the American correspondent for the New York *Tribune*, George Smalley, who echoed Lady Warwick's observations.

[33] Winston Churchill, *op. cit.*

[34] Frank Harris, *Contemporary Portraits.*

[35] Henry Lucy, *Diary of a Journalist.* Lucy was a close friend of Randolph, and broke with him about this time, but later renewed his friendship, as few others did. Lucy later reported Randolph's closest supporter and friend, Louis Jennings, as having said to him, 'It's an odd thing Randolph has just as many friends today as he had a week ago. He has regained you and he has lost me.'

[36] Carson afterward asked Winston what he thought of his (Carson's) speech that day in Parliament. 'I concluded from it, sir, that the ship of state is struggling in heavy seas,' Winston answered.

[37] Winston Churchill, *op. cit.*

[38] Blenheim Palace Papers.

[39] A. J. P. Taylor gives a good account of this period in *Bismarck*. Shortly after this time, Prince Otto von Bismarck was confined to a carriage, then to a wheelchair. He had told Sir Charles Dilke, 'The rule of kings is the rule of women; the bad women are bad and the good are worse.' His son Herbert's involvement in the divorce scandal had seriously affected his career.

[40] *Reminiscences of Lady Randolph Churchill.*

[41] In *Thoughts and Adventures,* Winston Churchill wrote: 'I suppose if I were to relive my life, I ought to eschew the habit of smoking. Look at all the money I've wasted on tobacco. Think of it all invested and mounting up in compound interest, year after year. I remember my father, in his most sparkling mood, his eyes gleaming through the haze of his cigarette, saying, "Why begin? If you want to have an eye that is true and a hand that does not quiver, if you are never to ask yourself a question as you ride at a fence, don't smoke."'

[42] Interview with Peregrine Churchill.

[43] She worried about Winston's blood being out of order and the boils on his back, wrote him details about political campaigns, and refused invitations elsewhere for weekends when Winston was home.

[44] Winston Churchill, *op. cit.*

[45] John, Viscount Morley, *Recollections*. The exact date was March 13, 1894.

[46] Lord Rosebery, *Lord Randolph Churchill.*

[47] Interview with Sir Shane Leslie.

[48] Harris, *My Life and Loves*. Guy de Maupassant also died of syphilis, with madness in the final stages.

[49] Wilfred Scawen Blunt, *My Diaries: Being a Personal Narrative of Events, 1888–1914*. Part One: 1888–1900.

## Chapter 17

*Reminiscences of Lady Randolph Churchill*, supplemented by her frequent letters to her sisters and her sons, offers the most complete account of the round-the-world trip, which was never fully realized.

The Buzzard Papers of Dr Thomas Buzzard have a detailed discussion of the final stages of Randolph's disease, and the letters of Dr Robson Roose have much to add.

Winston Churchill has some moving accounts of this time in *My Early Life* and so does Sir Shane Leslie in several of his books, particularly *Salutation to Five*.

There are only a few fragments in *The Life of Sir William Harcourt* by A. G. Gardiner, Vol. II, and *Uncensored Celebrities* by E. T. Raymond, but they are interesting to look at.

Dr A. L. Baron's *Man Against Germs* is still the best explanatory book on syphilis that I have found.

Newspaper and magazine accounts of this period are necessary background. There is an excellent collection of representative articles from *The New York Times* describing the United States at this time in *America's Taste*, ed. Marjorie Longley and others.

[1] Buzzard Papers. Dr Thomas Buzzard was brought in by Dr Robson Roose as the new consultant on Lord Randolph's case. Dr Buzzard, a specialist in diseases of the nervous system, was the consulting physician to London's National Hospital for the Paralysed and Epileptic. He and Dr Roose advised both Lord and Lady Randolph that they had reassessed the case and decided that a trip through the United States would be too hot in June, and a prolonged trip, in any case, was inadvisable. Instead, they suggested a fishing trip to Norway. Randolph refused to change his plans.

[2] Dr George E. Keith had just returned from New York where he had been house surgeon at the Women's Hospital. He was ten years older than Lady Randolph.

[3] Winston Churchill, *My Early Life*.

[4] Frank Harris, *My Life and Loves*.

[5] Mrs John Sloane reported this as one of the anecdotes passed down in the Travers and Jerome families.

[6] *The New York Times* many years later recorded that during her visit to New York, Lady Randolph Churchill 'created and named' the Manhattan cocktail. 'She conceived the notion of blending bourbon with a lesser portion of herb-piqued wine [sweet vermouth] and aromatic bitters.'

[7] The magazine from which the clipping came is unclear, but the date is July 21, 1894. The article referred to Lord Randolph as 'the Clemenceau of the English House of Commons' and goes on to say, 'In point of beauty, Lady Churchill, who accompanies her husband here, has long been acknowledged one of the fairest women in America. Only as long ago as the April drawing room, London correspondents described her as one of the most beautiful and distinguished women to make their bows to the Queen. . . . The charming suavity of her manner and a generous fund of tact and diplomacy have won for her the highest respect of all Englishwomen, who have unconsciously grown to consider her an Englishwoman to the manner born. . . . By a clever and ingenious method of pulling the political wires, [she] contrives to make herself of invaluable service to His Lordship.'

[8] They travelled by private railroad car, which they first thought was a generous gesture of the Canadian railroad owner, but which they soon discovered they had to pay for.

[9] *Reminiscences of Lady Randolph Churchill.* Unless otherwise stated, all quotations in this chapter attributed to Jennie are from this source.

[10] In coming years, Winston Churchill repeatedly said he expected to 'peg out early' and probably die before his thirties. A family friend remarked that Churchill probably said this because he felt he had somehow inherited his father's disease. The spectre of syphilis conceivably explains a possible wary attitude toward sex and the fact that he did not marry until he was thirty-three years old.

[11] Lady Randolph reported that King Thebaw at Rangoon presented three princesses—two pretty ones, completely covered and the third, old and ugly, hardly wearing any clothes at all. The princesses presented Lady Randolph with some cheroots which they hoped she would smoke.

[12] Dr A. L. Baron, in *Man Against Germs,* writes, 'When the brain is invaded by the germs, the last act of syphilis may be ended suddenly, or it may drag on for many dreary years. The fragile blood vessels of the brain are eroded, eventu-

ally the blood will spurt out and the fatal apoplectic stroke will terminate syphilis.'

[13] The coffin was lead-lined to prevent the deterioration of the body in the tropical heat.

[14] His fiancée was 21-year-old Countess Elisabeth Wolff Metternich zur Gracht, a cousin of the Empress of Austria.

[15] E. T. Raymond, in *Uncensored Celebrities,* makes the point that Winston Churchill's 'extra touch of recklessness' and 'an unbridled tendency to naked "bossing" of any "show" ' might well have been a characteristic inherited from his American mother.

[16] A. G. Gardiner, *The Life of Sir William Harcourt,* Vol. II, notes somebody saying to Harcourt of Randolph Churchill, 'Why, he isn't even an educated man.'

'No,' answered Harcourt pleasantly. 'If he were educated, he would be spoiled.'

[17] Allen Andrews, *The Splendid Pauper.*

[18] Blenheim Palace Papers.

[19] Shane Leslie, *Salutation to Five.*

[20] Describing her lying in bed, Sir Shane remembered vividly, 'Her black, brushed hair and pallor of death reflected in her own face—with those eyes, needing no jewels—the most beautiful vision of a woman I had ever seen.'

# Index